THE SOCIO-
ECONOMICS
OF CRIME
AND JUSTICE

Studies in Socio-Economics

MORALITY, RATIONALITY, AND EFFICIENCY
NEW PERSPECTIVES ON SOCIO-ECONOMICS
Richard M. Coughlin, editor

SOCIO-ECONOMICS
TOWARD A NEW SYNTHESIS
Amitai Etzioni and Paul R. Lawrence, editors

INSTITUTIONAL CHANGE
THEORY AND EMPIRICAL FINDINGS
Sven-Erik Sjöstrand, Editor

THE MORAL PHILOSOPHY OF MANAGEMENT
FROM QUESNAY TO KEYNES
Pierre Guillet de Monthoux

THE SOCIO-ECONOMICS OF CRIME AND JUSTICE
Brian Forst, editor

THE SOCIO-ECONOMICS OF CRIME AND JUSTICE

EDITOR
Brian Forst

M.E. Sharpe
ARMONK, NEW YORK
LONDON, ENGLAND

Library of Congress Cataloging-in-Publication Data

The socio-economics of crime and justice / Brian Forst, editor.
p.   cm.—(Studies in socio-economics)
Includes bibliographical references and index.
ISBN 1–56324–074–2.—ISBN 1–56324–025–4 (pbk.)
1. Crime—Social aspects—United States.
2. Crime—Economic aspects—United States.
3. Criminal justice, Administration of—Social aspects—United States.
4. Criminal justice, Administration of—Economic aspects—United States.
I. Forst, Brian.
II. Series.
HV6030.S63   1993
364.2—dc20
93–23797
CIP

Printed in the United States of America

The paper used in this publication meets the minimum requirements
of American National Standard for Information Sciences—
Permanence of Paper for Printed Library Materials,
ANSI Z39.48–1984.

BM (c) 10   9   8   7   6   5   4   3   2   1
BM (p) 10   9   8   7   6   5   4   3   2   1

To Judith,

my wife and best friend

Contents

List of Figures and Tables   ix

Foreword
Amitai Etzioni   xi

1. Socio-Economics, Crime, and Justice
    Brian Forst   3

PART I: Foundations

2 Justice and Punishment: Philosophical Basics
    Hugo Adam Bedau   19

3 Economic Perspectives on Criminality: An Eclectic View
    Llad Phillips   37

4 The Limits of Legal Sanctions
    Graham Hughes   51

PART II: The Community in the Human

5 Crime, Conscience, and Family
    Joan McCord   65

6 Crime and Ethnicity
    Darnell Hawkins   89

7 Women, Crime, and Justice
    Rita Simon   121

PART III: Offenders and Offenses

8 Juvenile Delinquency, Juvenile Justice
    Carl E. Pope   157

9   Community Responses to Crime and Fear of Crime
Bonnie Fisher   177

10   Social Structure and Spouse Assault
Jeffrey Fagan   209

11   School Violence and the Breakdown of Community Homogeneity
Jackson Toby   255

PART IV: The Criminal Justice System

12   "Good" Policing
James J. Fyfe   269

13   The Prosecutor and the Public
Brian Forst   291

14   The Honest Politician's Guide to Sentencing Reform
Norval Morris   303

Author Index   311
Subject Index   321
About the Contributors   327

List of Figures and Tables

Figures

3.1 Optimal Control Model Analogy of Dynamic Changes in
    Preferences over the Life Cycle of an Individual   41

Tables

6.1 Theoretical Perspectives on Ethnicity, Race, and Crime   94

7.1 Changes in Labor Force Participation Rates of Married
    Women with Children: 1948–87   122

7.2 Percentage of Earned Degrees Conferred upon Women:
    1950–85   123

7.3 Occupational Distributions by Race and Sex: 1970, 1980, 1986   124

7.4 Percentages of Females Arrested among Total Arrests for All
    Serious (Type I) Crimes and for All Violent and Property
    (Type I) Crimes: 1963–87   126

7.5 Females Arrested As Percentage of All Arrests for Type I
    Offenses: 1963–87   128

7.6 Other Crimes: Females Arrested As Percentage of All People
    Arrested for Various Crimes: 1963–87   130

7.7 Rank Order of Offenses for Which Females and Males Are
    Most Likely to Be Arrested: 1972, 1980, 1987   132

7.8 New York: Percentage of Prosecutions in Upper and Lower
    Courts Resulting in Conviction by Type of Offense and
    Sex: 1982–87   134

7.9 Pennsylvania: Percentage of Prosecutions Resulting in
    Convictions by Type of Offense and Sex: 1981–86   135

7.10 Females As a Percentage of All Sentenced Prisoners by Type
    of Institution: 1971–87   136

7.11 Adult Inmate Population by Security Level and Sex:
June 30, 1988   137

7.12 California: Persons Convicted in Superior Courts and
Sentenced to Prison by Type of Offense and Sex: 1982–87   138

7.13 New York: Persons Convicted in Upper Courts and
Sentenced to Prison by Type of Offense and Sex: 1982–87   140

7.14 Pennsylvania: Persons Convicted in All Courts and
Sentenced to Incarceration by Type of Offense and Sex:
1981–86   144

7.15 Offense Distribution of State Prison Inmates by Sex: 1979
and 1986   146

7.16 Age and Education of Inmates in Federal and State
Correctional Institutions: 1960, 1970, 1980   147

7.17 Occupational Status of Inmates in Federal and State
Correctional Institutions: 1960, 1970, 1980   148

8.1 Summary of Theoretical Perspectives Concerning the
Etiology of Delinquency   160

9.1 Motivation for Police and Public Participation in Different
Community Responses to Crime and Fear   188

10.1 Participation of Any Adult Household Members in Spouse
Assault by Social and Demographic Characteristics,
Controlling for Area Size   214

10.2 Spouse-Assault Offending Rates for Adult Household
Members by Social and Demographic Characteristics   216

10.3 Logistic Regression on Participation of Any Adult
Household Member in Spouse Assault, Controlling
for Area Size   218

Foreword

Attention to public safety is the first duty of the state. In many areas, however, the American government no longer discharges this duty effectively. The prison population, already the highest among the industrial nations, is growing, but crime has not been curbed. Criminals swing through turnstile courts; courts are overwhelmed, and the streets remain unsafe.

Behind the cops-and-robbers news about some drug dealer captured this week and the fine police work by this or that agent lies the fact that millions continue to use illegal drugs and open markets often exist for those who cater to this illicit clientele.

Moreover, in some areas public authorities seem to have abandoned any attempts to provide public safety. A typical example is the response of the police to a wave of carjacking in late 1992. Drivers were jerked out of their cars—in a growing number of instances, shot—and their cars taken away at gunpoint. Carjacking has been particularly scary to the citizenry because it occurs at unpredictable places and times and hence leaves people with the feeling that they are not safe any place, any time. The police response has been to tell people to lock their cars from the inside, to leave a front light on, so that when they come home they can see if anybody is lurking about, and so on, all suggestions that together amount to the message—you are on your own; there's not much we can do to protect you.

A citizenry that feels abandoned is a dangerous sociological mix. Sooner or later some politician will be elected who promises to be "strong" against crime if he or she will just be allowed a free hand. We already have a rising chorus calling for shooting drug dealers on sight, for "suspending the constitution until the war against drugs is won," and for more vigilantism. We badly require constructive, well-thought-out, workable treatments of crime.

The social sciences have a major role to play in attending to this social need. This volume offers no quick solutions or easy answers, but it does provide some of the best social science thinking on the subject, and does so largely in a new vein, that of socio-economics.

The underlying conceptual issue here concerns the qualities of human nature and the sources of social order. Some neoclassical economists and other social scientists who share the neoclassical paradigm (for example, specialists in the fields of law and economics, public choice) have argued that criminals are not different from the rest of us, that the same people could just as easily become reliable bank tellers if their cost and revenue flows were structured differently. We are all said to be driven by self-interest, and criminals are people who find that given their circumstances crime pays better than, say, going to work. All we need to do is to change the probability of being caught and serving time—increase the costs—and criminals will desist.

Socio-economics sees, in addition, social structures that disadvantage some groups of people and isolate them from the dominant culture, failure of the educational system, and defects in the community mechanisms whose goal is to introduce the young into the prevailing values of their society and encourage adults to abide by the values of their peers.

The reader will find here an unusually rich and varied attempt to grapple with these issues, either directly by explaining the underlying assumptions about persons and society, the place of culture and institutions, or indirectly by dealing with the implication of social forces and crime. I know of no better way to broach our subject while avoiding simplistic, often dangerous solutions.

Amitai Etzioni

THE SOCIO-
ECONOMICS
OF CRIME
AND JUSTICE

BRIAN FORST

Socio-Economics, Crime, and Justice

Is crime essentially a rational pursuit, as many have argued, or is it practiced largely out of nonrational motives? This question has more than just curiosity value. How we deal with offenders and how we go about preventing crime in the first place are matters of profound social consequence throughout the world.

In the United States alone, tens of thousands of people lose their lives to crime each year; hundreds of thousands of additional lives are damaged, many beyond repair. The Department of Justice estimates the total costs of crime and justice to be in the hundreds of billions of dollars each year.[1] If we can come to better understand why people commit crime, we may be better able to control crime and reduce its terrible consequences.

Throughout most of the twentieth century, our primary response to the problem of crime has been to expand police and court resources and to increase substantially our prison and jail populations. That approach has not been adequate; many see it as counterproductive. Crime has not gone away. By most objective standards it has resisted containment, leaving society with the worst of both worlds: high crime rates and huge prison populations. It is becoming increasingly clear that ever more criminal justice resources generally, and more prisons in particular, are by themselves no solution at all.

Contemplating Crime

Social problems of such magnitude require, perhaps above all else, careful reflection. That is the central message of James Q. Wilson's *Thinking About Crime*, one of the most influential books on crime and what to do about it in this century.[2] Wilson recalls that when a presidential commission called on criminologists and sociologists to guide public officials to a response to rapidly rising crime rates in the mid-1960s, those thinkers certainly offered some reflection, but they were unable to provide much more than beliefs without solid empirical support. "Social scientists did not carry the day."[3]

Wilson observed that policy makers were interested particularly in information about "the consequences of differences in the certainty and severity of penalties on crime rates" and that "to an increasing extent, that inquiry is being furthered by economists rather than sociologists."[4] The economists' advice was based on the conventional neoclassical model: Assume that offenders are responsible persons who respond to incentives just like people who engage more exclusively in legitimate activities; raise the cost of committing crimes by increasing the likelihood and severity of punishment, and the supply of crimes committed should decline.

This theory was supported with some statistical evidence. The evidence consisted of analyses of nonexperimental data on crime rates, sanction levels, and other prospective determinants of crime, with observations both across jurisdictions and over time. The analyses generally revealed an inverse relationship between the levels of crime and punishment. Scrutiny of this evidence, however, raised serious questions about both the accuracy of the data and the validity of the methods used to derive inferences about deterrence.[5] The economists were well in front of the criminologists in producing sophisticated statistical reductions that impressed policy makers, but the court of scholarly opinion on the worthiness of the evidence for policy purposes has to this day been mostly skeptical.

This is not to suggest that the econometric approach is incorrect. Clearly, if no one were imprisoned, the number of crimes committed outside of prisons would increase, and if everyone were imprisoned, it would decline to zero. In between, however, the possibilities are countless and the estimates of deterrence highly unreliable.

The question of imprisonment has to do primarily with whether society is served, on balance, by greater use of prisons and jails for various classes of offenders. A utilitarian might frame the question as follows: What sentence minimizes the total cost of crime and punishment for each class of offense and offender, taking into account the deterrent and incapacitation effects of each punishment option for that class of offense and offender and all the pertinent criminal justice costs and costs to prospective victims? Such a question is useful primarily for making explicit the relevant parameters of the problem of imprisonment. Our knowledge of the values of those parameters is too hopelessly incomplete to allow us to base real-world imprisonment policy on such ponderings.

The Insufficiency of the Neoclassical Economic Model

The question of imprisonment has dominated the crime-and-justice policy debate for too long. It is not an unimportant question; reliance on imprisonment may indeed be bad policy, and decisions to imprison some offenders and not others certainly stand to be vastly improved. But the question of imprisonment has preoccupied policy makers at the expense of crime-and-justice issues that may be more critical. Even if one accepts the model of neoclassical economics—and there is ample reason not to ignore it—it is in order to question whether it is *sufficient* to view official sanctions as the sole, or even the principal, component of the cost side of the decision-to-commit-crimes calculus.

There is nothing about the economic model that suggests that it should be restricted to the deterrent effect of formal punishment, excluding sanctions imposed informally by individuals and society, but that is nonetheless how it has been traditionally applied.[6] For most people, *informal* social sanctions weigh heavily in the calculus of costs, too, as do moral considerations that are *internal* to the decision maker, considerations that induce people not to commit crime even when they are certain they would not be caught.[7] People often "do the right thing" even when that means faring less well than they would otherwise.

Amitai Etzioni has made the point as follows:

> The position advanced here is *not* the opposite of the Public Choice or the neoclassical position. The I&We paradigm does *not* hold that people simply internalize their society's moral code and follow it, impervious to their own self-interest, or allow it to be defined by the values of their society. The position is (1) that individuals are, simultaneously, under the influence of two major sets of factors—their pleasure, and their moral duty (although both reflect socialization); (2) that there are important differences in the extent each of these sets of factors is operative under different historical and societal conditions, and within different personalities under the same conditions. Hence, a study of the dynamics of the forces that shape both kinds of factors and their relative strengths is an essential foundation for a valid theory of behavior and society, including economic behavior, a theory referred to as socio-economics.[8]

The case for the insufficiency of the neoclassical model has been made by others as well. Jane Mansbridge, for one, has assembled an impressive collection of essays in *Beyond Self-Interest*, essays that

> reject the increasingly prevalent notion that human behavior is based on self-interest, narrowly conceived. [The essays] argue for a more complex view of both individual behavior and social organization—a view that takes into account duty, love, and malevolence. . . . When people think about what they want, they think about more than just their narrow self-interest.[9]

One of the more compelling chapters in the Mansbridge volume is by Robert H. Frank. Frank begins his essay by reviewing the mutually self-destructive pursuit of vengeance by the Hatfields and McCoys in the late nineteenth century. He then observes that we ignore our narrow self-interest as we

> trudge through snowstorms to cast our ballots, even when we are certain they will make no difference. We leave tips for waitresses in restaurants in distant cities we will never visit again. We make anonymous contributions to private charities. We often refrain from cheating even when we are sure we would not be caught. We sometimes walk away from profitable transactions whose terms

we believe to be "unfair." We battle endless red tape merely to get a $10 refund on a defective product. And so on.[10]

These notions of the insufficiency of the neoclassical model had received empirical validation specifically in the domain of criminal behavior several years earlier. Grasmick and Green interviewed 390 persons, focusing on two basic aspects of deterrence or self-interest—the certainty and severity of punishment—as well as a third motive, the moral justification for behaving within the law. They found both of those aspects of deterrence to be significantly correlated with the moral justification for refraining from illegal behavior. Grasmick and Green thus obtained evidence in support of the basic notion that both self-interest and moral commitment influence one's predisposition to commit crime.[11]

James Q. Wilson, despite his acknowledgment of the strength of the economic approach to analyzing crime and justice, had been among the first to recognize the insufficiency of the neoclassical model in explaining crime. Wilson has identified "character"—largely ignored by that model—as the central determinant of criminal behavior. In a 1985 *Public Interest* essay, Wilson bemoaned the contemporary emergence of self-expression over an old-fashioned morality that emphasized self-control and other-regardingness; he noted that the neoclassical model failed to address this core determinant of behavior:

> What economics neglects is the important subjective consequence of acting in accord with a proper array of incentives: people come to feel pleasure in right action and guilt in wrong action. These feelings of pleasure and pain are not mere "tastes" that policy analysts should take as given; they are the central constraints on human avarice and sloth, the very core of a decent character. A course of action cannot be evaluated simply in terms of its cost-effectiveness, because the consequence of following a given course—if it is followed often enough and regularly enough—is to teach those who follow it what society thinks is right and wrong.[12]

What can be said about this critical dimension—character—that has been so long overlooked by the neoclassical model? Suppose we agree that the development of "decent character" is the hallmark of a healthy society; what then are the essential characteristics of such a society?

In a healthy society, families and communities establish social sanctions that impose costs that are greater than those imposed by the criminal justice system. In a healthy society, the criminal justice system is properly viewed as a last resort, offering a safety net that deals with people who, for one reason or another, lack an effective internal system of moral beliefs—people whose experience of social sanctions from within a family or community unit is insufficient, or who experience the sanctions but do not respond to them as other people do.

The question that is more important than imprisonment has to do with the moral dimension, the question that asks: What developments explain the decline in the effectiveness of social sanctions? What can be done to restore the prominence of social sanctions over criminal sanctions for large portions of our society? Is it possible to overcome one of the tragic ironies of crime, its tendency to destroy the very communities and families that were once successful in controlling it?

This book focuses on such questions. We do not deny the importance of punishment as a necessary sanction to maintain social order. Nor do we intend to suggest, as have others before us, that the primary choice is between punishing offenders and rehabilitating them. The issue at hand has more to do with areas in which *society* can be rehabilitated than it does with the rehabilitation of offenders. We seek insights that will lead to the restoration of a social integrity that, throughout the history of humankind, has been far more effective than punishment in preventing crime.

The chapters that follow offer a tapestry of perspectives on crime and justice—from economics to sociology, from philosophy to the law—focusing on the nonpunitive side of the issue. A common thread runs through the tapestry: that our ability to meet the immense challenge of crime revolves around our ability to restore a fundamental sense of compassion and strengthen basic social institutions—the family, the school, the community. This approach to crime control, which has been largely overlooked by those who shape public policy, is likely to be more effective in the long run than the punitive approach on which we have come to rely so extensively.

We can prefer this approach for another, more compelling reason: it conforms more closely to basic standards of decency and humanity. Most humans prefer environments in which people are sensitive to the needs of others, irrespective of concerns about crime.

Although the media tend to suggest otherwise, serious crime is still the exception rather than the rule in most neighborhoods. It is the exception in rural and suburban communities throughout the United States and in metropolitan areas throughout most of the world. Serious crime is still a relatively infrequent occurrence even in many big-city neighborhoods in the United States. The epidemic nature of murder rates in so many of our inner cities—the spectacle of a Middle East battlefield being safer for Americans than some inner-city locations—is, in fact, the exception.

It is, nonetheless, an exception that cannot be ignored. One cannot ignore the fact that homicide has become the leading cause of death for young black men. Nor can one ignore the fact that crime has destroyed much of the residential and commercial vitality of our cities. The horror of such an extraordinary level of serious crime, and its vast costs, captures our attention; crime cannot be ignored. It deserves the best thinking we can give.

Organization of the Book

This book addresses the problem of crime and our response to it in four stages. We discuss, in Part I ("Foundations"), fundamental principles underlying crime and justice. In Part II ("The Community in the Human"), we consider forces that shape human behavior generally and the inclination to commit crime in particular. In Part III ("Offenders and Offenses"), we focus on specific classes of offenders and offenses. We conclude, in Part IV ("The Criminal Justice System"), by examining the three principal components of the criminal justice system. Let us look at each of these sections in more detail.

Foundations

In Part I we consider pertinent foundations of crime and justice: philosophical, economic, and legal. Hugo Bedau's chapter on philosophy, justice, and punishment provides a thoughtful survey of the standard justifications for criminal sanctions. Noting that the classical Cartesian "foundations" approach offers little promise for the development of sentencing policy, Bedau reviews the dominant themes that have shaped the debate over criminal sanctions up to the present time: the retributivist or just-deserts model, and the consequentialist or utilitarian model, which includes general and special deterrence, incapacitation, and rehabilitation. Bedau then states the fundamental justification for punishment: the authorized deprivation of a person's rights supported by the judgment that that person criminally violated the rights of others. Bedau develops the argument that sanctions based on such a justification are more likely to be liberal, non-paternalistic, and respectful of individual autonomy than sanctions not so grounded.

The next chapter, by Llad Phillips, reconsiders the economic model of crime and justice. Phillips begins by citing the work of those who laid foundations for the neoclassical theory of criminal behavior: Jeremy Bentham and Gary Becker. He observes that cross-disciplinary approaches—such as Albert Hirschman's exit-voice-loyalty model and Jack Katz's sensual-rewards-of-crime theory—tend to be richer in explanatory power than the neoclassical economic model. He notes that the neoclassical model is too parsimonious; among other things, it ignores moral suasion and assumes that tastes are given and that the offender population responds to incentives as a somewhat homogeneous group.

Phillips does not reject the neoclassical model; indeed, he argues that it offers a framework to explain such important forces as altruism within the family, which can strongly induce individuals to avoid participation in criminal activity. He cautions, however, that the decline in the family unit and growth in economic inequality represent serious threats to the transmission of altruistic behavior in society and, in turn, to the very peace and prosperity of humankind.

Chapter 4, by Graham Hughes, addresses the limits of the criminal law. He describes a desperate preoccupation of lawmakers and criminal justice officials with an alphabet soup of draconian laws, such as those aimed at drug "kingpins" involved in Continuing Criminal Enterprises (CCE) and those aimed at offenders involved in Racketeer Influenced and Corrupt Organizations (RICO). Noting that the passage of such laws reflects frustration with crime and reliance on deterrence as a substitute for the failed goal of rehabilitation, Hughes observes that the law enforcement, prosecution, and adjudication of those offenses consume enormous resources, and that the arbitrariness of enforcement of these laws produces contempt for the system. He suggests that policy makers' newly found faith in the god of deterrence—built on an altar of belief that offenders adhere to the economists' rational man model—may turn out to be as misplaced as their earlier faith in the god of rehabilitation. Hughes sees hope in the prospect of shifting power from today's centralized, bureaucratic adjudicative institutions to local community participation in crime control, perhaps following the model of Inner London's seventeen magistrate courts.

The Community in the Human

The next set of chapters focuses on the processes that shape the individual's moral belief system. Joan McCord begins this discussion by considering the role of family in instilling an individual's internal moral system. Reviewing the literature on the socialization practices commonly found in American families, she finds strong effects of family interaction on the perceptions of children. The important question, according to McCord, has to do with specific mechanisms that link dysfunctional families to crime.

McCord identifies three common errors in thinking about why intervention programs fail to produce desired changes: (1) assuming that human nature is inherently egoistic; (2) assuming that socialization practices and biological conditions have universal, independent effects on child development; and (3) believing that rewards and punishments are effective for teaching children, while ignoring the role of reinforcements in teaching children what to *value*. She posits a "construct theory" for understanding the socialization process, a theory that holds language as key to thought, including thoughts about values, beliefs, hopes, and pain. McCord holds that children are more likely to be well socialized in families in which they are respected and communicated with accordingly, in families that offer consistent guidance, and in families that use reason and consideration along with the guidance.

Chapter 6, by Darnell Hawkins, focuses on the relationships among crime, ethnicity, and community. He organizes his essay around two theoretical constructs—"economic deprivation/inequality" (crime attributable to poverty) and "cultural variance" (crime related to cultural value systems). Hawkins describes some of the myriad difficulties in finding meaningful relationships between ethnicity/race and crime—from measuring crime and offending behavior to disentangling alternative theories for predicting or explaining relationships between ethnicity and crime. He compares earlier ethnicity-and-crime controversies, involving Irish and Sicilian populations, with those of more recent times, involving African-Americans and Latinos. Hawkins raises critical questions throughout; he makes a disturbing, yet compelling, case on behalf of the difficulty of resolving them.

His recommendations are practical—for example, in examining relationships between crime and ethnicity, analysts should focus less on crime and race as aggregates and more on specific crime categories and ethnic groups and subcultures. And they are sweeping—Hawkins observes that solutions to the problem of crime in minority communities are likely to lie both in interventions that focus on culture (for example, mentoring, community empowerment) and in programs that work to reduce poverty.

In chapter 7, Rita Simon focuses on male-female differences in crime rates and factors that lie beneath the differences. Simon observes gender differences in arrest, court, and prison statistics over time, relative to other changes in the role of women in society. She notes that over a fifty-year period in which the labor force participation rate of married women soared from 17 percent to 56 percent, arrests and convictions of those women for criminal activity increased as well, especially in nonviolent offenses. Simon sees no reason to expect an abatement of these trends. Women may or may not be inherently more compassionate, but they are not immune from inducements to participate in crime.

Offenders and Offenses

The next section examines issues related to specific categories of offenders and crimes. It begins with chapter 8, by Carl Pope, on juvenile crime and justice. Pope categorizes the theories of juvenile delinquency along three lines: structural theories, relating to societal factors such as unemployment; control theories, relating to society's social and legal inhibitors to crime; and reaction theories, focusing on the behavior of juveniles. He sees the high rates of criminality among minority youths getting worse before they get better. Pope argues that public policy, if it is to succeed, cannot confine itself to the criminal justice system alone; it must deal with structural and social aspects of delinquency as well.

In chapter 9, "Community Responses to Crime and Fear of Crime," Bonnie Fisher explores the prospects for community self-help in light of the neoclassical and communitarian models, the available evidence about what has been tried, limitations in that evidence, and a consideration of possibilities that have not been tried. Fisher catalogues an array of public and private responses, from a variety of community policing tactics to private security systems, from Crime Stopper and neighborhood-watch programs to citizen patrols. She explores what citizens should do when justice authorities can do little, whether there is any hope for community self-help programs, and what appears to have been wrong, and what right, with contemporary community self-help tactics. Throughout, she examines the contribution of the communitarian point of view to contemporary thought about public policy toward the control of street crime.

In chapter 10, Jeffrey Fagan considers the effect of the community on spouse assault. He begins by exposing the popular notion that family violence is a classless problem, afflicting all sectors of society about equally, as a myth. He reports the results of an analysis of national survey data showing that both the likelihood and frequency of spouse assault are influenced by socioeconomic factors, especially income and unemployment, and that the likelihood of such assault is higher in African-American households. Of particular importance, however, is Fagan's finding of how much stronger all of those effects are in the inner city than in rural or suburban settings.

Fagan finds an explanation for these findings in the ineffectiveness of the two principal deterrents to spouse assault—legal and social sanctions—in inner-city minority settings. He goes on to discuss the relative unimportance of "social capital" for these populations. Many inner-city assailants have little to lose in beating their partners; because of greater mobility, anonymity, heterogeneity, and separation from mainstream society, they are less likely to suffer job loss, social stigmatization, or other setbacks faced by people in other community contexts. Poor social cohesion also prevents aware neighbors from getting involved. Arrest, still the exception in spouse-assault episodes, does not appear to carry the same degree of deterrent value for these offenders as for people in other settings. Fagan sees little hope for immediate solutions; he urges that research be conducted to provide a more detailed anatomy of community effects in domestic violence.

In chapter 11, Jackson Toby looks at the problem of school crime in a multicultural society. Noting that cross-cultural understanding requires knowledge of cultural context, Toby observes that "school" has different meanings for different subcultures. He argues that the original purposes of compulsory school attendance have little relevance for some of these groups. Our current system traps a large corps of unwilling teenagers who have no stake in conformity in a setting they have no desire to align with. The result is a high rate of violence in many urban schools, with homicide not uncommon in some districts.

Toby finds the conventional solutions—more security guards and metal detectors in schools—unsatisfactory. He argues for a more basic solution: At the very least, we should stop compelling youths to attend school; we might do better to expel all students who do not meet fairly high standards of performance, behavior, and attendance. Toby says that the costs of using schools as rehabilitation centers for delinquents, in terms of both crime and lost education opportunities for real students, who are deprived of a healthy learning environment, are simply too great to continue to bear.

The Criminal Justice System

The concluding section focuses on three primary components of the justice system: the police, the prosecutor, and the courts. James Fyfe, in chapter 12, challenges the idea that the police can and should be able to solve the crime problem. He observes that such expectations are at sharp odds with the ambiguity of the role of policing. The police are called upon to handle not only street crimes but also domestic violence, vagrancy, and a limitless variety of social ills. To the extent that individual departments have been showcased for their reforms, it has been largely in communities with less serious crime problems in the first place. "Model" police departments succeed not so much because of their reforms as because of their relatively well behaved citizens. The crime explosion that began in the 1960s was not the product of police failure; it was largely the result of the replacement of relatively cohesive communities with impersonal, densely populated housing projects and related social upheaval, forces that go beyond the sphere of policing and that have tended to widen the psychic distance between the police and the community.

Fyfe sees the role of the police defined largely by the incentive systems that influence their behavior. The incentive systems currently used by most police departments, especially the nearly universal adoption of arrest statistics to measure police effectiveness, work primarily to retard genuine crime prevention activity. In the absence of better measures of performance and of a clearly defined role, most police officers give their loyalty primarily to their peers rather than to police managers and the community that pays their salaries. In the end, the most reliable definition of policing, according to Fyfe, is likely to come from the line police officers themselves.

In chapter 13, I consider the relationship between the prosecutor and the public in the United States. Prosecutors have been criticized for abuses in the exercise of discretion by liberals and conservatives alike. The chapter begins with a focus on the question of accountability: Is the prosecutor in the United States held sufficiently accountable to the public? If not, what can be done about it? Increased use of guidelines is considered as a possible solution to excesses in the exercise of prosecutorial discretion.

The chapter then focuses on the question of accountability by inquiring about the prospect of greater prosecutor–community integration. Two offices are examined that have reorganized their attorneys specifically with a view to the community, with case assignments based on the location of the crime rather than type of crime. The goals: to become sensitive to the unique problems and needs of various communities within the jurisdiction, to improve coordination with the police, and, in the end, to improve service to the community. While the prospects are encouraging, it remains to be seen how this new perspective on prosecution will work out and, if it succeeds, how long it will take to catch on in other jurisdictions.

In chapter 14, Norval Morris reexamines our sentencing policy with a view ultimately toward the interests of the community. Revisiting a form and title used in two earlier classics coauthored with Gordon Hawkins, Morris discusses the extraordinary rate of incarceration in the United States and its principal determinants: politicization of crime and failure to develop effective policies for dealing with its causes.[13] Morris discusses the recent twenty-five-year history of sentencing reform: a scholarly documentation of unwarranted disparity in sentences, a resulting decline in the indeterminacy of punishment, the development of measures designed to reduce the disparity, and the eventual neglect in the development of a comprehensive system of fair and efficient sentences. He then enumerates the disastrous results of this neglect and outlines a straightforward solution to the problem. Morris's chapter provides a fitting note on which to end this book: He observes that the ultimate goal of criminal justice policy is a healthier community.

Where from Here?

The authors of these chapters have attempted to reconsider standard criminological themes from a particular point of view, combining conventional notions of rationality with notions of compassion and community. We have only scratched the surface of critical issues to be dealt with from this perspective. Specific topics not addressed here that warrant similar treatment include the proliferation of firearms, drugs, white-collar and organized crime, gang-related crime, rape, drunk driving, street crime, hate crime, prostitution, terrorism, and a host of other issues.

We must also probe more deeply into some fundamental questions: How can a more cohesive social infrastructure be created, one that builds "character," inducing all members of the community to behave with compassion and respect for others? How, specifically, can individuals be encouraged to take a stand against the acceptability of crime, to take actions that will discourage crime? How, in turn, can the criminal justice system be induced to work more effectively with members of the community to prevent crime? What information is needed, and how can it be organized to support the development of guidelines and policies that will enable the courts to select offenders more effectively for alternatives to incarceration?

Unfortunately, much of what is already known about these issues has not been put to good use—a matter that policy makers must confront. But much remains to be learned about each of the issues—a matter for social scientists. The breadth and nature of the issues require scientific inquiry that transcends narrow academic disciplines; no single perspective is likely to succeed in resolving such a rich variety of matters.

These are high-stakes issues. Successful inquiry can contribute significantly to the reduction of crime. Of greater importance, it can contribute to the creation of a more robust, more nourishing, and more decent society.

Notes

1. Bureau of Justice Statistics, *Report to the Nation on Crime and Justice*, pp. 114–15.
2. James Q. Wilson, *Thinking About Crime*.

3. Ibid., p. 60. Earlier, Wilson notes: "When social scientists were asked for advice by national policy-making bodies, they could not respond with suggestions derived from and supported by their scholarly work . . . such advice as was supplied tended to derive from their general political views as modified by their political and organizational interaction with those policy groups and their staffs" (p. 42). And this: "Sociological theories of crime, widely known and intensely discussed in the 1960s, have certain features in common. All sought to explain the causes of delinquency, or at least its persistence. All made attitude formation a key variable. All stressed that these attitudes are shaped and supported by intimate groups—the family and close friends. . . . *But none could supply a plausible basis for the advocacy of public policy*" (p. 45, emphasis in the original).

4. Ibid., p. 50. This is not to imply that Wilson is especially enamored of the economists' rationalistic worldview or their empirical findings. He remarks, "To the extent that policymakers and criminologists have become less hostile to the idea of altering behavior by altering its consequences, progress has been made. . . . But long-term changes in crime rates exceed anything that can be explained by either rational calculation or the varying proportion of young males in the population" (Wilson, "The Rediscovery of Character: Private Virtue and Public Policy").

5. A National Academy of Sciences panel, reviewing the evidence, found several sources of bias in the finding of a negative correlation between crimes and punishments, as well as error in the measurement of crime, a confounding of deterrent and incapacitation effects, and simultaneous effects that made the inference of deterrence virtually impossible. The panel concluded in its report: "In summary, therefore, we cannot yet assert that the evidence warrants an affirmative conclusion regarding deterrence. We believe scientific caution must be exercised in interpreting the limited validity of the available evidence and the number of competing explanations for the results" (Alfred Blumstein, Jacqueline Cohen, and Daniel Nagin, eds., *Deterrence and Incapacitation: Estimating the Effects of Criminal Sanctions on Crime Rates*, p. 7.)

6. Gary Becker established himself as chief architect of the economic model of crime and punishment with his landmark "Crime and Punishment: An Economic Approach." He concludes the article as follows:

> This essay uses economic analysis to develop optimal public and private policies to combat illegal behavior. The public's decision variables are its expenditures on police, courts, etc., which help determine the probability (p) that an offense is discovered and the offender apprehended and convicted, the size of the punishment for those convicted (f), and the form of the punishment: imprisonment, probation, fine, etc.

7. Harold Grasmick and Donald Green have found both deterrence and moral commitments to affect people's predisposition to commit crimes or violate moral values. See "Deterrence and the Morally Committed," pp. 1–14.

8. Amitai Etzioni, *The Moral Dimension: Toward a New Economics*, p. 63.

9. Jane Mansbridge, *Beyond Self-Interest*, p. ix.

10. Robert H. Frank, "A Theory of Moral Sentiments," p. 72. Frank's essay was adapted from his *Passions Within Reason: The Strategic Role of the Emotions*.

11. Grasmick and Green, "Deterrence."

12. Wilson, "The Rediscovery of Character," p. 16.

13. Morris and Hawkins, *The Honest Politician's Guide to Crime Control*; Morris and Hawkins, *Letter to the President on Crime Control*.

References

Becker, Gary. "Crime and Punishment: An Economic Approach." *Journal of Political Economy* 76 (March/April 1968): 189–217.

Blumstein, Alfred; Cohen, Jacqueline; and Nagin, Daniel, eds. *Deterrence and Incapacitation: Estimating the Effects of Criminal Sanctions on Crime Rates*. Washington, D.C.: National Academy of Sciences, 1978.

Bureau of Justice Statistics. *Report to the Nation on Crime and Justice*, 2d edition. Washington, D.C.: U.S. Department of Justice, 1988.

Etzioni, Amitai. *The Moral Dimension: Toward a New Economics*. New York: Free Press, 1988.

Frank, Robert H. *Passions Within Reason: The Strategic Role of the Emotions*. New York: W.W. Norton, 1988.

———. "A Theory of Moral Sentiments." In Jane Mansbridge, ed., *Beyond Self-Interest*. Chicago: University of Chicago Press, 1990.

Grasmick, Harold, and Green, Donald. "Deterrence and the Morally Committed." *Sociological Quarterly* 22 (1981): 1–14.

Mansbridge, Jane, ed. *Beyond Self-Interest*. Chicago: University of Chicago Press, 1990.

Morris, Norval, and Hawkins, Gordon. *The Honest Politician's Guide to Crime Control*. Chicago: University of Chicago Press, 1970.

———. *Letter to the President on Crime Control*. Chicago: University of Chicago Press, 1977.

Wilson, James Q. "The Rediscovery of Character: Private Virtue and Public Policy." *Public Interest*, no. 81 (Fall 1985).

———. *Thinking About Crime*, 2d edition. New York: Basic Books, 1983.

Part I

Foundations

2

HUGO ADAM BEDAU

Justice and Punishment: Philosophical Basics

As the next millennium approaches, we find ourselves in an intellectual environment in which philosophers have told us, across the board—in logic, epistemology, philosophy of science, philosophy of mind, ethics, political theory—that there are no "foundations" for our beliefs and theories. Reasons and rationalizations, themes and theories, models and metaphors, there are galore, no one denies. But foundational reasons of the classic Cartesian or Kantian sort—reasons that compel rational assent because they are, or are based on, a priori truths that serve as the necessary presuppositions of any possible substantive policy or practice—such reasons are unavailable. Foundationalism, at least of that sort, despite having been a powerfully attractive and occasionally prevailing assumption of most Western philosophers during much of this century, is on the defensive today. In its place, especially in the English-speaking philosophical world, we find a resurgence of various forms of pragmatism, which since its inception more than a century ago (beginning with Pierce, then James, and especially Dewey), has been the very model of an empiricist, naturalistic, and realistic antifoundationalist philosophy. In Europe, where foundationalism has had less of a grip on philosophical thinking in the past century, antifoundationalism can be seen as an inevitable by-product of less naturalistic—existentialist, phenomenological, and post-structuralist—thought.

Insofar, therefore, as one seeks from philosophy the foundations for substantive penal policies—the axioms, as it were, on which the governing norms of justice and punishment are based and from which penal policy can be derived—one runs against the current tide. I am not myself wholly without sympathy for the antifoundationalist temper of the times, and the remarks that follow, I believe, reflect this. I do not argue directly, however, for any version of antifoundationalism in the theory of punishment. Instead, I merely warn readers that lying in the background of my argumentative strategy is a form of antifoundationalism, unarticulated and undefended in the body of my remarks though it may be. To put it another way, the account of justice in punishment that I offer must, in the last analysis, be given an antifoundationalist interpretation, despite what may seem to be occasional appearances to the contrary.

The theory I propose emerges out of the most influential developments over the past half century in the prevailing understanding of punishment in our culture. As a background to the theory, those developments are worth a brief review.

A Recent History of Punishment

The current state of philosophical reflection on punishment has helped cause, and is itself partially an effect of, developments in the understanding (I hesitate to say the theory) of punishment that have taken place outside the academy in the real world of the nation's political life. Two decades ago sociologists and penologists—not to mention the general public and politicians—became disenchanted with the rehabilitative effects (as measured by reduced offender recidivism) of programs conducted in prisons aimed at this end.[1] This led directly to skepticism about the feasibility of the very aim of rehabilitation within the framework of existing penal policy. To this was added skepticism over general deterrence and even special deterrence as effective goals to pursue in punishment. That left exactly two rational aims to pursue in the practice of punishment under law: social defense through incapacitation, and retribution. Public policy advocates insisted that the best thing to do with convicted offenders in order to reduce crime was to incarcerate them, in the belief that the most economical way to reduce crime was to incapacitate known recidivists via incarceration, or even death.[2] Whatever else may be true, this aim at least has been achieved on a breathtaking scale, as the enormous growth in the number of state and federal prisoners in the United States (including over 2,500 on "death row") during the past decade attests.

At the same time that enthusiasm for incarceration was growing on incapacitative grounds, dissatisfaction with the indeterminate sentence on grounds of fairness led policy analysts to search for another approach. Sentencing fairness seemed most likely to depend on determinate rather than indeterminate sentencing.[3] But even determinate sentencing would not be just unless the sentences it authorized were the punishments that convicted offenders deserved. Thus was born the doctrine of "just deserts" in sentencing, which effectively combined the two ideas.[4] By this route the goals of incapacitation and retribution came to dominate, and in some quarters completely supersede, the goals of rehabilitation and deterrence in the minds of politicians and social theorists.

Concurrently with these broadly sociolegal developments (to which might be added the despair of practitioners that reached its peak with the police assault on rioting prisoners in New York's Attica prison twenty years ago), philosophers were crafting their own arguments, reviving classic views associated with the names of Kant and Hegel, to establish two principal ideas that fit surprisingly well with those reviewed above. First, philosophers argued that reformation of convicted offenders (especially in its more medically inspired modes) is not the aim, or even a subsidiary aim among several, of the practice of punishment. Aside from being an impractical goal, it is morally defective because it fails to respect the convicted offenders' autonomy.[5] Second, justice in punishment is the essential task of sentencing, and a just sentence takes its character from the culpability of the offender and the harm the crime caused the victim.[6] In short, just punishment is retributive punishment. Philosophers reached these conclusions because they argued that there were irreducible retributive aspects to punishment—in the very definition of the practice, in the norms governing justice in punishment, and in the purpose of the practice as well.

As a result, the ground was cut out from under the dominant penal policy of mid-century, the indeterminate sentence, the type of sentence hitherto deemed a necessary feature of any effective, rehabilitative scheme conducted with offenders in prison. Probation as the essential nonincarcerative alternative sanction received an expanded role, but parole release came to a virtual end. In its place, at least in theory, was uniform determinate sentencing, which would avoid the follies of unachievable rehabilitative goals and ensure both incapacitation and even-handed justice for all offenders. That was, of course, before the political process distorted these aims. The culmination of this trend appears in the Sentencing Reform Act of 1984, which spawned the United States Sentencing Commission and its Federal Sentencing Guidelines. The doctrine has not been without its critics, early and late,[7] both in theory and in practice. But as the century ends, no alternative approach shows any signs of supplanting the just-desserts sentencing philosophy.

There has been a third development concurrent with the two outlined above, far less influential in the formation of actual penal policy even if it is of equal theoretical importance.[8] I refer to the reconceptualization of the practice of punishment arising from the work of Michel Foucault in the mid-1970s. Foucault invited us to view the practice of punishment as subject to general forces in society that reflect the dominant forms of power—the power to threaten, coerce, suppress, destroy, transform—that prevail in any given epoch. And he also cultivated a deep suspicion toward the claims that contemporary society had significantly humanized the forms of punishment by abandoning the savage physical brutality that prevailed in the bad old days, in favor of the hidden carceral system of the modern era.

Foucault's insights arose from a historical, socioeconomic, and psychodynamic approach to punishment. Professed goals of punishment, norms constraining the use of power in the pursuit of these goals, the aspiration for justice in punishment—all these, if Foucault is right, turn out to mask other (not necessarily conscious) intentions among reformers that belie the ostensible rationality (not to say rationalization) of their aims in the modern era. Thus, the movement against capital punishment in the late eighteenth century is not explained (or, presumably, justified) by the influence of conscious, rational, utilitarian calculations of the sort that Beccaria and Bentham argued had persuaded them to oppose the death penalty.[9] It is explained instead by disenchantment with the theatrical, dramaturgical, aspects of public executions and a self-deceiving humanitarian impulse that merely shifted but otherwise left unaltered the nature and locus of the power wielded over criminals by society—perfectly embodied in Bentham's own enthusiastic scheme of the Panopticon.

Two features at least of Foucault's explorations into the practice of punishment in Western society deserve brief mention here. First, he ignored the analytical distinctions that philosophers in the Anglo-American tradition had made familiar. None plays any visible role in his account of the practice of punishment. Some interpreters might explain this by arguing that Foucault offers no philosophical views about punishment at all—because conceptual and normative analysis and the search for principles on which to rest policy are so obscurely pursued in his writings. Instead, so this view declares, he is just a social theorist (or some other form of sociologist or historian).[10] But this would be an error. Foucault's views are, at least in part, unmistakably philosophical; not only do they issue in claims that are not obviously testable empirical hypotheses, they involve large-scale reinterpretations of human nature and of the point of our punitive practices.

Second, Foucault implicitly challenges the very idea of any form of justification of the practice of punishment. He is, in his way, a paradigmatic thinker whose views about punishment are what I have earlier called antifoundationalist. What emerges from his account is the view that justification of punishment (as with any other social practice) is inextricably tied up with assumptions, beliefs—in short, with ideology—that have no independent rational foundation. The very idea that penal institutions can be justified is suspect, self-delusive. Foucault, more than any other recent thinker who has reflected on the institutions of punishment in our society, has brought historicist, antianalytic, and antifoundationalist convictions together, thus sowing deep uncertainty over how and even whether to address the task of justifying punishment.

In all these respects, Foucault must be seen as the modern successor to Friedrich Nietzsche—Foucault's great albeit unacknowledged predecessor in the philosophy of punishment. More than any other modern thinker, Nietzsche understood the way punishment is "overdetermined by utilities of every sort" and survives now under this, now under that interpretation of its purposes—because the desire to punish (and thereby subordinate, coerce, transform) is so deeply rooted in human nature.

The cumulative effects of these forces, political and intellectual, has been to undermine the classic liberal view of punishment. Perhaps this is an exaggeration; one might argue that since it is quite unclear just what a liberal view of punishment really is, successfully undermining it is equally uncertain. Liberalism in punishment, it is true, has no canonical formulation; instead, it has been multiply ambiguous during its career of some two centuries, as Beccaria's influential proposals for reform at the apex of the Enlightenment show.[11] What is needed, I believe, is a reassertion, reformulation, and redeployment of recognizably liberal ideas in the theory of punishment—and that is what I endeavor to offer in the argument that follows.

Theory of Punishment

I want to start by reminding us of the central features of the modern theory of punishment developed by analytic philosophers roughly forty years ago. The theory of punishment in the Anglo-American philosophical world was and still is governed by a small handful of basic conceptual distinctions, self-consciously deployed by virtually all theorists no matter what substantive views they also hold about punishment. We can date the terminus a quo of these ideas in the mid-1950s with the influential writings of (among others) H.L.A. Hart in England and John Rawls in this country. Though both Hart and Rawls pass muster as centrist liberals, they understood these analytic distinctions to be ideologically neutral in nature. I do not think this particular quest for "neutral principles" was self-deluding.

(1) *Defining* the concept of punishment must be kept distinct from *justifying* the infliction of a punishment. A definition of punishment is, or is supposed to be, value-neutral, incorporating no norms or principles that surreptitiously tend to justify whatever falls under the definition itself. To put it another way, punishment is not supposed to be justified, or even partially justified, by packing its definition in a manner that virtually guarantees this result.

(2) Justifying the *practice* or institution of punishment must be kept distinct from justifying any given *act* of punishment. For one thing, it is possible to have a practice of punishment ready and waiting without having occasion to inflict punishment on anyone (for example, because there are no convicted criminals). For another, allowance must be made for the possibility that the practice might be justified even though not all of the acts that instantiate the practice are justified. (The converse possibility may be ignored.)

(3) Justification of any act of punishment is to be done by reference to the *norms* (rules, standards, principles) defining the institutional practice of punishment. Justification of the practice itself, however, necessarily has reference to very different considerations—social purposes, values, or *goals* of the community in which the practice is rooted. The values and considerations appropriate to justifying acts are often assimilated to those that define judicial responsibility, whereas the values that bear on justifying the punitive institution are akin to those that govern legislation.

(4) Justifying the practice of punishment must be done either by reference to *consequentialist* criteria—punishment seen entirely as a means to one or more

future ends, such as the utilitarian end of increasing overall net social welfare—or by reference to *deontological* criteria—punishment seen as a good in itself, an instance of justice that makes a direct claim on our allegiance. Or, as a third alternative, the justification of the practice must be found in some hybrid combination of these two ostensibly independent and exhaustive alternatives.

Acknowledgment of this quartet of distinctions seems to me essential to anything that might be regarded as a tolerably adequate (liberal) theory of punishment.

Two substantive conclusions have been reached by most philosophers based in part on these considerations. First, although it is possible to criticize the legitimacy or appropriateness of various individual punitive acts, or of various modes of punishment, the practice of punishment itself is clearly justified—and, in particular, justified within a liberal constitutional democracy. Second, this justification requires some accommodation both to consequentialist and to deontological considerations. A strait laced purely retributive theory of punishment is as unsatisfactory as a sprawling purely consequentialist theory. Punishment, to put the point another way, rests on a plurality of values, not some one value to the exclusion of others.

Although the philosophers who pioneered this general approach to punishment never developed their views in a full-scale manner, many others more or less under their influence have done so.[12] The task, if carried out properly, is a considerable one, because it requires identifying and using central elements of liberal political philosophy that lie in the background and have no direct reference to punishment theory at all. In what follows, I shall proceed on the assumption that the task of justifying punishment is to be carried out by reference to the role it plays in a liberal democratic constitutional republic, rather than in some other sort of society or in a manner that has no reference whatever to the larger sociopolitical setting in which the practice of punishment is fixed.

So much by way of review of the recent past as a stage setting for what is to follow. What I propose to do now is sketch what I take to be the best general approach to the problem of justifying punishment.

Justifications for Punishment

As a first step we need a *definition* of punishment in light of the conceptual distinctions suggested above. Can a definition be proposed that meets the test of neutrality (that is, does not prejudge any policy questions)? I suggest this: Punishment is *the authorized deprivation of the rights of a person because the person has been found guilty of a criminal violation of the rights of others.*

This definition, although imperfect (if only) because of its brevity, does bring out several essential points. First, punishment is authorized, not incidental or accidental, harm. It is an act of the legitimate political authority in the community. Second, it is constituted by some form of deprivation of rights. "Deprivation" has no covert or essentially subjective reference; punishment is an objectively (or at least intersubjectively) judged loss. Hence the reference to rights as what is lost. Third, punishment is a human or personal institution, not a natural event. Its practice requires persons cast in various socially defined roles according to public rules. Fourth, it is imposed on someone because of his or her alleged (and adjudicated) wrongdoing. Being found guilty by persons authorized to make such a finding, and based on their belief in the person's guilt, is the necessary condition of justified punishment. Actually being guilty is not. Fifth, no explicit purpose or aim is built by definition into the practice of punishment. The practice, as Nietzsche was the first to notice, is consistent with several functions or purposes (though it is not consistent with having no purposes or functions whatever). Sixth, not all socially authorized deprivations count as punishments; only deprivations inflicted on a person previously found guilty of a crime (rather than guilty only of a tort or a contract violation) count as punishments. Finally, although the practice of punishment under law may be the very perfection of punishment in human experience, most of us learn about punishment well before any encounters with the law (thus "authorized deprivation" must not be interpreted so narrowly as to rule out parental or other forms of "punishment" familiar to children), and the proffered definition is consistent with this fact.

Let us begin the justification for punishment by noticing three reasons that punishment needs to be justified:

(1) Punishment—especially punishment under law, by officers of the government—is a human institution, not a natural fact; it is deliberately and intentionally organized and practiced. Yet it is not a basic social institution that every society must have; it is a testimony to human frailty, not to the conditions necessary to implement human social cooperation. It also has no more than historical or biological affinity with retaliatory harm or other aggressive acts to be found among nonhuman animals or (despite thinkers from Butler to Strawson to the contrary) with the natural resentment that unprovoked aggression characteristically elicits.

(2) The practice or institution of punishment is not necessary, conceptually or empirically, to human society. It is conceivable even if impracticable that society should not have the practice of punishment, and it is possible—given the pains of punishment—that we might even decide to do without it, or at least that some radical social thinkers would from time to time advocate its abolition.[13]

(3) Punishment under law, and especially in a society like ours, incurs considerable costs for everyone involved in carrying it out, whatever the net benefits may be. Some rationale must be provided by a society that deliberately chooses to continue to incur these costs. The matter is aggravated to the extent that we prefer to incur them rather than the costs of alternative social interventions with personal liberty in order to prevent crime or heal its wounds.[14]

By way of expansion on some of the considerations alluded to above, I would draw attention to the fact that punishment by its very nature involves some (those who punish) having dominant coercive power over others (those being punished). To seek to be punished, because one likes it, is pathological, an inversion of the normal response, which is to shun or endure one's punishment. (Only among the Raskolnikovs of the world is one's deserved punishment welcomed.) To try to punish another without first establishing control over the would-be punished is doomed to failure. But the power to punish—as distinct from merely inflicting harm on another—cannot be adventitious; it must be authoritative, legitimate, institutionalized under the prevailing political regime. Finally, because the infliction of punishment is normally intended to cause, and usually does cause, some form of deprivation for the person being punished, the infliction of punishment provides unparalleled opportunity for abuse of power. To distinguish such abuses both from the legitimate deprivations that are essential to punishment and from the excesses of sentences that embody cruel and inhumane punishments, one must rely on the way the former are connected (and the latter disconnected) to whatever constitutes the sentence as such and whatever justifies it.[15] This is especially true where punishment through the legal system is concerned, since the punishments at the system's disposal—as well as the abuses—are typically so severe.

The general form of any possible justification of punishment involves several steps. They start from realizing that punishing people is not intelligibly done entirely or solely for its own sake, as are, say, playing cards or music, writing poetry or philosophy, or other activities of intrinsic worth to their participants. (Nietzsche and Foucault are among those who would, for various reasons, dispute this claim, and they may have history on their side. They think that human nature is such that we do get intrinsic even if disguised satisfactions out of inflicting authorized harm on others. I regard this as a perversity of human nature, not its natural expression—but I cannot argue the point here.) Instead, we practice punishment in order to achieve certain goals, ends, or results.

Although punishment can be defined without any reference to its purposes, it cannot be justified without such reference. Accordingly, to justify punishment we must specify, first, what our goals are in establishing (or perpetuating) the practice itself. Second, we must show that when we punish we achieve these goals. Third, we must show that we cannot achieve these goals unless we punish (and, moreover, perhaps punish in certain ways and not in others) or cannot achieve them with comparable efficiency and fairness in any other way. Fourth, we must show that achieving these goals is itself justified. Justification thus is closed over these four steps; roughly, to justify the practice of punishment it is necessary and sufficient to carry out these four tasks.

Unsurprisingly, no matter what actual society we find ourselves in, we can contest each of these steps, especially the fourth. Just as there is no theoretical limit to the demands that can be made in the name of any or all of these tasks, there is also no bedrock on which to stand as one undertakes either a critique of existing systems of punishment or the design of an ideal system. As a result, the foundations of punishment imitate the topology of a Moebius strip—if any path is pursued far enough, it will return to itself, and one loses one's grip on what is inside and what outside the justification. Metaphor apart, the inescapable forensic quality of justification defeats all forms of what might be called linear— whether top-down or bottom-up—foundationalism. How this guides the actual justification of punishment I shall shortly attempt to explain.

Consequentialist or Deontological Justification

For some decades, philosophers have (over)simplified the picture of possible forms of normative justification in ethics, politics, and law into two alternatives: consequentialist and deontological. They have also undertaken to apply this distinction to the justification of punishment. It is clear from what I have said above that the approach I take is not anticonsequentialist. I have insisted that punishment as an institution is justified because, and only because, it accomplishes certain goals or ends, and not because of its very "nature."

However, I do not think a purely consequentialist theory of punishment is defensible, and the liberal theory I am sketching here is not purely consequentialist. By a purely consequentialist theory, I mean a theory that imposes no constraints on what counts as my fourth step in justification, mentioned above. The pure consequentialist views punishment as justified to the extent that its practice achieves (or is reasonably believed to achieve) whatever end-state the theorist specifies. Instead, I shall argue that the goals of punishment must be achieved under certain constraints, whether or not these constraints can be justified on consequentialist grounds. In my view, the most important part of the theory of punishment in need of careful articulation is the norms that provide these constraints, and their rationale—a point to which I will return later.

I shall also argue that individual acts of punishment—typically, a judge's sentencing of a convicted offender—cannot be justified on purely consequentialist grounds, principally for two reasons: First, sentencers lack sufficient information about all the actual effects of inflicting one rather than another punishment on a given offender at a given time. Second, as a result sentencers must content themselves with a purely procedural justification of most of the sentences they impose. That is, insofar as the system of punishment on which they rely is essentially just, none of the sentencing acts that implement this institution are unjust.

My approach to punishment is also obviously not purely retributivist. The retributive justification of punishment is founded on an a priori norm (the guilty deserve to be punished) and an empirical epistemological claim (we know what punishments the guilty deserve).[16] It is arguable, however, whether the guilty do always deserve to be punished; it is also arguable whether, even when they do, they ought always to get what they deserve; and it is further arguable whether when they ought to be punished as they deserve, the punisher always knows what it is that they deserve (except in the purely procedural sense alluded to above; see also below).[17] We cannot meet these challenges to the deontological retributivist by insisting that punishment is nothing more than a necessary, conceptual consequence of living under the rule of law.[18]

Let me focus on but one of the preceding points here. Despite considerable efforts, retributivists have no nonarbitrary way of deciding what sentence the guilty offender deserves as punishment. Retributivists, ancient and modern, have always been lured by one or another form of lex talionis,[19] despite objections dating from post biblical times to the present. Nor does it suffice to abandon like-for-like retaliation in punishment in favor of restating the basic retributive principle in nontalionic form: Severity in punishment must be proportional to the gravity of the offense. The proportionality principle still leaves us with a spectrum of alternatives, marked at one end by a positivistic legalism (offenders deserve whatever the penal code provides as their punishment) and at the other end by an inchoate moralism (offenders deserve whatever accords with their moral culpability and the harm they have caused).

All actual attempts to specify the penalty schedule on purely retributive grounds fail because the retributive principle underdetermines the penalty schedule.[20] There is no nonarbitrary way to locate either the end points of maximum and minimum severity on the scale of punitive severity or the intervals appropriate to different punishments.[21] Without more information, it is impossible to calculate which crimes deserve which punishments; an infinite number of different penalty schedules are equally consistent with the retributivist's proportionality principle. And retributivism cannot supply the further information needed. Consequently, every existing penalty schedule purportedly incorporating the basic retributive principle fails to the extent that it is not and cannot be uniquely determined by this principle. It must contain arbitrary decisions throughout.

But the basic insights of retributivism and consequentialism cannot be merely brushed aside. There is a role for desert in a liberal theory of punishment, but it needs careful definition. The retributivist relies on the assumption that the criminal laws whose violation makes one eligible for punishment protect genuine individual rights. Were this not so, the retributivist could not claim that justice requires punishment for violation of the law. Nor could the retributivist claim that the resentment or indignation directed toward offenders is fitting, rather than mere anger. Retributivism, whether in law or morals, without an appeal, tacit or express, to the justice of punishment is inconceivable—or inconceivably distinct from mere retaliation or revenge.[22]

But as soon as this is acknowledged, there emerges an unmistakable forward-looking point to introducing liability to punishment for law violation, publication of this liability so that it works as a threat, and expectation of increased compliance with the law because of the dislike of the perceived punitive threat by most people and their unwillingness to risk incurring what is threatened for noncompliance. Thus, risk of punishment provides an incentive for any normal person to comply with just laws protecting individual rights. No purely backward-looking conception of the practice of punishment, focused exclusively on the desert of the offender, can accommodate provisions for this incentive.

On the view sketched above, a system of punishment under law is a technique of social control,[23] and its employment is justified to the extent that it actually protects such social justice as society through its laws has achieved. This purpose is external, not internal, to the practice of punishment. To accept this conception of punishment is to concede the central claim of the consequentialist, not that of the retributivist. The institution of punishment so conceived is thus not justified on purely deontological or consequential grounds, because it manifests some features of each line of consideration. Nevertheless, punishment has essentially retributive elements in it, conceptually and normatively. Any given act of punishment may look starkly retributive to the one who undergoes it—the sentence imposed is a deprivation inflicted on someone found guilty, and not on anyone else, and it is imposed solely because of that finding. What could be more retributive than this?

Against this background, we can now consider a step-by-step argument for the liberal justification of punishment. Although I have sketched the general idea before,[24] most of what follows has been presented in various forms and fragments over the past quarter century by many others.[25]

Liberal Justification

We can begin with an empirical generalization of unimpeachable reliability: Some kinds of intentional human conduct are harmful to others, and it is inappropriate to expect (teach, require) people who have been victimized by such harm either to forgive those who harmed them, to suffer the harm in silence, or to retaliate. In a just society, undeserved victimization is understood to violate individual rights and is therefore prohibited by law and is punishable. Thus the color and texture of any possible justification for punishment will depend upon more general political and moral theory, consistent with the responsibilities for legal protection afforded by a just society. Justification for punishment under law thus emerges as a contingent matter, inescapably dependent on other and deeper normative considerations that only a general theory of social justice can provide.[26]

To repeat, in a society that takes justice seriously, such intentionally harmful conduct is to be prohibited by law and, when and if it occurs, condemned under the law. To do otherwise is to fail to vindicate the rights of individuals that the criminal law is principally designed to protect. The central instrument of such condemnation is the penal sanction attached to the law that defines certain harmful acts as crimes.

In a just society that is also a rational society, unlawfully harmful conduct is preferably prevented before the fact rather than punished after the fact. From society's point of view, compliance under threat is much to be preferred to noncompliance followed by arrest, trial, conviction, sentencing, and punishment. (There are exceptions to this rule, of course; justified civil disobedience is one of them.) But compliance is not so valuable that it is worth trying to increase at any price, especially at the price of irreparable invasions of liberty. Thus, willing compliance with the law as a consequence of internalization of the norms of a just society is preferable to unwilling compliance or noncompliance. But if willing compliance is not forthcoming, then society must settle for unwilling compliance, since that is preferable to noncompliance. Prohibition by law plays an essential role in securing grudging compliance, and the principal vehicle for such prohibition is the punitive sanction attached to the criminal law. No doubt, nondeterrent effects of the sanction system are more important for general compliance than the deterrent effects. Still, once such sanctions are in place, they create *liability* to authorized punishment.

Even in a just society, not every person will comply with the law, and not everyone who does comply will do so out of respect for the rights of others, that is, out of recognition of others as persons with rights deserving mutual respect. Here we encounter in another form the fundamental nondeontological principle on which the system of punishment is built: It is better to increase law compliance by liability to sanctions of those who otherwise would violate the law than it is to permit them to act on their perverse autonomy without any socially imposed cost to themselves, since that would require us to tolerate an increase in the victimization of the innocent. For this reason, rational self-interested persons would choose to impose on themselves and on others a liability to criminal sanctions for certain law violations.

If the punitive sanction is to function effectively as a preventive of noncompliance, then it must be perceived not only as a legitimate threat but also as a credible threat. Its legitimacy is established by its protection of individual rights, its authorization by constitutional procedures, and its administration through due process of law. Its credibility is established by its being generally perceived to be both reasonably severe (hence unpleasant) and effectively enforced (hence a likely consequence for anyone who does not comply).

There are constraints, however, in the use of penal threats and coercion even to preserve a just social system. Four are particularly important for a liberal theory of punishment:[27]

(1) Punishments may not be so severe as to be inhumane or (in the familiar language of the Bill of Rights) "cruel and unusual."

(2) Punishments may not be imposed in ways that violate the rights of accused and convicted offenders ("due process of law" and "equal protection of the laws").

(3) Punitive severity must accord with the principle of proportionality: The graver the crime, the more severe the deserved punishment.

(4) Punitive severity is also subject to the principle of minimalism (less is

better), that is, given any two punishments not ruled out by any of the prior three principles and roughly equal in retributive and incapacitative effects for a given offense and a given class of offenders, the less severe punishment is to be preferred to the more severe.

Conviction of an accused offender under laws that satisfy the foregoing criteria establishes individual *eligibility* for punishment. All and only punishments that are the product of a system of law consistent with the foregoing constraints may be said to be deserved by the offender. Deserved punishment, insofar as it exists at all, thus emerges as a result of "pure procedural justice."[28] That is, we have only the vaguest idea of the just or deserved punishment for a given offender guilty of a given crime apart from the sentencing schedule provided by the laws of a just society (and thus laws that conform to the constraints above). The punishment deserved is the punishment authorized under a fair penalty schedule; no other conception of deserved punishment can be defended. The perennial lure of an illusory independent criterion for desert, founded ultimately on intuition, as well as of utilitarian calculations, must be resisted. Given this account of desert, anyone both liable and eligible for punishment deserves to be punished, and ceteris paribus ought to be punished (for example, in the absence of forgiveness by the victim).[29]

The argument for imposing deserved punishments so defined on guilty offenders is thus in part an argument from consistency: It is inconsistent to specify liability and eligibility conditions for punishment and then not apply the sanctions so authorized when the facts in a given case show that they are warranted. It is unfair to the law-abiding for law-breakers to incur no socially approved cost for their conduct; it is unfair because it would create a class of harmful free riders in the society. The socially approved costs of crime imposed on offenders consist mainly in the deprivations authorized by the punitive sanction.

The creation of a punitive sanction in the name of fairness and under the circumstances specified above is justified. So is the infliction of such a sanction in the name of compliance with the law. Therefore, the practice of punishment, including creating liability to punishment, using sanctions as a threat and incentive for compliance, and actually inflicting the punishment where eligibility conditions are met, is justified.

Conclusion

The foregoing argument incorporates retributive and consequentialist (and to that extent, utilitarian) considerations. It is better than a pure retributivism because it shows why a system of punishment is needed, and how that system is to be nested into the larger political and moral concerns of social justice. It allots a clear and defensible function to punishment without yielding to atavistic demands for retaliation or to illusory deontological demands for pure retributive justice, and without pretending that the punishments it metes out are "deserved" in any fundamental sense. The argument acknowledges the sovereign choices of the individual without invoking any awkward and paradoxical "right to be punished."[30] It is better than a pure consequentialism, because it constrains punitive interventions with individual liberty to the bare minimum. Through the punishment system, all are given fair warning that they put their own rights at risk if they intentionally engage in certain kinds of harmful conduct.[31]

The system of punishment that emerges under this theory is liberal and non-paternalistic, respects the nominal autonomy of all persons equally, and acknowledges the contingency of its justification as applied in any given case.

It is also true that the system of punishment that emerges under this theory leaves punishment in any actual individual case something of a ritual—in some cases an empty ritual, and in any case a highly formalized act whose exact retributive and incapacitative effects are uncertain. Acts of punitive deprivation must be imposed on each convicted offender without the comfort of believing, much less knowing, that the purposes for which the system of punishment was designed and maintained will really be advanced by inflicting the deserved punishment. Some have been led by this fact to view punishment with considerable distrust, because we cannot count on it having any beneficial effect on the punished.[32] Others are less troubled by this because they focus on how the "expressive function" of punishment under law serves society by making punishment a "symbol of infamy," whatever its other effects may be.[33]

Notice, finally, that the entire argument for the justification of punishment unfolds in the belief that alternative, nonpunitive methods of social control have been examined and rejected on the ground that they will not work—or will not work as well as punitive methods in securing compliance with just laws.[34]

Many details remain to be specified before we have a comprehensive liberal theory of punishment in hand. Philosophy can, of course, help supply certain desiderata of the theory of punishment such as specification of the quality and quantity of deprivations (the modes of punishment) appropriate to include in the penalty schedule; construction of the penalty schedule coordinate with the class of crimes; identification of subordinate norms to supplement those already mentioned, which serve as constraints on the penalty schedule and the imposition of sanctions on any given offender; and specification of the norms that make it appropriate to reduce or even waive punishment in favor of some nonpunitive alternative response in a given case.[35] But philosophy alone cannot provide the necessary details; philosophical argument by itself would underdetermine a penal code and has no means to administer one. Yet the heart of a liberal theory of punishment in practice lies in its code of sanctions and their fair administration. Further development of this theory, and its full implications for policy, must be left for another occasion.

Notes

1. Robert Martinson, "What Works?—Questions and Answers About Prison Reform."
2. James Q. Wilson, *Thinking About Crime.*

3. Francis A. Allen, *The Decline of the Rehabilitative Ideal*; Marvin E. Frankel, *Criminal Sentences: Law Without Order*.

4. Twentieth Century Fund, *Fair and Certain Punishment*; Andrew von Hirsch, *Doing Justice: The Choice of Punishments*; Richard G. Singer, *Just Deserts: Sentencing Based on Equality and Desert*.

5. Herbert Morris, "Persons and Punishment"; Nicholas Kittrie, *The Right to Be Different*.

6. Claudia Card, "Retributive Penal Liability"; Andrew von Hirsch, *Doing Justice: The Choice of Punishments*, and *Past or Future Crimes: Deservedness and Dangerousness in the Sentencing of Criminals* ; Robert Nozick, *Philosophical Explanations*.

7. Frank E. Zimring, "Making the Punishment Fit the Crime"; Barbara Hudson, *Justice Through Punishment: A Critique of the "Justice" Model of Corrections*.

8. Though see Christopher Harding and Richard W. Ireland, *Punishment: Rhetoric, Rule, and Practice*; David Garland, *Punishment and Modern Society: A Study in Social Theory*.

9. Hugo Adam Bedau, "Bentham's Utilitarian Critique of the Death Penalty" and "Beccaria."

10. Garland, *Punishment and Modern Society*.

11. Bedau, "Beccaria."

12. See Ted Honderich, *Punishment: The Supposed Justifications*; C.L. Ten, *Crime, Guilt, and Punishment*; David Hoekema, *Rights and Wrongs: Coercion, Punishment, and the State*; Nicola Lacey, *State Punishment: Political Principles and Community Values*.

13. B.F. Skinner, *Walden Two*; H.A. Bedau, "Punitive Violence and Its Alternatives."

14. Elliot Currie, *Confronting Crime: An American Challenge*.

15. Hugo Adam Bedau, "Penal Theory and Prison Reality Today."

16. Igor Primoratz, *Justifying Legal Punishment*.

17. Hugo Adam Bedau, "Retribution and the Theory of Punishment."

18. Herbert Fingarette, "Punishment and Suffering."

19. Michael Davis, "Making the Punishment Fit the Crime."

20. Hugo Adam Bedau, "Retribution" and "Classification-Based Sentencing: Some Conceptual and Ethical Problems."

21. Edmund Pincoffs, "Are Questions of Desert Decidable?"

22. Nozick, *Philosophical Explanations*.

23. Jack Gibbs, *Crime, Punishment, and Deterrence*.

24. Bedau, "Retribution" and "Capital Punishment."

25. See Henry M. Hart, Jr., "The Aims of the Criminal Law"; John Rawls, "Two Concepts of Rules"; H.L.A. Hart, "Prolegomenon to the Principles of Punishment"; Joel Feinberg, "The Expressive Function of Punishment"; Richard A. Wasserstrom, "Punishment"; Hyman Gross, *A Theory of Criminal Justice*; David A. J. Richards, *The Moral Criticism of Law*; Hoekema, *Rights and Wrongs*; Lacey, *State Punishment*.

26. John Rawls, *A Theory of Justice*.

27. Hugo Adam Bedau, "Capital Punishment" and "The Eighth Amendment, Human Dignity, and the Death Penalty."

28. Rawls, *Theory of Justice*.

29. There seems to be a sharp contrast between the role that forgiveness of offenders may properly play in our personal lives, and the narrow or even nonexistent role it ought to play in a punishment system under law. Deserved mercy, apart from being an oxymoron, may have a role to play in the latter, but it is not the same thing as deserving to be forgiven or deserving to be excused.

30. Hugo Adam Bedau, "Prisoners' Rights."

31. H.L.A. Hart, "Prolegomenon to the Principles of Punishment."

32. R.A. Duff, *Trials and Punishments.*
33. Feinberg, "The Expressive Function."
34. Bedau, "Punitive Violence."
35. Kathleen Dean Moore, *Pardons: Justice, Mercy, and the Public Interest.*

References

Allen, Francis A. *The Decline of the Rehabilitative Ideal.* New Haven: Yale University Press, 1981.

Beccaria, Cesare. *On Crimes and Punishments* (1764), tr. David Young. Indianapolis: Hackett Publishing, 1986.

Bedau, H.A. "Beccaria." In Lawrence C. Becker and Charlotte B. Becker, eds., *Encyclopedia of Ethics*, vol. 1, pp. 81–82. Hamden, Conn.: Garland Publishing, 1992.

———. "Bentham's Utilitarian Critique of the Death Penalty." *Journal of Criminal Law and Criminology* 74 (1983): 1033–65.

———. "Capital Punishment." In Tom Regan, ed., *Matters of Life and Death*, pp. 148–82. New York: Random House, 1980.

———. "Classification-Based Sentencing: Some Conceptual and Ethical Problems." In J. Roland Pennock and John W. Chapman, eds., *Criminal Justice: Nomos XXVII*, pp. 89–118. New York: New York University Press, 1985.

———. "The Eighth Amendment, Human Dignity, and the Death Penalty." In Michael J. Meyer and William A. Parent, eds., *The Constitution of Rights*, pp. 145–77. Ithaca, N.Y.: Cornell University Press, 1992.

———. "Penal Theory and Prison Reality Today." *Juris Doctor* 2 (December 1972): 40–43.

———. "Prisoners' Rights." In Fredrick Elliston and Norman Bowie, eds., *Ethics, Public Policy, and Criminal Justice*, pp. 321–46. Cambridge, Mass.: Oelgeschlager, Gunn & Hain, 1982.

———. "Punitive Violence and Its Alternatives." In James B. Brady and Newton Garver, eds., *Justice, Law, and Violence*, pp. 193–209. Philadelphia: Temple University Press, 1991.

———. "Retribution and the Theory of Punishment." *Journal of Philosophy* 75 (1978): 601–20.

Butler, Joseph. "Sermon Upon Resentment" (1723). In Butler, *Works*, vol. 2, pp. 87–98. Oxford: Oxford University Press, 1850.

Card, Claudia. "Retributive Penal Liability." *American Philosophical Quarterly Monographs* no. 7 (1973): 17–35.

Currie, Elliot. *Confronting Crime: An American Challenge.* New York: Pantheon Books, 1985.

Davis, Michael. "Making the Punishment Fit the Crime." In J. Roland Pennock and John W. Chapman, eds., *Criminal Justice: Nomos XXVII*, pp. 156–64. New York: New York University Press, 1985.

Duff, R.A. *Trials and Punishments.* Cambridge: Cambridge University Press, 1986.

Feinberg, Joel. "The Expressive Function of Punishment" (1965). Reprinted in Feinberg, *Doing and Deserving: Essays in the Theory of Responsibility.* Princeton, N.J.: Princeton University Press, 1970.

Fingarette, Herbert. "Punishment and Suffering." *Proceedings of the American Philosophical Association* (1978): 499–525.

Foucault, Michel. *Discipline and Punish: The Birth of the Prison.* New York: Pantheon Books, 1977.

Frankel, Marvin E. *Criminal Sentences: Law Without Order.* New York: Hill & Wang, 1973.

Garland, David. *Punishment and Modern Society: A Study in Social Theory.* Chicago: University of Chicago Press, 1990.

Gibbs, Jack. *Crime, Punishment, and Deterrence.* New York: Elsevier, 1975.

Gross, Hyman. *A Theory of Criminal Justice.* Oxford: Oxford University Press, 1979.

Harding, Christopher, and Ireland, Richard W. *Punishment: Rhetoric, Rule, and Practice.* London: Routledge, 1989.

Hart, H.L.A. "Prolegomenon to the Principles of Punishment" (1959). Reprinted in Hart, *Punishment and Responsibility: Essays in the Philosophy of Law.* Oxford: Oxford University Press, 1968.

Hart, Henry M., Jr. "The Aims of the Criminal Law." *Law and Contemporary Problems* 23 (1958): 401–41.

Hoekema, David. *Rights and Wrongs: Coercion, Punishment, and the State.* Selinsgrove, Pa. Susquehanna University Press, 1986.

Honderich, Ted. *Punishment: The Supposed Justifications*, revised edition. New York: Penguin Books, 1976.

Hudson, Barbara. *Justice Through Punishment: A Critique of the "Justice" Model of Corrections.* New York: St. Martin's Press, 1987.

Kittrie, Nicholas. *The Right to Be Different.* Baltimore: Johns Hopkins University Press, 1971.

Lacey, Nicola. *State Punishment: Political Principles and Community Values.* London: Routledge, 1988.

Martinson, Robert. "What Works?—Questions and Answers About Prison Reform." *The Public Interest* 10 (1974): 22–54.

Moore, Kathleen Dean. *Pardons: Justice, Mercy, and the Public Interest.* Oxford: Oxford University Press, 1989.

Morris, Herbert. "Persons and Punishment" (1968). Reprinted in Morris, *On Guilt and Innocence: Essays in Legal Philosophy and Moral Psychology.* Berkeley: University of California Press, 1976.

Nietzsche, Friedrich. *On the Genealogy of Morals* (1887), tr. Walter Kaufmann. New York: Vintage Books, 1969.

Nozick, Robert. *Philosophical Explanations.* Cambridge, Mass.: Harvard University Press, 1981.

Pincoffs, Edmund. "Are Questions of Desert Decidable?" In J. B. Cederblom and William Blizek, eds., *Justice and Punishment.* Cambridge, Mass.: Ballinger Publishing, 1977.

Primoratz, Igor. *Justifying Legal Punishment.* Atlantic Highlands, N.J.: Humanities Press International, 1989.

Rawls, John. *A Theory of Justice.* Cambridge, Mass.: Harvard University Press, 1971.

———. "Two Concepts of Rules." *The Philosophical Review* 64 (1955): 3–32.

Richards, David A.J. *The Moral Criticism of Law.* Encino, Calif.: Dickenson Publishing, 1977.

Singer, Richard G. *Just Deserts: Sentencing Based on Equality and Desert.* Cambridge, Mass.: Ballinger Publishing, 1979.

Skinner, B.F. *Walden Two.* New York: Macmillan, 1948.

Strawson, Peter F. "Freedom and Resentment" (1962). Reprinted in Strawson, *Freedom and Resentment and Other Essays.* London: Methuen, 1974.

Ten, C.L. *Crime, Guilt, and Punishment.* Oxford, England: Clarendon Press, 1987.

Twentieth Century Fund. *Fair and Certain Punishment.* New York: McGraw-Hill, 1976.

United States Sentencing Commission. *Federal Sentencing Guidelines Manual.* St. Paul, Minn.: West Publishing, 1990.

von Hirsch, Andrew. *Doing Justice: The Choice of Punishments*. New York: Hill & Wang, 1976.

————. *Past or Future Crimes: Deservedness and Dangerousness in the Sentencing of Criminals*. New Brunswick, N.J.: Rutgers University Press, 1985.

Wasserstrom, Richard A. "Punishment." In Wasserstrom, *Philosophy and Social Justice*. Notre Dame, Ind.: University of Notre Dame Press, 1980.

Wilson, James Q. *Thinking About Crime*. New York: Basic Books, 1975.

Zimring, Frank E. "Making the Punishment Fit the Crime." *Hastings Center Report* 6 (December 1976): 17.

3

LLAD PHILLIPS

Economic Perspectives on Criminality: An Eclectic View

Until the revival of interest among economists occasioned by Gary Becker's treatment of crime and punishment, criminology was more the province of sociologists and psychologists;[1] however, the notion that economists are trespassing on criminology turf is arguable from a historical perspective, because Jeremy Bentham, who applied the cost/benefit calculus to offensive behavior, was also one of the fathers of utility theory.[2] Since the Second World War, economists have applied their paradigm to many new areas, a process that Jack Hirshleifer has compared to imperialism.[3] Of course, imperialists may be influenced by, and adopt, indigenous ways and ideas. This chapter focuses on one imperialist venture, the economic analysis of crime and, in particular, what many economists call the supply of offenses, or the generation of crime.

The topic of thinking about crime causality can be approached from many perspectives. One perspective is the microeconomic analysis of how an individual decides to participate in legitimate work or illegal activity, and how many hours to supply to each. Another perspective is Jack Katz's argument that many illegal acts are committed for the sensual thrill of the act and the excitement of the lifestyle or demeanor of the criminal role player.[4] Both these perspectives, apparently so different, revolve around individual behavior. A perspective that provides some bonds across different disciplinary approaches, and at a more aggregate level, is outlined in Albert Hirschman's *Exit, Voice, and Loyalty.*

Hirschman uses *exit* to capture the economic notion of choice in the impersonal market: switching brands and employers, for example, voting with one's feet. *Voice* is the political act, attempting to influence the outcome through persuasion. *Loyalty* to product, organization, or community can influence one's decision to combine the economic and political approaches in achieving an end. The threat of exit may empower voice. The use of voice may moderate the need for exit.

The notion of voice is embodied in the philosophy of the law, in the idea of codifying a behavior as illegal in an attempt to persuade potential perpetrators that it is not in the larger social interest. Consideration of the expected sanction for committing the offense brings us full circle to Jeremy Bentham and the forces affecting choice in the market context as represented by exit.

Of course, if the law embodies both concepts of control, that is, exit and voice, or deterrence and persuasion, should not theories of individual attitudes toward committing a criminal act embody both concepts of control as well? Some studies have. Control of drunk driving has not lost sight of the moral issue; strict legislation against drunk driving in Scandinavia, for example, was strongly influenced by the temperance parties.[5] It is not difficult to incorporate moral suasion, even in an economic model of participation and supply of effort. Most paradigms are malleable, even imperialistic ones, and can incorporate indigenous ideas. This is the importance of exit and voice, a blend of the economic and political models, a reminder arguing for balance, especially for models of behavior in the criminal and legal realms.

Another important idea derivative of exit, voice, and loyalty is the notion that sanctions such as imprisonment, exile, and banishment are a form of forced exit. Of course, these can be thought of as events happening to an individual. At a more aggregate level, society in the United States imprisons disproportionate numbers of African-American and Hispanic adults. If such large groups experience forced exit in adult life, what preceded this in their adolescent years? Perhaps voluntary exit or dropout from school? Is this estrangement from society something that characterizes the criminal subgroup over much of its life cycle?

Economic Models of Crime

Various economic models have been influential in directing thinking about, and analyzing criminal behavior. Gary Becker's article "Crime and Punishment: An Economic Approach," stimulated interest among some economists in the issue of deterrence. This was pursued empirically by Isaac Ehrlich, among others. Ehrlich's time series analysis of the deterrent effect of the death penalty in the United States led to a controversy that is central to criminology today.[6] Do we understand criminal behavior well enough to control for the causes of crime sufficiently to separately identify the control effects of deterrence?

Two theoretical approaches from labor economics are particularly useful in establishing a framework for thinking about an individual's involvement in crime. The first is the demand for leisure or, equivalently, the supply of labor. The second is investment in human capital and earning power, achieved both through education and from learning through the experience of working for income. An individual will supply labor if the expected earnings exceed a certain amount, known in economics as the individual's "reservation wage." Applied to the evaluation of expected illegal earnings, deterrent variables such as the probability of arrest and imprisonment will decrease expected illegal earnings. The reservation wage is a threshold affected by tastes and values. Hence, moral suasion may lead to a very high threshold, or reservation wage, for participating in an effort to obtain illegal gains. Of course, in the case of legal gains, an individual's expected earnings will be greater, the larger his or her stock of human capital: education and job experience play important roles in determining an individual's socioeconomic success. Experience and knowledge, including knowledge of opportunities, may affect the amount of an individual's expected illegal earnings, as well.

Economic models of criminal behavior that incorporate notions of deterrence, labor supply, and human capital could be broad enough or sufficiently eclectic to embrace the concept of moral suasion as a factor determining tastes and the reservation wage for participating in crime or not. It is all a matter of emphasis, and this is where the concepts of exit and voice provide illumination of the literature. It is natural for economists to see how far economic variables such as price and income can be pressed to explain behavior, especially in empirical studies.[7] Economists tend to emphasize market forces and market variables—in other words, to rely on exit. The difficulty is that this may provide a mental model of the crime problem that relies too heavily on market forces for a solution.

An interesting example is provided by Eli Ginzberg in *The School/Work Nexus: Transition of Youth from School to Work*. Ginzberg reports on a verbal exchange with Theodore Schultz, a founder of human capital theory, who expressed the view that youth unemployment could be solved by letting young people grow into their twenties, when they would get jobs. The issue is not only whether youth unemployment is a problem, as argued by Ginzberg, but also whether it is a phenomenon that time and the market will take care of.

A similar question can be posed about individuals engaged in criminal behavior. Will growing older and getting jobs draw these people out of criminality? Is only one set of experiences over the life cycle relevant to thinking about crime, the experience of education and then work? Is the population basically homogeneous, differing only in each individual's initial endowment of abilities at birth but facing similar opportunities for socially provided education and for work? Or is a more complex abstraction necessary? In this regard, it is interesting to note that in some of their studies of recidivism, Peter Schmidt and Ann Witte have postulated and applied split-population models, explicitly recognizing the heterogeneity of the imprisoned criminal population.[8]

Whether or not specific empirical studies account for the possibility of population heterogeneity or the influence of moral suasion on crime participation is relevant to assessing the explanatory significance of these factors. However, conceptually, the basis of the law and the criminal justice system encompasses both punishment and education through codification. The social approach is a mixture of voice and exit. Consequently, models of aggregate and individual criminal behavior should provide for the influence of both persuasion and price.

Some Empirical Studies Using Individual Data

The economic models of crime are explanations of individual choice. Much of the early work utilized aggregate data that raised issues such as ecological fallacy and the identification of causality among mutually dependent variables. Increasingly, there has been a call for empirical studies of individuals to inform the argument about the relevance to criminal choice of economic concepts such as (1) deterrence, (2) the supply of labor, (3) human capital, and (4) state dependence.[9]

In recent years, more studies of crime based on individual data have been published. Findings include the weak explanatory power of supply of labor (or allocation of time) applied to participation in crime, as well as the limited explanatory power of human capital variables such as investment in education. However, the importance of moral suasion has been observed in several studies.

Phillips and Votey applied the same model to participation in crime as to participation in work for youths from the National Longitudinal Survey. They found that human capital variables such as years of schooling and work experience had much less explanatory power for participation in crime than for participation in work.[10] In contrast, individual attributes such as being raised in a religious faith and church attendance significantly decreased participation in crime. Similar findings were reported by Tauchen, Witte, and Griesinger using cohort data from Philadelphia.[11] Attainment of a high school degree had no effect on the probability of arrest, although a higher intelligence quotient significantly decreased the probability. Attendance at a parochial high school also decreased the probability.

There are connections between labor market experience and crime. Farrington et al. found that the rate of offending for youths was higher during their periods of unemployment than during their periods of employment. This state dependence effect was observed using longitudinal data composed mainly of white, urban, working-class males of British origin.[12] Phillips and Votey reported that the probability of employment decreased for school dropouts if they had been involved in remunerative crime, controlling for the fraction of time worked between the annual interviews.[13]

Metapreferences

A useful analytical framework for thinking about the economic analysis presented in this essay is Albert Hirschman's concept of metapreferences, as discussed in *Rival Views of Market Society*.[14] Economists usually conduct their analyses using individual preferences or tastes, which determine the demand for goods and services. Metapreferences are the set of values that underlie individual tastes. These values are determined by an individual's experience within the family and the culture. Metapreferences serve as a reference against which an

Figure 3.1 Optimal Control Model Analogy of Dynamic Changes in Preferences over the Life Cycle of an Individual

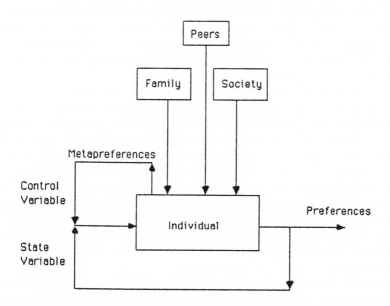

individual's tastes can be checked for consistency. A change in individual tastes or preferences may be accomplished by the formation or change of an individual's metapreferences. Using an analogy of an optimal control model, with an individual's preferences as the state variable and the individual's metapreferences as the control variable, the various influences of family, peers, and society on the values of the individual are illustrated in Figure 3.1.

One important application of the concept of metapreferences is the possibility that moral suasion can influence metapreferences and change tastes and thereby change the reservation wage for participating in crime. An analogous argument could be made about changing the values of individuals through investment in human capital by education and job experience and hence affecting the threshold at which a person would participate in school or work.

Another important application of metapreferences is at the aggregate rather than the individual level. It concerns the struggle for people's minds by political parties, social movements, ethnic and gender splinter groups, and special interests concerned about specific aspects of behavior such as drunk driving or drug abuse. These advocates hope to change behavior and policy by influencing values and metapreferences.

Exit, Voice, and Models of Criminal Behavior

In *Rival Views of Market Society*, Hirschman argues that the rational-man approach to economic behavior is too parsimonious.[15] Economists that rely solely on price and income to explain criminal behavior, and ignore moral suasion, are ignoring the philosophical basis of the law as it may apply to their models. Aristotle argues that the purpose of legislation is to induce good habits in the citizens. A difficulty with the economic argument that tastes are given, and the only policy tool is price, especially as applied to criminal behavior, is that it ignores the possibility of changing behavior by changing values.

The "war on drugs" certainly reflects the fact that criminal justice policy in the United States has been a blend of persuasion and deterrence. More recently, public campaigns to "just say no" and public programs such as DARE have tried to alter tastes. For much of this century, public policy toward substance abuse has attempted to stigmatize the behavior by making it illegal. However, this country's experience with Prohibition and Repeal and, more recently, with the war on drugs suggests that the best social policy to deal with substance abuse remains debatable. While crimes of violence and taking clearly injure others against their will, this may not always be the case with substance abuse. If this behavior is not unambiguously antisocial, then should it be stigmatized by making it illegal?

The use of voice by means of making behavior illegal is not the only drug policy emphasis in question. There have been cycles in the enforcement of drug abuse laws. Recent years have seen a large increase in the proportion of new arrivals to prison accounted for by violation of drug laws. Yet these offenders are often viewed as less serious, in terms of length of sentence or average time served, compared to violent and property offenders, whom they are tending to displace on the crowded prison rolls. I would argue that in the case of substance abuse, the use of voice through the law rather than by means of education and propaganda is questionable, and that going further and emphasizing exit by means of deterrence and incapacitation is a waste of our scarce prison capacity.

Exit, Voice, Loyalty, and the Underclass

The increase in per capita rates of imprisonment for the population during the decade of the eighties was accompanied by disproportionate increases in imprisonment for minorities. This is not a new phenomenon in our society. In a study examining the historical evidence from this century and the last, Myers and Sabol showed that African-Americans have long had higher rates of imprisonment than whites, especially in the northern states.[16]

Roger Masters identifies imprisonment, as well as enslavement, as a form of ostracism, which he, in turn, defines as a form of coerced exit.[17] He goes further and links Hirschman's concepts of exit, voice, and loyalty to clusters of emotions in animal behavior discovered by contemporary ethology, namely flight, threat, and bonding, respectively. Fred Kort points out that ostracism can also be understood as the inverse of civil rights and liberties and, in the case of imprisonment, part of the administration of criminal justice.[18]

Time in prison is part of the experience of their twenties and thirties in the life cycle of those so ostracized. The reason for forcing the exit of felons from society is, of course, no mystery and lies in the antisocial behavior that led the individual to run afoul of society: violence or taking. We can wonder, though, about the forced exit of disproportionate numbers of minorities, of African-Americans and Hispanics. Was there a linkage to behavior earlier in their life cycle, perhaps a voluntary exit from society?

Any group that is subject to discrimination because of easily discernible physical characteristics such as sex or color may question whether it is possible to make socioeconomic progress and achieve upward mobility through individual effort. Depending on one's trust, or distrust, in the efficacy of individual striving, it is logical to embrace the normal paths that lead to socioeconomic status, such as investing in human capital or, alternatively, to rebel. Hirschman noted that one of the novelties of the black power movement in America is that it rejected upward social mobility for the individual, or successful exit from one's group, as the answer for the masses in the black ghetto.[19] Jerome H. Barkow, in "The Elastic Between Genes and Culture," argues that individual success or exit also deprives the rest of an oppressed group of capable leadership, similar to Hirschman's point that exit can be ineffective for the group, while voice is weakened by the exit of talented potential leaders.[20]

Consequently, in African-American and Latino societies today, there are countervailing voices. Some leaders, perhaps more identified with the middle class, urge individual responsibility and effort and extol the virtues of education, family, and work. Other voices, perhaps most appealing to those least well off, reject the normal pathways to success and call for identification with the collective welfare of the disadvantaged group. If we examine African-American and Latino culture today, we must realize that there are various voices supporting different social norms. Depending on the messages adolescents hear and on their interpretation of their own experiences within the context of these countervailing views of society, the educational ideal of the dominant group may seem irrelevant. Loyalty plays a part in this process, and rival groups and cultures compete for the loyalties of young minds.

Barkow identifies culture as a pool of organized information transmitted within and across generations. He argues that social inequality will likely lead to conflict among factions or social strata about the information that is transmitted by culture.[21] This conflict about information can certainly be costly to the society. A recent eruption of this conflict in the realm of higher education has been the attack on western civilization courses as offering too Europocentric a view of the culture to be transmitted to the next generation of college graduates.

To the degree that conflict over information precipitated by perceptions and fear of discrimination may lead to the rejection by some of the ideal of individual progress through education, the costs of dropping out may retard growth in the economic and social welfare of society. Today, we bear large burdens to support those without the human capital to support themselves and to protect ourselves from those we have been forced to ostracize through imprisonment. In economic terms, inequality carries a cost in inefficiency and lost production and growth opportunities.

The Serious Offender

The concept of the serious offender, defined as an individual who commits serious offenses at a high annual rate, is important for a number of reasons. First of all, it once again recognizes the heterogeneity of the population, the fact that some offenders do not participate in crime and have a zero rate, while others may have a low rate and, last, that a small group of high-rate offenders may account for much of the crime. Second, the notion that the offending rate varies across individuals, coupled with the possibility that these individuals could be identified, has been a basis for arguing for incarceration of serious offenders as a foundation for criminal justice policy. This has been particularly important in an era during which some scholars have questioned the empirical support for deterrence as a basis for policy. Third, the serious offender concept focuses attention on state dependence and the intrinsically dynamic nature of criminal behavior over an individual's life cycle.

If we concentrate for a moment on the behavior of serious offenders, those individuals with high rates of committing offenses, we could, conceptually, find them in three states: (1) free and offending, (2) incarcerated, and (3) rehabilitated.[22] The probabilities of moving from one state to another are affected not only by the individual's criminal behavior, as measured by the rate of offending and the probability of being rehabilitated and ceasing offending, but also by the response of the system as measured by the probability of arrest plus conviction, and the probability of incarceration given conviction.

This conceptual framework is sufficiently flexible that it can be used to model policy under the assumption that only incapacitation is effective, or it can be extended to allow for the effects of deterrence on criminal behavior. If typical or average transition probabilities among the states are used, it can capture the evolution of aggregate or cohort behavior over time. Alternatively, if each probability or rate is presumed to vary over each individual, this conceptual framework can be applied to the study of individual behavior.

An important aspect of the serious offender model for the purposes of the argument in this essay is a focus on violence. The serious offender model does not exclude consideration of serious property crimes and other offenses, but the most serious offenses, with the highest costs per offense to society and, correspondingly, the longest sentences for convicted offenders, are crimes of violence.

In sum then, the serious offender model, and the evolution of an individual's behavior with the passage from one state to another, has a perspective of time dependence in common with the economic model of the dynamics of human capital formation and accumulation.

A Synthesis of Facts and Perspectives

Instead of beginning with innocent infants and pondering crime causality among adolescents, it is possible, using a dynamic framework, to use a point of departure closer to the end of the life cycle and work backwards. If we focus on prison populations, we will not necessarily encompass all aspects of criminal behavior, but we will be dealing with the graver aspects of the social problem. Prison populations may not be homogeneous always, but a considerable proportion of prisoners will be difficult to rehabilitate and keep out of prison for more than two or three years. This subgroup of serious offenders has a high rate of offending when released from prison, with consequent exposure to a high risk of arrest, conviction, and being returned to prison. There is a set of stylized facts about these serious offenders. Compared to the general population, they will be ill-educated, with little work experience, likely violent, and disproportionately drawn from minority groups.

Examining these ostracized prisoners, we may gain more of a clue to their probable history by thinking about the African-American or Latino violent offender than about a poor white drug offender or burglar, even though their earlier experiences may not be that different. Society forces the exit of the serious taker as well as the violent offender, but society reserves the most severe sanctions and ostracism for the latter, and minority membership provides a visible link between the prisoner and the gang member.

Not every offender is a former gang member, but violence is the currency of the gang, its measure of value. The gang has its own subculture and has rejected the values of the dominant society. It is only a matter of time, therefore, before society in self-defense will ostracize the gang member. It is a point of controversy whether an individual had a meaningful choice in deciding to join a gang, or was left no meaningful alternative by society. Gang members have questioned the attractiveness of the gang lifestyle and the notion that they sought out this choice.[23] This at least raises the question of whether they saw pursuing the pathways to mainstream society as a meaningful alternative. This is the issue of focus in the following argument.

In the economic model, the model embodying the values of the dominant society, the individual pursues an education, stockpiling human capital and potential earning power, in preparation for entering the labor force. Why would a rational individual ever drop out? Why do the values of the dominant society become irrelevant to adolescents and why are so many of these dropouts Latinos and African-Americans?

Hirschman points out that the rural-to-urban migration of minorities during the fifties and sixties was accompanied by urban white flight to the suburbs, and that this weakened the social services provided in the cities.[24] This combination of exit and voice, or the weakening of the latter, contributed to the deterioration of public education and decreased its relevance to minorities living in communities with below-average public schools.

Yet the question persists, why do many minority youths voluntarily exit from school when no *economically* attractive alternative exists for a great number of them? Gangs, violence, and prison may offer a seductive lifestyle for some individuals in pursuit of sensual thrills. Jack Katz argues in *Seductions of Crime* that the positive sensual rewards of the criminal lifestyle are often neglected in discussions of the causal factors of crime.[25] However, as applied to our aggregate situation, are these individual tastes peculiarly associated with underclass minorities?

Returning to Barkow's argument, perhaps inequality between the dominant group and underclass minorities has led to a conflict in values and a disagreement about the information content of the culture to be transmitted from one generation to the next. Youth may be dropping out of school and rejecting mainstream paths to socioeconomic success, not only out of their own perceptions of the irrelevance of school, but, in addition, because of the reinforcement or inculcation of similar values from their families. In this regard, special forms of communication, such as songs and graffiti, and the double and hidden meanings of words from the subcultures, may provide clues to the strength and prevalence of ideas counter to the mainstream culture.

The Family, Altruism, and Economic Growth

These thoughts about inequality and the conflict among subgroups of society over the control of the content of culture may be relevant for another economic model as well as for the economic models of crime, labor supply, and investment in human capital. Gary Becker has extended the usual economic model of self-interested or selfish behavior to encompass parents who value the welfare of their children as well as their own.[26] These values, in conjunction with use of the promise and the threat, provide a strong model for social control within the confines of the family. The parents, if sufficiently altruistic, can keep the peace within the family by promising a behest or reward if the children, possibly selfish in motive, behave themselves, and by threatening disinheritance as a consequence if the children succumb to selfish temptations. Thus the wise parent can induce cooperative behavior in offspring who might otherwise act in a selfish manner, destructive to the family welfare. Two social institutions, the family and the law, make their contributions to individual and collective safety.

Since Adam Smith, economists have inquired into the sources and the causes of the wealth of nations. What accounts for differential rates of growth of output per capita in various countries? Will our own country continue to prosper or fade? There are different theories of what the engine of growth might be, and these have been reviewed by Isaac Ehrlich.[27] One possibility is altruism within the family.

If parents are sufficiently altruistic, they will want a higher standard of living for their children than for themselves. They may provide this by consuming less, saving, and investing in the human capital of their children, ensuring that their progeny will be better educated and more prosperous than themselves. If these altruistic family preferences are sufficiently prevalent in a society, then there will be an intergenerational transfer of wealth, and the economy will grow and the society will prosper.

To the extent that the family is threatened as a social institution in a society, conflict, crime, and violence may increase; investment in education may decrease; and the future prosperity of the entire society may be threatened. The threat to the family may be not only its sundering or dissolution but also any diminution in coherence and feelings of concern by parents about the welfare of their children.

Socioeconomic inequality may threaten the transmission of values in a culture from one generation to the next. To the extent that the values that are threatened are those of the family, and especially the feelings of parental interest in the welfare of their children, investment in the education of these children may be diminished. Even if this occurs principally within subcultures, the peace and future prosperity of the whole society may be threatened.

Notes

1. See Gary Becker, "Crime and Punishment: An Economic Approach."
2. Llad Phillips and Harold L. Votey, Jr., in *The Economics of Crime Control*, chapter 2, discuss Bentham's contribution to the economic model of crime.
3. Jack Hirshleifer, in "The Expanding Domain of Economics," deals with many topics mentioned in this essay, including economic man, self-interest, altruism in the family, contributions to the economic model of crime.
4. See Jack Katz, *Seductions of Crime.*
5. Johannes Andenaes, in "General Prevention—Illusion or Reality," discusses whether the preventive effect of drunk driving legislation might have been due to a change in attitude associated with the legislation as well as to deterrence.
6. See Isaac Ehrlich, "The Deterrent Effect of Capital Punishment: A Question of Life and Death." For a critique of research on deterrence, see Alfred Blumstein, Jacqueline Cohen, and Daniel Nagin, eds., *Deterrence and Incapacitation: Estimating the Effects of Criminal Sanctions on Crime Rates.*
7. In "Rational Choice Models of Crime by Youth," Llad Phillips and Harold L. Votey, Jr., verified that the usual economic variables of years of schooling and job experience explain individual decisions to participate in work but found these variables had less explanatory power in explaining individual participation in crime. This is discussed in more detail in the next section.
8. See Peter Schmidt and Ann Witte, *An Economic Analysis of Crime and Justice* and "Predicting Criminal Recidivism Using 'Split Population' Survival Time Models."

9. For example, see David Farrington et al., "Unemployment, School Leaving and Crime," p. 336, and Pamela Lattimore and Ann Witte, "Models of Decision Making under Uncertainty: The Criminal Choice," p. 131.

10. See Phillips and Votey, "Rational Choice Models," pp. 170–84.

11. See Helen Tauchen, Ann Witte, and Harriet Griesenger, "Deterrence, Work and Crime: Revisiting the Issues with Birth Cohort Data."

12. See Farrington et al., "Unemployment, School Leaving and Crime."

13. See Phillips and Votey, "Rational Choice Models," pp. 151–70.

14. Albert O. Hirschman, *Rival Views of Market Society.*

15. Ibid.

16. See Samuel L. Myers, Jr., and William Sabol, "Business Cycles and Racial Disparities in Punishment."

17. See Roger Masters, "Ostracism, Voice, and Exit: The Biology of Social Participation."

18. See Fred Kort, "The Politics of Ostracism."

19. See Albert O. Hirschman, *Exit, Voice, and Loyalty*, p. 109.

20. Jerome H. Barkow, "The Elastic Between Genes and Culture."

21. Ibid.

22. See Alfred Blumstein and Daniel Nagin, "On the Optimal Use of Incarceration for Crime Control," for development of a model of two states, free and incarcerated, and David F. Greenberg, *Mathematical Criminology*, for a model that includes the possibility of rehabilitation.

23. See Leon Bing, *Do or Die.*

24. See Hirschman, *Rival Views*, p. 90.

25. Katz, *Seductions of Crime.*

26. See Gary Becker, *A Treatise on the Family*, chapter 8.

27. See Isaac Ehrlich, "The Problem of Development: Introduction."

References

Andenaes, Johannes. "General Prevention—illusion or Reality." In Stanley E. Grupp, ed., *Theories of Punishment.* Bloomington: Indiana University Press, 1971.

Barkow, Jerome H. "The Elastic Between Genes and Culture." *Ethology and Sociobiology* 10 (1989): 111–29.

Becker, Gary. "Crime and Punishment: An Economic Approach." *Journal of Political Economy* 76 (March/April): 189–217.

———. *A Treatise on the Family.* Cambridge, Mass: Harvard University Press, 1981.

Bentham, Jeremy. *The Principles and Morals of Legislation.* New York: Hafner, 1948.

Bing, Leon. *Do or Die.* New York: Harper Collins, 1991.

Blumstein, Alfred; Cohen, Jacqueline; and Nagin, Daniel, eds. *Deterrence and Incapacitation: Estimating the Effects of Criminal Sanctions on Crime Rates.* Washington, D.C.: National Academy of Sciences, 1978.

Blumstein, Alfred, and Nagin, Daniel. "On the Optimal Use of Incarceration for Crime Control." In James A. Fox, ed., *Models in Quantitative Criminology.* San Francisco: Academic Press, 1981.

Ehrlich, Isaac. "The Deterrent Effect of Capital Punishment: A Question of Life and Death." *American Economic Review* 63, no. 3 (June 1975): 397–417.

———. "The Problem of Development: Introduction." *Journal of Political Economy* 98, no. 5 (1990): 51–511.

Farrington, David; Gallagher, Bernard; Morley, Lynda; St. Ledger, Raymond; and West, Donald. "Unemployment, School Leaving and Crime," *British Journal of Criminology* 26, no. 4 (October 1986): 335–56.

Ginzberg, Eli. The School/Work Nexus: *Transition of Youth from School to Work*. Bloomington, Ind: Phi Delta Kappa Educational Foundation, 1980.

Greenberg, David F. *Mathematical Criminology*. New Brunswick, N.J.: Rutgers University Press, 1979.

Hirschman, Albert O. *Exit, Voice, and Loyalty*. Cambridge, Mass.: Harvard University Press, 1979.

———. Rival Views of Market Society. New York: Viking, 1986.

Hirshleifer, Jack. "The Expanding Domain of Economics." *American Economic Review* (December 1985): 53–68.

Katz, Jack. *Seductions of Crime*. New York: Basic Books, 1988.

Kort, Fred. "The Politics of Ostracism." *Ethology and Sociobiology* 7 (1986): 367–77.

Lattimore, Pamela, and Witte, Ann. "Models of Decision Making under Uncertainty: The Criminal Choice." In Derek Cornish and Ronald Clarke, eds., *The Reasoning Criminal*. New York: Springer-Verlag, 1986.

Masters, Roger. "Ostracism, Voice, and Exit: The Biology of Social Participation." *Ethology and Sociobiology* 7 (1986): 379–95.

Myers, Samuel L., Jr., and Sabol, William. "Business Cycles and Racial Disparities in Punishment." *Contemporary Policy Issues* 5, no. 4 (October 1987): 189–209.

Phillips, Llad, and Votey, Harold L. Jr., *The Economics of Crime Control*. Beverly Hills: Sage, 1981.

———. "Rational Choice Models of Crime by Youth." *The Review of Black Political Economy* 16, nos. 1, 2 (Summer/Fall 1987): 129–87.

Schmidt, Peter, and Witte, Ann. *An Economic Analysis of Crime and Justice*. San Francisco: Academic Press, 1984.

———. "Predicting Criminal Recidivism Using 'Split Population' Survival Time Models." National Bureau of Economic Research, Working Paper No. 2445, Cambridge, Mass., 1987.

Smith, Adam. *Wealth of Nations*. New York: Random House, 1937.

Tauchen, Helen; Witte, Ann; and Griesinger, Harriet. "Deterrence, Work and Crime: Revisiting the Issues with Birth Cohort Data." National Bureau of Economic Research, Working Paper No. 2508, Cambridge, Mass., 1988

4

GRAHAM HUGHES

The Limits of Legal Sanctions

In 1970 Congress passed a criminal statute[1] aimed at those who held executive positions in large illegal drug-selling enterprises, known as the offense of conducting a "continuing criminal enterprise" (CCE). The law applied to defendants who occupied a supervisory or managerial position in a drug operation in which at least five other people participated. Such an offender was made subject to a mandatory minimum term of ten years' imprisonment (without possibility of parole) for committing a drug felony as part of a series of offenses. The provisions of this statute were soon interpreted by prosecutors and courts in the most expansive fashion, so that its stringent penalties, although clearly designed only for drug "kingpins," came to be applied also to lesser lights in the drug business.

With CCE's penalties now applying to a broad range of run-of-the-mill drug defendants, Congress revisited the question in 1988, again seeking to isolate kingpins for its special wrath. It did not do this, as one might have expected, by tightening the definition of CCE so as to exempt lesser players from the ten-year minimum sentence. Instead, it increased the minimum sentence for this now devalued category to twenty years while creating a further category of super kingpins, defined as "principal administrators, organizers or leaders of the enterprise," and enacting a new sentence of mandatory life imprisonment for such offenders. Not content with this, the 1988 law went on to create a federal death penalty for one who kills while working for a CCE.

This statute exemplifies both good and bad aspects of a recent expansion of sanctions in our criminal justice systems. The scope of sanctions, in the sense of how we define prohibited conduct, calls for constant review, both to prune out conduct that we conclude we should no longer condemn criminally and to draft new prohibitions to meet newly complex forms of criminality. The federal system has recently been energetic in meeting the second need. Finding classic crimes, even with the loose offense of conspiracy to hand, to be clumsy tools for attacking criminal combinations, it has devised new offenses, the essence of which is participation in the affairs of a criminal enterprise. Here we find the celebrated RICO (Racketeer Influenced and Corrupt Organizations) offense[2] and allied crimes such as CCE.

The new crimes have been linked with powerful new sanctions based on the forfeiture of proceeds and profits of crime in whatever form they are found. Joined with other new offenses with respect to money laundering and requirements of notification of large cash transactions, prosecutors have found these new laws to be an attractive addition to their arsenal. Their energetic application has certainly consigned a small number of defendants to long terms of imprisonment and may have succeeded in shaking the foundations of some long-established crime families. But there is no empirical evidence to suggest that they have had a substantial deterrent impact on the overall incidence of the kinds of criminality at which they aim. The enormous drain on investigative and prosecutorial resources in mounting an organized-crime trial (and most of these cases go to trial) means that few prosecutions can be carried through. In this way, elaborate new constructs in the criminal law have a self-defeating element built in.

This development has other negative aspects. A combination of loosely drafted statutes, an overly pressing prosecution, and courts with narrow vision has given some of the new offenses a grossly overblown interpretation. The progressively draconian development of CCE is, indeed, a fairly typical instance of modern American criminal legislation, characterized by a periodic escalation of penalties in response to mounting perceptions of the incapacity of the criminal justice system to reduce the volume of crime. This tendency received a general expression in the radical changes in federal sentencing introduced by the Sentencing Reform Act of 1984, which abolished parole and established narrow ranges of sentencing guidelines for categories of crime. Reducing judicial discretion to a minimum, the federal guidelines (unlike those in some states) enact a generally rather severe pattern of sentences that, in turn, is frequently preempted by the even more severe mandatory minimum sentences required by such statutes as CCE.

This determination to appear hard on crime has also taken root in the courts, receiving its most dismal and unproductive expression in two decisions of the Supreme Court, one of which validated the execution of the death penalty on the mentally retarded,[3] while the other declined to condemn as unconstitutional the execution of the death penalty on teenagers[4]—decisions that painfully echo judgments to the same effect by the Nazi German courts.[5]

Sanctions and Deterrence

There are many explanations for this trend. The most cynical points to the political advantages for legislators (and even judges) in making repeated rhetorical declarations of their adamant stand against crime. More rationally, the trend no doubt owes a good deal to the modern disenchantment with rehabilitative goals and the substitution of the overall aim of giving criminals their "just deserts," though there can be much disagreement about exactly what these amount to. Again, some sentencing escalations will be justified by the belief that there are hardened criminals who, as a measure of social defense, ought to be incapacitated through detention for a very long period of time.

Side by side with these contestable claims there runs the perennial appeal to the general justification of criminal sanctions as deterrents to crime. This appeal will always have force, for it seems intuitively correct that large-scale removals or weakening of penalties or law enforcement would produce an increase in the rate of commission of at least some offenses. The claim is hard to document, however, for we have no "state of nature" with which to make a comparison. The conditions of modern social and commercial life presuppose a high degree of law and order, so that the amount of crime we might have if there were no criminal justice system is disorienting to imagine and impossible to quantify. Occasional illuminations, such as the upswing in crime that may go along with a police strike, are not very informative, since a long period of time with a settled expectation of no law enforcement would be necessary to yield a clear picture, and this is hardly an experiment that social scientists will be allowed to conduct. General deterrence is thus dauntingly difficult to measure.

Even granted the centrality of general deterrence as a sine qua non of social order, measuring increments of deterrence obtained by making sanctions more severe has, for a variety of reasons, also proved difficult, although attempts have been made in specific areas, such as capital punishment, drunk driving, and tax evasion. It is true that, assuming reasonably zealous law enforcement, more severe sanctions will result in convicts spending more time in prisons. But determining what effect this has on the volume of crime is very problematic. Harsher sanctions certainly may reduce some crimes, at least for a time, but the impact depends, among other factors, on the nature of the offense, the social situation in which it occurs, and the baseline from which the sanction was raised.[6] It would certainly be quite unwarranted to suppose that more severe sanctions will always further reduce crime. With respect to some crimes that are economically very attractive, such as drug vending, it may be that the harshest penalties only breed out the weaker and less skillful operators (who end up spending a good deal of their lives in prison) and promote the natural selection of the hardiest and wiliest entrepreneurs who more effectively insulate themselves from the reach of the law. In this way hard laws may sometimes make criminals more efficient.

Criminological literature certainly displays little enthusiasm for the incremental deterrent power of sanctions as a general remedy. In the important collection of essays published in 1983 under the title *Crime and Public Policy*,[7] the editor, James Q. Wilson, in summarizing the studies presented by the authors, has little to say about sanctions. Perhaps, he suggests, some impact could be made by more sophisticated profiling of career offenders who would then be targeted for rigorous prosecutions; by making bail more difficult for dangerous offenders; by developing more stringent laws on the abuse of alcohol and guns; by scrutinizing rules restricting the admission of evidence; and by streamlining the appellate process. To an extent, some of these proposals have been implemented, even though some of them also carry the suspicion of constitutional violation. While there now may be a decline in the rate of commission of some crimes, it is impossible to be confident about any causal links. "What needs to be done is difficult, complex and costly, and the gains will be deferred and moderate."[8]

There are other practical difficulties. The demand for harsher sanctions naturally is heard when the crime rate is high or increasing. But the most typical impact of an increasing crime rate is deterioration or breakdown in the workings of the criminal justice system. A high crime rate is rarely a problem of the criminal justice system, but it is certainly a problem *for* the system. With respect to "ordinary" crimes of violence and offenses against property that cause so much concern, law enforcement is often unable in the great run of cases to make a very effective investigation, so that the chances of being subject to a sanction may be quite small. Also, with respect to the criminals who are caught, the application of harsh penalties threatens to wreck already-strained prison systems, so that prosecutors often feel compelled to avoid them through charge reductions or other forms of plea bargaining. Thus, even if deterrent effects could be established at low levels of crime, as the crime figures worsen, the risk factor for the potential criminal is likely to diminish.

The deterrent effect of sanctions is substantially weakened as this gap between bark and bite inculcates lack of respect, even contempt for the system. Those who have a firm belief in the efficacy of increasing deterrents point to such factors as an explanation of why the system does not work well. If we were really serious in their application, they argue, sanctions would work. This point of view is also beset with problems. Obviously, if all the criminals were in jail, there would be no more crime. But this would not happen even under a vigorously enforced system of harsh sanctions. First, the best of all law enforcement systems would still leave a large number of crimes unsolved and a substantial number of criminals uncaught and continuing to function. Second, even with limitless prison facilities and long sentences that were actually served, we cannot say what impact there would be on reinforcements growing up into the criminal ranks. Third, though there are no measurements here, one may perhaps presume that a point can be reached when the percentage of the population that is in prison reaches so high a level that a degree of economic and social deterioration sets in. The cost of incarcerating a high percentage of citizens may be as great as or greater than enduring a large volume of crime.

In sum, sanctions, viewed as a deterrent, play an indispensable role as a fundamental feature of an authoritative system of criminal prohibitions, certainly providing a degree of crime prevention even if it cannot be precisely calculated. The study of the effectiveness of sanctions is a matter of individual crimes and the penalties attached to them. No doubt there are instances in which increasing severity of sanctions might yield a dividend in effective deterrence. Possibly drunk driving, tax fraud, and domestic violence fall into this category. With other crimes we have surely reached or passed the point at which increasing sanctions yields an efficient return—at least within the concept that we have of a criminal justice system. We can, perhaps without much difficulty these days, imagine dragnets, death squads, a war on crime *à outrance* that would propel "sanctions" to a height so far unknown. But then, of course, they would not be sanctions within a criminal justice system.

The point is that the impact of sanctions is limited not only by empirical constraints but also by justice concepts implicit in the notion of what it means to have a criminal justice system. Such a system involves natural-justice concepts of sanctions being applied only for the breach of rules when the breach has been determined by some due process, and when the sanction bears a degree of reasonable proportionality to the nature of the breach. In turn, such values inescapably call for complex and expensive procedures that limit the number of cases that can be fully processed. Thus, the criminal sanction (if viewed as a means of controlling crime) seems repeatedly to bump against natural ceilings. The preoccupation with deterrence through increasingly severe sanctions leads to disappointment, as the only tools it recognizes for crime control become ever more blunted by the very phenomenon they seek to control.

Incentives and Attitudes

An approach that analyzes criminal behavior primarily as a calculated response to sanctions faces theoretical problems as well as practical ones. The "economic" model makes the central assumption that people calculate comparative incentives for acting or not acting in a certain way and are influenced in their conduct by the final computation of the contribution to their well-being. This approach does not, of course, assert that everyone always follows this process, but, if it is to have important connections with reality and a practical application, the model must and does take the position that the assessment of incentives is an important, indeed a central, characteristic of human action.

By expressing the incentive equation in a mathematical mode (that may be used for prediction), the economic approach opens up a valuable perspective. In application it tends to lead us to scrutinize in detail the clusters of different social circumstances that surround the commission of different crimes and therefore depends on intensive empirical studies, which often prove illuminating. For example, such studies teach us that it is a mistake to look in a monocular fashion at sanctions and their deterrent impact alone in order to reduce crime. The balance of incentives is shifted just as much or more by the chances of apprehension and conviction. Certainty of justice is thus an important consideration. Also, the balance of incentives can be shifted by making crimes more difficult to commit, thus increasing the cost of commission. In this way we have learned that in some areas opportunity blocking, as with theft-proof devices or better security measures, can do much more to reduce some crime rates than elevating sanctions.

But there remains a major theoretical difficulty with the economic approach. This arises once we ask how we should count different impulses and inclinations in the individual's decision-making process. Some factors are capable of a simple monetary evaluation: How much money can I make by committing a crime compared with the money I can make by legitimate work, discounted by the chance of conviction and the estimate of punishment if convicted? But psychic and moral considerations fit less comfortably. It is surely clear that a welter of impulses and influences impels people to commit crimes. There is the natural rebelliousness and experimentalism of youth, involving the conscious defiance of authority, so that the threat of sanctions may be an alluring challenge rather than a deterrent. There is the sense of reinforcement and elation that comes when a group acts together. There is the break in tedium and for many the sense of having wrung something pleasurable out of a system that makes an unfair allocation of advantages. And of course there is the spur of rage. Against these often struggle the individual's assimilated feelings of social and moral condemnation of criminal acts. How shall all these be counted alongside monetary profit and loss?

The economic approach does not (at least in its later versions) speak simply of plain cash values. It recognizes the psychic tilt that comes from degrees of risk aversion or risk preference; it acknowledges that people must and do weigh their moral impulses in deciding whether an act will contribute to their well-being. The problem remains of how such different concepts can be usefully combined in explicating, by way of any formula, the process of people embarking on action. If there is no common denominator by which we may translate the weight of moral positions, or the weight of inhibitions formed by acculturation, into terms that permit their assimilation in the same equation with assessments of financial gain or loss, then we are left with an intractable difficulty.

The difficulty is central since we may intuitively and sensibly assume the impact of moral positions. Knowing the imperfections and uncertainties of the criminal justice system, we may guess that the reasonable degree of security that most people enjoy in social living has much to do with the fact that many people habitually refrain from crime, in spite of the possibility at times of considerable financial reward, for reasons that are connected with the moral repugnancy of the acts involved. Some people will not commit some crimes no matter how affirmative the calculation of risk appears in financial terms. For them the moral force is transcendent and could only be thought of mathematically as an infinity.

The economic model is based on the assumption that most people most of the time act rationally. But of course we think that people who refrain from crime for moral reasons have acted rationally. One way of looking at this will be to say that rationality is a variable construct for each individual, changing with each person's psychic makeup—so that theft is rational for the person without strong moral scruples but irrational for one who labors under moral inhibitions. Looked at this way, murder would be a perfectly rational act for the person with overwhelming impulses of rage. But if attitudes and impulses (psychic and moral) are powerful contributors to action and people are variously constituted with respect to them, and if at the same time they cannot be measured objectively and universally in monetary terms, then behavior is very unpredictable. This imperils the economic model by positing so many varying concepts of well-being, intruding so weightily, that we shall be unable to predict schematically. The economic response is to de-emphasize attitudes and to insist on the centrality of calculating well-being in the sense of looking to wealth-type incentives.

This is a dangerous path to follow, since society rests on a special recognition of that species of rationality that operates through moral judgments. We profess to count moral values higher than a desire for wealth or the satisfaction of envy or anger. In the civic context we view moral repugnancy toward crime as especially meritorious and regard it as a pillar of the social order. To classify such aversion to crime as an attitude that must in practice be discounted, because it is not susceptible to the hard measurements of economic models, is to embrace a stunted view of human action and to evince a lack of interest in what should be one of the most urgent concerns of crime fighting: the question of how to fortify the social and moral rejection of criminal acts that traditionally makes social living possible.

The Decline of Legitimacy

The concentration on incentives in a theory of deterrence perhaps contributes to lawmakers' preoccupation with inflating sanctions. Attention is diverted from the important association of norms with feelings of legitimacy. Crime signifies the weakened legitimacy of public norms—a loss of feelings of obligation and validity, a failure to connect public morality with responses instilled by acculturation. This is not to be confused with a repudiation of national values. Criminals, as has often been pointed out, do not for the most part reject the society's deepest values. They simply pursue them in ways that are officially disapproved, though, it is believed, widely followed. Much crime does aim at either material success or the alleviation of material distress. To be rich—or at least free from poverty—is a cherished goal in American society, perhaps so cherished that it attracts compellingly even when the risk is great.

Indeed, the legitimacy of publicly expressed, authoritatively packaged norms of conduct is weakened precisely because they often appear to conflict with, or be irrelevant to, the successful pursuit of national values. Many people do emerge from poverty and live well by dealing in drugs. Reported news conveys the impression that many successful business people and many successful politicians commit crimes. Nationally prominent political and business families owe their initial fortunes to organized criminal activity only a generation or two ago. An intelligent inference from closely following the news in America might be that crime is a shortcut to success and esteem, but that one ought to be clever and careful about the manner of its commission.

Such perceptions certainly weaken the deterrent impact of sanctions by underscoring the economic attractions of crime. But it would be a mistake to view them solely in economic terms. Just as important, they create a disjunction between authority and obligation, showing that behavior indicated by authoritative norms is often devalued by those who are admired. Responses of legitimacy may be further weakened by the substantial gap between public rhetoric about criminal sanctions and the reality of the system. It is hard to be respectful toward or even to take seriously a system that veers wildly between inflicting, in some cases, the harshest sentences in the Western world, and, on the other hand, in a great run of cases of some seriousness, exacting in practice a light punishment if any at all. A national commitment to hypocrisy creates a confusion of values that makes crime seem a less serious matter.

Skepticism about national commitment to consistent lawful conduct may be deepened for many by other aspects of the operations of the criminal justice systems in the United States. Sporadic but troubling reports recur about illegalities committed by the police. Even when not plainly illegal, police street practices are often seen as harassing and discriminatory with respect to minorities and the poor. In many cities the criminal courts that have the most contact with the public conduct their business in a disorderly, perfunctory, and indifferent manner. It is rare that the accused or spectators get the impression of a dignified, judicious, and just resolution. The defendant is likely either to feel aggrieved at being treated as a mere object of a bureaucratic exercise or to feel contemptuous of a system that lets him loose so quickly when he has committed a serious offense. With respect to serious business crimes or crimes of corruption by officials, one has the impression that many people believe such crimes to be rife, and are skeptical of the motives that lead investigators and prosecutors to selected targets. As a Supreme Court Justice once wrote, we suspect that a prosecutor may "pick the people he thinks he should get rather than pick cases that need to be prosecuted."[9]

Recognition that crime owes more to the complex deterioration of the legitimacy of public norms than to an inadequate structure of sanctions does not have encouraging implications. If such an acknowledgment means that we must turn back to the old liberal verities, and confess that crime may recede substantially only when we tear out the weeds of criminogenic social conditions—improve education, provide more decent jobs, eradicate glaring inequalities, replace poor housing, end homelessness—then, with no such great changes apparently in the offing, the landscape appears bleak. Wholesale changes in American values, mores, and leadership are beyond the powers of criminal justice reformers and do not seem to be on the horizon. While much is made of crime in public rhetoric, it nevertheless seems unwarranted to expect that deep changes in economic arrangements, in class and race relations, would be pursued merely because of the crime rate. Those who profit most from present arrangements are also those who are best protected from crime, so that the incentive is not keen. In any event, the price for a quick improvement may be too high; a rising crime rate is not the worst thing in the world. What the Establishment might offer to reduce crime may be worse than the disease. The installation of oppressive, sometimes tyrannical, regimes has reputedly been known to bring a sharp reduction in crime. But this is an example we should not want to emulate.[10]

Community Action

How, then, shall we promote the ideals of civic virtue in the South Bronx, in political offices, and in the boardrooms of great corporations? In the short run, what better techniques than sanction boosting are to hand for confronting crime? There are recent suggestions that the relegitimation of public norms can best be effected by engagement of the public at the local level. Under this view, reawakening is likely to manifest itself first in the limbs and not in the head. If penal norms are to have a vital meaning, then the organs that express disapproval must be local and must be seriously censorious—local and vocal. This now fashionable wisdom may spring in part from a disgust with city, state, and national governments that often appear to do nothing or to act wastefully or ineptly. No doubt it also owes much to sociological and criminological teachings to the effect that felt that deracination and community change and breakdown are important criminogenic factors that can be countered only by action within small communities.[11]

A source of concern about such proposals is that community action must to some extent entail the decentralization of governmental and criminal justice functions. Decentralization is often associated in the United States with negative images of local corruption and inefficiency. This is a risk to be run in any community program. It will be at its lowest in programs involving not much administration or expenditure, as with community policing techniques that enlist the cooperation and initiative of the community in a variety of crime-checking procedures. It would be at its highest if communities were given a large measure of control over a wide range of criminal justice operations, including, conceivably, the police, the prosecution service, legal aid, the appointment or election of magistrates, and the administration of courts. The risk might still be worth running.

Which services or agencies might most helpfully be decentralized will present hard questions. It may be a positive factor to break up huge prosecutorial offices and inaugurate a system of local prosecutors elected by relatively small districts of a city (as already happens in less heavily populated areas), while, on the other hand, perhaps the magistracy should continue to be appointed on a citywide or statewide basis in order to remove the judicial arm from entanglement with parochial politics.

Comparative observations do suggest the possibility of engendering a healthier climate with some degree of decentralization. For example, New York City has a criminal court for each borough, constituting five criminal courts in all, and four for the great mass of the city's population. By contrast, Inner London has seventeen magistrates courts. This larger number of courts reduces the operation of each to a more manageable level and scales down the size of the calendar and the defendant population to more human dimensions. There is more of the feeling of moving round a town than roaming through a continent. Police and magistrates get to know each other and the population and character of the neighborhood in which they are located. A feel for the kind of crime that is endemic, with its frequency and violence, develops. In this way it is possible to focus on the problems of a particular neighborhood.

Decentralization is also likely to bring home more vividly any shortage of resources or defects in the operation of the criminal justice system, so that political pressure can be organized more effectively than when the problem is thinly diffused through a borough containing several million people, as in New York. The activities of judges and prosecutors are exposed to daily scrutiny by a public that is not vast and remote but local and engaged. Doing justice may be more suited to being a cottage industry than to the methods of mass production.

If there is an overall point to be made, it is the old one that the capacity of a criminal justice system to control crime is inherently limited. The proper role of a criminal justice system is to dispense justice. Its most important potential for affecting behavior is emblematic—by being calm, dignified, and just, it can reinforce feelings of validity and obligation with respect to the norms that it enforces. The escalation of sanctions, with the inevitable evasions and inconsistencies that accompany such movements, may be counterproductive by undermining respect for the system and consequently for the norms of conduct it purports to guard.

Notes

1. Title 21, U.S.C., Section 848.
2. Title 18, U.S.C., Sections 1961–1968.
3. In *Penry v. Lynaugh*, 492 U.S. 302 (1989), the court held that the imposition of the death sentence on a mentally retarded accused was not categorically prohibited by the Eighth Amendment's cruel and unusual punishments clause.
4. In *Thompson v. Oklahoma*, 487 U.S. 815 (1988), although the imposition of the death sentence on a defendant who was fifteen when he committed the crime was reversed by the court, only four justices (two of whom have since retired) took the view that imposing the death penalty on juveniles was unconstitutional.
5. Richard Grunberger, in *The Twelve-Year Reich*, p. 123 (citing *Frankfurter Zeitung*, 29 May 1937), states that in 1927 the German Supreme Court extended the death penalty to those whose unsound mind indicated diminished responsibility. During the war, relying

on the extraordinary times, the German Supreme Court held that death sentences could be executed on those aged sixteen. This was lowered to fourteen in 1944. Andreas Frittner, *Deutsches Geistesleben und Nationalsozialismus*, p. 166, cited in Grunberger, p. 123.

6. For a summary of difficulties in measuring deterrent impact, see Johannes Andenaes, "Deterrence," vol. 2 *Encyclopedia of Crime and Justice* (1983), p. 591.

7. James Q. Wilson, ed., *Crime and Public Policy* (1983).

8. Ibid., p. 274.

9. Robert H. Jackson, "The Federal Prosecutor," vol. 31 *Journal of Criminal Law and Criminology* pp. 3,5 (1940).

10. The assumption of power by the Nazis in Germany was followed by a sharp decline in most ordinary crimes. In 1933, 590,165 crimes were recorded in Germany. In 1939, this had fallen to 335,162. Franz Ehrenwirth, *Statistiches Handbuch fur Deutschland 1928–1944*, p. 633. The usual explanation for this is that a sense of regeneration of commitment and engagement to the community came along with the Nazi assumption of power, though the fall in crime was likely also in part due to improving economic conditions.

11. For a summary of this line of criminological scholarship, see Albert K. Cohen, "Crime Causation: Sociological Theories," p. 342.

References

Andenaes, Johannes. "Deterrence." *Encyclopedia of Crime and Justice* 2 (1983): 591.

Cohen, Albert K. "Crime Causation: Sociological Theories." *Encyclopedia of Crime and Justice* 1 (1983): 342.

Ehrenwirth, Franz. *Statistiches Handbuch fur Deutschland 1928–1944.* 1949.

Frittner, Andreas. *Deutsches Geistesleben und Nationalsozialismus.* Tubingen, 1965.

Grunberger, Richard. *The Twelve-Year Reich.* New York: Holt, Rinehart and Winston, 1971.

Jackson, Robert H. "The Federal Prosecutor." *Journal of Criminal Law and Criminology* 31 (1940): 3, 5.

Wilson, James Q., ed. *Crime and Public Policy.* San Francisco: Institute for Contemporary Studies, 1983.

Part II

The Community in the Human

5

JOAN MCCORD

Crime, Conscience, and Family

Responding to Socrates's attempts to understand justice, Thrasymachus declared: "If one reasons rightly, it works out that the just is the same thing everywhere, the advantage of the stronger."[1] Many a criminal would agree. I will argue that perception of justice as nothing but the interest of the stronger can result from socialization practices commonly found in American families.

Although there is disagreement about how the influence works, there is little reason to doubt that family interaction affects what children view as proper behavior. We know that there are intergenerational links between criminality and aggression.[2] We know also that parental conflict is highly criminogenic and may account for apparent relationships between broken homes and crime.[3] Parental rejection and inattention, too, are related to crime.[4] Yet we do not understand what mechanisms link dysfunctional families to crime.

Families that are dysfunctional in terms of conflict tend to be the same families in which a parent is alcoholic and rejecting and aggressive. Such families are likely to present models for egocentrism and to fail to provide clear, reasonable guidance. We do not know under which, if any, of these descriptions of collinear conditions dysfunctional families cause crime.

The fact that intervention programs typically fail to bring about the changes in behavior for which they were designed suggests that there are errors in contemporary theories about the process of socialization. Three such errors are considered below.

Error One: Egoistic Theory

The first error is that of assuming that human nature is naturally egoistic. This egoistic theory claims that people choose always and only according to their own

An earlier version was presented at the American Society of Criminology Annual Meeting in San Francisco, November 20–23, 1991. The author wishes to thank Brian Forst, editor of this volume, for his helpful criticisms of that paper.

interests. The theory suggests, as Hobbes was careful to point out, that social benefit derives from convincing individuals that their own interests coincide with those of the group.[5] This argument, I believe, is false and dangerous.

In a famous attack on psychological hedonism, Bishop Joseph Butler noted that any cogent description of human nature must account for the appearance of benevolence, of filial love, and of a disposition to friendship. He argued that if self-love were the only motivation for friendship, we would not take pleasure in the well-being of one person rather than another. He also pointed out that by any account, happiness requires the satisfaction of specific desires. What is desired, say food or the well-being of another, could not be the happiness itself, or we would not have those specific appetites, the satisfaction of which (sometimes) produces happiness.[6] A theory that attributes choice to hedonic calculus could not explain specific desires. Yet an explanation of specific desires is a necessary part of a theory of choice, even of one that invokes a hedonic calculus. More will be said about specific desires below. Butler's criticisms of psychological hedonism included the observation that we often make moral judgments about actions when there is no possibility that we could be affected.[7]

In a similar vein, David Hume pointed out that animals frequently show extreme kindness, and it is implausible to attribute "refined deductions of self-interest" to them. In addition, the sacrifice of parents for their children, expressions of gratitude, and the generosity of sentiment sometimes found between a man and woman appear to be benevolence without self-interest. Hume concluded: "These and a thousand other instances are marks of a general benevolence in human nature, where no real interest binds us to the object."[8]

Those who espouse psychological hedonism confuse the results of achieving a goal with the goal, of being pleased because an experiment has worked and doing the experiment in order to be pleased. Some people receive pleasure from benefiting others or pursuing justice; some people receive pleasure from being praised or made wealthy; some people get pleasure from being beaten with a whip. Psychological hedonism cannot distinguish among such different sets of motives. Although altruism and egoism are attached to motivation in the same way, as identifying objects of desire, they lead to quite different types of actions—and a theory of motivation that cannot distinguish them must be an inadequate theory.

Psychological hedonism confounds the assumption that a voluntary action must be motivated, that the agent must want to do it (under some description), with a belief that voluntary actions must be motivated by self-interested desires. This confusion provides the underpinning for an assumption that children must be taught to behave socially by appeals to their self-interests. Such appeals are misguided.

Observations of infants have shown that at very young ages children have social interests.[9] Between twelve and eighteen months, their level of altruistic behavior seems to stabilize.[10] Correlations of measures of altruism between monozygotic (identical) twins are about twice those between dizygotic twins,[11] suggesting that there may be some genetically transmitted basis for altruism. Socialization practices that increase altruism, like those that increase aggression, include imitation of the behavior children see.[12] Helpful behavior is increased by exposure to nurturing adults who model helping and give altruistic reasons for their actions.[13]

Recognition of an altruistic motive undercuts the fundamental assumption of reinforcement theories.[14] The existence of such a motive demonstrates that appeals to self-interest are at least sometimes unnecessary. In fact, they may be counterproductive. However lofty may be the motive, inappropriate rewards may generate avarice and punishments provide models for giving pain.

Error Two: Universal Scope and Unidirectionality of Influence

The second error is the tacit assumption that socialization practices and biological conditions have independent and universal effects on child development. The view that a child's behavior is completely under control of socializing personnel seems to have been derived from the philosophy of John Locke, father of modern empiricism, who had argued that all materials for thinking come ultimately from perceptions and reflections upon them.

Although ideas, according to Locke, were ultimately drawn entirely from experience, his psychological theories recognized the importance of emotions. In *Some Thoughts Concerning Education*, he urged that the use of ordinary punishments would produce "an aversion to that which it is the tutor's business to create a liking to." Education, Locke believed, must play with the child's higher motives: "To make a good, a wise, and a virtuous man, it is fit he should learn to cross his appetite, and deny his inclination to riches, finery, or pleasing his palate, &c. whenever his reason advises the contrary and his duty requires it."[15]

Most theories of socialization presuppose that a given practice will have similar effects on all children. This view overlooks evidence that mood, temperament, and expectancies affect responses. Some of these relationships were demonstrated in an experiment by Carlsmith, Lepper, and Landauer, who showed twenty-five girls and twenty-seven boys in preschool one of two films about an experimenter. In one, the experimenter was punitive and in the other, supportive. Several days later, the children were individually shown either a film that aroused anxiety or one that was neutral; then the experimenter seen in the earlier film asked the child to pick up 150 tennis balls. Anxious children were more helpful for a negative experimenter, although children shown the neutral film were more helpful to a supportive experimenter.[16] In a 1983 study, I found that the types of parental behavior that apparently influenced 113 more aggressive boys to become criminals differed from the types of parental behavior that apparently influenced 114 less aggressive boys to become criminals.[17]

Not only do similar socialization practices vary in effects for different children, but also characteristics of children can affect the socialization practices of parents. Differences in size, health, attractiveness, intelligence, responsiveness, sex, and temperament affect how adults respond to children.

Cantor and Gelfand trained twelve children to be responsive with some female college students and unresponsive with others. Forty-eight adult–child pairs were observed through one-way mirrors as the adult assisted the child in building with Tinker Toys and drawing with Etch-a-Sketch. Observers blind to the purpose of the study found that children who were being responsive received more attention.[18] Other studies have used pictures of attractive or unattractive children attached to short descriptions of misbehavior to test how looks affect judgments. These yield evidence that adults judge attractive children as more honest and less likely to misbehave.[19]

Some differences in behavior may have genetic origins. Several studies have found evidence of heritability for activity level, impulsivity, aggression, and desire for excitement.[20] Goodman and Stevenson found a considerable amount of heritability for hyperactivity among the twins they studied. The authors suggested that genetically determined hyperactivity might cause poor socialization practices.[21]

Richard Bell suggested a variety of ways that differences among newborns might affect their social environments. Crying babies can make it difficult for mothers to sleep, thereby influencing their child-rearing behaviors; illness might make it difficult for children to digest food or nurse; and poor abilities to communicate might produce failures of parental responsiveness.[22] Rutter and Garmezy suggested that a child's misbehavior could promote marital discord, which, in turn, could increase conduct disorder.[23] In a test of this hypothesis, however, I found no evidence that misbehavior of the child produced parental conflict, although contemporaneous misconduct and conflict were strongly related.[24]

Although bidirectionality of influence between children and parents has been acknowledged over an extended period of time,[25] only a handful of studies has pinned down specific relationships. Maccoby and Jacklin showed that mothers respond to their infants' difficult behavior with reductions in pressure to conform, and low levels of pressure to conform increase infants' difficult behavior.[26] Barkley and Cunningham showed that methylphenidate-induced changes in the behavior of hyperactive children produced changes in the mothers' behavior.[27]

Anderson, Lytton, and Romney watched as thirty-two boys between the ages of six and eleven interacted with their own and other boys' mothers individually. Half the boys were classified as conduct disordered, according to criteria set forth by the American Psychiatric Association's Diagnostic and Statistical Manual. Mothers of both conduct-disordered and normal children tended to be more negative toward the conduct-disordered children.[28]

Adults differ, of course, in their responses to children. To study the differences, Bugental, Caporael, and Shennum used four boys trained to act cooperatively or uncooperatively in an experimental situation. Sixteen mothers and sixteen female undergraduates interacted with a responsive and an unresponsive boy, counterbalanced for order. The content of the adults' conversation was masked in order to code their conversation for assertiveness when communicating positive, negative, and neutral messages. Differences in the adults' locus of control produced opposite reactions to uncooperative behavior of the children. Adults with an internal locus of control reduced assertiveness, and those with an external locus of control increased assertiveness when conveying affectively neutral messages to the uncooperative child.[29] After extending their studies to include naturally occurring interacting effects of mother's and child's personalities, Bugental and Shennum concluded: "Our results suggest that the mother who questions her own caregiving ability behaves in such a way as to maintain or exacerbate child uncontrollability."[30]

Error Three: Belief in Single Effects of Punishments and Rewards

The degree to which children care about their own pleasures and pains and what they consider pleasurable and painful are largely functions of experience. Many believe that rewards and punishment should be used to teach children, ignoring the role of reinforcements in teaching them what to value.

Effects of subtle rewards can be found even among newborn babies. Thoman, Korner, and Benson-Williams randomly assigned eighteen first-born healthy newborns to conditions in which one-third were held whenever they awakened over a two-day period. As anticipated, the babies who were held subsequently spent more time with their eyes open. Unexpectedly, they also spent more time crying. The authors suggest that these infants had been taught to associate crying with the comfort of being held.[31]

In another study of newborns, Riese compared forty-seven pairs of monozygotic, thirty-nine pairs of same-sex dizygotic, and seventy-two pairs of opposite-sex dizygotic twins. She found significant correlations for both same- and opposite-sex dizygotic twins, indicating shared environmental influences. Correlations among the monozygotic pairs were not significantly larger than those among dizygotic pairs. Comparisons included tests for irritability, resistance to soothing, activity level when awake, activity level when asleep, reactivity to a cold disk on the thigh and to a pin prick, and response to cuddling. Riese concluded that "environment appears to account for most of the known variance for the neonatal temperament variables."[32]

Just as neonates can learn to cry in order to be picked up, children learn to notice what to consider painful. Variability in recognizing sensations as painful has been dramatically evidenced through studies of institutionalized infants. After observing children who received little attention, Goldfarb reported how when one child closed a door on her hand, injuring her finger so severely that it turned blue, she did not cry or otherwise show pain. Another child had a steel splinter removed from her cornea that had been embedded there for two days without any report of pain. Another sat on a radiator too hot for the teacher to touch, and yet another was observed cutting the palm of his own hand with sharp scissors. Contrary to an interpretation that the children lacked normal pain receptors, all the children gave pain responses to a pin prick. Goldfarb reasonably concluded: "The perception of pain and the reaction to pain-arousing stimuli are episodes far more complex than is implied in the concept of pure, unencumbered sensation."[33]

Children also can be positively motivated by the prospect of reinforcements typically considered to result in pain.[34] The influence of both models and role play have been shown to affect pain threshold for receiving shocks.[35]

Wahler and Dumas suggest that some children misbehave in order to generate negative feedback, a consequence of valuing predictability. If families are more predictable in their punitive behavior, they argue, punishments take on positive valence.[36]

In developing the Opponent Process Theory, Solomon demonstrated that over a range of behaviors, pain-giving consequences acquire positive value through exposure.[37] Experiences with punishments are also likely to desensitize. Cline, Croft, and Courrier compared galvanic skin response and blood volume change among boys watching nonviolent and violent segments of movies. Twenty of the boys customarily watched violent television, whereas twenty-one watched little. The two groups were equivalent during nonviolent segments, but the boys who rarely watched violent television showed greater blood volume change and increased GSR while watching a chase scene and a violent segment of a boxing movie.[38] Similar results are reported from controlled exposure to violence in the laboratory.[39]

Experimental studies of transgression shed light on the ways in which experience with punishments influence preference. Aronson and Carlsmith asked forty-four preschool children, individually, to compare five toys until they established stable transitive preferences. The experimenter then said he had to leave the room for a few minutes and placed on a table the toy ranked second-favorite by the child. The child was told not to play with that toy, but that playing with the others was permissible. Half of the children were randomly assigned to each of two conditions. In the "mild threat" condition, the experimenter said he would be annoyed if the child played with the forbidden toy. In the "severe threat" condition, the experimenter said that if the child played with the forbidden toy, the experimenter would be very angry and would take all the toys and never come back. The experimenter left the child for ten minutes. Approximately forty-five days later, the children were again asked to rank the five toys. For this ranking, eight of those who were told merely that the experimenter would be annoyed had decreased their preference for the forbidden toy, whereas none of the children who were threatened with punishment had decreased their preference for it.

Conversely, four of the children from the mild-threat condition ranked the forbidden toy as a favorite, whereas fourteen of those in the severe-threat condition regarded the forbidden toy as the favorite. In sum, punishment tended to enhance the value of the forbidden.[40]

In a near replication, after asking children to rank the toys, Lepper told two groups not to play with the toy ranked second in preference, with one group told that the experimenter would be a little annoyed if the child played with the toy and the other that the experimenter would be very upset and angry with the child. A third group was not forbidden to play with a toy. Three weeks later, the children played another game and were to report their own scores, which were two points less than required to win a prize. Honesty in reporting their scores was greatest among children without any threats, followed by those given mild threats, and least among children who had been severely threatened. Denigration of the toy that had been forbidden occurred only among children in the mild-threat condition. Again punishment increased forbidden behavior, in this case, dishonesty.[41]

Punishments are invoked only when rules are disobeyed, so that telling a child about rules in conjunction with information about punishments for infractions informs a child that he or she has a choice: obey, or disobey and receive punishment. This choice may account for the fact that increased misbehavior appears to be a consequence of punishment.[42]

Similarly, rewards are used only if an activity would not attract on its merits. Hence, the implication of using rewards is diminution of the value of what requires reward.

The extent to which preferences can be shaped by the use of punishments and rewards has been demonstrated through arbitrarily arranged activities. Lepper et al. used imaginary foods dubbed "hupe" and "hule." Twenty-eight preschool children were told short stories about Johnny or Janie, depending on the sex of the child, being given new foods. For half the children, the mother in the story offered first one and then the other (in counterbalanced order) to the child in the story; for the other half, the mother in the story explained to her child that (s)he could have one (hupe or hule for different children) if (s)he ate the other. In the contingency condition, in which it seemed as though hupe (or hule) was a reward for eating the other, the children judged the second preferable and gave as their reason that the second dish tasted better. No such preference appeared in the noncontingent condition. The effect for preferences under contingency options was replicated with another group of forty children using felt pens and pastels rather than imaginary foods.[43]

Identifying something as a reward tends to enhance its value while diminishing that of the rewarded behavior.[44] Many studies show that rewarding children for performing an activity they already enjoy tends to reduce the children's interest in that activity.[45] Outside the laboratory, a study of seventy-two children showed that those accustomed to receiving rewards were less likely to be helpful without rewards than those not accustomed to receiving them.[46]

The mistaken belief that by manipulating rewards and punishments one can generate social interest has a dangerous consequence. The manipulations create the impression that children ought to consider only their own interests. Desires for reward and avoidance of punishment are selfish motivations. Their use by parents increases the salience of egocentric motives. This, as Kant noted, "is the most objectionable of all . . . for it puts the motives to virtue and those to vice in the same class."[47]

Conscience and Family

Empirical research into socialization of children coincided with widespread acceptance of Freudian notions describing development of the superego. Those who accepted Freud's theory "bought into" ideas about the pleasure principle, universality of an Oedipus complex, and the necessity for punishments in the course of identification with socializing agents. These assumptions, I believe, have lived beyond their usefulness and considerably beyond their support in research.

Some keys to the types of socialization practices conducive to social welfare have been found in a variety of studies. These show that experiences in families where a child is treated as a reasoning, though inexperienced, colleague tend to promote social responsibility.

In one study, thirteen (of thirty-nine) randomly selected mothers of preschoolers were trained to respond to their children's requests and to avoid directing them during a specified period of time each day for one week. After a week of "practice," their children complied with more of the mother's requests in the laboratory than the comparison group of children, whose mothers used reinforcement training.[48] The results are mirrored in natural settings.

Stayton, Hogan, and Ainsworth observed twenty-five infants at three-week intervals, for four hours of home visits. Measures for discipline and control included frequency of verbal commands, frequency of physical intervention, and extent of floor freedom permitted the child. These were unrelated to the infant's compliance. The authors concluded that "infants who have the most harmonious relations with their mothers and hence who have the least reason to fear loss of love, are the most readily compliant with their mothers' wishes and commands."[49]

In another study based on home observations of sixteen infants initially either fifteen or twenty months old, over a period of nine months, Zahn-Waxler, Radke-Yarrow, and King found that mothers who explained consequences to their child had children who were more altruistic, especially if the explanations included the importance of not hurting others. Neutral explanations, withdrawal of love, and physical punishments, however, were ineffective techniques for teaching children cooperative, helpful behavior.[50]

Harrington, Block, and Block report on a longitudinal study of thirty-three girls and fifth-three boys in California. When the children were three or four years old, both the father and the mother described their child-rearing practices. The children were again studied as students in the ninth grade. After a decade, those from early home environments that supported psychological comfort and freedom were most intellectually active, had high aspirations, and valued autonomy.51

Children tend to treat other children as they are treated. This was demonstrated in an experiment in which sixteen children between the ages of six and seven years were taught how to use a marble drop by use of rewards only, punishments (fines), both, or neither. These children were then told to teach a child a year younger than themselves. Only the children who had been taught using fines used them, though the possibility for doing so was mentioned to half the children who had been taught without them.[52]

Clearly, children learn without the use of external rewards or punishments. Their use of language serves as a constant reminder of this. Even if children could learn words by being rewarded for producing them (which seems implausible), they could not be taught the infinite variety of sentences through use of reinforcements.[53] Yet they do learn to speak and to understand what others say, even in unfamiliar contexts with unfamiliar sentences.

What I have called Construct Theory suggests a means for integrating understanding how children learn a language with how they learn how to act. In brief, Construct Theory claims that children learn what to do and what to believe in the process of learning how to use language.[54] The theory is an extension, one might say, of Wilfrid Sellars's observation that "to be a language user is to conceive of oneself as an agent subject to rules."[55]

Construct Theory postulates that children learn by constructing categories organized by the concepts of the language in their culture. These categories can be identified by descriptions, much as one might identify jacket labels in a filing system. Some categories are collections of objects, but others have labels such as "To be done," "To be avoided," "To be believed," or "To be doubted." Through these categories, the child organizes perceptions and behaviors and feelings. For some categories, such as "painful" and "pleasant," the label identifies types of events for which there are dispositional styles of noticing and responding. For others, the categories identify motivational components for acting.

The idea that learning a language involves categorizing objects can be traced to Plato. In "Cratylus," Socrates notes that speaking is a sort of action involving placing things in their proper classes in order to communicate about them. After testing a variety of possibilities, the dialogue ends with the suggestion that truth is related to naming and depends on both convention and reality.[56] This was not, however, the theory that came to dominate social science. The assumptions of those studying human behavior were derived from empiricists and Logical Positivists.

Empiricists, in a quest for certainty upon which to build a science of probability,[57] constructed an ontology that could not yield knowledge about the world or enable an adequate theory of communication. Empiricists insisted that meaningful statements were verifiable, and criteria of evidence depended on private sense data.[58] This view of language neglected a fundamental condition. According to Quine, "Language is a social art. In acquiring it we have to depend entirely on intersubjectively available cues as to what to say and when."[59]

The Construct Theory is an attempt to make sense of socialization, with its heavy dependency on communication. Socialization involves teaching children what to expect in the world and how to talk about it. An adequate theory of socialization cannot, therefore, require apprehension of elaborate, elusive, or private events.

Frege recognized that "we cannot come to an understanding with one another apart from language."[60] And, in showing that reference could not depend on thought, Frege paved the way to a theory of language that could be tied to knowledge.[61] Building on the work of Frege, Tarski indicated how things in a public world could be related to a language of description, and proposed that his semantic definition of truth could be extended to cover other intentional concepts.[62]

Quine and Sellars showed that the foundations of empiricism could not bear its weight.[63] Wittgenstein tore the heart out of the idea that language could exist privately, that we could know what we mean even without expressing it.[64] Austin showed that meaning and use were intricately entwined and that language involved doing much more than stating beliefs.[65]

In "Truth and Meaning," Donald Davidson developed Tarski's definition of truth into a theory of meaning. "It is a misfortune that dust from futile and confused battles . . . has prevented those with a theoretical interest in language . . . from recognizing in the semantical concept of truth (under whatever name) the sophisticated and powerful foundation of a competent theory of meaning," he wrote.[66] On Davidson's account, the truth conditions provided meaning. He explained, "The truth of an utterance depends on just two things: what the words as spoken mean, and how the world is arranged."[67]

Philosophers as divergent on other issues as Quine, Sellars, Dummett, Follesdal, Searle, and Dennett agreed that language could not be used as it is used were there not some public criteria of meaning to enable one to communicate, approve, oppose, promise, command, and perform a variety of other "illocutionary" and "perlocutionary" acts.[68] "The proper role of experience or surface irritation is as a basis not for truth but for warranted belief," suggested Quine, adding that this interface "makes scientific method partly empirical rather than solely a quest for internal coherence."[69]

Empiricism had provided grounding for learning theories, theories that appear on the evidence discussed above to be faulty. Contemporary analytic philosophy provides a foundation for analyzing the process of socialization as one in which the teaching of language, behavior, and belief are intertwined. If meanings of sentences in a language come from truth conditions for assertion, there would be no way to teach the concepts pertaining to values, beliefs, hopes, and pains unless they were at least partially public.[70]

Learning a language requires learning not only what to count as tables and chairs, cars and trucks, but also what to count as painful and pleasant, undesirable and desirable, and worth avoiding or pursuing. In learning how to name and to reidentify, children construct classifications. The classification systems they develop will permeate what they notice and how they act as well as what they say. Actionable categories differ, of course, from assent categories, so socialization must involve teaching children not only to assent to moral propositions, but also to act upon them.

Learning a language involves learning to formulate sentences as well as how to use words. Sentences are constructed by linking predicates (which can be thought of as classes) and functional relations. Perhaps no component of a sentence is so critical to the relation between language and action as the connective "if . . . then." This connective gives linguistic expression to what neonates learned when they cried and were picked up (if I cry, then I will be picked up), what an infant learns by shaking a rattle (if I shake it, then it will make noise), and what the child learns when discovering natural consequences in the physical world.

When children recognize the logical equivalence between the conditional, "if x then y," and the disjunctive, "either not-x or y," rewards and punishments weaken the force of a rule by introducing choices. In learning how to use the language, children learn the logical force of material implication. Told that if they stay out late (x), their parents will punish them (y), children can choose to stay out late and devalue the pains their parents impose. Told that if they eat their carrots, they will be allowed to eat dessert, children may decide the dessert is not very appetizing and therefore choose not to eat the carrots. If parents intend to teach a child to come home at a certain time and to eat vegetables, they stand a better chance of doing so by telling the child why this is important.

A child also perceives that the intention of the person who punishes is to give pain. This knowledge may decrease the child's desire to be with the person who punishes or to care how the person who punishes feels, thus further reducing the influence of a socializing agent.

Because rewards are designed to give pleasure to the child and punishments are designed to give the child pain, their use teaches children that they ought to value their own pleasure and to attempt to reduce their own pain. Punishments and rewards teach children to focus on their own pains and pleasures in deciding how to act.

Children do not require punishments if they are given consistent guidance. Nor do they require rewards if intrinsic values of what they ought to do are made apparent to them. Of course, children will not always do as their parents wish, whether or not punishments are used. Yet children can be taught to follow reasonable rules and to be considerate—and the likelihood that particular children will learn these things is directly related to the use of reason in teaching them and to the consideration they see in their surroundings.

Notes

1. Plato, "Republic" 339.

2. For example, Justin D. Call, "Child Abuse and Neglect in Infancy: Sources of Hostility Within the Parent–Infant Dyad and Disorders of Attachment in Infancy"; Byron Egeland and Alan Sroufe, "Developmental Sequelae of Maltreatment in Infancy"; Leonard D. Eron et al., "Aggression and Its Correlates over 22 Years"; David P. Farrington, "The Family Backgrounds of Aggressive Youths" and "Environmental Stress, Delinquent Behavior, and Convictions"; Richard J. Gelles, "Violence in the Family: A Review of Research in the Seventies"; Sheldon Glueck and Eleanor T. Glueck, *Unraveling Juvenile Delinquency*; Roy C. Herrenkohl and Ellen C. Herrenkohl, "Some Antecedents and Developmental Consequences of Child Maltreatment"; L.Rowell Huesmann and Leonard D. Eron, "Cognitive Processes and the Persistence of Aggressive Behavior"; Ernest N. Jouriles, Julian Barling, and K. Danise O'Leary, "Predicting Child Behavior Problems in Maritally Violent Families"; Dorothy O. Lewis et al., "Biopsychosocial Characteristics of Matched Samples of Delinquents and Nondelinquents"; Mary Main and Ruth Goldwyn, "Predicting Rejection of Her Infant from Mother's Representation of Her Own Experience: Implications for the Abused-Abusing Intergenerational Cycle"; Joan McCord, "Some Child-Rearing Antecedents of Criminal Behavior in Adult Men" and "A Longitudinal Study of Aggression and Antisocial Behavior"; David R. Offord, "Family Backgrounds of Male and Female Delinquents"; Lea Pulkkinen, "Search for Alternatives to Aggression in Finland"; Lee N. Robins, *Deviant Children Grown Up*; Cathy S. Widom, "Child Abuse, Neglect, and Adult Behavior: Research Design and Findings on Criminality, Violence, and Child Abuse."

3. Robert E. Emery, "Interparental Conflict and the Children of Discord and Divorce"; Farrington, "Family Backgrounds" and "Stepping Stones to Adult Criminal Careers"; Travis Hirschi, *Causes of Delinquency*; Rolf Loeber and Magda Stouthamer-Loeber, "Family Factors As Correlates and Predictors of Juvenile Conduct Problems and Delinquency"; Joan McCord, "A Longitudinal View of the Relationship between Parental Absence and Crime" and "Aggression in Two Generations."

4. John Bowlby, "The Influence of Early Environment on Neurosis and Neurotic Character" and "Maternal Care and Mental Health"; Sanford M. Dornbusch et al., "Single Parents, Extended Households, and the Control of Adolescents"; William Goldfarb, "Psychological Privation in Infancy and Subsequent Adjustment"; John Hirschi, *Causes of Delinquency*; John H. Laub and Robert J. Sampson, "Unraveling Families and Delinquency: A Reanalysis of the Gluecks' Data"; Alan E. Liska and Mark D. Reed, "Ties to Conventional Institutions and Delinquency: Estimating Reciprocal Effects"; Rolf Loeber and Magda Stouthamer-Loeber, "Family Factors"; H.W. Newell, "The Psycho-Dynamics of Maternal Rejection" and "A Further Study of Maternal Rejection"; L. Edward Wells and Joseph H. Rankin, "Direct Parental Controls and Delinquency."

5. Thomas Hobbes, *Leviathan*.

6. Joseph Butler, "Fifteen Sermons."

7. Ibid.

8. David Hume, *An Enquiry Concerning the Principles of Morals*, p. 143.

9. Harriet Rheingold and Gena N. Emery, "The Nurturing Acts of Very Young Children"; Carolyn Zahn-Waxler and Marian Radke-Yarrow, "The Development of Altruism: Alternative Research Strategies"; Carolyn Zahn-Waxler et al., "The Early Development of Prosocial Behavior."

10. E.Mark Cummings et al., "Early Organization of Altruism and Aggression: Developmental Patterns and Individual Differences."

11. J.Phillipe Rushton et al., "Altruism and Aggression: The Heritability of Individual Differences."

12. Albert Bandura, Dorothea Ross, and Shiela A. Ross, "Transmission of Aggression through Imitation of Aggressive Models"; Leonard Berkowitz et al., "Experiments on the Reactions of Juvenile Delinquents to Filmed Violence"; James H. Bryan and Perry London, "Altruistic Behavior by Children"; Nancy Eisenberg, *Altruistic Emotion, Cognition, and Behavior*; Leonard D. Eron and L. Rowell Huesmann, "The Relation of Prosocial Behavior to the Development of Aggression and Psychopathology" and "The Role of Television in the Development of Prosocial and Antisocial Behavior"; David P. Farrington, "The Family Backgrounds of Aggressive Youths"; Lynette Kohn Friedrich and Althea H. Stein, "Aggressive and Prosocial Television Programs and the Natural Behavior of Preschool Children"; Jeffrey H. Goldstein and R.L. Arms, "Effects of Observing Athletic Contests on Hostility"; McCord, "A Longitudinal Study"; D. Rosenhan and G.M. White, "Observation and Rehearsal As Determinants of Prosocial Behavior"; J. Phillipe Rushton, "Effects of Prosocial Television and Film Material on the Behavior of Viewers"; Ervin Staub, *Positive Social Behavior and Morality: Socialization and Development*; Glenn M. White, "Immediate and Deferred Effects of Model Observation and Guided and Unguided Rehearsal on Donating and Stealing"; Widom, "Child Abuse"; Judy L. Wilkens, William H. Scharff, and Robert S. Schlottman, "Personality Type, Reports of Violence and Aggressive Behavior"; Carolyn Zahn-Waxler, Marian Radke-Yarrow, and Robert A. King, "Child-Rearing and Children's Pro-Social Initiations toward Victims of Distress."

13. Marian-Radke Yarrow, Phyllis M. Scott, and Carolyn-Zahn Waxler, "Learning Concern for Others."

14. Joan E. Grusec and Sandra L. Skubiski, "Model Nurturance Demand Characteristics of the Modeling Experiment and Altruism"; Martin L. Hoffman, "Is Altruism Part of Human Nature?"; Lauren Wispé, "Introduction" in *Altruism, Sympathy, and Helping: Psychological and Sociological Principles*.

15. John Locke, *Some Thoughts Concerning Education*.

16. J. Merrill Carlsmith, Mark R. Lepper, and T.K. Landauer, "Children's Obedience to Adult Requests: Interactive Effects of Anxiety Arousal and Apparent Punitiveness of the Adult."

17. McCord, "A Longitudinal Study."

18. Nancy L. Cantor and Donna M. Gelfand, "Effects of Responsiveness and Sex of Children on Adults' Behavior."

19. Karen Dion, "Physical Attractiveness and Evaluation of Children's Transgressions."

20. For example, Eron et al., "Aggression and Its Correlates"; H.H. Goldsmith and I.I. Gottesman, "Origins of Variation in Behavioral Style: A Longitudinal Study of Temperament in Young Twins"; Huesmann and Eron, "Cognitive Processes"; Nancy L. Pederson et al., "Neuroticism, Extraversion, and Related Traits in Adult Twins Reared Apart and Reared Together."

21. Robert Goodman and Jim Stevenson, "A Twin Study of Hyperactivity."

22. Richard Q. Bell, "The Effect on the Family of a Limitation in Coping Ability in a Child: A Research Approach and a Finding," "A Reinterpretation of the Direction of Effects in Studies of Socialization," and "Parent, Child, and Reciprocal Influences."

23. Michael Rutter and Norman Garmezy, "Developmental Psychopathology."

24. McCord, "Aggression in Two Generations."

25. For example, Willard W. Hartup, "The Social Worlds of Childhood"; Hugh Lytton, "Child and Parent Effects in Boys' Conduct Disorder: A Reinterpretation"; John

B. Reid, G.R. Patterson, and Rolf Loeber, "The Abused Child: Victim, Instigator, or Innocent Bystander?"; Michael Rutter et al., "Genetic Factors in Child Psychiatric Disorders—I. A Review of Research Strategies"; Robert R. Sears, Eleanor E. Maccoby, and Harry Levin, *Patterns of Child Rearing*; Leon J. Yarrow, "Research in Dimensions of Early Maternal Care."

26. Eleanor E. Maccoby and Carol N. Jacklin, "The 'Person' Characteristics of Children and the Family As Environment."

27. Russell A. Barkley and Charles E. Cunningham, "The Effects of Methylphenidate on the Mother-Child Interactions of Hyperactive Children."

28. K.E. Anderson, Hugh Lytton, and D.M. Romney, "Mothers' Interactions with Normal and Conduct-Disordered Boys: Who Affects Whom?"

29. Daphne B. Bugental, Linda Caporael, and William A. Shennum, "Experimentally Produced Child Uncontrollability: Effect on the Potency of Adult."

30. Daphne B. Bugental and William A. Shennum, " 'Difficult' Children As Elicitors and Targets of Adult Communication Patterns: An Attributional-Behavioral Transactional Analysis," p. 52.

31. Evelyn B. Thoman, Anneliese F. Korner, and Lynn Benson-Williams, "Modification of Responsiveness to Maternal Vocalization in the Neonate."

32. Marilyn L. Riese, "Neonatal Temperament in Monozygotic and Dizygotic Twin Pairs," p. 1236.

33. William Goldfarb, "Pain Reactions in a Group of Institutionalized Schizophrenic Children" and "Psychological Privation in Infancy," pp. 780–81.

34. Ronald Gallimore, Roland G. Tharp, and Bryan Kemp, "Positive Reinforcing Function of 'Negative Attention' "; Kenneth L. Witte and Eugene E. Grossman, "The Effects of Reward and Punishment upon Children's Attention, Motivation, and Discrimination Learning."

35. K.D. Craig and Stephen M. Theiss, "Vicarious Influences on Pain-Threshold Determinations"; Steven A. Kopel and Hal S. Arkowitz, "Role Playing As a Source of Self-Observation and Behavior Change."

36. Robert G. Wahler and Jean E. Dumas, "Maintenance Factors in Coercive Mother–Child Interactions: The Compliance and Predictability Hypothesis" and " 'A Chip off the Old Block': Some Interpersonal Characteristics of Coercive Children across Generations."

37. Richard L. Solomon, "The Opponent-Process Theory of Acquired Motivation: The Costs of Pleasure and the Benefits of Pain"; Elliot Aronson, J. Merrill Carlsmith, and John M. Darley, "The Effects of Expectancy on Volunteering for an Unpleasant Experience"; Robert A. Rosellini and R.L. Lashley, "Opponent-Process Theory: Implications for Criminality"; Thomas E. Shipley, Jr., "Opponent Process Theory"; Elaine Walster, Elliot Aronson, and Zita Brown, "Choosing to Suffer As a Consequence of Expecting to Suffer: An Unexpected Finding."

38. Victor B. Cline, Roger G. Croft, and Stevenneth Courrier, "Desensitization of Children to Television Violence."

39. Margaret H. Thomas et al., "Desensitization to Portrayals of Real-Life Aggression As a Function of Exposure to Television Violence."

40. Elliot Aronson and J. Merrill Carlsmith, "Effect of the Severity of Threat on the Devaluation of Forbidden Behavior."

41. Mark R. Lepper, "Dissonance, Self-Perception and Honesty in Children."

42. David P. Farrington and Donald J. West, "The Cambridge Study in Delinquent Development (United Kingdom)"; Joan McCord, "Family Relationships, Juvenile Delinquency, and Adult Criminality."

43. Mark R. Lepper et al., "Consequences of Superfluous Social Constraints: Effects on Young Children's Social Influences and Subsequent Intrinsic Interest."

44. Ann K. Boggiano and Deborah S. Main, "Enhancing Children's Interest in Activities Used As Rewards: The Bonus Effect."

45. For example, David Greene and Mark R. Lepper, "Effects of Extrinsic Rewards on Children's Subsequent Intrinsic Interest"; Mark R. Lepper, David Greene, and Robert E. Nisbett, "Undermining Children's Intrinsic Interest with Extrinsic Rewards"; Michael Ross, Rachel Karniol, and Mitch Rothstein, "Reward Contingency and Intrinsic Motivation in Children: A Test in the Delay of Gratification Hypothesis."

46. Richard A. Fabes et al., "Effects of Rewards on Children's Prosocial Motivation: A Socialization Study."

47. Immanuel Kant, *Foundations of the Metaphysics of Morals*, p. 61.

48. Mary Parpal and Eleanor E. Maccoby, "Maternal Responsiveness and Subsequent Child Compliance."

49. Donald J. Stayton, Robert Hogan, and Mary D. Ainsworth, "Infant Obedience and Maternal Behavior: The Origins of Socialization Reconsidered," p. 1067.

50. Zahn-Waxler, Radke-Yarrow, and King, "Child-Rearing."

51. David M. Harrington, Jeanne H. Block, and Jack Block, "Testing Aspects of Carl Rogers' Theory of Creative Environments: Child-Rearing Antecedents of Creative Potential in Young Adolescents."

52. Donna Gelfand et al., "The Effects of Adult Models and Described Alternatives on Children's Choice of Behavior Management Techniques."

53. But see Skinner, "The Operational Analysis of Psychological Terms," for a different opinion. Skinner acknowledges difficulties in the identification of psychological terms but challenges psychologists to come up with a reasonable analysis to "account for the functional relation between a term, as a verbal response, and a given stimulus," p. 594.

54. Joan McCord, "Questioning the Value of Punishment."

55. Wilfred Sellars, "Language As Thought and As Communication," p. 48.

56. Plato, "Cratylus."

57. See, for example, C.I. Lewis, *An Analysis of Knowledge and Valuation*.

58. For example, A.J. Ayer, *Language, Truth and Logic*; R.M. Chisholm, *Perceiving: A Philosophical Study*; Lewis, *An Analysis*; H.H. Price, *Perception*; Ludwig Wittgenstein, *Tractatus Logico-Philosophicus*.

59. Willard V.O. Quine, *Word and Object*.

60. Gottlob Frege, "On Concept and Object," p. 45.

61. Gottlob Frege, "On Sense and Reference."

62. Alfred Tarski, "The Semantic Conception of Truth and the Foundations of Semantics."

63. Willard V.O. Quine, *From a Logical Point of View*; Wilfred Sellars, "Empiricism and the Philosophy of Mind."

64. Ludwig Wittgenstein, *Philosophical Investigation*.

65. J.L. Austin, *How to Do Things with Words*.

66. Donald Davidson, "Truth and Meaning," p. 310.

67. Donald Davidson, "A Coherence Theory of Truth and Knowledge," p. 309.

68. Willard V.O. Quine, *Ontological Relativity and Other Essays*; Sellars, "Language As Thought and As Communication"; M. Dummett, "The Social Character of Meaning"; D. Follesdal, "Meaning and Experience"; John R. Searle, *Intentionality: An Essay in the Philosophy of Mind;* Daniel C. Dennett, *The Intentional Stance*.

69. Willard V.O. Quine, *Theories and Things*, p. 39.

70. This point was brought home many years ago. My five-year-old had been misbehaving. I asked him what to do to stop the bad behavior. He suggested I spank him. Not knowing what he had in mind because he had never been spanked, I asked and then followed his instructions, but with cupped hand to make a sound without giving pain.

When I finished, I asked if he was ready to be a good boy. He said, "No, not until after the crying part."

References

American Psychiatric Association, Committee on Nomenclature and Statistics. *Diagnostic and Statistical Manual of Mental Disorders*, 3d edition. Washington, D.C., 1980.

Anderson, K.E.; Lytton, Hugh; and Romney, D.M. "Mothers' Interactions with Normal and Conduct-Disordered Boys: Who Affects Whom? *Developmental Psychology* 22, no. 5 (1986): 604–609.

Aronson, Elliot, and Carlsmith, J. Merrill. "Effect of the Severity of Threat on the Devaluation of Forbidden Behavior." *Journal of Abnormal and Social Psychology* 66, no. 6 (1963): 584–88.

Aronson, Elliot; Carlsmith, J. Merrill; and Darley, John M.. "The Effects of Expectancy on Volunteering for an Unpleasant Experience." *Journal of Abnormal and Social Psychology* 66, no. 3 (1963): 220–24.

Austin, J.L. *How to Do Things with Words*. Oxford: Clarendon Press, 1962.

Ayer, A.J. *Language, Truth and Logic*. New York: Dover Publications, 1946.

Bandura, Albert; Ross, Dorothea; and Ross, Shiela A. "Transmission of Aggression through Imitation of Aggressive Models." *Journal of Abnormal and Social Psychology* 63 (1961): 575–82.

Barkley, Russell A., and Cunningham, Charles E. "The Effects of Methylphenidate on the Mother–Child Interactions of Hyperactive Children." *Archives of General Psychiatry* 36 (1979): 201–8.

Bell, Richard Q. "Age-Specific Manifestations in Changing Psychological Risk." In D.C. Farren and J.D. McKinney, eds., *Risk in Intellectual and Psychosocial Development*. Orlando, Fla.: Academic Press, 1986.

———. "The Effect on the Family of a Limitation in Coping Ability in a child: A Research Approach and a Finding." *Merrill-Palmer Quarterly* 10 (1964): 129–42.

———. "Parent, Child, and Reciprocal Influences." *American Psychologist* 34, no. 10 (October 1979): 821–26.

———. "A Reinterpretation of the Direction of Effects in Studies of Socialization." *Psychological Review* 75 (1968): 81–95.

Berkowitz, Leonard; Parke, Ross D.; Leyens, Jacques P.; West, Stephen; and Sebastian, Richard J. "Experiments on the Reactions of Juvenile Delinquents to Filmed Violence." In L.A. Hersov and M. Berger, eds., *Aggression and Anti-Social Behaviour in Childhood and Adolescence*, pp. 59–71. Oxford: Pergamon Press, 1978.

Boggiano, Ann K., and Main, Deborah S. "Enhancing Children's Interest in Activities Used As Rewards: The Bonus Effect." *Journal of Personality and Social Psychology* 31, no. 6 (1986): 1116–26.

Bowlby, John. "The Influence of Early Environment on Neurosis and Neurotic Character." *International Journal of Psychoanalysis* 21 (1940): 154–78.

———. "Maternal Care and Mental Health." *Bulletin of the World Health Organization* 3 (1951): 355–534.

Bryan, James H., and London, Perry. "Altruistic Behavior by Children." *Psychological Bulletin* 73, no. 3 (1970): 200–211.

Bugental, Daphne B.; Caporael, Linda; and Shennum, William A. "Experimentally Produced Child Uncontrollability: Effect on the Potency of Adult." *Child Development* 51, no. 2 (June 1980): 520–28.

Bugental, Daphne B., and Shennum, William A. " 'Difficult' Children as Elicitors and Targets of Adult Communication Patterns: An Attributional-Behavioral Transactional

Analysis." *Monographs of the Society for Research in Child Development*, Serial No. 205, vol. 49, issue 1.

Butler, Joseph. "Fifteen Sermons" (including "Three Sermons Upon Human Nature"). In *The Works of Joseph Butler*, ed. Rt. Hon. W.G. Gladstone. Oxford, 1897.

Call, Justin D. "Child Abuse and Neglect in Infancy: Sources of Hostility within the Parent–Infant Dyad and Disorders of Attachment in Infancy." *Child Abuse and Neglect* 8, no. 3 (1984): 185–202.

Cantor, Nancy L., and Gelfand, Donna M. "Effects of Responsiveness and Sex of Children on Adults' Behavior." *Child Development* 48 (1977): 232–38.

Carlsmith, J. Merrill; Lepper, Mark R.; and Landauer, T.K. "Children's Obedience to Adult Requests: Interactive Effects of Anxiety Arousal and Apparent Punitiveness of the Adult." *Journal of Personality and Social Psychology* 30, no. 6 (1974): 822–28.

Chisholm, Roderick M. *Perceiving: A Philosophical Study*. Ithaca, N.Y.: Cornell University Press, 1957.

Cline, Victor B.; Croft, Roger G.; and Courrier, Stevenenneth. "Desensitization of Children to Television Violence." *Journal of Personality and Social Psychology* 27, no. 3 (1973): 360–65.

Craig, K.D., and Theiss, Stephen M. "Vicarious Influences on Pain-Threshold Determinations." *Journal of Personality and Social Psychology* 19, no. 1 (1971): 53–59.

Cummings, E. Mark; Hollenbeck, Barbara; Iannotti, Ronald; Radke-Yarrow, Marian; and Zahn-Waxler, Carolyn. "Early Organization of Altruism and Aggression: Developmental Patterns and Individual Differences." In C. Zahn-Waxler, E.M. Cummings, and R. Iannotti, eds., *Altruism and Aggression: Biological and Social Origins*, pp. 165–88. Cambridge: Cambridge University Press, 1986.

Davidson, Donald. "A Coherence Theory of Truth and Knowledge." In E. LePore, ed., *Truth and Interpretation: Perspectives on the Philosophy of Donald Davidson*, pp. 307–19. Oxford: Basil Blackwell, 1986.

————. "Truth and Meaning." *Synthese* 17, no. 3 (1967): 304–23.

Dennett, Daniel C. *The Intentional Stance*. Cambridge, Mass.: MIT Press, 1987.

Dion, Karen. "Physical Attractiveness and Evaluation of Children's Transgressions." *Journal of Personality and Social Psychology* 24, no. 2 (1972): 207–13.

Dornbusch, Sanford M.; Carlsmith, J. Merrill; Bushwall, Steven J.; Ritter, Philip L.; Leiderman, Herbert; Hastorf, Albert H.; and Gross, Ruth T. "Single Parents, Extended Households, and the Control of Adolescents." *Child Development* 56 (1985): 326–41.

Dummett, Michael. "The Social Character of Meaning." In Dummett, ed., *Truth and Other Enigmas*, pp. 420–30. Cambridge, Mass.: Harvard University Press, 1978.

Egeland, Byron, and Sroufe, Alan. "Developmental Sequelae of Maltreatment in Infancy." In R. Rizley and D. Cicchetti, eds., *Developmental Perspectives on Child Maltreatment, New Directions for Child Development*, pp. 77–92. San Francisco: Jossey-Bass, 1981.

Eisenberg, Nancy. *Altruistic Emotion, Cognition, and Behavior*. Hillsdale, N.J.: Lawrence Erlbaum, 1986.

Emery, Robèrt E. "Interparental Conflict and the Children of Discord and Divorce." *Psychological Bulletin* 92 (1982): 310–30.

Eron, Leonard D., and Huesmann, L. Rowell. "The Relation of Prosocial Behavior to the Development of Aggression and Psychopathology." *Aggressive Behavior* 10, no. 3 (1984): 201–11.

————. "The Role of Television in the Development of Prosocial and Antisocial Behavior." In D. Olweus, J. Block, and M. Radke-Yarrow, eds., *Development of Antisocial and Prosocial Behavior*, pp. 285–314. New York: Academic Press, 1986.

Eron, Leonard D.; Huesmann, L. Rowell; Dubow, Eric; Romanoff, Richard; and Yarmel,

Patty. "Aggression and Its Correlates over 22 Years." In D.H. Crowell, I.M. Evans, and C.R. O'Donnell, eds., *Childhood Aggression and Violence: Sources of Influence, Prevention, and Control*, pp. 249–62.) New York: Plenum Press, 1987.

Fabes, Richard A.; Fultz, Jim; Eisenberg, Nancy; May-Plumlee, Traci; and Christopher, F. Scott. "Effects of Rewards on Children's Prosocial Motivation: A Socialization Study. *Developmental Psychology* 25, no. 4 (1989): 509–15.

Farrington, David. "Environmental Stress, Delinquent Behavior, and Convictions." In I.G. Sarason and C.D. Spielberger, eds., *Stress and Anxiety*, vol. 6, pp. 93–106. New York: John Wiley, 1979.

———. "The Family Backgrounds of Aggressive Youths." In L.A. Hersov and M. Berger, eds., *Aggression and Anti-social Behaviour in Childhood and Adolescence*, pp. 73–93. Oxford: Pergamon Press, 1978.

———. "Stepping Stones to Adult Criminal Careers." In D. Olweus, J. Block, and M. Radke-Yarrow, eds., *Development of Antisocial and Prosocial Behavior*, pp. 359–384. New York: Academic Press, 1986.

Farrington, David P. and West, Donald J. "The Cambridge Study in Delinquent Development (United Kingdom)." In S.A. Mednick and A.E. Baert, eds., *Prospective Longitudinal Research: An Empirical Basis for Primary Prevention*, pp. 137–45. Oxford: Oxford University Press, 1981.

Follesdal, D.. "Meaning and Experience." In S. Guttenplan, ed., *Mind and Language*, pp. 25–44. Oxford: Clarendon Press, 1975.

Frege, Gottlob. "On Concept and Object." In P. Geach and M. Black, eds., *Translations from the Philosophical Writings of Gottlob Frege*, pp. 42–55. Oxford: Basil Blackwell, 1960.

———. "On Sense and Reference." In P. Geach and M. Black, eds., *Translations from the Philosophical Writings of Gottlob Frege*, pp. 56–78. Oxford: Basil Blackwell, 1960.

Friedrich, Lynette Kohn, and Stein, Aletha Huston. "Aggressive and Prosocial Television Programs and the Natural Behavior of Preschool Children." *Monographs of the Society for Research in Child Development* 38, no. 4 (Serial No. 151, 1973): 1–64.

Gallimore, Ronald; Tharp, Roland G.; and Kemp, Bryan. "Positive Reinforcing Function of 'Negative Attention.'" *Journal of Experimental Child Psychology* 8 (1969): 140–46.

Gelfand, Donna; Hartmann, Donald; Lamb, Ann; Smith, Cathleen; Mahon, Mary Ann; and Paul, Steven. "The Effects of Adult Models and Described Alternatives on Children's Choice of Behavior Management Techniques." *Child Development* 45 (1974): 585–93.

Gelles, Richard J. "Violence in the Family: A Review of Research in the Seventies." *Journal of Marriage and the Family* 42, no. 4 (1980), 873–85.

Glueck, Sheldon, and Glueck, Eleanor T. *Unraveling Juvenile Delinquency*. New York: Commonwealth Fund, 1950.

Goldfarb, William. "Pain Reactions in a Group of Institutionalized Schizophrenic Children." *American Journal of Orthopsychiatry* 28 (1958): 777–85.

———. "Psychological Privation in Infancy and Subsequent Adjustment." *American Journal of Orthopsychiatry* 15 (1945): 247–55.

Goldsmith, H.H., and Gottesman, I.I. "Origins of Variation in Behavioral Style: A Longitudinal Study of Temperament in Young Twins." *Child Development* 52 (1981): 91–103.

Goldstein, Jeffrey H., and Arms, R.L. "Effects of Observing Athletic Contests on Hostility." *Sociometry* no. 1 (1971):83–90.

Goodman, Robert, and Stevenson, Jim. "A Twin Study of Hyperactivity. 2. The

Aetiological Role of Genes, Family Relationships and Perinatal Adversity." *Journal of Child Psychology and Psychiatry and Allied Disciplines* 30, no. 5 (1989): 691–710.

Greene, David, and Lepper, Mark R. "Effects of Extrinsic Rewards on Children's Subsequent Intrinsic Interest." *Child Development* 45 (1974): 1141–45.

Grusec, Joan E., and Skubiski, Sandra L. "Model Nurturance Demand Characteristics of the Modeling Experiment and Altruism." *Journal of Personality and Social Psychology* 14, no. 4 (1970): 352–59.

Harrington, David M.; Block, Jeanne H.; and Block, Jack. "Testing Aspects of Carl Rogers' Theory of Creative Environments: Child-Rearing Antecedents of Creative Potential in Young Adolescents." *Journal of Personality and Social Psychology* 52, no. 4 (1987): 851–56.

Hartup, Willard W. "The Social Worlds of Childhood." *American Psychologist* 34, no. 10 (1979): 944–50.

Herrenkohl, Roy C. and Herrenkohl, Ellen C. "Some Antecedents and Developmental Consequences of Child Maltreatment." In R. Risley and D. Cicchetti, eds., *Developmental Perspectives on Child Maltreatment*, pp. 57–76. San Francisco: Jossey-Bass, 1981.

Hirschi, Travis. *Causes of Delinquency*. Berkeley: University of California Press, 1969.

Hobbes, Thomas. *Leviathan* (1651). Reprint. Buffalo, N.Y.: Prometheus, 1988.

Hoffman, Martin L. "Is Altruism Part of Human Nature?" *Journal of Personality and Social Psychology* 40, no. 1 (1981): 121–27.

Huesmann, L. Rowell, and Eron, Leonard D. "Cognitive Processes and the Persistence of Aggressive Behavior." *Aggressive Behavior* 10 (1984): 243–51.

Hume, David. *An Enquiry Concerning the Principles of Morals* (1777). Reprint. La Salle, Ill.: Open Court, 1960.

Jouriles, Ernest N.; Barling, Julian; and O'Leary, K. Danise. "Predicting Child Behavior Problems in Maritally Violent Families." *Journal of Abnormal Child Psychology* 15, no. 2 (1987): 165–73.

Kant, Immanuel. *Foundations of the Metaphysics of Morals* (1785), tr. L.W. Beck. Reprint. Indianapolis: Bobbs-Merrill, 1959.

Kopel, Steven A., and Arkowitz, Hal S. "Role Playing as a Source of Self-Observation and Behavior Change." *Journal of Personality and Social Psychology* 29, no. 5 (1974): 677–86.

Laub, John H., and Sampson, Robert J. "Unraveling Families and Delinquency: A Reanalysis of the Gluecks' Data." *Criminology* 26, no. 3 (1988): 355–80.

Lepper, Mark R. "Dissonance, Self-Perception and Honesty in Children." *Journal of Personality and Social Psychology* 25, no. 1 (1973): 65–74.

Lepper, Mark R.; Greene, David; and Nisbett, Robert E. "Undermining Children's Intrinsic Interest with Extrinsic Rewards." *Journal of Personality and Social Psychology* 28, no. 1 (1973): 129–37.

Lepper, Mark R.; Sagotsky, Gerald; Dafoe, Janet L.; and Greene, David. "Consequences of Superfluous Social Constraints: Effects on Young Children's Social Influences and Subsequent Intrinsic Interest." *Journal of Personality and Social Psychology* 41, no. 1 (1982): 51–65.

Lewis, C.I. *An Analysis of Knowledge and Valuation*. LaSalle, Ill.: Open Court, 1946.

Lewis, Dorothy O.; Pincus, Jonathan; Lovely, Richard; Spitzer, Elinor; and Moy, Ernest. "Biopsychosocial Characteristics of Matched Samples of Delinquents and Nondelinquents." *Journal of the American Academy of Child and Adolescent Psychiatry* 26, no. 5 (1987): 744–52.

Liska, Alan E., and Reed, Mark D. "Ties to Conventional Institutions and Delinquency: Estimating Reciprocal Effects." *American Sociological Review* 50 (August 1985): 547–60.

Locke, John. *Some Thoughts Concerning Education.* vol. 8, 9th edition. London: T. Longman, 1794.

——. *Two Treatises of Civil Government* (1690). Reprint. London: J.M. Dent, 1924.

Loeber, Rolf, and Stouthamer-Loeber, Magda. "Family Factors As Correlates and Predictors of Juvenile Conduct Problems and Delinquency." In M. Tonry and N. Morris, eds., *Crime and Justice*, vol. 7, pp. 29–149. Chicago: University of Chicago Press, 1986.

Lytton, Hugh. "Child and Parent Effects in Boys' Conduct Disorder: A Reinterpretation." *Developmental Psychology* 26, no. 5 (1990): 683–97.

Maccoby, Eleanor E., and Jacklin, Carol N. "The 'Person' Characteristics of Children and the Family As Environment." Paper presented at the Conference on Interaction of Person and Environment, Stockholm, June 1982.

Main, Mary, and Goldwyn, Ruth. "Predicting Rejection of Her Infant from Mother's Representation of Her Own Experience: Implications for the Abused-Abusing Intergenerational Cycle." *Child Abuse and Neglect* 8, no. 2 (1984): 203–17.

McCord, Joan. "Aggression in Two Generations." In L.R. Huesmann, ed., *Aggressive Behavior: Current Perspectives.* New York: Plenum, 1993.

——. "Family Relationships, Juvenile Delinquency, and Adult Criminality." *Criminology* 29, no. 3 (1991): 397–417.

——. "A Longitudinal Study of Aggression and Antisocial Behavior." In K.T. VanDusen and S.A. Mednick, eds., *Prospective Studies of Crime and Delinquency*, pp. 269–75. Boston: Kluwer-Nijhoff, 1983.

——. "A Longitudinal View of the Relationship between Paternal Absence and Crime." In J. Gunn and D. P. Farrington, eds., *Abnormal Offenders, Delinquency, and the Criminal Justice System*, pp. 113–28. Chichester: John Wiley, 1982.

——. "Longterm Effects of Parental Absence." In L.N. Robins and M. Rutter, eds., *Straight and Devious Pathways from Childhood to Adulthood*, pp. 116–34. Cambridge: Cambridge University Press, 1990.

——. "Questioning the Value of Punishment." *Social Problems* 38, no. 2 (1991): 167–79.

——. "Some Child-Rearing Antecedents of Criminal Behavior in Adult Men." *Journal of Personality and Social Psychology* 37 (1979): 1477–86.

Newell, H. W. "A Further Study of Maternal Rejection." *American Journal of Orthopsychiatry* 6 (1936): 576–89.

——. "The Psycho-Dynamics of Maternal Rejection." *American Journal of Orthopsychiatry* 4 (1934): 387–401.

Offord, David R. "Family Backgrounds of Male and Female Delinquents." In J. Gunn and D.P. Farrington, eds., *Abnormal Offenders, Delinquency, and the Criminal Justice System*, pp. 129–51. Chichester: John Wiley, 1982.

Parpal, Mary, and Maccoby, Eleanor E. "Maternal Responsiveness and Subsequent Child Compliance." *Child Development* 56 (1985): 1326–44.

Pederson, Nancy L.; Plomin, Robert; McClearn, G.E.; and Friberg, Lars. "Neuroticism, Extraversion, and Related Traits in Adult Twins Reared Apart and Reared Together." *Journal of Personality and Social Psychology* 55, no. 6 (1988): 950–57.

Plato. "Cratylus." In B. Jowett, trans., *The Dialogues of Plato*, vol. 1, pp. 173–229. New York: Random House, 1937.

——. "The Republic." In Edith Hamilton and Huntington Cairns, eds., Paul Shorey, trans., *The Collected Dialogues of Plato*, pp. 575–844. New York: Pantheon Books, 1961.

Price, H.H. *Perception.* London: Methuen, 1954.

Pulkkinen, Lea. "Search for Alternatives to Aggression in Finland." In A.P. Goldstein and M.H. Segall, eds., *Aggression in Global Perspective*, pp. 104–44. Elmsford, N.Y.: Pergamon Press, 1983.

Quine, Willard V.O. *From a Logical Point of View.* Cambridge, Mass.: Harvard University Press, 1961.
————. *Ontological Relativity and Other Essays.* New York: Columbia University Press, 1969.
————. *Theories and Things.* Cambridge, Mass.: Harvard University Press, 1981.
————. *Word and Object.* Cambridge, Mass.: Harvard University Press, 1960.
Reid, John B.; Patterson, G.R.; and Loeber, Rolf. "The Abused Child: Victim, Instigator, or Innocent Bystander?" In D.J. Bernstein and H.E. Howe, eds., *Proceedings of the Nebraska Symposium on Motivation: Response Structure and Organization.* Lincoln, Neb.: University of Nebraska Press, 1982.
Rheingold, Harriet, and Emery, Gena N. "The Nurturing Acts of Very Young Children." In D. Olweus, J. Block, and M. Radke-Yarrow, eds., *Development of Antisocial and Prosocial Behavior*, pp. 75–96. New York: Academic Press, 1986.
Riese, Marilyn L. "Neonatal Temperament in Monozygotic and Dizygotic Twin Pairs." *Child Development* 61, no. 4 (1990): 1230–37.
Robins, Lee N. *Deviant Children Grown Up.* Baltimore: Williams and Wilkins, 1966.
Rosellini, Robert A., and Lashley, R.L. "Opponent-Process Theory: Implications for Criminality." In J. McCord, ed., *Facts, Frameworks, and Forecasts: Advances in Criminological Theory*, vol. 3, pp. 47–62. New Brunswick, N.J.: Transaction Press, 1991.
Rosenhan, D., and White, G.M. "Observation and Rehearsal As Determinants of Prosocial Behavior." *Journal of Personality and Social Psychology* 5 (1967): 424–31.
Ross, Michael; Karniol, Rachel; and Rothstein, Mitch. "Reward Contingency and Intrinsic Motivation in Children: A Test in the Delay of Gratification Hypothesis." *Journal of Personality and Social Psychology* 33 (1976): 442–47.
Rushton, J. Philippe. "Effects of Prosocial Television and Film Material on the Behavior of Viewers." In L. Berkowitz, ed., *Advances in Experimental Social Psychology*, vol. 12, pp. 321–51. New York: Academic Press, 1979.
Rushton, J. Philippe; Fulker, David W.; Neale, Michael C.; Nias, David K.B.; and Eysenck, Hans J. "Altruism and Aggression: The Heritability of Individual Differences." *Journal of Personality and Social Psychology* 50, no. 6 (1986): 1192–98.
Rutter, Michael; Bolton, P.; Harrington, R.; Couteur, A.L.; Macdonald, H.; and Simonoff, E. "Genetic Factors in Child Psychiatric Disorders—I. A Review of Research Strategies." *Journal of Child Psychology and Psychiatry and Allied Disciplines* 31, no. 1 (January 1990): 3–37.
Rutter, Michael, and Garmezy, Norman. "Developmental Psychopathology." In E.M. Hetherington, ed., *Handbook of Child Psychology*, Vol. IV: *Socialization, Personality and Social Development*, pp. 775–912. New York: John Wiley, 1983.
Searle, John R. *Intentionality: An Essay in the Philosophy of Mind.* Cambridge: Cambridge University Press, 1983.
Sears, Robert R.; Maccoby, Eleanor E.; and Levin, Harry. *Patterns of Child Rearing.* Evanston, Ill.: Row, Peterson, 1957.
Sellars, Wilfrid. "Empiricism and the Philosophy of Mind." In Sellars, ed., *Science, Perception and Reality*, pp. 127–96. London: Routledge and Kegan Paul, 1963.
————. "Language As Thought and As Communication." In P. Kurtz, ed., *Language and Human Nature: A French-American Philosophers' Dialogue*, pp. 41–62. St. Louis, Mo.: Warren H. Green, 1971.
Shipley, Thomas E., Jr. "Opponent Process Theory." In H.T. Blane and K.E. Leonard, eds., *Psychological Theories of Drinking and Alcoholism*, pp. 346–87. New York: Guilford Press, 1987.
Skinner, B.F. "The Operational Analysis of Psychological Terms." In H. Feigl and M.

Brodbeck, eds., *Readings in the Philosophy of Science*, pp. 585–95. New York: Appleton-Century-Crofts, 1953.

Solomon, Richard L. "The Opponent-Process Theory of Acquired Motivation: The Costs of Pleasure and the Benefits of Pain." *American Psychologist* 35, no. 8 (1980): 691–712.

Staub, Ervin. *Positive Social Behavior and Morality: Socialization and Development*, vol. 2. New York: Academic Press, 1979.

Stayton, Donald J.; Hogan, Robert; and Ainsworth, Mary D. "Infant Obedience and Maternal Behavior: The Origins of Socialization Reconsidered." *Child Development* 42, no. 4 (1971): 1057–69.

Tarski, Alfred. "The Semantic Conception of Truth and the Foundations of Semantics." In H. Feigl and W. Sellars, eds., *Readings in Philosophical Analysis*, pp. 52–84. New York: Appleton-Century-Crofts, 1949.

Thoman, Evelyn B.; Korner, Anneliese F.; and Benson-Williams, Lynn. "Modification of Responsiveness to Maternal Vocalization in the Neonate." *Child Development* 48 (1977): 563–69.

Thomas, Margaret H.; Horton, Robert W.; Lippincott, Elaine C.; and Drabman, Ronald S. "Desensitization to Portrayals of Real-Life Aggression as a Function of Exposure to Television Violence." *Journal of Personality and Social Psychology* 35, no. 6 (1977): 450–58.

Wahler, Robert G., and Dumas, Jean E. " 'A Chip off the Old Block': Some Interpersonal Characteristics of Coercive Children across Generations." In P.S. Strain, M.T. Gunalnick, and H.M. Walker, eds., *Children's Social Behavior: Development, Assessment, and Modification*, pp. 49–91. New York: Academic Press, 1986.

———. "Maintenance Factors in Coercive Mother–Child Interactions: The Compliance and Predictability Hypothesis." *Journal of Applied Behavior Analysis* 19 (1986): 13–22.

Walster, Elaine; Aronson, Elliot; and Brown, Zita. "Choosing to Suffer as a Consequence of Expecting to Suffer: An Unexpected Finding." *Journal of Experimental Social Psychology* 2 (1966): 400–406.

Wells, L. Edward, and Rankin, Joseph H. "Direct Parental Controls and Delinquency." *Criminology* 26, no. 2 (1988): 263–85.

White, Glenn M. "Immediate and Deferred Effects of Model Observation and Guided and Unguided Rehearsal on Donating and Stealing." *Journal of Personality and Social Psychology* 21, no. 2 (1972): 139–48.

Widom, Cathy S. "Child Abuse, Neglect, and Adult Behavior: Research Design and Findings on Criminality, Violence, and Child Abuse." *American Journal of Orthopsychiatry* 59, no. 3 (July 1989): 355–67.

Wilkens, Judy L.; Scharff, William H.; and Schlottman, Robert S. "Personality Type, Reports of Violence and Aggressive Behavior." *Journal of Personality and Social Psychology* 30, no. 2 (1974): 243–47.

Wispé, Lauren. "Introduction." In L. Wispé, ed., *Altruism, Sympathy, and Helping: Psychological and Sociological Principles*, pp. 1–8. New York: Academic Press, 1978.

Witte, Kenneth L., and Grossman, Eugene E. "The Effects of Reward and Punishment upon Children's Attention, Motivation, and Discrimination Learning." *Child Development* 42, no. 2 (1971): 537–42.

Wittgenstein, Ludwig. *Philosophical Investigation*, tr. G.E.M. Anscombe. New York: Macmillan, 1953.

———. *Tractatus Logico-Philosophicus*. London: Routledge and Kegan Paul, 1960.

Yarrow, Leon J. "Research in Dimensions of Early Maternal Care." *Merrill-Palmer Quarterly* 9 (1963): 101–14.

Yarrow, Marian Radke; Scott, Phyllis M.; and Waxler, Carolyn Zahn. "Learning Concern for Others." *Developmental Psychology* 8, no. 2 (1973): 240–60.

Zahn-Waxler, Carolyn, and Radke-Yarrow, Marian. "The Development of Altruism: Alternative Research Strategies." In N. Eisenberg, ed., *The Development of Prosocial Behavior*, pp. 109–37. New York: Academic Press, 1982.

Zahn-Waxler, Carolyn; Radke-Yarrow, Marian; and King, Robert A. "Child-Rearing and Children's Pro-Social Initiations toward Victims of Distress." *Child Development* 50 (1979): 319–30.

Zahn-Waxler, Carolyn; Radke-Yarrow, Marian; Wagner, Elizabeth; and Pyle, Claudia. "The Early Development of Prosocial Behavior." Paper presented at the International Conference of Infant Studies (ICIS) meetings, Washington, D.C., April 1988.

6

DARNELL HAWKINS

Crime and Ethnicity

One of the pervasive facts of life in late twentieth-century America is the disproportionate representation of African-Americans, Native Americans, and Latinos among those arrested, convicted, and punished for crime. On the other hand, Americans of Chinese and Japanese descent have sometimes been labeled "model minorities" partly in response to their comparatively low rates of reported crime. Although their rates of reported crime are low today, historical accounts suggest high rates of criminal involvement during the past for many white ethnic groups. Notwithstanding such accounts and despite an increasing belief in the accuracy of official statistics as a measure of modern group-crime-rate differences,[1] attempts to explain varying rates of crime across ethnic/ racial groups have been largely abandoned, avoided, or ignored by social scientists during the last two to three decades.[2]

This inattention may reflect a concern for the political and social volatility that often accompanies discussions of presumed linkages among ethnicity, nationality, race, and crime. In addition, scientific analysts of ethnic and racial group differences in crime have had to confront the obvious truth that "criminality" and "crime" are culture-bound concepts. Being part of each society's cultural heritage, definitions of crime and criminal labels are neither universal nor immutable. To the extent that the boundaries of those entities labeled as "races" or "ethnic" groups are coterminous with distinct cultural heritages, analysts are confronted with a dilemma. This dilemma is most evident when attempts are made to conduct cross-societal, quantitative comparisons of crime and criminality. Similar conceptual/methodological problems arise for intergroup comparisons in the United States, where ideology suggests that various ethnic/racial groups may stem from diverse heritages but now share a common, binding legal culture.[3]

In this chapter, I utilize an approach partially derived from the work of Charles Tittle and associates to review and provide a critique of the conceptual and theoretical bases for observed and expected differences in the level of involvement in crime across various American racial and ethnic groups. Most attention is paid to reported rates of crime among Americans of African, Irish, and Italian ancestry. I conclude with a discussion of unanswered questions. Let us begin by considering the work of Tittle.

Social Class and Criminality: Tittle's Perspective

Tittle notes that a pervasive theme in sociology and criminology has been that law violation is linked to the individual's position in the social structure. Specifically, criminal behavior is thought to be concentrated in the lowest socioeconomic strata. He identifies at least eight different theories, or schools of thought, that might be interpreted as implying a negative association between socioeconomic status and the rate of criminal behavior. Anomie, socialization/psychodynamic, subcultural, differential association, community/ecological, radical/conflict, utilitarian/deterrence, and labeling theories were all interpreted by Tittle to predict a concentration of criminality within the lowest social classes. After an examination of the premises underlying each, he concludes that none actually provides a sufficient rationale for predicting that criminal behavior varies inversely with social class.[4]

Moreover, in earlier works, Tittle and associates provide systematic crime data that they argue call into question the assumption that crime is essentially a lower-class phenomenon.[5] Their major premise is that social-class groupings do not differ in their rates of actual involvement in criminal and antisocial behaviors. The persistence of the belief in the excessive criminality of the poor in the face of questionable theory and contradictory data is attributed to a number of factors. These include stereotypes of the lifestyles of the poor that are held by predominantly middle-class social scientists and media representatives. Tittle suggests that perceptions of the moral and intellectual inferiority of the poor predate the development of social science and are deeply ingrained in public opinion. He does not propose that the poor and nonpoor are equally likely to be punished for crime. He acknowledges the accuracy of various labeling and conflict perspectives that suggest that there are class differences in the ability to influence the formulation and enforcement of law, and in the ability to conceal one's criminality.[6]

To the extent that Tittle offers a potential model for the examination of the relationship among ethnicity, race, and criminal behavior, we may ask:

(1) How adequate is the evidence on ethnic/racial group differences in criminality?

(2) What are the conceptual and theoretical bases for the expectation of higher rates of criminal behavior among some ethnic/racial groups than among others?

(3) Does belief in ethnic/racial crime-rate differences, like belief in social-class differences, persist despite inadequate theory and problematic empirical evidence?

Before attempting to address these queries, let us briefly discuss some of the conceptual and methodological problems encountered in the study of ethnicity/race and crime.

Ethnicity and Race As Social Statuses

Like one's social-class standing, one's race or ethnicity can be a measure of status within the social structure. Indeed, since in most multi-ethnic, multiracial societies social-class status is highly correlated with ethnic/racial identity, the attributes are not separable within these societies. Cross-cultural or historical comparisons may pose difficulties, however. For example, while persons of lower socioeconomic status occupy a position in the social structure that (by definition) varies little from society to society, the level of privilege or disadvantage attached to membership in a given ethnic or racial group varies considerably across different temporal and societal contexts. This difference between social class and ethnic/racial status has meant that social theorists who have attempted to link the latter to law violation have had first to determine the sociohistorical significance of a given racial/ethnic trait within the society at issue. On the basis of theory, a given trait may be considered potentially "criminogenic" in one social structural context but not in another.

Analysts of racial and ethnic differences in crime have also had to confront and attempt to discount biological/genetic explanations of social conduct. Most early analysts began their discussions of the connections between ethnicity/race and crime by attempting to define "race" or "ethnicity" from the viewpoint of social science. While racial differences in social behavior are more likely than ethnic differences to be perceived as determined by biology/genetics, ethnic variations in social conduct have been similarly perceived.[7] What are commonly called ethnic groups today were frequently thought to constitute distinct "races" during the recent past.

Yet, even if one assumes that race and ethnicity are largely "social statuses," one must confront the multiplicity of problems encountered in attempting to use these groupings for research purposes. The self-identification methods used to ascertain race and ethnic heritage in the United States census illustrate the impreciseness and inconsistency of such categorizations.[8] Governmentally determined categories pose other problems. Frequently, politically relevant demographic labels mask the cultural distinctiveness that concerns social researchers. For example, national groupings characterized by considerable "ethnic" cleavage within their countries of origin are often treated as undifferentiated populations within the United States and many other modern industrial societies to which they migrate. Racial categorizations conceal even more subgroup variation in culture and place of origin. They often conceal both nationality and ethnic group differences. Steinberg has proposed that ethnic and racial distinctions among Americans stem less from cultural differences than from the politics of intergroup relations.[9] Nowhere is the influence of politics more evident than in the measurement of group differences in the rate of crime in the United States.

Enumerating Misbehavior: The Science and Politics of Ethnic/Racial Counts of Crime

As previously noted, one of the most consistently reported findings has been the high rate of crime found among African-Americans. Because they represent the largest nonwhite minority, and given the legacy of tumultuous black-white relations in the United States, African-American crime has been of considerable interest. On the contrary, the measurement of crime across ethnic groupings has not been a major preoccupation of government despite much political and public scrutiny of ethnic differences during the nineteenth century. Anyone who has used official arrest, adjudication, or imprisonment statistics in the United States is aware of the limited extent to which these measure the criminal behavior of the diverse groups of European ancestry found in the United States. This problem is related, of course, to the historic failure of the federal censuses to enumerate white ethnics. Attempts to count the crime of white ethnic groups have been limited to the enumeration of crime among the "foreign-born." Federal governmental surveillance of crime of newly arrived immigrants within the United States was conducted by immigration and other government officials during the late 1800s and early 1900s.[10] Crime data for "native" and "foreign-born" whites were also collected by the FBI during the first eight years of the Uniform Crime Reports (UCR).

This politically motivated categorization of criminal offenders (foreign-born versus native) is of limited usefulness for the study of ethnic differences in criminal behavior. Distinctly different white ethnics are grouped together as "natives," and the "foreign-born" categorization "captures" only a portion of the population of interest to analysts of ethnic differences in the rate of crime. The crime of the foreign-born may be different from others within their ethnic group. For example, Quinney reports that "though immigrants themselves have tended to have offense patterns similar to those of the home country, their children have tended to be arrested for offenses characteristic of the areas in which they have settled."[11] He also notes (citing Van Vechten, "The Criminality of the Foreign-Born") that the extent to which the crime rates of ethnic and nationality groups conform to that of the native white population varies with the time such groups have been in the United States. Also observed is the tendency of younger immigrants to take on the crime rates of native whites more quickly than older immigrants.[12]

Current federal crime statistics (UCR) enumerate arrests for an undifferentiated white population, except for Hispanics; a Native American category (American Indian and Alaskan native); African-Americans; and a category that combines Asians and Pacific Islanders. Apart from historical accounts of white ethnic-group crime, primarily in the Northeast during the nineteenth century, our knowledge of ethnic/racial differences in crime has come from data utilizing the current categories.[13] Like those for white ethnics, governmental categories for nonwhites fail to take into account the great ethnic/cultural diversity found among these groups.

These data collection patterns have obvious implications for attempts to devise theories to predict or explain patterns of criminality across ethnic/racial lines in the United States. They have obviously limited the kind of empirical work that can be done in this area of research. Because viable social theory is usually based on known social facts, the unavailability of official crime data for white ethnic groups and limited data for most nonwhites has sometimes led to ungrounded theory. Once devised, theories cannot be adequately tested.[14]

For the present discussion it suffices to say that the lack of accurate data for diverse types of crime has prevented researchers from answering many questions that might help test the various theoretical perspectives outlined in this chapter. Among these questions are the following:

(1) How do/have the various white ethnic groups in the United States differ(ed) in terms of their rates of involvement in crime?

(2) How do historical and contemporary rates for various subgroups of the white population compare to those found among African-Americans, Japanese-Americans, Chinese-Americans, Native Americans, and Latinos/Hispanics?

(3) How do crime rates vary among those diverse populations now classified as Asians Hispanics? Do all segments of these populations have comparable rates of crime?

(4) How have rates for various ethnic/racial groups changed over time?

Having noted the conceptual and methodological problems associated with the study of ethnicity and race as social statuses, let us now examine the competing perspectives that have been used to predict or explain intergroup differences in rates of crime.

Theoretical Perspectives on the Study of Ethnicity, Race, and Crime

For the purposes of the present discussion, theoretical approaches to the analyses of ethnic/racial differences in criminal behavior are grouped into *two* broad, but internally cohesive categories. The first is derived largely from the social-class theory reviewed by Tittle.[15] Within this perspective, ethnicity and race are treated as proxies or near-proxies for social-class status. Although they provide many variations on the theme, proponents of this view generally attribute higher rates of crime for certain ethnic/racial groups to their marginal socioeconomic status. I refer to this approach as the *economic-deprivation/inequality* perspective.

Advocates of the second perspective argue that those differences in "culture" that

Table 6.1

Theoretical Perspectives on Ethnicity, Race, and Crime

Economic Deprivation/Inequality

1. Basic tenets

  a. Rates of crime are highest among those ethnic/racial groups characterized by economic deprivation and marginality.

  b. In many instances, the economic marginality of subordinate groups is maintained by the social and political oppression of the privileged.

  c. As the economic condition of a group improves, its rate of involvement in crime will decrease.

  d. Law, crime, and criminality are not generally considered as culture-bound concepts.

2. Supportive Evidence

  a. Researchers note the strong historical association between poverty and crime, primarily as shown through the use of ecological analyses.

  b. Current research and theory emphasize the importance of "relative deprivation."

  c. Past high rates of crime among impoverished, white immigrant groups are frequently compared to much lower, contemporary rates of crime among their more privileged descendants . Similarly used is evidence of lower rates of crime among middle-class segments of contemporary "high crime rate" groups, e.g., African-Americans and Hispanics.

3. Principal Advocates

  a. Contemporary views stem partly from earlier cartographic/ecological traditions in Europe and the U.S.

  b. Aspects of the ideas of Emile Durkheim and Karl Marx have also been influential.

  c. Advocates include: Sanborn/DuBois (1904), Sellin (1928), Johnson (1941), Shaw and McKay (1969), Bonger (1943), Frazier (1957), Ferdinand (1967), Merton (1968), Nelli (1970), Wolfgang and Cohen (1970), Monkkonen (1975), Lane (1979), Blau and Blau (1982), and Steinberg (1989).

4. Policy Implications

  a. A reduction in the level of economic inequality/deprivation, and, hence, in the rate of crime is a natural product of the gradual integration of ethnic or racial groups into the American mainstream. Few proactive policies are needed.

  b. Residential longevity within American society does not always lead to economic integration. Policies designed to reduce levels of societal inequality and concomitant crime may be required.

Table 6.1 *Continued*

Cultural Variance

1. Basic Tenets

a. Rates of crime are highest among those ethnic/racial groups that are not part of the American cultural mainstream. Such groups may be relative newcomers to the United States or may represent long-term, persisting subcultures. In either instance, their cultural heritages represent norms and values that are inconsistent with those of the mainstream culture.

b. As these groups become more fully acculturated, their rates of crime will decrease.

c. Law, crime, and criminality are recognized as culture-bound concepts by the earliest theorists, but such considerations are largely ignored by later theorists.

2. Supportive Evidence

a. Data showing higher rates of crime among "foreign-born" as compared to "native" populations have been the principal form of evidence.

b. Also cited is the gradual reduction in the rate of crime among several white ethnic populations during the last century.

c. Some effort has been made to show that current groups having high rates of crime possess distinct subcultures with values and norms that promote criminal activity.

3. Principal Advocates

a. Much of the earlier tradition was grounded in anthropology-like research and theory.

b. Within sociology and criminology, Durkheim's **anomie** concept has been frequently cited in support of some tenets of the perspective.

c. More recent advocates include Sutherland (1924), Sellin (1938), Miller(1958), Wolfgang and Ferracuti (1982), Hackney (1969), Gastil (1971, 1990), Curtis (1975), and Katz (1988).

4. Policy Implications

Proponents appear to share some of the assimilationist views of many advocates of the economic-inequality/deprivation perspective: i.e., the belief that ethnic/racial groups will "naturally" assimilate, thus removing the criminogenic influences of cultural variance or conflict. This view seems to have less applicability to African-Americans than to European immigrants or some Hispanics. Various methods aimed at "mainstreaming" and/or "empowering" nonwhite minority populations may be implied.

distinguish ethnic and racial groups are the source of differential rates of crime. Whether cultures are viewed as geographically and socially isolated, as relatively equal value systems, or as subcultures, cultural difference is said to be linked to the etiology of crime. This grouping of theories is labeled the *cultural-variance* perspective. While these two sets of perspectives are closely related and are often combined in the work of many writers, for heuristic purposes they are analyzed separately. In the remainder of the chapter I review the explanations offered by advocates of these two broad perspectives, briefly assess the adequacy of proof for ethnic/racial differences in the rate of involvement in crime, and discuss issues left unresolved by extant theory and empirical research. Table 6.1 summarizes the tenets, supportive evidence, principal advocates, and policy implications for each perspective.

Part I
The Economic-Deprivation/Inequality Perspective:
Historical and Contemporary Accounts

As Tittle and Vold and Bernard have observed, the idea that poverty is a major cause of criminal conduct is as old as the study of crime and society.[16] Similarly, the belief that certain ethnic and racial groups in the United States have comparatively high rates of crime because of their social/political subordination and/or economic deprivation has been a prominent theme in the criminological and sociological literatures. In this section I use historical and contemporary accounts of racial and ethnic differences in the rate of crime to illustrate how this theme has developed. Because accounts of the causes of high rates of crime among African-Americans differ in some respects from similar accounts for white ethnics, these groups are discussed separately.

White Ethnics, Deprivation, and Crime

The Irish were one of the first white ethnic minority groups in the United States, and their criminal conduct was a frequent target of public debate and policy. In the Northeast and portions of the Midwest, perceptions of the criminality of Irish immigrants during the late 1700s and into the early twentieth century were very similar to current perceptions of African-Americans.[17] As early as 1796, a French observer of the United States, M. de Saint-Mery, said:

> In the latter state (Pennsylvania) out of ten convicts, seven at least are in general strangers, and in particular natives of Ireland, who bring with them from their own country little besides poverty, ignorance and habits of indolence, the seeds of every kind of vice. . . .[18]

An 1860s account in *Harper's* magazine stated that the Irish "have so behaved themselves that nearly 75 percent of our criminals are Irish, that fully 75 percent of the crimes of violence committed among us are the work of Irishmen. . . ."[19]

Scholarly analysts have made similar observations. In a discussion of crime rates in Boston between 1849 and 1951, Ferdinand concluded:

> Boston was inundated in the nineteenth century, first, by the starving yeomen of Ireland and, then, by the impoverished peasants of Sicily and southern Italy. These immigrants were eventually assimilated by the city, but both the immigrants and the city suffered grievously in the process. There can be little doubt that the gradual adjustment of the descendants of the Irish and Italian immigrants to the urban patterns of Boston has resulted in a gradual reduction in the city's crime rate. And by the same token, the fact that the city, like most American communities, has enjoyed a gradually rising standard of living during nearly the entire period of this study must have had a significant effect upon its crime rate.[20]

Alexander reported that during a period in which both African-Americans and foreign-born Irish were a small percentage of Philadelphia's population (1794 to 1900), together they constituted 68.3 percent of convicted criminals. The Irish alone accounted for 37 percent of all convictions, but were less than 10 percent of the city's population.[21] Similar over-representation of the Irish and free blacks among persons arrested or imprisoned was reported for Boston between 1790 and 1865.[22] As the Irish population of Philadelphia, Boston, and other American cities grew during the decades preceding the Civil War, so did concerns about their disproportionate involvement in crime. Alexander and Handlin attribute the high rate of crime found among the Irish and free blacks to their poverty.

Most of the public concern about crime among foreign-born Irish and other white immigrant groups centered on their involvement in typical, common-law violations. As in Elizabethan England,[23] offenses against property were the type of crime most frequently associated with the "dangerous class" in the United States during the eighteenth and nineteenth centuries.[24] Also of great concern were various "public order" and "vice" offenses. Violent behavior was of much less concern, unless, of course, such was directed against the more affluent. This likelihood was minimized due to the development of slums, ghettos, and other segregated enclaves to house newly arrived immigrants and the small populations of free blacks.

In addition to the "unorganized" criminal activity of the masses, various white ethnic groups have been associated with organized crime. Nelli suggests that Americans reacted to crime among Italians with a frenzy of emotion aroused by no other immigrant group. He notes that official reports, books, pamphlets, and magazine and newspaper articles decried "Southern" criminality, a code word for the activities of the Black Hand or Mafia.[25] A distinction was made between Sicilians and those from Southern Italy, and those from other regions. Entering the United States during a period when the rates of crime among the Irish and other earlier immigrant groups had decreased substantially, Southern Italians and Sicilians were especially vulnerable to such labeling. Haller, among others, has noted that while the Irish had played a crucial role during the late nineteenth century in organizing gambling and arranging political protections, by the twentieth century Jews and Italians had begun to rise rapidly in the world of organized crime. Since the organized crime activities of more recent immigrants often invaded the "turf" of established groups, these crimes often received far more attention than did the unorganized crime of the foreign-born masses.[26]

Steinberg observed that by the turn of the century the connection between immigration and crime had nearly become a national obsession. He cites the 1911 study of the United States Immigration Commission, which collected crime data in New York, Chicago, and Massachusetts. The commission described various "races and nationalities" as "exhibiting clearly defined criminal characteristics."[27] The commission depicted Italians as prominently involved in crimes of personal violence, the Irish in drunkenness and vagrancy, and Jews and the French in prostitution. Jews were also noted to have high rates of crimes against property. High rates for some offenses were noted for Greeks, as well.[28]

It was in response to these ethnic-group crime patterns that the economic-deprivation/inequality perspective on the etiology of ethnic/racial crime in the United States first emerged among various white ethnic populations. These observations have been coupled with a view of a largely "law-abiding" white ethnic population in the United States during the last half century. Steinberg, an advocate of this perspective, says:

> That crime in immigrant communities was primarily a response to economic disadvantage, and not a product of deeper cultural abnormalities, is easier to see now that these groups have attained middle-class respectability. To realize this should make it easier to avoid confusion of social class with culture and ethnicity when considering the problems of minorities today.[29]

In response to both the rise and the decline of criminal activity among American white ethnics, proponents of this perspective have generally argued the following:

> (1) The economic and social marginality of ethnic newcomers, as compared to natives or more settled immigrants, resulted in a greater likelihood of their engaging in criminal conduct.
> (2) Such marginality (due to poverty, deprivation) rather than any persisting social characteristics unique to a given ethnic population accounts for the comparative over-involvement in crime found among some groups.
> (3) As members of various ethnic/immigrant groups improve their comparative economic status, their rate of involvement in crime will be reduced, thus reducing the gap between their ethnic grouping and others who preceded them.

African-Americans and Crime

Sanborn used arrest, conviction, and imprisonment data to study patterns of crime among blacks in the South after the Civil War. His work was aimed at refuting racist contentions during the period that slavery suppressed the innate criminality of blacks and that freedom fostered crime among them. He acknowledged a high rate of crime among blacks, and, like many other scholars of the period, he attributed such crime to the "pauperism" produced by several centuries of slavery. But while acknowledging that blacks had higher rates of crime than whites, Sanborn suggested that these rates were not so high as to warrant a conclusion that blacks were significantly more criminal than all groups of whites or other nonwhite groups. For example, he offers imprisonment data for 1890 showing the Chinese and American Indian populations to have rates of confinement surpassing that for blacks. He also noted the great variability in the rate of crime among blacks, for example, in urban compared to rural and northern compared to southern areas.[30]

Sellin's account is similar to that of Sanborn, but he reaches a somewhat different conclusion. In discussing the high rate of crime among American blacks, he says:

> Practically all writers, Negro or white, who have studied the question of Negro criminality have admitted the existence of an apparently higher crime rate for the Negro than for the white.[31]

After reviewing empirical studies and official criminal justice statistics for the period, Sellin warns his readers that these statistics "picture only the *apparent* and not the *real* criminality of the Negro."[32] By this he meant, of course, that one must consider the role that race prejudice and discrimination plays in producing the statistics observed. But after a discussion of police and judicial bias, Sellin concludes:

> Nothing in the above pages points to a conclusion that the Negro's *real* criminality is lower or as low as the white's. The American Negro lacks education and earthly goods. He has had very little political experience and industrial training. His contact with city life has been unfortunate, for it has forced him into the most dilapidated and vicious areas of our great cities. Like a shadow over his whole existence lies the oppressive race prejudice of his white neighbor, restricting his activities and thwarting his ambitions. It would be extraordinary, indeed, if this group were to prove more law-abiding than the white, which enjoys more fully the advantages of a civilization the Negro has helped to create.[33]

Bonger made comparable observations in his study of race and crime in various parts of the world. In a section of the study devoted to a discussion of black American criminality, he says:

> Crimes committed by Negroes are more frequently prosecuted than those committed by whites. Negroes are less well able to defend themselves legally, they are less often in a position to secure a good lawyer, and they are more promptly sentenced to prison. . . .[34]

But, like Sellin, after considering sentencing and imprisonment data for Americans during 1910, he concludes:

> These figures leave no room for doubt: crime among the Negroes is significantly higher than among the whites. It is three or four times higher among the women. To me, this appears to eliminate the idea that the actual criminality among the Negroes is no greater than among whites—even if the above mentioned causes make it appear greater than it is.[35]

Consistent with his Marxist orientation, Bonger attributes this racial differential in crime to the economic and social disadvantages found among the African-American population.[36]

Similar conclusions have been reached by other researchers.[37] More recently, Hindelang, in response to questions of racial bias in the administration of justice, concluded that official (UCR) crime statistics accurately measure the extent of black over-involvement in common-law personal crimes. That is, the high rate of reported crime among blacks is not due to racial discrimination in the administration of justice. Hindelang, like many other analysts of the modern era, documents a high rate of black crime while offering few explanations for the persistence of racial differences.[38]

Wolfgang and Cohen are somewhat more skeptical than either Sellin or Bonger regarding the extent to which official crime data measure *real* criminality. They note the perennial problems of undetected and unrecorded crime, the low clearance rates, and the absence of data for white-collar crime and their relevance for the study of racial differentials.[39] They conclude that "we do not know with certainty the actual amount of crime among whites, Negroes, Puerto Ricans or any other group."[40] In attempting to explain the seemingly high rate of crime among blacks, Puerto Ricans, and Mexican-Americans, they rely primarily on the work of subcultural theorists, especially the subcultural-structural approach of Merton.[41] They emphasize the etiological importance of socioeconomic conditions, such as low income, unavailability of employment opportunities, family disruption, poor education, and so on.[42] Pope made similar observations in his examination of black-white crime differentials.[43]

Other Deprivation-Related Explanations

Tittle identifies several other theoretical approaches to the class/crime phenomenon that have relevance for the attempted explanation of ethnic and racial differences in the rate of involvement in crime. These include anomie, socialization, and community/ecological theory, some of which are sometimes referred to as "strain theories"[44] or as "process theories."[45] Anomie and socialization theories attempt to specify the processes by which social structural stressors, such as class status, poverty, or subordination, become patterns of individual behavior. In the present discussion, these three sets of theories have largely been subsumed under the economic-deprivation/inequality heading. But they provide additional theoretical/conceptual approaches to the study of ethnic and racial differences in the rate of crime. As a consequence of, or in addition to, being poor, ethnic and racial minorities are said to experience anomie,[46] to have dysfunctional families,[47] and to live under unfavorable ecological conditions and/or disorganized communities.[48] All of these conditions/traits have been linked to high rates of criminal behavior.

During recent years, considerable attention has been paid to the effects of high rates of single-parent and "broken" families on the criminal involvement of minority, especially African-American, youth in the United States. Because such "dysfunctional" families are seen to be concentrated disproportionately among the underclass, they are said to be consequences or correlates of economic deprivation. Other researchers stress the causal significance of normative factors and discuss ways in which such family patterns affect the socialization and value systems of the poor and minorities. These normative correlates of poverty are then linked to criminal conduct. In many respects, these more recent elaborations of strain and process theories are derived less from the economic deprivation/inequality tradition than from the cultural-variance perspective.

Part II

The Cultural-Variance Perspective

A related, but clearly distinctive, theoretical linkage among ethnicity, race, and crime also emerges from the historical and contemporary literature on ethnic and racial crime patterns. This research tradition emphasizes the etiological importance of cultural difference in explaining rates of crime across ethnic and racial groups. An early statement of the cultural-variance (and economic-deprivation) approach came from Sutherland:

> A general comparison of the negroes and whites is a comparison not only of races, but also of different economic and cultural groups. If a valid comparison is to be made, it would be necessary to compare negroes of a certain educational and cultural status with whites of the same status. There is nothing in the previous discussion of the frequency of crimes of negroes that proves any racial, as contrasted with cultural, differences between whites and negroes.[49]

While Sutherland speaks of cultural groups in terms that may include considerations of social-class status, his observations also apply to broader meanings of "culture," such as those used to designate ethnic groups.

The classic statement of the cultural-variance perspective comes from Sellin. He proposed that the clashing of conduct norms among divergent cultures often leads to actual antisocial conduct or perceptions of such conduct among members of the subordinate cultural grouping.[50] Both Sellin and Sutherland suggested that the gradual assimilation of subordinate groups into the cultural mainstream of the dominant groups reduces disparities in rates of criminal activity and the differential perception of criminality.[51] That is, while the proponents of the economic-deprivation perspective emphasize the importance of economic assimilation for reducing the criminality of ethnic newcomers, advocates of the cultural-variance approach attribute such a reduction to the effects of cultural assimilation.

For its early advocates, this theory seemed ideally suited to explain the disproportionally high rates of crime found among Irish, Italian, and other immigrant groups in an Anglo-dominated America. Sellin argued that the existence of high crime rates of the foreign-born, as compared to more culturally assimilated groups in the United States, supported his basic premises.[52] With its emphasis on assimilation as a remedy for high rates of crime among immigrant and minority groups, the theory has had great appeal for many American academics and policy makers. It appeals to American political and economic ideals by suggesting that the criminality of immigrant groups will diminish as they "assimilate" into the American economic, political, and social mainstream.[53] The effects of assimilation have been said to account for the reduction over time in rates of crime among Americans of Irish and Italian ancestry.[54]

Sellin stressed the primacy of culture conflict as opposed to economic deprivation as factors in crime causation:

> Poverty in the home, a broken home, delinquency on the part of parents, etc., etc., are not in themselves important in this connection. The research student must find to what extent these factors are specifically created wholly or in part by the *cultural* heritage of the immigrant. If the immigrant's conduct norms are different from those of the American community and if these differences are not due to his economic status, but to his *cultural origin* then we can speak of conflict of norms drawn from different cultural systems or areas.[55]

Sellin and other cultural-variance advocates propose that the poverty of certain ethnic groups, and hence their poverty-related criminality, may be *caused* by the clashing of cultural heritages. Thus, cultural attributes rather than poverty constitute the "primary" cause of ethnic group differences in the rate of crime. However, Sellin does imply that poverty itself may lead impoverished groups to possess conduct norms that conflict with those of the larger society. This is a strand of thought that will later be more fully developed by "subculture" theorists. On the other hand, Sellin rejects the kind of "ethnic traits" approach that holds that some national/cultural groupings are more prone to criminality than others in the absence of culture conflict.[56]

Sellin's theory has been applied to the explanation of high rates of crime among some Hispanics and other recent arrivals in the United States, such as Asians. At times his thesis has been used to explain high rates of crime among Native Americans and African-Americans. The thrust of such arguments has been that the cultural heritages of these groups, perhaps more so than those of white ethnics, clash with the dominant Anglo-Saxon cultural heritage of the United States. One product of this clash is a higher rate of crime. The validity of this explanation for high rates of African-American crime has sometimes been questioned on the basis that the African heritage was largely destroyed by slavery. The debate between E. Franklin Frazier and Melville Herskovits reflected the split among academic analysts of African-American life over this issue.[57] Other analysts seem to assume that even if culture conflict explained black crime rates during slavery, such conflict was not evident in the post-slavery era.

In response to high rates of crime among African-Americans, Sellin noted that culture conflicts need not always result from recent immigration. He described the conflict between white and black norms in the United States as of "indigenous origin."[58] He later refers to such indigenous conflicts as "secondary" culture conflicts as opposed to the "primary" culture conflicts that new immigrants experience.[59] Despite this observation, Sellin cited few examples of black-white value/culture difference that could be said to account for differential involvement in crime.

Others question whether either an indigenous or a nonindigenous form of culture conflict exists between native blacks and whites. Johnson argues for the inapplicability of the culture-conflict thesis as an explanation for black crime when he says:

> We shall assume that, in view of the advanced stage of the process of acculturation in the United States, culture conflict arising from the clash of the Negro's African heritage with his European heritage is not vital enough to be regarded as an important causative factor in Negro crime.[60]

Despite these observations, later researchers have incorporated a cultural-variance perspective into the study of black crime. However, rather than utilizing an idea of "culture conflict" to explain rates of crime among African-Americans, they stress the significance of "subculture."

Subcultures and Crime

Sellin's notion of secondary culture conflicts may have led later analysts to develop the notion of subcultures to account for ethnic/racial differences in the rate of involvement in crime. The notion of a culture or subculture of poverty is said to be derived from the anthropological writings of Lewis, but it can also be traced to the work of Miller, who discussed the etiology of crime. Both Lewis and Miller suggested that the poor, because of their isolation from the larger society, have developed cultural norms and values found only among them.[61] Such normative constructs, not just their levels of economic distress, are said to lead to antisocial and criminal conduct. Some analysts attribute the high rates of crime among impoverished white ethnic groups during the past to the effects of a poverty-based subculture.

Although the concept of subcultures has been applied to the examination of African-American crime, the process has been somewhat circuitous. Given perceptions that blacks do not possess an African cultural heritage, theorists initially sought to situate them within subcultural heritages that shaped their lives but were also shared by other Americans. The "subculture of violence" explanation for high rates of southern (white and black) and lower-class crime represents the classic formulation of this kind of perspective.[62] One result is that these researchers pay considerably less attention to the causes of black violence than to that of other groups subsumed under their "subculture" label. An exception is the work of Curtis, who attempted to demonstrate the impact of uniquely African-American cultural traditions on the incidence of violence among them.[63]

Despite the circuitous and tangential application of subcultural theory to the analysis of black crime, it remains perhaps the most popular explanation for the high rates of crime found in African-American communities today. It has found adherents among those analysts who discount inequality/deprivation views and stress such factors as socialization/learning and dysfunctional families within the context of "subcultures of poverty." Particularly targeted by these analysts is the high and growing rate of crime in urban areas.

Urban Life and Criminal Behavior: A Question of Subculture?

Since the earliest ecological studies of crime, researchers have noted a greater concentration of crime in cities as compared to rural areas, and within certain areas of the city. Beginning with the Chicago School of sociology, urban life, particularly inner-city residence, has been linked to increased levels of sociopathology.[64] Both Clinard and Monkkonen also argued that urbanization leads to patterns of social disorganization. Such disorganization is said to be a major cause of elevated levels of criminal conduct in these areas. Clinard further noted that even offenders from rural backgrounds/residence had "urban lifestyles" that contributed to their involvement in crime.[65] The urbanization-induced effects of normative change rather than economic deprivation are said to account for higher rates of crime in cities than in small towns or rural areas.

The fact that both nineteenth-century white ethnic immigrants and twentieth-century African-Americans have tended to settle in inner-city locations in the United States has led to speculation that the cultural variance that characterizes such settings may explain their higher rates of crime. Such thinking about the normative effects of urbanization, perhaps more than Sellin's notion of "culture conflict" or Miller's "culture of poverty," is said by some to have led to the development of subcultural theory within American social science. On the other hand, the notion of an "urban subculture of crime" has not been widely accepted in the study of crime causation, nor as an explanation for ethnic/racial differences in the rate of involvement in crime. Yet the continuing existence of higher rates of many types of crime among groups found in urban areas, as compared to their economically deprived counterparts in small towns and rural areas does lead to speculation regarding the importance of urban life as a source of cultural variance that is linked to the etiology of crime.

Reconsideration of the Central Issues

In the remainder of the chapter I provide a limited critique of the two sets of perspectives discussed above. Like Tittle, I do not attempt to provide a general assessment of these perspectives. Many such assessments already exist in the literature. Each perspective is discussed primarily in terms of its grounding in the historical research and empirical data on ethnic/racial differences in the rate of involvement in crime. The discussion is centered around a listing of issues and questions left unresolved by each perspective. Some issues/questions concern theoretical substance; others address matters of conceptualization and methodology in the study of ethnicity, race, and crime.

Issue 1: How conclusive is the proof of ethnic/racial difference in the rate of involvement in crime in the United States? To what extent do ethnic/racial groups differ in the type of crime committed?

Despite an awareness of the enormous diversity of the behaviors and omissions that are in violation of the criminal law, many criminological theorists tend to treat "crime" as a singular, undifferentiated entity. This practice has important implications for the study of the etiology of crime, as well as the study of ethnic/racial differences. Even if one accepts the definition of crime as limited only to acts violative of the criminal law (as opposed to violations of conduct norms or other markers of societal sanctioning), it makes little sense to speak of the etiology of *all* categories of crime as many criminological theorists frequently do. Similarly, theories or perspectives that purport to explain group differences for *all* types of criminal acts are questionable. The generic conceptualization and use of the term *crime* in many of the theories included in the perspectives described above may limit our understanding of the ethnic/racial crime differences.

Some official data suggest that ethnic and racial group differences may be substantial for some categories/types of crime, while nonexistent for others. In addition, some groups with low aggregate rates of reported crime may have rates for individual offenses that surpass those rates found among groups with overall high rates of crime. The reverse may also be true. Despite the overall high rate of crime found among black Americans reported by the Uniform Crime Reports, the black-white gap is quite low for some offenses. For other offenses, the white rate of offending has exceeded that found for blacks during some years. The UCR has historically shown a smaller discrepancy between the races for property offenses than for violent crime, and an even smaller gap for many other, miscellaneous categories of offenses.

Using official data, Flowers found no significant difference between black and white arrest rates for liquor law violations and drunkenness.[66] This pattern has been evident since the beginning of the UCR. Similarly, small black-white gaps can be found for such categories as offenses against family and children, runaways, driving under the influence, vandalism, forgery, counterfeiting, embezzlement, and fraud. The latter four offenses may reflect the tip of the iceberg of white-collar crimes, whose nondocumentation distorts both social-class[67] and racial comparisons of the rate of involvement in crime.

The current over-representation of Native Americans as criminal offenders is limited to a narrow range of offenses. Conversely, Asians, who have an overall low rate of crime, appear to be involved in some forms of property crime at rates equal to those of some white populations.[68] On the other hand, sizable racial gaps persist for such offenses as murder, rape, and robbery. The black rate is much higher than that found for whites, Asians, Native Americans, or Hispanics. If UCR data were available for a broad array of ethnic/racial groups, they might reveal the existence of interesting differences in crime-type involvement for a variety of groups.

Historical accounts of ethnic differences in criminal involvement also reveal differences in the type of crime committed by various groups.[69] The 1911 study of the United States Immigration Commission noted that Irish, Italian, French, Jewish, and Greek immigrants and native whites were differentially involved in various categories of crime. Indeed, it may be argued that each tended to offend within its own niche or area of crime specialization. Such seeming specialization may be linked to cultural differences among groups, or other factors may explain them. Because of the way that access to crime is socially distributed in society, very seldom will a single ethnic/racial group "monopolize" all categories of criminal behavior. Both spatial/ecological and political/socioeconomic barriers prevent any one group from doing so. Only by ignoring, through law and public opinion, the existence and societal impact of certain categories of crime (for example, white-collar and corporate crime today) will it appear that the over-representation of a single group extends across all crimes. Of course, differential law enforcement and the ability to avoid detection also affect the past and present distribution of various types of crime across ethnic/racial lines.

The potential inaccuracy of historical crime data has led some to challenge the adequacy of the data purported to show higher rates of crime among the Irish and Italians than those found among other white ethnic groups during the nineteenth century. Hearsay, stereotype, and anecdotal evidence often constituted "proof" of such differences. The reliability and validity of official measures of criminality used in a pre-UCR era can also be questioned. For example, much of the evidence used to show higher rates of criminal behavior among ethnic groups (or the foreign-born) consisted of imprisonment statistics. The bias inherent in custody statistics is well known. When arrest or conviction data were available, they sometimes challenged accepted beliefs.

Nelli acknowledges a high rate of crime among Chicago's Italian-Americans between 1880 and 1930.[70] However, arrest and conviction data for the city during 1913 showed both foreign-born Italians and Irish to have rates about equal to their shares of the city's population. Left unresolved by such data is the question of whether the foreign-born had patterns different from their American-born descendants, as Quinney suggests.[71] Nelli does note a high rate of crime among Italian youth in Chicago during this period.[72] Also unresolved is the question of whether these groups had lower rates of crime by 1913 than they did during the decades before the turn of the century. Nelli's and similar observations nevertheless raise questions regarding the evidence of greater levels of crime among some ethnic/racial groups than among others.

The work of conflict theorists such as Quinney and Chambliss and Seidman also raises questions as to whether the Irish and Italians, like nonwhite minorities today, were subjected to greater levels of social control than more dominant ethnic/racial groups.[73] Quinney describes the determinants of the criminality of African-Americans and white ethnics in very similar terms. These include differential treatment by the criminal justice system.[74] Brown and Warner report that by the turn of the last century the increasing numbers of immigrants represented political, economic, and cultural threats to native middle- and upper-class Americans.[75] In many of the largest cities indigenous Americans used the police to attempt to control various undesirable aspects of the "foreign" community's lifestyle. What were the effects of such patterns of social control on the reported rates of crime among these groups?

Even if differences exist in rates of actual crime across ethnic/racial groups in the United States, factors other than those frequently proposed might explain such differences. For example, in her study of immigrants in Philadelphia between 1870 and 1920, Golab reported that Poles, having arrived later, found that many of the better-paying jobs were monopolized by other immigrant groups. Thus, the settlement of Poles in that city was somewhat selective. Only the most highly skilled chose to compete for jobs in Philadelphia, while those with few skills settled in smaller towns or rural areas in the western part of Pennsylvania.[76] Such pre- and post-immigration selectivity in settlement may explain why historical accounts, conducted mainly in selected urban areas of the Northeast and Midwest, highlight the criminality of the Irish and Italians as opposed to Germans, Poles, and other groups. In Pennsylvania, the crime of poor Irish and Italian peasants living in Philadelphia may have been both more prevalent and more visible to the public and scholars than the crime of either highly skilled urban Poles or unskilled populations living in small towns. Pre-immigration selectivity has, of course, been shown to be a factor in the recent comparative economic standing in the United States of such groups as Russian Jews and Caribbean blacks.[77]

tives previously discussed? Do they invalidate any of the presumptions or tenets of the theories discussed above? While not sufficient to completely discount them, they may suggest that the devising of theories to explain ethnic/racial differences in criminal behavior might best proceed on the basis of a consideration of individual crime categories rather than "crime" as a composite of all lawbreaking acts. The utility of this approach for the study of crime causation has been noted by many commentators, including Wolfgang in his study of homicide patterns.[78] These observations also suggest that conflict and social-control perspectives must be an integral part of any analysis of ethnic/racial differences in the rate of involvement in crime.

Research using these approaches may show that ethnic/racial differences are real in some instances and, therefore, require explanations. In other instances, the absence of differences may negate the need for explanation. I propose that some offenses, such as homicide, do show evidence of having distinct ethnic/racial patterns both during the past and today.[79] That is, during a given period, some groups show higher rates of offending than others. Such ethnic/racial differences are not likely found across the whole range of common-law personal crimes, as Hindelang suggests.[80] To the extent that interpersonal violence or other categories/types of crime show clear-cut ethnic or racial differences not caused by selective detection or law enforcement, such differences require explanation. Are groups that display higher rates characterized by culture conflict or greater levels of deprivation? If not, what factors explain the differences?

On the other hand, many categories of property crime—for example, theft of various kinds—show less evidence of ethnic/racial difference. Often, bias in the formulation of the substantive criminal law and in the administration of justice accounts for what appear to be ethnic/racial differences in behavior. Ethnic/racial groups may differ in their access to (or choice of) various forms of theft and conversion, but it is likely that the overall "take" is very similar within any given group. Indeed, the "take" is undoubtedly much greater among higher social classes or among ethnic/racial groups in dominant positions in society than for lower-status groups or classes. For instance, American society suffers a much greater loss from white-collar theft than from "street" theft during any given year.

Issue 2: To what extent do ethnic/racial groups with similar levels of economic deprivation/inequality or cultural variance have similar rates of criminal behavior?

This question goes to the core of these perspectives and the criticisms of them. Let us begin by examining the "proof" of higher rates of crime among the economically deprived. In addition to the work of Tittle and his associates,[81] numerous studies have challenged the idea that the highest rates of crime are found among the poorest segments of the population. Indeed, this has been one of the most hotly debated topics within criminology for some years. Messner has of the most hotly debated topics within criminology for some years. Messner has concluded that neither absolute nor relative deprivation alone or together can fully explain the distribution of homicide in contemporary, urban America.[82] Other studies have challenged the idea that comparative levels of economic well-being account for the distribution of other crimes. If Tittle, Messner, and similar analysts are correct, the idea that the crime of white ethnics or contemporary American nonwhite minorities is attributable to their social-class standing is debatable and lacks empirical support. If the poor do not have higher rates of crime than other social classes, then greater comparative concentrations of poverty among some ethnic/racial groups than among others do not explain differential rates of crime.

In support of this view, a number of empirical studies, both historical and contemporary, raise questions about whether similar levels of deprivation lead to similar rates of criminal involvement across ethnic/racial groupings. Lane reported that rates of homicide in nineteenth-century Philadelphia varied substantially across seemingly similarly situated white immigrant populations. Irish and Italian immigrants had high rates of violence, while Jews and eastern Europeans had much lower rates.[83] Interestingly, Powell reported that blacks in Buffalo, New York, prior to the Civil War appeared to have lower rates of violent crime than did the Irish of that city.[84]

Studies of this sort show the need for more historical studies of ethnicity/race and crime to test the tenets of the two perspectives outlined in this chapter. Many questions remain unanswered. For example, if the Irish and Italian populations in nineteenth-century America can be shown to have high rates of involvement in crime, can it be shown that they also were comparatively more disadvantaged or culturally marginal than other immigrant groups? The available evidence does not seem to support the idea that various other groups of northern, southern, or eastern Europeans in America were more economically privileged than the Irish or Italians during the late nineteenth century. It is possible, but not likely, that the free black population of Buffalo during the period studied by Powell was more economically advantaged than were the Irish. On the other hand, while segments of the populations of English, Scotch, Welsh, or German ancestry were economically marginal during this period, their overall socioeconomic status was likely higher than that of the Irish and Italians.

Neither is Sellin's culture-conflict approach consistent with all of the historical data. For example, while Lane found low rates of violence among Germans, a more settled immigrant population, Lane reports that most foreign-born ethnic groups (Italians excepted) in Philadelphia were less inclined to violence than native, white Americans.[85] In the absence of data showing that the ethnic/racial differences cited by Lane and Powell were due to significant differences in the socioeconomic status of these groups, their varying rates of crime seem to call into question a pure "economic deprivation" explanation. These differences also question the accuracy of a "culture-conflict" model of group crime-rate differences.

Similar questions can be raised regarding ethnic/racial differences in reported crime today. For example, in terms of official measures of economic well-being for the 1980s, several ethnic/racial groups fared worse than African-Americans. These include Native Americans, Vietnamese, Mexican-Americans, and Puerto Ricans. All have rates of reported crime lower than that for blacks, and in some cases, substantially lower. Yet, all have rates higher than those for the majority white population, a fact that may lend support to the deprivation perspective. On the other hand, the cultural variance/conflict-of-conduct norms perspective also fails to explain the higher rate of crime found among these nonwhite groups as compared to blacks. Native Americans, Hispanics, and Asians, including Japanese and Chinese, arguably experience greater levels of cultural variance/conflict than do blacks. Indeed, despite the potential for culture conflict, some populations of recently arrived Asians have rates of crime lower than those of long-term white residents of the United States.

If current crime data were collected so as to measure white ethnic differences in the rate of criminal activity, findings might also emerge to challenge some of the tenets of the perspectives discussed above. For example, it has been shown that southern whites, most of whom historically stem from populations of English, Irish, or Scottish ancestry, have relatively high rates of violent and aggressive behavior and also comparatively high rates of property crime. As a result, the black-white gap for many of the crimes listed on the UCR is much smaller in the southern states than in states outside of the South. Some observers have suggested that modern southern whites constitute a distinct cultural group. A belief in a distinct cultural heritage in the South among both whites and blacks is the basis for the southern subculture of violence hypothesis first advocated by Hackney.[86] On the other hand, in support of the economic-deprivation/inequality perspective, it may be proposed that similarities in rates of crime among southern blacks and whites result from shared economic disadvantages.

To what extent would disaggregated data reveal ethnic "pockets" of high (or low) crime in the United States? Regional statistics show comparatively low rates of violent and property crime in states with large German and Scandinavian enclaves, for example, Wisconsin, Minnesota, the Dakotas. The WASP-dominated states of upper New England have similarly low rates of crime. On the other hand, pockets of violent crime can be found among many states in the southern and western United States. Similar concentrations can be found in other regions. To what extent are such patterns associated with cultural concentrations?

Recent international homicide statistics also raise questions that may apply to our understanding of the causes of ethnic crime-rate patterns in the United States. Fingerhut and Kleinman compared homicide rates per 100,000 population for males, fifteen to twenty-four years of age in several countries. Rates ranged from 0.3 percent in Austria to 21.9 percent in the United States. As expected, rates were highest for African-Americans. However, several comparative national rates were of interest. Rates in Scotland and New Zealand were more than four times higher than rates in such countries as West Germany, Denmark, and Portugal, and were about ten times higher than rates for Japan and Austria.[87] To what extent are such differences due to socioeconomic as opposed to cultural factors? Do other factors explain the differences?

Issue 3: What explains temporal changes in crime within and across ethnic/racial groups?

Both the economic-deprivation/inequality and cultural-variance perspectives presume or predict temporal changes in the level of criminal activity among ethnic/racial groups. A defining tenet of the deprivation/inequality perspective is the presumption that improvements in economic well-being will reduce the criminality of the deprived. Cultural-variance approaches suggest that either through acculturation or other forces that alter the culture or subculture of a given group, there can be a reduction in criminality. Analyses of rates of crime among Irish- and Italian-Americans offer case studies for the testing of these propositions. Official crime statistics collected in the United States during the last half century show little evidence of disproportionate rates of crime among persons of Irish and Italian ancestry.

Which of the two perspectives seems to best account for the transition among these two ethnic groups from a law-breaking underclass to a law-abiding bourgeoisie? This is largely a rhetorical question. Even if there are separate and distinct effects of acculturation/assimilation versus economic betterment, these effects cannot be disentangled in retrospect. Nonetheless, the question of what accounted for the "success" of these immigrant groups is frequently asked by scholars and the public. And, despite an inability to definitively resolve the question, the ideological/political stances taken by questioners have much relevance for the nature of the public's response to America's contemporary crime problems.

Recent data show Irish Catholics to have average incomes higher than those for most white ethnic groups in the United States. Italian-American median income figures also compare favorably to those of other white ethnic groups. The average income for Irish Catholics during the 1970s was nearly equal to the income of Jewish Americans and higher than that earned by German Americans.[88] Both the Irish and the Italians are often cited as evidence of the "natural" process by which ethnic groups have culturally and economically assimilated into the American mainstream, leaving behind their legacy of over-involvement in crime. Of principal concern to many analysts and policy makers is the relevance of the "success story" of the Irish and Italians for our understanding of what can be done about high rates of crime among some ethnic/racial groups today.

Lane notes that one of the questions most frequently asked by social researchers and the public concerns reasons for the continuing rise of crime among blacks. He notes that while both African-American and white ethnic crime rates were elevated during the middle to late 1800s in Philadelphia, only African-American rates have remained at those levels or surpassed them.[89] Of course, other observers have noted similar patterns in other American cities. During the 1980s, both the media and academicians have documented the shockingly high rates of violent crime and imprisonment found among African-American males. With homicide the leading cause of death among young black males and their rate of confinement perhaps the highest in the world, politicians and policy makers are beginning to seek solutions. Much of their understanding of black crime and its solutions is rooted in their perceptions of the success achieved by white immigrants in reducing their rates of crime.

Steinberg is one of a handful of scholars who confronts head-on the multiplicity of ideological/political responses to the persisting high rate of black crime. He challenges the usefulness of the "immigrant analogy" for understanding the current plight of African-Americans and criticizes the culture-of-poverty thesis, especially its reformulation by Banfield.[90] His work also contributes to the economic-deprivation/inequality versus cultural-variance debate. He documents reports of high rates of crime during the nineteenth century not only among the Irish and Italians but also among other groups not commonly associated with criminal activity. After describing crime in most nineteenth-century American cities as characterized by "ethnic succession in all areas of crime," Steinberg says:

> Today, of course, it is blacks, Puerto Ricans, and Chicanos who are blamed for high rates of crime, and as before, crime is treated as a cultural aberration rather than a symptom of class inequality. No doubt, the incidence of crime in immigrant ghettos was lower than it is today; nor, perhaps were homicides and other crimes of violence as prevalent. But neither were immigrants mired in poverty over many generations. On the contrary, having entered an expanding economy, most immigrants were on the threshold of upward mobility. Yet if the Irish, Italians, Jews and others produced as much crime as they did in a single generation, what could have been expected of these groups had they remained in poverty for five, or eight or ten generations, like much of the nation's black population?[91]

Despite the eloquence of Steinberg's call for historical correctness in the study of ethnicity/race and crime, his conclusions are not accepted by all commentators. A common concern has been not whether economic deprivation is a major factor affecting rates of crime among blacks, but rather why the black underclass has remained mired in poverty for so many generations. During the last two decades, some have begun to question the causal significance of the two most commonly cited reasons for black-white inequality—slavery and its legacy, and continuing inequality and discrimination. The legal reforms of the 1960s are cited as evidence of the demise of slavery-produced social institutions and practices in the United States. One consequence of such lines of argument is a persisting belief that high rates of black crime and other "sociopathology" result from either deeply entrenched cultural traits or biological/genetic racial differences.[92]

Even for commentators who do not share those conclusions, the persistence of rates of "street" crime among blacks surpassing those of other nonwhites and whites has been puzzling. Some have sought answers in the work of current analysts of the "underclass." William Wilson has attributed higher rates of black crime, single-parent families, and similar problems to the social dislocations caused by the demise of blue-collar jobs in the United States over the last two decades.[93] Whatever the academic and public response to them, large segments of the population of urban African-Americans have become the "dangerous class" of the 1990s in the United States.

Conclusion

To a great extent, the debate in this chapter represents merely a recasting of the perennial "materialism" versus "ideology/culture" argument so common in social science. One of the few widely accepted canons of social science is the assertion that human societies are characterized by the existence of values and norms that both inhibit and condone those behaviors labeled as "crimes." On the other hand, social researchers have achieved much less success in identifying the various social contexts that determine which of these sets of values will predominate and, if predominant, whether such values will significantly affect actual behavior. Social class and ethnic/racial statuses represent macrolevel contexts within which criminal behavior emerges. And, as this chapter has illustrated, much conceptual and empirical confusion reigns within social science regarding the connections among social class, ethnicity/race, and crime.

Despite its unsettled state, social science thinking about ethnicity, race, and crime does offer some insights. It has relevance for assessing the potential utility of many recently advocated public policy initiatives aimed at remedying America's crime problem. The seeming "lawlessness" of some segments of the American population has prompted questions that emanate from ideas about inequality and cultural difference. Given the current association of crime and criminality with identifiable ethnic/racial groupings, the perspectives and research findings reported in this chapter are extremely salient today.

The similarities between the criminal patterns of the white ethnic underclass during the past and the black underclass today have received considerable notice. Media coverage of violence associated with drug trafficking in black communities is frequently reminiscent of the coverage of organized crime during the 1920s and 1930s. The successful arrest, indictment, and conviction of black "drug kingpins" in Chicago, Los Angeles, Detroit, and other major cities resulted from investigatory methods first used against the Mafia. In addition, media accounts and public discourse regarding "unorganized" black crime resemble similar accounts of the crime of the foreign-born dangerous classes of the past.

Many of the recent attempts to explain such patterns of crime appear to be based on the belief that ethnic/racial communities (or at least disadvantaged sectors within them) differ in their comparative levels of civic mindedness, community consciousness, moral and ethical values, and so forth. Such tenets are the core of the cultural-variance view of ethnic/racial crime-rate differences, especially certain notions of subculture. In response to perceived normative deficits within some portions of African-American communities, many observers and policy makers currently seek alternatives to the "dysfunctional" values of black youth. Interventions that involve "Afrocentricity," "community empowerment," "community policing," "self-help," "re-socialization," "mentoring," and similar concepts have been advocated during the last two decades as methods of reducing black crime rates. To greater or lesser degrees, each one of these proposed remedies is derived from aspects of the two perspectives discussed in this chapter. Taken as a whole, they appear to owe more to conceptualizations of cultural variance than economic inequality. Each appears to presume that elevated levels of black crime are "caused" by the absence of prosocial values and/or the embeddedness of criminogenic values within lower-class black communities. Many academicians, politicians, community activists, and others bemoan the breakdown of family life and erosion of values in these communities. Interestingly, these are themes quite similar to those presented by black and white observers of black life during the decades after the Civil War.[94]

The discussion in this chapter lends some support to the idea that these and similar methods of intervention have potential utility as responses to currently high rates of crime among African-Americans and other groups. It also raises doubt about the effectiveness of such approaches if they are pursued in isolation from the other forces that encompass the socioeconomics of crime in society. While the current targeting of the criminogenic values and norms of the black underclass is grounded in some theory, it may simply be one more reflection of the politics surrounding race relations and welfare policy in the United States today. The kinds of public expenditures on the disadvantaged that characterized the War on Poverty are, for many, an unthinkable option today. On the other hand, arguments in favor of such expenditures can be made on the basis of research and theory presented in this chapter.

To the extent that the experiences of American white ethnics offer a model for today, it may be proposed that the currently lower rates of crime found among them may have resulted less from normative change than from the achievement of middle-class economic status. Much the same conclusion may apply to evidence of comparatively low rates of crime among middle-class African-Americans, many of whom only recently achieved such status. Policies that advocate reductions in levels of societal inequality are as grounded in theory and may offer as much potential for change in the rates of crime among African-Americans, Native Americans, Puerto Ricans, and other groups as are those policies that focus on cultural values. It may well be that reductions in levels of deprivation/inequality across ethnic/racial groups will not completely eliminate group differences in rates of involvement in crime. But public policies and programs aimed at such reductions are a social experiment worth pursuing.

Notes

1. Michael J. Hindelang, "Race and Involvement in Common Law Personal Crimes."
2. Darnell F. Hawkins, "Black and White Homicide Differentials: Alternatives to an Inadequate Theory" and "Explaining the Black Homicide Rate."
3. For example, Richard Quinney, *The Social Reality of Crime*; William J. Chambliss and Robert B. Seidman, *Law, Order, and Power.*
4. Charles Tittle, "Social Class and Crime: A Critique of the Theoretical Foundation," p. 334.
5. Charles Tittle and Wayne J. Villemez, "Social Class and Criminality"; Charles Tittle, Wayne J. Villemez, and D. Smith, "The Myth of Social Class and Criminality: An Empirical Assessment of the Empirical Evidence."
6. Tittle, "Social Class and Crime," p. 335.
7. Stephen J. Gould, *Mismeasure of Man.* The purpose of this paper is not to contribute to the nature–nurture controversy. However, the recent work of James Q. Wilson and Richard J. Herrnstein, *Crime and Human Nature*, shows that the debate is still evident among those who study the etiology of crime, including racial differences in the amount of criminal behavior. In this discussion, I limit my review to the conceptualizations and theories that propose that ethnic and racial group differences in criminal behavior are products of social forces rather than biological ones. Like Tittle, in "Social Class and Crime," I also limit my discussion to theories of the etiology of criminal behavior as opposed to various perspectives that stress the importance of group differences in the administration of justice.
8. Ira S. Lowry, "The Science and Politics of Ethnic Enumeration."
9. Stephen Steinberg, *The Ethnic Myth: Race, Ethnicity and Class in America.*
10. For example, see U.S. Immigration Commission, "Immigration and Crime"; National Commission on Law Observance and Enforcement, *Report on Crime and the Foreign-Born.*
11. Quinney, *Social Reality of Crime*, p. 221.
12. Quinney, *Social Reality of Crime*; C.C. Van Vechten, "The Criminality of the Foreign-Born." The point raised by Quinney requires investigation. If, as many suggest, second- and third-generation ethnics had higher rates of crime than the first generation, the focus on the crime of the foreign-born was misguided.
13. Much of the seeming inattention to the counting of crime along ethnic lines may stem from the fact that the Uniform Crime Reports and other official measures of crime and punishment began during the 1920s and 1930s. This was a period during which the previously heightened interest in white ethnic crime-rate differences was waning.
14. All of the "blame" for a lack of attention to white ethnic crime in the United States cannot be placed on the unavailability of national data. Social scientists studying crime in specific localities can collect data on the ethnic characteristics of offenders, especially where such populations are residentially segregated or otherwise identifiable. Few attempts have been made to collect these kinds of data.
15. Tittle, "Social Class and Crime."
16. Ibid.; George B. Vold and Thomas J. Bernard, *Theoretical Criminology*, pp. 130–42.

17. Oscar Handlin, *Boston's Immigrants, 1790–1865: A Study in Acculturation*; E.A. Hobbs, "Criminality in Philadelphia: 1790–1810 Compared with 1937"; Theodore N. Ferdinand, "The Criminal Patterns of Boston since 1849"; John K. Alexander, "Poverty, Fear and Continuity: An Analysis of the Poor in Late Eighteenth-Century Philadelphia"; Roger Lane, *Violent Death in the City*; Steinberg, *The Ethnic Myth*.

18. As quoted in Hobbs, "Criminality in Philadelphia," p. 202.

19. Andrew M. Greeley, *That Most Distressed Nation: The Taming of the American Irish*, p. 225.

20. Ferdinand, "Criminal Patterns," p. 98.

21. Alexander, "Poverty, Fear and Continuity," pp. 19–20.

22. Handlin, *Boston's Immigrants*.

23. Joel Samaha, *Law and Order in Historical Perspective: The Case of Elizabethan Essex*.

24. Eric H. Monkkonen, *The Dangerous Class: Crime and Poverty in Columbus, Ohio, 1860–1885*; Alexander, "Poverty, Fear and Continuity."

25. Humbert S. Nelli, *Italians in Chicago, 1880–1920*, p. 125.

26. Mark H. Haller, "Recurring Themes," p. 285.

27. Steinberg, *The Ethnic Myth*, p. 116.

28. U.S. Immigration Commission, "Immigration and Crime."

29. Steinberg, *The Ethnic Myth*, p. 117.

30. Frank M. Sanborn, "Negro Crime," e.g., p. 11.

31. Thorsten Sellin, "The Negro Criminal: A Statistical Note," p. 52.

32. Ibid., p. 53.

33. Ibid., p. 64.

34. Willem A. Bonger, *Race and Crime*, p. 43.

35. Ibid.

36. Ibid., pp. 43–51.

37. Nathaniel Cantor, "Crime and the Negro"; Guy B. Johnson, *The Negro and Crime: The Annals of the American Academy of Political and Social Science*; Herman Canady, "The Negro in Crime"; E. Franklin Frazier, *The Negro in the United States*, chapter 25.

38. Hindelang, "Race and Involvement."

39. Marvin Wolfgang and Bernard Cohen, *Crime and Race: Conceptions and Misconceptions*, p. 100.

40. Ibid.

41. Robert K. Merton, *Social Theory and Social Structure*.

42. Ibid., pp. 94–97.

43. Carl E. Pope, "Race and Crime Revisited."

44. Vold and Bernard, *Theoretical Criminology*.

45. Tittle, "Social Class and Crime."

46. Merton, *Social Theory*.

47. Patrick P. Moynihan, *The Negro Family: The Case for National Action*.

48. Clifford R. Shaw and Henry D. McKay, *Juvenile Delinquency and Urban Areas*.

49. Edwin H. Sutherland, *Criminology*, p. 106.

50. Sellin, "The Negro Criminal."

51. Ibid. and Sutherland, *Criminology*.

52. Sellin, "The Negro Criminal," pp. 74–107.

53. Ibid., pp. 99–100.

54. Ferdinand, "Criminal Patterns."

55. Sellin, "The Negro Criminal," pp. 104–5.

56. Sellin, "The Negro Criminal."

57. Frazier, *The Negro in the United States*; Melville J. Herskovits, *The Myth of the Negro Past.*

58. Sellin, "The Negro Criminal," p. 62.

59. Ibid., pp. 104–5.

60. Johnson, *The Negro and Crime*, p. 93.

61. Oscar Lewis, *Five Families*; Walter B. Miller, "Lower Class Culture As a Generating Milieu of Gang Delinquency."

62. S. Hackney, "Southern Violence"; Marvin Wolfgang and Franco Ferracuti, *The Subculture of Violence: Towards an Integrated Theory in Criminology*; Raymond D. Gastil, "Homicide and a Regional Subculture of Violence"; Steven F. Messner, "Poverty, Inequality and the Urban Homicide Rate: Some Unexpected Findings."

63. Lynn Curtis, *Violence, Race, and Culture.*

64. Robert Park, Edward W. Burgess, and R.D. McKenzie, *The City*; Shaw and McKay, *Juvenile Delinquency.*

65. Marshall B. Clinard, "The Process of Urbanization and Criminal Behavior"; Monkkonen, *The Dangerous Class*, p. 9.

66. Ronald B. Flowers, *Minorities and Criminality.*

67. Tittle and Villemez, "Social Class and Criminality."

68. Flowers, *Minorities and Criminality.*

69. Lane, *Violent Death in the City.*

70. Nelli, *Italians in Chicago*, pp. 144–47.

71. Quinney, *Social Reality of Crime.*

72. Nelli, *Italians in Chicago*, p. 144.

73. Quinney, *Social Reality of Crime*; Chambliss and Seidman, *Law, Order, and Power.*

74. Quinney, *Social Reality of Crime*, p. 222.

75. M. Craig Brown and Barbara D. Warner, "Immigrants, Ethnic Politics and Urban Policing at 1900."

76. Caroline Golab, "The Immigrant and the City: Poles, Italians, and Jews in Philadelphia, 1870–1920."

77. Richard T. Schaefer, *Racial and Ethnic Groups.*

78. Marvin E. Wolfgang, *Patterns in Criminal Homicide.*

79. This observation is not meant to suggest that racial-ethnic differentials do not change over time. Some groups with comparatively high homicide rates during the past have much lower rates today and vice versa. Of course, overall societal levels of offending may also change. The point is that in any given historical period, rates often vary markedly across ethnic/racial lines.

80. Hindelang, "Race and Involvement."

81. Tittle, "Social Class and Crime"; Tittle and Villemez, "Social Class and Criminality"; Tittle, Villemez, and Smith, "The Myth of Social Class."

82. Messner, "Poverty, Inequality and the Urban Homicide Rate."

83. Lane, *Violent Death*, p. 102.

84. Elwin H. Powell, "Crime As a Function of Anomie."

85. Sellin, *Culture Conflict*; Lane, *Violent Death*, pp. 102–3.

86. Hackney, "Southern Violence."

87. Lois A. Fingerhut and Joel C. Kleinman, "International and Interstate Comparisons of Homicide Among Males."

88. Andrew M. Greeley, *Ethnicity in the United States: A Preliminary Reconnaissance*, pp. 42–43; Schaefer, *Racial and Ethnic Groups*, pp. 129–43.

89. Roger Lane, *Roots of Violence in Black Philadelphia, 1860–1900.*

90. Steinberg, *The Ethnic Myth*; Edward Banfield, *The Unheavenly City Revisited.*

91. Steinberg, *The Ethnic Myth*, p. 117.
92. Hawkins, "Explaining the Black Homicide Rate."
93. William J. Wilson, *The Truly Disadvantaged: The Inner City, the Underclass, and Public Policy.*
94. W.E.B. DuBois, *Proceedings of the Ninth Atlantic Conference for the Study of Negro Problems.*

References

Alexander, John K. "Poverty, Fear and Continuity: An Analysis of the Poor in Late Eighteenth-Century Philadelphia." In Allen F. Davis and Mark H. Haller, eds., *The Peoples of Philadelphia: A History of Ethnic Groups and Lower-Class Life, 1790–1940*, pp. 13–35. Philadelphia: Temple University Press, 1973.

Banfield, Edward. *The Unheavenly City Revisited.* Boston: Little, Brown, 1974.

Blau, Judith R., and Blau, Peter M. "The Cost of Inequality: Metropolitan Structure and Violent Crime." *American Sociological Review* 57 (1982): 114–29.

Bonger, Willem A. *Race and Crime.* New York: Columbia University Press, 1943.

Brown, M. Craig, and Warner, Barbara D. "Immigrants, Ethnic Politics and Urban Policing at 1900." Paper presented at the annual meeting of the American Sociological Association, Cincinnati, Ohio, 1991.

Canady, Herman. "The Negro in Crime." In Vernon C. Branham and Samuel B. Kutash, eds., *Encyclopedia of Criminology.* New York: Philosophical Library, 1949.

Cantor, Nathaniel. "Crime and the Negro." *Journal of Negro History* 16 (1931): 61–66.

Chambliss, William J., and Seidman, Robert B. *Law, Order, and Power.* Reading, Mass.: Addison-Wesley, 1971.

Clinard, Marshall B. "The Process of Urbanization and Criminal Behavior." *American Journal of Sociology* 48 (1942): 202–13.

Curtis, Lynn. *Violence, Race, and Culture.* Lexington, Mass.: D.C. Heath, 1975.

DuBois, W.E.B., ed. *Proceedings of the Ninth Atlantic Conference for the Study of Negro Problems.* Atlanta: Atlanta University, 1904.

Duff, John B. *The Irish in the United States.* Belmont, Calif.: Wadsworth, 1971.

Ferdinand, Theodore N. "The Criminal Patterns of Boston since 1849." *American Journal of Sociology* 73 (July 1967): 84–99.

Fingerhut, Lois A., and Kleinman, Joel C. "International and Interstate Comparisons of Homicide Among Males." *Journal of the American Medical Associations* 263 (June 1990): 3292–95.

Flowers, Ronald B. *Minorities and Criminality.* New York: Greenwood Press, 1988.

Frazier, E. Franklin. *The Negro in the United States.* New York: Macmillan, 1957.

Gastil, Raymond D. "Lower-Class Behavior: Cultural and Biosocial." *Human Organization* 32, no. 4 (1990): 349–61.

———. "Homicide and a Regional Subculture of Violence." *American Sociological Review* 36 (1971): 412–26.

Golab, Caroline. "The Immigrant and the City: Poles, Italians, and Jews in Philadelphia, 1870–1920" In Allen F. Davis and Mark H. Haller, eds., *The Peoples of Philadelphia: A History of Ethnic Groups and Lower-Class Life, 1790–1940*, pp. 203–30. Philadelphia: Temple University Press, 1973.

Gould, Stephen J. *Mismeasure of Man.* New York: W.W. Norton, 1981.

Greeley, Andrew M. *Ethnicity in the United States: A Preliminary Reconnaissance.* New York: John Wiley, 1974.

———. *That Most Distressed Nation: The Taming of the American Irish.* Chicago: Quadrangle Books, 1972.

Hackney, S. "Southern Violence." In H. Graham and T. Gurr, eds., *Violence in America*, pp. 393–410. Beverly Hills: Sage Publications, 1969.

Haller, Mark H. "Recurring Themes." In Allen F. Davis and Mark. H. Haller, eds., *The Peoples of Philadelphia: A History of Ethnic Groups and Lower-Class Life, 1790–1940*. Philadelphia: Temple University Press, 1973.

Handlin, Oscar. *Boston's Immigrants, 1790–1865: A Study in Acculturation*. Cambridge, Mass.: Harvard University Press, 1941.

Hawkins, Darnell F. "Black and White Homicide Differentials: Alternatives to an Inadequate Theory." *Criminal Justice and Behavior* 10 (December 1983): 407–40.

———. "Explaining the Black Homicide Rate." *Journal of Interpersonal Violence* 5 (June 1990): 151–63.

Herskovits, Melville J. *The Myth of the Negro Past*. New York: Harper and Row, 1941.

Hindelang, Michael J. "Race and Involvement in Common Law Personal Crimes." *American Sociological Review* 43 (1978): 93–109.

Hobbs, E.A. "Criminality in Philadelphia: 1790–1810 Compared with 1937." *American Sociological Review* 8 (February 1943): 198–202.

Johnson, Guy B. *The Negro and Crime: The Annals of the American Academy of Political and Social Science* 217 (1941): 93–104.

Katz, Jack. *Seductions of Crime: Moral and Sensual Attractions in Doing Evil*. New York: Basic Books, 1988.

Lane, Roger. *Roots of Violence in Black Philadelphia, 1860–1900*. Cambridge, Mass.: Harvard University Press, 1986.

———. *Violent Death in the City*. Cambridge, Mass.: Harvard University Press, 1979.

Lewis, Oscar. *Five Families*. New York: Basic Books, 1959.

Loftin, Colin, and Hill, Robert. "Regional Subculture of Homicide." *American Sociological Review* 39 (1974): 714–24.

Lowry, Ira S. "The Science and Politics of Ethnic Enumeration." In Winston A. Van Horne, ed., *Ethnicity and Public Policy*, vol. 1. Madison: University of Wisconsin, 1982.

Merton, Robert K. *Social Theory and Social Structure*. Glencoe, Ill.: Free Press, 1968.

Messner, Steven F. "Poverty, Inequality and the Urban Homicide Rate: Some Unexpected Findings." *Criminology* 20 (1982): 103–14.

———. "Regional and Racial Effects on the Urban Homicide Rate: The Subculture of Violence Revisited." *American Journal of Sociology* 88 (1983): 997–1007.

Messner, Steven F., and Tardiff, K. "Economic Inequality and Levels of Homicide: An Analysis of Urban Neighborhoods." *Criminology* 24 (1986): 297–318.

Miller, Walter B. "Lower Class Culture As a Generating Milieu of Gang Delinquency." *Journal of Social Issues* 14 (1958): 5–19.

Monkkonen, Eric H. *The Dangerous Class: Crime and Poverty in Columbus, Ohio, 1860–1885*. Cambridge, Mass.: Harvard University Press, 1975.

Moynihan, Patrick P. *The Negro Family: The Case for National Action*. Office of Policy Planning and Research, United States Department of Labor, Washington, D.C.: U.S. Government Printing Office, 1965.

National Commission on Law Observance and Enforcement. *Report on Crime and the Foreign-Born*. Washington, D.C.: U.S. Government Printing Office, 1931.

Nelli, Humbert S. *Italians in Chicago, 1880–1920*. New York: Oxford University Press, 1970.

Park, Robert; Burgess, Edward W; and McKenzie, R.D. *The City*. Chicago: University of Chicago Press, 1928.

Pope, Carl E. "Race and Crime Revisited." *Crime and Delinquency* 25 (July 1979): 347–57.

Powell, Elwin H. "Crime As a Function of Anomie." *Journal of Criminal Law, Criminology, and Police Science* 57 (1966): 151–71.

Quinney, Richard. *The Social Reality of Crime.* Boston: Little, Brown, 1970.

Samaha, Joel. *Law and Order in Historical Perspective: The Case of Elizabethan Essex.* New York: Academic Press, 1974.

Sanborn, Frank M. "Negro Crime." In W.E.B. DuBois, ed., *Proceedings of the Ninth Atlantic Conference for the Study of Negro Problems.* Atlanta: Atlanta University, 1904.

Schaefer, Richard T. *Racial and Ethnic Groups.* Boston: Little, Brown, 1979.

Sellin, Thorsten. *Culture Conflict and Crime.* New York: Social Science Research Council, 1938.

———. "The Negro Criminal: A Statistical Note." *The Annals of the American Academy of Political and Social Science* 140 (1928): 52–64.

Shaw, Clifford R., and McKay, Henry D. *Juvenile Delinquency and Urban Areas.* Chicago: University of Chicago Press, 1969.

Steinberg, Stephen. *The Ethnic Myth: Race, Ethnicity and Class in America.* Boston: Beacon Press, 1989.

Sutherland, Edwin H. *Criminology.* Philadelphia: J.B. Lippincott, 1924.

Tittle, Charles. "Social Class and Crime: A Critique of the Theoretical Foundation." *Social Forces* 62 (December 1983): 334–58.

Tittle, Charles, and Villemez, Wayne J. "Social Class and Criminality." *Social Forces* 56 (December 1977): 474–502.

Tittle, Charles; Villemez, Wayne J.; and Smith, D. "The Myth of Social Class and Criminality: An Empirical Assessment of the Empirical Evidence." *American Sociological Review* 43 (October 1978): 643–46.

U.S. Immigration Commission. "Immigration and Crime," vol. 36. Washington, D.C.: Government Printing Office, 1911.

Van Vechten, C.C. "The Criminality of the Foreign-Born." *Journal of Criminal Law, Criminology, and Police Science* 32 (July–August 1941): 139–47.

Vold, George B., and Bernard, Thomas J. *Theoretical Criminology.* New York: Oxford University Press, 1986.

Wilbach, Harry. "The Thread of Crime in New York City." *Journal of Criminal Law, Criminology, and Police Science* 29 (1938): 62–75.

Wilson, James Q., and Herrnstein, Richard J. *Crime and Human Nature.* New York: Simon and Schuster, 1985.

Wilson, William J. *The Truly Disadvantaged: The Inner City, the Underclass, and Public Policy.* Chicago: University of Chicago Press, 1987.

Wolfgang, Marvin E. *Patterns in Criminal Homicide.* New York: John Wiley, 1958.

Wolfgang, Marvin, and Cohen, Bernard. *Crime and Race: Conceptions and Misconceptions.* New York: Institute of Human Relations, 1970.

Wolfgang, Marvin, and Ferracuti, Franco. *The Subculture of Violence: Towards an Integrated Theory in Criminology.* Beverly Hills: Sage Publications, 1982.

7

Rita Simon

Women, Crime, and Justice

Almost twenty years have gone by since I wrote *Women and Crime*, in which I argued that women's greater opportunities and skills, as a function of their increased participation in the labor force and years of schooling, have increased their propensity to commit criminal acts, especially property and white-collar offenses.[1] This chapter analyzes trends in women's involvement in criminal activities, reviewing recent arrest, judicial, and prison statistics and examining the changes, if any, that have occurred vis-à-vis women's socioeconomic status.

Turning first to various indices of women's socioeconomic status, we note that between 1940 and 1987, the percentage of women in the labor force increased from 27 to 55 percent, and the percentage of married women in the labor force increased from 17 to 56 percent. Indeed, as shown in Table 7.1, as of 1987 there is a higher percentage of women than ever before—including those who are married and have preschool children—who are working full time.

In addition to their increased participation in the labor force, women are completing baccalaureate and postgraduate degrees in greater numbers. Between 1950 and 1985, the percentage of women who earned bachelor's degrees increased from 23.9 to 49.4 percent. In 1950, only 29.3 percent of the master's degrees were earned by women, but by the 1980s, women were receiving half of the degrees conferred. Although women still lag far behind men at the doctoral level, there has been a major increase there as well; women were the recipients of one-third of the doctorate degrees in the 1980s, compared to 9 percent in the 1950s.

Not only are more women receiving higher academic degrees and working outside their homes than at any other time since the end of the Second World War, but higher proportions of them also occupy positions that involve more training, responsibility, and authority than they have in the past. Table 7.3 shows the proportions of black males, white males, black females, and white females in different occupational categories in the years 1970, 1980, and 1986.

But along with women's greater educational achievements, participation in the labor force, and promotion to higher-status positions, there is a greater percentage of single-headed female households in which women are the caretakers

Table 7.1.

Changes in Labor Force Participation Rates of Married Women with Children: 1948–87[a]

Year	Total	No Children Under 18	Children 6–17 (None < 6)	Children Under 6
1948	22.0	28.4	26.0	10.3
1949	22.5	29.7	27.3	11.0
1950	23.8	30.3	28.3	11.9
1951	25.2	31.0	30.3	14.0
1952	25.3	30.9	31.1	13.9
1953	26.3	31.2	32.2	15.5
1954	26.6	31.6	33.2	14.9
1955	27.7	32.7	34.7	16.2
1956	29.0	35.3	36.4	15.9
1957	29.6	35.6	36.6	17.0
1958	30.2	35.4	37.6	18.2
1959	30.9	35.2	39.8	18.7
1960[b]	30.5	34.7	39.0	18.6
1961	32.7	37.3	41.7	20.0
1962	32.7	36.1	41.8	21.3
1963	33.7	37.3	41.5	22.5
1964	34.4	37.8	43.0	22.7
1965	34.7	38.3	42.7	23.3
1966	35.4	38.4	43.7	24.2
1967	36.8	38.9	45.0	26.5
1968	38.3	40.1	46.9	27.6
1969	39.6	41.0	48.6	28.5
1970	40.8	42.2	49.2	30.3
1980	50.1	46.0	61.7	45.1
1982	51.2	46.2	63.2	48.7
1983	51.8	46.6	63.8	49.9
1984	52.8	47.2	65.4	51.8
1985	54.2	48.2	67.8	53.4
1986	54.6	48.2	68.4	53.8
1987	55.8	49.4	70.6	56.8

Source: U.S. Bureau of the Census, *Historical Statistics, Colonial Times to 1970,* series D 63–84 (Washington, D.C.: Government Printing Office, 1975), table D 63–74; *Statistical Abstract of the U.S. (Washington, D.C.: Government Printing Office, 1988), p. 374, table 624.*

[a]Married women in the labor force as percentage of married women in the population.
[b]First year for which figures include Alaska and Hawaii.

Table 7.2

Percentage of Earned Degrees Conferred upon Women: 1950–85

	Bachelor's		Master's		Doctorate		Total	
	Total Number	Percent Women	Total Number	Percent Women	Total Number	Percent Women	Total Number	Percent Women
1950	434	23.9	58	29.3	6.6	9.1	499	24.4
1955	288	36.1	58	32.8	8.8	9.1	354	35.0
1960	395	35.1	75	32.0	9.8	10.2	479	34.2
1965	539	40.6	112	32.1	16.5	10.9	668	38.5
1970	833	41.5	209	39.7	29.9	13.4	1,073	40.4
1974	1,009	42.5	278	43.2	33.9	19.2	1,321	42.0
1975	988	43.5	294	44.9	34.1	21.4	1,316	43.2
1976	998	43.6	313	46.3	34.1	22.9	1,345	43.8
1977	993	44.4	318	46.9	33.3	24.3	1,344	44.6
1978	998	45.4	313	47.9	32.2	26.4	1,342	45.7
1979	1,000	46.6	302	50.0	32.8	28.0	1,335	46.7
1980[a]	999	47.3	298	49.3	32.6	29.8	1,330	47.4
1981[a]	1,007	48.0	296	50.3	32.9	31.0	1,336	48.2
1982[a]	1,025	48.6	296	50.7	32.7	32.1	1,353	48.8
1983[a]	1,042	49.1	290	50.0	32.8	33.2	1,365	48.9
1984[a]	1,049	49.0	285	49.5	33.3	33.6	1,366	48.8
1985[a]	1,055	49.4	286	50.0	32.9	34.0	1,374	49.3

Source: Adapted from U.S. Bureau of the Census, *Statistical Abstract of the U.S.* (Washington, D.C.: Government Printing Office, 1988), p. 149, table 254. Data from U.S. Department of Education, Center for Education Statistics, *Digest of Education Statistics*, annual.

Note: Numbers are in thousands. Except as noted, data include Puerto Rico. Beginning in 1960, data include Alaska and Hawaii.
[a] Data for fifty states and Washington, D.C.

of young children. In 1970, 10.8 percent of all families in the United States were headed by females. In 1975, the percent increased to 13 percent, in 1980 to 14.6 percent, and in 1988 to 16.3 percent. Other characteristics about the demographic status of women in American society indicate that from 1970 on, women delayed marriage longer than they did in the previous two decades, they were more likely to remain childless, and they were more likely to divorce. With these data as background for assessing the socioeconomic position of women in American society, we turn to the crime statistics.

Arrest Data

Table 7.4 traces the percentage of arrests of females for all serious offenses (Type 1, Uniform Crime Reports) and for all violent and property offenses from 1963 to 1987.

Table 7.3

Occupational Distributions by Race and Sex: 1970, 1980, 1986[a]

Distribution by Employment[b]

	Black Males (in percent)			White Males (in percent)			Black Females (in percent)			White Females (in percent)		
	1970	1980	1986	1970	1980	1986	1970	1980	1986	1970	1980	1986
Managerial, Professional and Technical:												
Executive, Managerial, and Administrative	2.9	5.7	6.7	10.8	13.5	14.1	1.7	4.7	5.9	4.0	7.8	9.8
Professional Specialty	4.3	5.9	6.3	10.6	11.5	12.2	9.8	11.8	10.8	13.7	14.6	14.9
Technicians and Related Support	1.1	2.0	1.7	2.6	3.1	2.9	2.5	3.3	3.7	2.1	3.1	3.2
TOTAL	8.3	13.6	14.7	24.0	28.1	29.2	14.0	19.8	20.4	19.8	25.5	27.9
Sales	2.9	3.9	5.2	10.4	9.8	11.9	4.4	6.1	8.7	11.8	12.0	13.6
Administrative Support	7.8	9.3	9.1	7.2	6.6	5.3	19.2	25.9	26.1	34.0	32.1	30.1
Service:												
Private Household	0.5	0.2	0.1	0.1	0.1	0.1	17.8	5.0	4.0	2.0	0.8	1.7
Protective Service	1.8	3.1	4.2	2.1	2.3	2.4	0.3	0.7	0.7	0.2	0.4	0.4
Other Service	14.0	13.6	13.0	5.3	5.9	6.1	23.8	23.6	23.8	14.9	15.1	15.1
TOTAL	16.3	16.9	17.3	7.5	8.3	8.6	41.9	29.3	28.5	17.1	16.3	17.2

Table 7.3 *continued*

Occupational Distributions by Race and Sex: 1970, 1980, 1986[a]

Distribution by Employment[b]

	Black Males (in percent)			White Males (in percent)			Black Females (in percent)			White Females (in percent)		
	1970	1980	1986	1970	1980	1986	1970	1980	1986	1970	1980	1986
Farming, Forestry, and Fishing	6.6	3.4	3.6	5.4	4.3	5.0	1.3	0.5	0.4	0.8	1.0	1.1
Precision Production and Crafts	15.5	15.6	15.9	21.5	21.2	20.4	2.4	2.3	2.6	2.7	2.3	2.2
Machine Operators and Assemblers	15.6	14.7	11.0	10.4	9.1	7.4	13.1	12.3	10.1	10.9	8.0	5.7
Transportation	11.6	11.1	9.7	7.2	6.9	6.5	0.5	0.9	1.2	0.5	0.8	0.9
Handlers, Helpers, and Laborers	15.4	11.5	13.5	6.4	5.7	5.7	3.2	2.9	2.0	2.4	2.0	1.3
TOTAL	100	100	100	100	100	100	100	100	100	100	100	100

Source: Adapted from Reynolds Farley and Walter R. Allen, The Color Line and the Quality of Life in America (New York: Russel Sage Foundation, 1987), pp. 272–73, table 9.2. Data from U.S. Bureau of the Census: 1980, PC80–1-C1-A, Table 89, PC80–1-D1-A, table 281, U.S. Bureau of Labor Statistics, Employment and Earnings, vol. 33, no. 5 (May 1986), table A–23.

[a] Employed persons sixteen and over.
[b] April data.

Table 7.4

Percentages of Females Arrested among Total Arrests for All Serious (Type I) Crimes and for All Violent and Property (Type I) Crimes: 1963–87

Year	Total Arrested for Serious Crimes	Percent Female	Total Arrested for Violent Crimes[a]	Percent Female	Total Arrested for Property Crimes[b]	Percent Female
1963	695,222	11.7	124,821	10.3	570,401	12.0
1964	780,501	12.6	137,576	10.4	642,925	13.0
1965	834,296	13.4	151,180	10.2	683,116	14.1
1966	871,962	13.9	167,780	10.1	704,182	14.8
1967	996,800	14.1	191,807	9.8	804,993	15.1
1968	1,047,220	14.2	201,813	9.5	845,407	15.4
1969	1,111,674	15.7	216,194	9.6	892,283	17.1
1970	1,273,783	16.9	241,905	9.6	1,028,858	18.7
1971	1,397,304	17.2	273,209	10.0	1,121,327	19.0
1972	1,417,115	18.0	299,221	10.0	1,114,908	20.2
1973	1,372,220	18.7	290,382	10.2	1,078,842	21.1
1974	1,474,427	19.0	294,617	10.2	1,177,584	21.2
1975	1,901,811	19.5	370,453	10.3	1,528,317	21.7
1976	1,787,106	19.8	338,849	10.5	1,445,607	22.1
1977	1,986,043	20.1	386,806	10.4	1,596,304	22.4
1978	2,169,262	19.9	446,122	10.2	1,723,140	22.4
1979	2,163,302	19.5	434,778	10.2	1,728,524	21.8
1980	2,198,077	18.8	446,373	10.0	1,751,704	21.0
1981	2,293,754	19.1	464,826	10.1	1,828,928	21.4
1982	2,152,480	19.7	443,860	10.4	1,708,620	22.1
1983	2,151,120	20.1	443,686	10.8	1,707,434	22.5
1984	1,834,348	20.8	382,246	10.7	1,452,102	23.4
1985	2,124,671	21.4	431,332	10.9	1,693,339	24.0
1986	2,167,071	21.1	465,391	10.9	1,701,680	23.9
1987	2,266,467	21.6	473,030	11.1	1,793,437	24.4

Overall Rates of Change

1963–87		0.85		0.08		1.03
1973–87		0.16		0.09		0.16
1980–87		0.15		0.11		0.16

Source: Uniform Crime Reports (Washington, D.C.: F.B.I., U.S. Department of Justice, 1963–87). Total Arrests, Distributed by Sex.
[a]Includes male and female arrests for criminal homicide, forcible rape, robbery, and aggravated assault.
[b]Includes males and females arrested for burglary, larceny-theft, and auto theft. As of 1979, arson also is included.

The pattern that began to form in the late 1960s and early 1970s has contin-ued. Women's participation in property and white-collar crime has continued and increased. In 1987, 31 percent of all larceny, 44 percent of all fraud, 34 percent of all forgery, and 38 percent of all embezzlement arrests were of women. The percentages of women arrested for robbery (8 percent) and burglary (8 percent) have also increased, but at nowhere near the levels for the other property offenses. Women's involvement in violent offenses has not deviated from the pattern established in the 1960s. In 1963, women accounted for 10.3 percent of the Type I violent offense arrests; in 1987, women accounted for 11.1 percent of those arrests. On the property side, in 1963 women accounted for 12 percent of the Type I property offenses and in 1987, for 24 percent.

Thus, the overall pattern of women's participation in criminal activities has not changed dramatically in the past decade. The increases observed in the 1980s have been for the same types of offenses reported earlier: property and white-collar offenses that women have greater opportunities to commit and the skills to carry out, as a result of their greater participation in the labor force and as a function of the types of positions they occupy.

Table 7.7 ranks the proportion of men and women who were arrested in 1972, 1980, and 1987 for the ten most frequently cited Type I and Type II offenses. These ten offenses account for 64.4 percent of all men and 66.4 percent of all women arrested in 1987.

Larceny has remained the number one offense for which women are arrested. In 1987, women were less likely than in earlier years to be arrested for drunken-ness and disorderly conduct, but more likely to be arrested for drunk driving. Given all of the media coverage that drug-related crimes receive, it is somewhat surprising that drugs account for only 6.3 percent of all female arrests. On the other hand, crimes that specifically involve alcohol, if combined, comprised 16.7 percent of all offenders in 1987, which was similar to the amount they comprised in 1972 (16.7 percent) and 1980 (18.4 percent).

Among men, the ordering has been even more stable. Except for a decline in the proportion arrested for drunkenness and disorderly conduct and an increase in arrests for drunk driving and narcotics, there have been no marked changes. If we combine all alcohol-related offenses, as we did for women, we find an interesting negative trend: alcohol-related offenses comprised 34.1 percent of male arrests in 1972, 30.8 percent in 1980, and only 25.9 percent in 1987. Among both men and women, the sharp decrease in arrests for drunken-ness and disorderly conduct and the increase in arrests for drunken driving may be as much, or even more, an indication of a shift in police behavior as in the behavior of men and women arrested.

In sum, the data tell us that the proportion of female arrests in 1987 was greater than the proportion of arrests one or two decades earlier; the increase in female arrest rates among the serious offenses was due almost entirely to greater participation in property offenses, especially larceny. In 1963, roughly one out of

Table 7.5

Females Arrested As Percentage of All Arrests for Type I Offenses: 1963–87

Year	Total Arrested for Criminal Homicide	Percent Female	Total Arrested for Robbery	Percent Female	Total Arrested for Aggravated Assault	Percent Female	Total Arrested for Burglary	Percent Female	Total Arrested for Larceny	Percent Female	Total Arrested for Auto Theft	Percent Female
1963	8,805	15.5	37,836	4.9	68,719	14.0	170,160	3.3	314,402	19.0	85,839	3.7
1964	9,097	15.5	39,134	5.3	79,895	13.6	187,000	3.7	358,569	20.3	97,356	4.2
1965	10,163	15.4	45,872	5.2	84,411	13.5	197,627	3.7	383,726	22.1	101,763	4.2
1966	10,734	15.3	47,031	5.0	98,406	13.2	199,781	3.9	398,623	23.1	105,778	4.1
1967	12,167	14.8	59,789	5.2	107,192	12.9	239,461	4.1	447,299	23.9	118,233	4.2
1968	13,538	14.7	69,115	5.6	106,475	12.4	256,216	4.2	463,928	24.4	125,263	4.9
1969	14,706	14.1	76,533	6.2	113,724	12.6	255,937	4.4	510,660	26.5	125,686	5.3
1970	15,856	14.5	87,687	6.1	125,971	12.6	285,418	4.7	616,099	27.9	127,341	5.1
1971	17,317	15.7	101,728	6.3	140,350	13.3	215,276	4.9	674,997	28.1	130,954	6.0
1972	18,035	14.8	109,217	6.5	155,581	13.2	314,393	5.2	678,673	29.7	121,842	5.7
1973	17,395	14.5	101,894	6.8	154,891	13.2	316,272	5.4	644,190	31.5	107,226	6.5
1974	16,044	14.3	108,481	6.8	154,514	13.4	340,697	5.4	729,661	30.7	120,224	7.0
1975	19,526	14.9	129,217	7.0	202,217	13.1	449,155	5.4	958,938	31.2	110,708	7.0
1976	16,763	14.1	110,296	7.1	192,753	13.1	406,821	5.2	928,078	31.2	135,196	7.0
1977	20,096	14.0	122,514	7.4	221,329	12.8	454,193	6.0	1,006,915	31.8	153,270	8.3

Table 7.5 continued

Females Arrested As Percentage of All Arrests for Type I Offenses: 1963–87

Year	Total Arrested for Criminal Homicide	Percent Female	Total Arrested for Robbery	Percent Female	Total Arrested for Aggravated Assault	Percent Female	Total Arrested for Burglary	Percent Female	Total Arrested for Larceny	Percent Female	Total Arrested for Auto Theft	Percent Female
1978	18,755	14.1	141,481	7.0	257,629	12.7	485,782	6.1	1,084,088	31.7	153,270	8.3
1979	18,264	13.7	130,753	7.4	256,597	12.4	468,085	6.3	1,098,398	30.3	143,654	8.9
1980	18,745	12.8	139,476	7.2	258,721	12.4	479,639	6.2	1,123,823	28.9	129,783	8.6
1981	20,432	12.7	147,396	7.2	266,948	12.6	489,533	6.3	1,197,845	29.1	122,188	8.9
1982	18,511	13.3	138,118	7.3	258,899	12.9	436,271	6.6	1,146,705	29.4	108,736	9.0
1983	18,064	13.3	134,018	7.4	261,421	13.5	415,651	6.8	1,169,066	29.5	105,514	8.9
1984	13,676	13.3	108,614	7.2	231,620	13.4	334,399	7.4	1,009,743	30.2	93,285	9.2
1985	15,777	12.4	120,501	7.6	263,120	13.5	381,875	7.4	1,179,066	31.0	115,621	9.3
1986	16,066	12.3	124,245	7.8	293,952	13.2	375,544	7.9	1,182,099	30.7	128,514	9.5
1987	16,714	12.5	123,306	8.1	301,734	13.3	374,963	7.9	1,256,552	31.1	146,753	9.7
Overall Rates of Change												
1963–87		−0.19		0.66		−0.05		1.42		0.64		1.60
1973–87		−0.14		0.19		0.01		0.46		−0.01		0.49
1980–87		−0.02		0.12		0.07		0.27		0.08		0.13

Source: Uniform Crime Reports (Washington, D.C.: F.B.I., U.S. Department of Justice, 1963–87). Total Arrests, Distribution by Sex.

Table 7.6

Other Crimes: Females Arrested As Percentage of All People Arrested for Various Crimes: 1963–87

Year	Total Arrested for Embezzlement	Percent Female	Total Arrested for Fraud	Percent Female	Total Arrested for Forgery/Counterfeiting	Percent Female	Total Arrested for Offenses against Family	Percent Female	Total Arrested for Narcotic Drug Law Violations	Percent Female	Total Arrested for Prostitution and Vice	Percent Female
1963[a]					30,610	17.6	58,228	9.1	29,604	14.2	26,124	76.9
1964	8,610	17.3	45,998	19.0	30,637	18.2	57,454	9.3	37,802	14.0	28,190	78.0
1965	7,674	17.2	52,007	20.3	30,617	18.4	60,981	8.8	46,069	13.4	33,987	77.5
1966	6,439	19.2	52,041	21.6	29,277	19.8	55,820	9.9	60,358	13.8	34,376	79.9
1967	6,073	19.2	58,192	23.2	33,462	20.8	56,137	8.9	101,079	13.7	39,744	77.7
1968	5,894	19.6	56,710	24.0	34,497	21.8	51,319	8.8	162,177	15.0	42,338	78.3
1969	6,309	20.8	63,445	26.2	36,727	22.7	50,312	9.2	232,690	15.5	46,410	79.6
1970	8,174	24.6	76,861	27.1	43,833	23.7	56,620	8.9	346,412	15.7	49,344	79.3
1971	7,114	24.9	95,610	28.6	45,340	24.5	56,456	8.6	400,606	16.3	52,916	77.7
1972	6,744	26.3	96,713	29.6	44,313	24.8	52,935	9.3	431,608	15.7	44,744	74.1
1973	5,612	23.7	85,467	31.2	41,975	26.7	42,784	9.2	484,242	14.5	45,308	75.5
1974	5,981	26.3	91,176	32.6	39,741	28.6	34,902	11.9	454,948	14.2	53,309	75.6
1975	9,302	31.1	146,253	34.2	57,803	28.9	53,332	11.7	508,189	13.8	50,229	74.3
1976	8,218	31.0	161,429	36.6	55,791	29.6	58,249	10.7	500,540	13.6	58,648	70.7
1977	6,607	22.7	216,672	35.6	67,984	29.1	53,385	10.3	569,293	13.9	77,115	70.7

Table 7.6 continued

Other Crimes: Females Arrested as Percentage of all People Arrested for Various Crimes: 1963–1987

Year	Total Arrested for Embezzlement	Percent Female	Total Arrested for Fraud	Percent Female	Total Arrested for Forgery/Counterfeiting	Percent Female	Total Arrested for Offenses against Family	Percent Female	Total Arrested for Narcotic Drug Law Violations	Percent Female	Total Arrested for Prostitution and Vice	Percent Female
1978	7,670	25.1	249,207	36.8	73,269	29.7	54,014	10.2	596,940	13.7	89,365	67.7
1979	7,882	25.3	243,461	40.4	70,977	30.9	53,321	9.9	519,377	13.5	83,088	67.5
1980	7,885	28.5	261,787	41.4	72,643	31.1	49,991	10.6	533,010	13.4	85,815	69.5
1981	8,170	28.5	272,900	41.2	81,429	32.1	51,908	10.5	586,646	13.2	103,134	73.4
1982	7,358	30.3	265,663	40.3	79,951	32.6	45,432	11.6	565,182	13.6	111,029	71.0
1983	7,604	32.4	261,844	40.2	74,508	33.4	46,111	11.1	616,936	14.0	119,626	70.2
1984	6,290	36.9	203,175	40.4	63,359	33.7	32,877	13.9	562,255	13.9	88,337	69.9
1985	9,799	35.6	286,941	42.6	75,281	33.2	48,699	12.7	702,882	13.8	101,167	69.5
1986	10,500	36.4	284,790	43.3	76,546	33.9	47,327	15.0	691,882	14.5	96,882	65.4
1987	10,639	38.1	280,809	43.5	78,817	34.4	48,002	17.4	811,078	14.9	100,950	64.8
Overall Rates of Change												
1963–87[b]		1.21		1.28		0.96		0.90		0.05		−0.16
1973–87		0.61		0.39		0.29		0.89		0.03		−0.14
1980–87		0.34		0.05		0.11		0.64		0.11		−0.07

Source: Uniform Crime Reports (Washington, D.C.: F.B.I., U.S. Department of Justice, 1963–87). Total Arrests, Distribution by Sex.

a In 1963, embezzlement and fraud were combined.
b For embezzlement and fraud, the rates are for the change from 1964 to 1987.

Table 7.7

Rank Order of Offenses for Which Females and Males Are Most Likely to Be Arrested: 1972, 1980, 1987

	1972				1980				1987		
Offense	Female[a]	Offense	Male[b]	Offense	Female[a]	Offense	Male[b]	Offense	Female[a]	Offense	Male[b]
Larceny-Theft	19.1	Drunkenness	21.6	Larceny-Theft	21.2	Drunk Driving	14.5	Larceny-Theft	20.4	Drunk Driving	14.0
Drunkenness	9.5	Drunk Driving	9.5	Drunk Driving	8.0	Drunkenness	11.9	Drunk Driving	8.6	Larceny-Theft	9.7
Disorderly Conduct	8.0	Disorderly Conduct	8.4	Disorderly Conduct	7.3	Larceny-Theft	9.8	Fraud	6.4	Drug-Abuse Violations	7.8
Narcotic Drug Laws	6.3	Larceny-Theft	8.0	Fraud	7.1	Disorderly Conduct	7.5	Drug-Abuse Violations	6.3	Drunkenness	7.2
Other Assaults	4.0	Narcotic Drug Laws	6.1	Drunkenness	5.2	Drug Abuse Violations	5.6	Disorderly Conduct	5.8	Other Assaults	6.4
Drunk Driving	3.9	Burglary	5.0	Drug-Abuse Violations	4.7	Aggravated Assault	5.5	Other Assaults	5.3	Disorderly Conduct	5.5

Table 7.7 *continued*

Rank Order of Offenses for Which Females and Males Are Most Likely to Be Arrested: 1972, 1980, 1987

	1972			1980				1987			
Offense	Female[a]	Offense	Male[b]	Offense	Female[a]	Offense	Male[b]	Offense	Female[a]	Offense	Male[b]
Prostitution	3.1	Other Assaults	4.5	Liquor Laws	4.2	Other Assaults	4.8	Liquor Laws	4.7	Liquor Laws	4.7
Embezzlement and Fraud	2.9	Liquor Laws	3.0	Other Assaults	4.1	Liquor Laws	4.4	Drunkenness	3.4	Burglary	3.9
Liquor Laws	2.8	Aggravated Assault	2.3	Prostitution and Vice	3.9	Aggravated Assault	2.8	Prostitution and Vice	3.4	Aggravated Assault	2.9
Aggravated Assault	2.0	Vandalism	2.0	Aggravated Assault	2.1	Vandalism	2.6	Aggravated Assault	2.1	Vandalism	2.3

Source: Uniform Crime Reports (Washington, D.C.: F.B.I., U.S. Department of Justice, 1963–87). Total Arrests, Distribution by Sex.

[a] Percent arrested out of all female arrests.
[b] Percent arrested out of all male arrests.

Table 7.8

New York: Percentage of Prosecutions in Upper and Lower Courts Resulting in Conviction by Type of Offense and Sex: 1982–87

Offense		1982	1983	1984	1985	1986	1987
Homicide	Female	61.7	67.0	59.9	69.2	60.0	50.0
	Male	67.8	69.5	70.4	70.7	65.7	55.0
Robbery	Female	58.2	60.0	58.2	53.8	53.7	51.1
	Male	63.6	67.3	65.8	63.2	62.3	57.2
Burglary	Female	61.9	61.8	62.0	57.5	59.4	60.3
	Male	72.4	73.5	72.7	71.7	71.3	69.6
Assault	Female	44.8	44.1	44.7	41.8	37.5	35.4
	Male	50.3	51.0	50.4	50.3	46.1	43.9
Larceny	Female	65.7	65.0	62.8	62.8	62.6	61.5
	Male	69.9	70.1	69.6	69.9	68.1	67.6
Drug-Law Violation	Female	63.1	65.4	67.6	69.7	69.3	73.3
	Male	70.1	71.2	72.1	73.4	72.8	74.5

Source: New York State Division of Criminal Justice Services, unpublished data.

five arrests for larceny involved a woman; since 1973, the proportion has been approximately one out of three. And contrary to impressions conveyed by the mass media, the proportion of female arrests for violent crimes has hardly changed over the past two and a half decades, as evidenced by stable female arrest rates for homicide and aggravated assault.

A more detailed examination of the female homicide rates reveals that between 1976 and 1987, 65.5 percent of all victims of female homicides were persons with whom the women had intimate ties (for example, spouses, lovers, or exes, children, or other family members), compared to 22.1 percent for the male offenders. And among those "intimate" victims, spouses, ex-spouses, lovers, and children accounted for 48.9 percent, compared to 11.8 percent for males. Only 6.2 percent of all felony murders and 4 percent of all robbery murders were committed by women during the same time span.[2] These data suggest that while women's motivations for committing property offenses are comparable to those of men, they commit acts of violence for different reasons. Women are much less likely to kill in the act of committing another offense; rather, they kill for personal and private reasons. In many instances, their victims are their former abusers. This statistic may change, however, as women gain greater economic independence and autonomy—they will be victims less frequently and will be

Table 7.9

**Pennsylvania: Percentage of Prosecutions Resulting in Convictions by
Type of Offense and Sex: 1981–86**

	1981	1982	1983	1984	1985	1986
Murder						
Female	59.2	71.1	70.3	75.5	72.6	67.2
Male	65.9	76.5	78.3	78.4	77.9	72.5
Robbery						
Female	37.7	48.8	58.5	47.3	30.4	36.5
Male	57.4	63.6	65.5	66.3	48.7	49.1
Burglary						
Female	37.2	54.6	61.8	55.6	45.7	43.3
Male	56.4	69.4	72.6	73.3	67.7	65.8
Aggravated Assault						
Female	26.4	35.2	38.1	33.6	26.4	25.2
Male	30.4	43.2	45.4	46.3	36.4	34.4
Other Assault						
Female	21.1	40.8	39.4	44.8	45.7	42.5
Male	28.1	53.9	56.2	57.0	57.8	55.9
Theft						
Female	38.0	71.8	68.4	66.2	63.5	62.1
Male	43.3	59.5	61.5	60.9	63.1	61.5
Forgery						
Female	45.0	63.4	60.2	58.0	58.0	61.4
Male	52.3	65.9	76.0	70.0	65.2	68.0
Fraud						
Female	32.0	43.8	52.7	49.9	60.4	56.9
Male	31.3	47.3	57.9	60.0	57.2	60.7
Drug Law Violations						
Female	40.7	49.6	57.1	60.5	58.7	59.1
Male	44.3	46.8	57.1	59.9	59.2	57.6

Source: Pennsylvania Commission on Crime and Delinquency, unpublished data.

more able to walk away from abusive relationships before they reach the desperation stage that eventually results in the death of the abuser.

Further probing of female arrest rates in the Type II offenses reveals that the offenses showing the greatest increases are embezzlement, fraud, and forgery—there are no other offenses, except prostitution, in which women are so highly represented. Should the rate of change continue, female arrest rates for fraud, embezzlement, and forgery will be commensurate with women's representation in society—in other words, roughly equal to male arrest rates for the same offenses—in the next one or two decades.

Table 7.10

**Females As a Percentage of All Sentenced Prisoners by
Type of Institution: 1971–87**

Date	Number of Sentenced Prisoners in All Institutions	Percent Female	Percent Female in Federal Institutions	Percent Female in State Institutions
1971	198,061	3.2	3.7	4.7
1972	196,183	3.2	3.7	3.1
1973	204,349	3.3	4.1	3.1
1974	229,721	3.5	4.4	3.2
1975	253,816	3.8	4.6	3.4
1976	262,833	3.8	5.4	3.8
1977	300,024	4.1	5.9	3.7
1978	306,602	4.2	6.2	3.9
1979	314,006	4.2	5.9	3.9
1980	328,695	4.1	5.8	4.0
1981	368,772	4.2	5.6	3.9
1982	414,362	4.3	5.5	4.2
1983	437,238	4.4	5.5	4.3
1984	462,442	4.5	5.8	4.4
1985	503,601	4.6	6.0	4.5
1986	546,659	4.9	6.4	4.7
1987	581,609	5.0	6.3	4.8

Source: U.S. Department of Justice, *Prisoners in State and Federal Institutions* (Washington, D.C.: Bureau of Justice Statistics, annual).

Note: Figures include all inmates sentenced for more than one year.

Judicial Data

In 1975, I reported the reactions of twenty-three criminal court judges interviewed in the Midwest and commented:

> Most of the judges treat women more leniently than they do men. They are more inclined to recommend probation rather than imprisonment, and if they sentence a woman, it is usually for a shorter time than if the crime had been committed by a man.[3]

Based on additional interviews conducted in 1989, I am still inclined to believe that judges treat women more gently than they do men, mostly at the sentencing stage.[4] There is some evidence to suggest that they are also more inclined to be lenient at the determination of guilt stage. Many trial court judges

Table 7.11

Adult Inmate Population by Security Level and Sex: June 30, 1988

	Federal Prisons		State Prisons	
	Men	Women	Men	Women
Maximum security				
Number	600	10	98,364	2,173
Percent	1.5	0.4	19.4	9.3
Close security				
Number	9,712	233	48,213	1,565
Percent	24.0	8.4	9.5	6.7
Medium security				
Number	11,012	698	195,178	11,117
Percent	27.2	25.1	38.5	47.4
Minimum security				
Number	14,213	1,613	131,741	7,013
Percent	35.1	58.0	26.0	29.9
Trusty				
Number	0	0	10,263	524
Percent	0.0	0.0	2.0	2.2
Other				
Number	4,994	228	22,906	1,049
Percent	12.3	8.2	4.5	4.5
Total				
Number	40,531	2,782	506,665	23,441
Percent	100.0	100.0	100.0	100.0

Source: American Correctional Association, 1989 *Directory* (Laurel, Md.), p. xxv.

believe today, as they did twenty years ago, that incarceration is far more degrading for a woman than for a man.

The federal judicial statistics and those available from the states of California, Pennsylvania, and New York reveal a pattern that is consistent with the recent arrest data, namely, that there has been a 6 percent increase in the number of women who have been charged and convicted in federal courts, from 10.8 in 1979 to 17.2 in 1987. Twenty percent of the fraud, 49 percent of the embezzlement, 24 percent of the larceny, and 29 percent of the forgery convictions were of women in 1987. In the state courts, women accounted for 23 percent of the larceny convictions in California, 26 percent in New York, and 24 percent in Pennsylvania. In each of those states, women were convicted for less than 10 percent of all Type I offenses in 1987.

Table 7.12

California: Persons Convicted in Superior Courts and Sentenced to Prison by Type of Offense and Sex: 1982–87

	Number Convicted	Percent Sentenced to Prison	Number Convicted	Percent Sentenced to Prison	Number Convicted	Percent Sentenced to Prison	Number Convicted	Percent Sentenced to Prison	Number Convicted	Percent Sentenced to Prison	Number Convicted	Percent Sentenced to Prison
Homicide[a]												
Female	97	71.1	87	64.4	86	67.4	101	75.2	100	75.0	100	73.0
Male	1,035	83.2	858	86.7	854	88.8	833	89.9	966	92.3	927	92.3
Robbery												
Female	241	41.1	254	44.5	216	45.8	231	51.9	272	52.2	262	55.7
Male	4,447	64.4	4,135	70.7	3,820	69.9	4,589	70.4	4,451	69.8	4,150	71.3
Burglary												
Female	397	29.5	428	32.2	543	35.7	613	37.8	651	37.5	658	39.7
Male	9,641	41.2	9,181	46.0	9,213	47.5	9,900	49.4	9,963	50.2	9,350	50.7
Assault												
Female	329	17.6	314	18.8	358	21.2	356	19.7	408	14.0	354	22.6
Male	3,750	29.5	3,475	33.3	3,635	34.6	4,071	36.2	4,342	37.5	4,013	38.9
Theft												
Female	1,635	9.8	1,879	13.6	2,200	12.7	2,622	14.8	2,426	19.8	2,206	18.4
Male	6,313	22.3	6,394	25.7	6,638	27.7	7,418	29.4	7,366	31.1	7,270	32.0

Table 7.12 continued

California: Persons Convicted in Superior Courts and Sentenced to Prison by Type of Offense and Sex: 1982–87

	Number Convicted	Percent Sentenced to Prison	Number Convicted	Percent Sentenced to Prison	Number Convicted	Percent Sentenced to Prison	Number Convicted	Percent Sentenced to Prison	Number Convicted	Percent Sentenced to Prison	Number Convicted	Percent Sentenced to Prison
Drug–Law Violations												
Female	1,132	7.6	1,417	10.5	1,675	11.2	2,392	10.0	3,115	13.2	3,883	12.5
Male	7,322	14.6	9,074	16.4	11,224	17.2	17,371	17.5	22,995	21.3	26,702	23.3
Total												
Female	3,831	15.4	4,379	17.6	5,078	17.6	6,315	17.8	6,972	20.2	7,463	19.5
Male	32,508	34.7	33,117	36.8	35,384	36.3	44,182	35.2	50,083	35.6	52,412	35.6

Source: California Department of Justice, Division of Law Enforcement, Bureau of Criminal Statistics, unpublished data.

[a] "Percent Sentenced to Prison" includes persons sentenced to death.

Table 7.13

New York: Persons Convicted in Upper Courts and Sentenced to Prison by Type of Offense and Sex: 1982–87

	1982		1983		1984		1985		1986		1987	
	Number Convicted	Percent Sentenced to Prison	Number Convicted	Percent Sentenced to Prison	Number Convicted	Percent Sentenced to Prison	Number Convicted	Percent Sentenced to Prison	Number Convicted	Percent Sentenced to Prison	Number Convicted	Percent Sentenced to Prison
Homicide												
Female	121	52.9	122	63.9	96	59.4	124	66.1	126	62.7	54	48.1
Male	1,716	78.7	1,650	80.6	1,544	79.5	1,430	78.7	1,387	81.5	778	76.9
Robbery												
Female	279	31.5	349	35.8	340	29.7	311	30.9	415	41.7	417	36.5
Male	6,392	60.5	8,149	60.2	7,378	58.9	6,768	58.8	7,497	59.7	6,900	62.3
Burglary												
Female	208	12.0	212	15.6	217	24.4	174	17.2	205	17.1	203	27.6
Male	6,124	34.7	6,928	39.4	6,009	40.0	5,961	39.7	6,220	42.7	5,854	43.7
Assault												
Female	155	16.8	139	20.1	158	17.7	192	19.3	176	18.2	127	18.1
Male	1,522	30.4	1,522	30.1	1,795	29.8	1,833	31.9	1,740	34.1	1,265	31.6

Table 7.13 continued

New York: Persons Convicted in Upper Courts and Sentenced to Prison by Type of Offense and Sex: 1982–87

	1982		1983		1984		1985		1986		1987	
	Number Convicted	Percent Sentenced to Prison	Number Convicted	Percent Sentenced to Prison	Number Convicted	Percent Sentenced to Prison	Number Convicted	Percent Sentenced to Prison	Number Convicted	Percent Sentenced to Prison	Number Convicted	Percent Sentenced to Prison
Larceny												
Female	437	11.4	600	9.5	545	14.7	567	16.6	619	13.1	453	12.1
Male	2,060	23.3	2,310	23.6	2,500	26.8	2,995	27.1	3,147	30.2	2,314	30.8
Drug–Law Violations												
Female	503	16.9	624	19.6	686	19.7	966	21.3	1,440	24.1	1,787	20.6
Male	4,651	37.6	4,823	38.0	5,655	42.7	6,760	41.7	11,219	43.0	12,026	38.1
Total												
Female	1,703	19.8	2,046	21.7	2,042	22.2	2,334	23.4	2,981	25.1	3,041	22.4
Male	22,465	44.7	25,382	46.5	24,881	46.6	25,747	45.4	31,210	46.9	29,137	45.2

Source: New York State Division of Criminal Justice Services, Bureau of Statistical Services, unpublished data.

The data in Tables 7.8 and 7.9 compare the percentages of prosecutions of men and women in New York (1982–87) and Pennsylvania (1981–86) that resulted in convictions for specific offenses. They show that for every type of offense in every year, a slightly but consistently higher percentage of men than women who faced prosecution were eventually convicted. These data support the impressions gained from interviews with judges who maintain that "justice" is not quite blind even at the determination of guilt stage. But in the absence of additional pertinent information, such as prior criminal record, circumstances surrounding the crime, and type of attorney, we cannot conclude that the higher conviction rates for men are solely a function of the judges' bias in favor of women.

Prison Data

In 1987, about 22 out of 100 people arrested for a serious crime were women. In the same year, approximately 10 out of 100 people convicted of a serious crime was a woman, but only about five out of every 100 people sentenced to a federal or state prison was a woman. The big differences in conviction rates between men and women are probably a function of prior criminal record, circumstances surrounding the crime, and judges' bias in favor of women. Many women arrive in the courtroom on their day of sentencing with young children (presumably theirs), whose presence may well influence the judge.

Table 7.10 shows the percentage of women compared to men who were sentenced to federal and state institutions for selected years from 1971 to 1987. As of December 1987, of the approximately 580,000 inmates in state and federal prisons, 29,000 were women. For the sixteen-year period shown, the percentage of women in federal prisons has ranged from 3.7 to 6.3; in state prisons, where the bulk of inmates have been housed, the percentage has ranged from 3.1 to 4.8. But the Uniform Crime Reports show that in 1970, 16.9 percent of all arrests for Type I offenses were women, and in 1987, 21.6 percent of all arrests for serious offenses were women. These data indicate that the rate of commitment to prison has not kept pace with the rate of female arrests: the percentage of women arrested for serious offenses has increased, but the rate at which they have been sentenced to state prisons has remained relatively stable.

Table 7.11 shows the types of institutions to which men and women have been committed at the federal and state levels. Three times as many men as women have been committed to maximum and closed institutions at the federal level and twice as many at the state level. In 1988, 15 percent of the women assigned to maximum security prisons were on death row. The percentage of women on death row ranged from 8 in 1981 to a high of 17 in 1987.[5]

By and large, however, the types of prisons to which men and women are sent reflect the types of offense for which they were committed. As the data in Tables

7.12 through 7.14 show, the absolute number of women sentenced to prison for homicide has usually been less than 125 per year in three of the most populous states—California, New York, and Pennsylvania. For every year, the data across all three states show that for each type of offense for which they have been found guilty, men have been more likely than women to be sentenced to prison.

Note also that within each state, the ordering of the types of crime for which defendants are most likely to receive a prison sentence does not differ noticeably between men and women, with homicide and robbery as the two most likely offenses. In Pennsylvania and California, those are followed by burglary; in New York, drug violation is the third most frequent offense for which men and women are likely to be sentenced to prison. In California, there is no difference in the rank ordering for all six types of offenses between men and women. The differences in Pennsylvania and New York are slight and cover offenses involving assault, burglary, theft, fraud, and drugs.

Table 7.15 compares the offenses for which men and women were sentenced to all state prisons in 1979 and 1986. In 1986, women represented a smaller percentage of the violent offenders than they did in 1979, 40.7 percent as opposed to 49.0 percent. For the violent offenses, murder and robbery are most frequently cited for both men and women. Among the property offenses, women are more likely to be committed for fraud and theft than they are for burglary, whereas men are most likely to be committed for burglary.

Table 7.16 shows the age and education of inmates of federal and state correctional institutions from 1960 to 1980 as recorded in the decennial U.S. Census report. Most notable is the increased educational levels of all inmates under custody. By 1980, approximately 27 percent of all male inmates and 22 percent of all females in federal institutions had attended college. State inmates show a similar pattern: In 1960, 4 percent of the males and 5 percent of the females had some college education; these percentages jumped to 18 percent for the men and 19 percent for the women in 1980. About one-third of all federal and state inmates had a high school education by 1980. In 1960, over 50 percent of the men and women had only an elementary school education. In 1980, that percentage dropped to 22 percent for the men and 20 percent for the women.

The age distribution of inmates has not changed much over the years, except for a shift from a smaller percentage of male and female inmates in the 30 to 39 age range and a larger percentage in the 20 to 24 age range.

Table 7.17 examines the occupational backgrounds of men and women under federal and state custody. We see that the number of incarcerated women who reported never having worked increased over the years. But with the high percentage of "absence of information" about work histories, it is difficult to make too much of that trend. We also see that among women for whom there are occupational data, the number reporting a white-collar occupation, especially in the professional, technical, and administration areas, increased, while the percentage reporting a blue-collar occupation declined. Although this trend seems

Table 7.14

Pennsylvania: Persons Convicted in All Courts and Sentenced to Incarceration by Type of Offense and Sex: 1981–86

	1981		1982		1983		1984		1985		1986	
	Number Convicted	Percent Incarcerated	Number Convicted	Percent Incarcerated	Number Convicted	Percent Incarcerated	Number Convicted	Percent Incarcerated	Number Convicted	Percent Incarcerated	Number Convicted	Percent Incarcerated
Murder												
Female	56	53.6	54	48.1	64	71.9	74	85.1	45	82.2	45	86.7
Male	428	75.9	469	81.9	499	87.6	522	85.1	398	89.7	371	90.0
Robbery												
Female	60	43.3	105	52.4	120	56.7	98	65.3	66	68.2	85	68.2
Male	1,941	74.4	2,456	73.7	2,173	80.1	2,460	83.6	1,608	84.6	1,648	87.0
Burglary												
Female	89	34.8	172	42.4	131	46.6	129	47.3	110	40.0	84	52.4
Male	3,058	62.2	4,486	60.3	4,394	68.9	4,207	73.5	3,212	77.0	2,945	78.1
Aggravated Assault												
Female	184	23.4	209	22.0	196	33.7	181	39.2	155	38.1	149	37.6
Male	1,609	40.5	1,725	43.4	1,494	56.0	1,552	60.4	1,231	61.3	1,224	67.3
Other Assault												
Female	260	15.4	304	21.1	329	21.0	358	24.9	335	26.3	314	23.2
Male	2,682	29.0	3,077	32.1	3,593	36.7	3,576	38.7	3,227	39.8	3,377	39.7

Table 7.14 continued

Pennsylvania: Persons Convicted in All Courts and Sentenced to Incarceration by Type of Offense and Sex: 1981–86

	1981		1982		1983		1984		1985		1986	
	Number Convicted	Percent Incarcerated	Number Convicted	Percent Incarcerated	Number Convicted	Percent Incarcerated	Number Convicted	Percent Incarcerated	Number Convicted	Percent Incarcerated	Number Convicted	Percent Incarcerated
Theft												
Female	539	18.7	2,947	11.7	2,195	20.0	2,048	21.5	1,822	25.9	1,673	27.2
Male	4,832	35.4	7,243	32.5	6,813	42.5	6,441	44.2	5,599	45.4	5,269	44.5
Forgery												
Female	238	27.7	229	32.8	206	35.4	246	41.1	233	44.6	281	38.1
Male	652	50.9	587	49.9	691	59.8	694	65.4	617	66.1	690	64.5
Fraud												
Female	388	19.8	225	20.0	289	28.4	295	33.6	411	31.1	393	26.2
Male	935	31.3	676	35.5	1,018	38.1	1,123	42.9	1,013	41.9	1,164	41.9
Drug–Law Violations												
Female	455	17.4	517	22.2	649	24.8	669	24.8	619	31.2	634	33.1
Male	3,108	28.3	3,121	31.3	3,606	37.5	3,791	38.6	3,686	40.7	4,133	46.6
Total												
Female	2,269	21.7	4,762	17.7	4,179	25.5	4,098	28.2	3,796	35.7	3,658	31.1
Male	19,245	43.2	23,840	44.0	20,675	44.5	24,366	54.0	20,591	53.9	20,821	53.6

Source: Pennsylvania Commission on Crime and Delinquency, unpublished data.

Table 7.15

Offense Distribution of State Prison Inmates by Sex: 1979 and 1986

	Percent of Prison Inmates(a)			
	1979		1986	
	Male	Female	Male	Female
Violent offenses				
Murder	12.2	15.5	11.2	13.0
Negligent manslaughter	3.8	9.8	3.0	6.8
Kidnapping	2.2	1.4	1.7	0.9
Rape	4.5	0.4	4.4	0.2
Other sexual assault	2.0	0.3	4.7	0.9
Robbery	25.6	13.6	21.3	10.6
Assault	7.7	7.6	8.1	7.1
Other violent offenses	0.3	0.4	0.8	1.2
TOTAL	53.3	49.0	55.2	40.7
Property offenses				
Burglary	18.6	5.3	17.0	5.9
Larceny-theft	4.5	11.2	5.6	14.7
Motor vehicle theft	1.5	0.5	1.4	0.5
Arson	0.6	1.2	0.7	1.2
Fraud	3.8	17.3	3.2	17.0
Stolen property	1.3	0.9	2.0	1.6
Other property offenses	0.8	0.4	0.5	0.4
TOTAL	31.2	36.8	30.4	41.3
Drug offenses				
Possession	1.5	2.7	2.9	4.0
Trafficking	4.3	7.1	5.3	7.3
Other drug offenses	0.4	0.7	0.2	0.7
TOTAL	6.2	10.5	8.4	12.0

Source: Adapted from Bureau of Justice Statistics, *Profile of State Prison Inmates* (Washington, D.C.: U.S. Department of Justice, 1986).

[a] Figures do not add up to 100 percent because two offense categories ("Public order offenses" and "Other offenses") were excluded from the table.

Table 7.16

Age and Education of Inmates in Federal and State Correctional Institutions: 1960, 1970, 1980

	1960 Federal		1960 State		1970 Federal		1970 State		1980 Federal		1980 State	
	Male	Female	Male	Female	Male	Female	Male	Female	Male	Female	Male	Female
					(percent)							
Age (years)												
<15	0.0	0.6	0.1	0.1	0.0	0.6	0.3	0.5	0.3	0.3	0.3	0.4
15–19	8.0	7.8	8.6	10.1	3.7	3.8	8.4	11.6	7.6	5.1	7.9	6.1
20–24	20.7	16.0	19.6	17.0	25.4	27.7	26.2	22.8	22.8	21.4	29.9	23.6
25–29	18.5	20.5	18.2	17.7	19.8	23.5	20.3	18.5	22.4	17.4	24.9	25.9
30–39	31.7	31.6	28.5	32.4	27.2	24.0	24.1	24.8	28.3	25.0	24.7	25.8
40–49	13.5	17.1	15.0	14.2	15.3	17.2	13.4	15.4	11.3	9.0	7.9	9.2
50–64	6.9	6.3	8.7	7.5	7.6	3.3	6.2	4.5	6.3	4.6	3.9	5.7
65+	0.7	0.0	1.4	0.9	1.0	0.0	1.0	1.9	1.0	17.2	0.5	3.3
Education (years)												
Elementary												
0–4	10.4	10.1	16.6	14.2	6.3	6.4	7.9	5.8	3.7	4.6	3.9	4.8
5–8	39.4	46.7	41.8	39.8	30.9	24.9	33.8	29.6	14.5	18.7	17.7	15.1
High school												
1–3	26.8	25.0	27.2	28.9	33.9	38.6	34.3	37.4	22.2	25.6	30.1	29.1
4	14.8	13.8	10.6	12.3	20.3	21.8	18.6	20.1	32.6	29.1	29.9	31.8
College												
1–3	7.0	3.3	3.1	3.8	6.1	6.0	4.6	5.6	18.3	14.6	15.1	15.5
4+	1.7	1.2	0.8	1.0	2.4	2.3	0.8	1.5	8.7	7.3	3.3	3.7

Sources: U.S. Bureau of the Census, 1960 Decennial Census, *Characteristics of Persons under Custody in Correctional Institutions*, tables 4 and 25; 1970 Decennial Census, *Persons in Institutions and Other Group Quarters*, tables 3 and 24; 1980 Decennial Census, *Persons in Institutional and Other Group Quarters*, table 14.

Table 7.17

Occupational Status of Inmates in Federal and State Correctional Institutions: 1960, 1970, 1980[a]

	1960				1970				1980			
	Federal		State		Federal		State		Federal		State	
	Male	Female	Male	Female	Male	Female	Male	Female	Male	Female	Male	Female
					(percent)							
Total with Occupation[a,b,c]	75.0	56.5	61.4	44.8	72.1	57.3	67.6	65.8	72.5	54.8	66.2	61.1
Never Worked	4.5	11.5	3.9	12.9	7.1	9.0	7.3	18.6	8.5	21.9	11.8	20.1
No Occupational Information[d]	20.6	31.9	34.7	42.3	20.8	33.6	25.0	15.6	19.0	23.3	22.0	18.8
Occupation Type												
White collar:												
Professional, technical, or administrative	9.1	6.0	3.8	4.4	12.8	17.9	5.8	5.3	9.2	13.2	6.2	11.4
Clerical	4.8	14.8	2.7	10.0	4.7	21.9	5.2	18.5	4.9	7.1	3.8	8.8
Sales	4.8	8.1	2.3	2.9	6.4	5.4	2.5	4.1	5.6	24.1	4.4	18.0
TOTAL	18.7	28.9	8.8	17.3	24.0	45.2	13.4	27.9	19.7	44.4	14.4	38.2
Blue Collar:												
Craft	18.7	3.8	12.9	0.4	18.9	0.0	21.3	2.9	20.6	6.5	22.8	3.7
Operatives/laborers[e]	35.1	20.0	39.3	18.6	41.5	14.0	48.5	24.2	37.6	15.3	40.5	21.6
Service[f]	9.5	36.0	8.3	49.7	10.4	39.6	12.7	41.7	14.7	28.2	15.1	32.9

Table 7.17 continued

Occupational Status of Inmates in Federal and State Correctional Institutions: 1960, 1970, 1980[a]

	1960				1970				1980			
	Federal		State		Federal		State		Federal		State	
	Male	Female	Male	Female	Male	Female	Male	Female	Male	Female	Male	Female
					(percent)							
Blue Collar (continued): Farming, forestry, or fishing[g]	6.2	2.5	6.5	2.6	5.2	1.2	4.1	3.3	7.3	5.5	7.3	3.6
TOTAL	69.5	62.3	67.0	71.3	76.0	54.8	86.6	72.1	80.2	55.5	85.7	61.8
No Occupation Reported	11.9	8.8	24.2	11.4	—	—	—	—	—	—	—	—

Sources: U.S. Bureau of the Census, 1960 Decennial Census, *Characteristics of Persons under Custody in Correctional Institutions*, table 25; 1970 Decennial Census, *Persons in Institutions and Other Group Quarters*, table 24; 1980 Decennial Census, *Persons in Institutional and Other Group Quarters*, table 14.

[a] Figures are not strictly comparable across years due to changes in occupational categorizations.
[b] For 1960 and 1970 totals include inmates fourteen years and older, but for 1980 totals include inmates sixteen years and older.
[c] For 1960 figures indicate the number of inmates who reported last working in 1950 or later; for 1970, 1960, or later; and for 1980, 1975, or later.
[d] Included in this category are inmates who last worked in 1959 or earlier and those who did not report the last year that they worked.
[e] Includes all nonfarm laborers and operatives. For 1980 figures include inmates who had been employed in the armed services.
[f] Includes private household workers.
[g] Includes all farm-related occupations, including farm owners and managers as well as laborers.

reversed for the men, again we cannot draw final conclusions based on these percentages because of the number not reporting their occupational category.

Inside Women's Prisons

The American prison system has been a target of the equal rights movement, because, by and large, it continues to provide separate facilities for men and women. Separate prisons were established for women in the 1880s to give them the same benefit of rehabilitation as was being sought for young men and boys in new reformatories.

Advocates of the Equal Rights Amendment who directed their interests at the female offender claimed that the same reasoning that was persuasive to the Supreme Court in *Brown v. the Board of Education* (that is, segregation denies to blacks equal opportunities and equality in their educational experiences) should apply to women and the maintenance of a separate prison system. Schools that segregate by race and prisons that segregate by sex are basically discriminatory. The authors of a note in the May 1973 *Yale Law Journal* claimed that, although the Supreme Court had as yet not made the same determination concerning segregation on the basis of sex that it made for segregation on the basis of color (separate, by its nature, cannot be equal), the passage of the ERA would compel such a result.[6]

The fact that women prisoners constitute only 5 percent of all inmates continues to influence the conditions of their incarceration in many important ways. Indeed, the effect begins from the moment a woman is sentenced. Because there are fewer female institutions, she is likely to be sent much farther from her community than is her male counterpart. Few states operate more than one female penal institution. Women inmates thus experience greater difficulty in keeping track of their families and their possessions. A letter from the superintendent at the California Institution for Women characterized the situation as follows:

> Almost all the women who come to prison have husbands and children. If a man goes to prison, the wife stays home and he usually has his family to return to and the household is there when he gets out. But women generally don't have family support from the outside. Very few men are going to sit around and take care of the children and be there when she gets back. So—to send a woman to prison means you are virtually going to disrupt her family. She knows that when she gets out she won't have a husband waiting for her. It really will mean starting her life over again.

The size of the female prison population also affects the heterogeneity of the populations within women's prisons. Women's prisons contain a more heterogeneous population than do prisons for men. They include a wider range of ages than do the male prisons, and there is less differentiation by types of offenders.

All but five states have more than one institution for male offenders, and the decision about which type of institution to commit an offender to is based on age and type of offense.

But not all of the differences between men's and women's institutions result in more negative treatment for women. The stereotypes of women in general provide some advantages to the female inmates. As Burkhart pointed out:

> Women just weren't considered as dangerous or as violent as men. So— rather than the mass penitentiary housing used for men—women's prisons were designed as a domestic model with each woman having a "room" of her own. Often no more than stretches of open fields or wire fences separate women prisoners and the "free world"—armed guards are rarely visible. Just like women outside, a woman prisoner would be confined to "the home."
>
> "The home" planned for women was a cottage that was built to house 20 to 30 women—who would cook their own food in a "cottage kitchen." The cottages in most states were built to contain a living room, a dining room, and 1 or 2 reading rooms.[7]

Physically, then, female institutions are usually more attractive and more pleasant than the security-oriented institutions for men. They tend to be located in more pastoral settings, and they are not as likely to have the gun towers, the concrete walls, and the barbed wire that so often characterize the male institutions. Women inmates usually have more privacy than men and tend to have single rooms. They may be allowed to wear street clothes rather than prison uniforms and decorate their rooms with bedspreads and curtains provided by the prison. Toilet and shower facilities also reflect a greater concern for women's privacy. Because women prisoners are perceived as less dangerous and less escape-prone than men, most states also allow them more trips outside the prison than they do their male counterparts. Women's prisons now offer academic classes, as well as a broad range of job training that helps female inmates find work once they are released from prison. Some prisons also have industries that offer women an opportunity to earn money while doing time.

Considering the statistics, which estimate that between 56 percent and 75 percent of incarcerated women have young children, however, the number of institutions accommodating the special needs of mothers with children are disproportionately low.[8] Based on a 1989 survey of women's prisons I conducted with a colleague, only 35 percent (thirteen) of the institutions have either "rooms with cribs, high chairs, or other 'baby equipment' " or "rooms in which to talk privately, read, listen to music with older children," and only 50 percent (nineteen) of the responding institutions report having "rooms with toys and other facilities for children up to six years of age." Even fewer, 30 percent (eleven), report having "places to prepare food for children."[9]

We also found a great disparity among the institutions in the amount of time allowed for mother–child visitations. Seven of the thirty-seven responding institutions allowed visitations seven days a week. Eleven of the facilities permitted visitations twice a month, and another two allowed visitations only once a month.

At least half (nineteen) of the institutions reported that they had a furlough program whereby mothers could visit their children at home or in halfway houses. Most often, however, these programs had stringent eligibility requirements and were available only to offenders on work release, those convicted of relatively minor crimes, or those within sight of their release dates.

Child visitation is even more problematic in the federal system than it is in the state system, because there are only twelve facilities to serve the population of federal female offenders. While there may be only one facility within a state that houses female offenders, women adjudicated under the federal system may be housed in any federal facility throughout the country and are more likely to be incarcerated outside their home states. Indeed, a large majority of the women incarcerated in the federal system reside in just two institutions, Alderson, West Virginia, and Lexington, Kentucky. This situation has obvious negative implications for the continuity of family life, for both men and women.

All of the federal facilities that house women have furlough programs for eligible mothers, and our surveys suggest that they are somewhat more liberal than those offered at the state level. In at least two of the facilities, an inmate may become eligible within two years of release, and at least one other allows eligibility within one year of release.

Concluding Remarks

Looking back over data compiled during the past twenty-five years, we see a higher percentage of women than ever before—including those who are married and have preschool children—working full time. Not only are more women working outside their homes, but they are occupying positions in the labor force that involve more training, responsibility, and authority than they had in the past. Along with women's greater participation in the labor force, promotion to higher-status positions, and increased representation in the professions, there is a higher percentage of female-headed households in which women are the caretakers of young children.

The crime rates for women, while not dramatic, also indicate increases over time for property and white-collar offenses. The judicial statistics from the states of California, Pennsylvania, and New York confirm this pattern of an increase in the percentage of women charged with and convicted of property crimes.

Women account for about 5 percent of the prison population, and they are more likely than men to be assigned to medium- and minimum-security institutions at both the federal and state levels. A major improvement has occurred over the past fifteen years in the facilities that are available for contacts and visits with female inmates' children. In addition, the vast discrepancies between women's and men's opportunities for vocational training and jobs for pay have diminished.

Looking ahead to the next twenty years, I do not see an abatement in the amount of property offenses women are likely to commit. As long as women continue to participate in the labor force and as long as they continue to move into more responsible positions, there is the likelihood that they will continue to commit the property offenses for which their jobs provide the opportunity and the skills. But violent crimes, I believe, will show a different pattern. To the extent that women are less likely to perceive themselves as victims or to be victimized by men, the likelihood of their committing violent acts will decline. Women who find themselves the victims of male aggression and cruelty will recognize that they have more options available than to bear such abuse and hope it will not get worse, or to kill or disable the perpetrator. Violent offenses by women are also likely to decline as they are more able to support themselves physically and emotionally. The higher levels of education attained by women and their greater participation in the labor force underlie this contention, just as the same demographic trends support the likelihood that women's involvement in property offenses will continue to increase.

Notes

1. Rita J. Simon, *Women and Crime.*
2. Elizabeth Rapaport, "The Death Penalty and Gender Discrimination."
3. Debra Anthony, *Judges' Perceptions of Women Offenders and Their Own Actions toward Women Offenders.*
4. Based on interviews conducted by Angela Musolio and reported in "Judges' Attitudes toward Female Offenders," unpublished manuscript, 1989.
5. American Correctional Association, *1989 Directory of Juvenile and Adult Correctional Departments, Institutions, Agencies, and Paroling Authorities.*
6. Ralph R. Arditi et al., "The Sexual Segregation of American Prisons: Notes."
7. Kathryn W. Burkhart, *Women in Prison*, p. 367.
8. See Clarice Feinman, *Women in the Criminal Justice System*, wherein she cites Glick and Neto as finding 56.2 percent with one or more children; Phyllis Jo Baunach, "Mothering from Behind Prison Walls," as finding 70.4 percent having one or more children; and Brenda McGowen and Karen Blumenthal, *Why Punish the Children: A Study of Children of Women Prisoners*, who wrote that on any given day, 70 percent of the women in prisons and jails are mothers.
9. Rita J. Simon and Jean Landis, *The Crimes Women Commit, the Punishments They Receive.*

References

American Correctional Association. *1989 Directory of Juvenile and Adult Correctional Departments, Institutions, Agencies and Paroling Authorities.* Laurel, Md.: ACA, 1988.
Anthony, Debra. *Judges' Perceptions of Women Offenders and Their Own Actions toward Women Offenders.* Unpublished master's thesis. Urbana-Champaign: University of Illinois, 1973.

Arditi, Ralph R.; Goldberg, F., Jr.; Hartle, M.M.; Peters, J.H.; and Phelps, W.R. "The Sexual Segregation of American Prisons: Notes." *Yale Law Journal* 82 (1973): 1229–73.

Baunach, Phyllis Jo. "Mothering from Behind Prison Walls." Paper presented at annual meeting of the American Society of Criminology, 1979.

Burkhart, Kathryn W. *Women in Prison*. New York: Doubleday, 1973.

Feinman, Clarice. *Women in the Criminal Justice System*. New York: Praeger, 1986.

Glick, Ruth M., and Neto, Virginia. *National Study of Women's Correctional Programs*. Washington, D.C.: U.S. Government Printing Office, 1977.

McGowen, Brenda, and Blumenthal, Karen. *Why Punish the Children: A Study of Children of Women Prisoners*. Hackensack, N.J.: National Commission on Crime and Delinquency, 1978.

Musolino, Angela. "Judges' Attitudes toward Female Offenders." Unpublished manuscript, 1989.

Rapaport, Elizabeth. "The Death Penalty and Gender Discrimination." *Law and Society Review* 25, no. 2 (1991): 366–83.

Simon, Rita J. *Women and Crime*. Lexington, Mass.: Lexington Books, 1975.

Simon, Rita J., and Landis, Jean. *The Crimes Women Commit, the Punishments They Receive*. Lexington, Mass.: Lexington Books, 1991.

Part III

Offenders and Offenses

8

CARL E. POPE

Juvenile Delinquency, Juvenile Justice

Problems associated with youthful misbehavior and indiscretion are not new to society. Historically every culture has faced the continuing problem of socializing children into acceptable patterns of behavior. Although expectations may differ across and within societies based on various ethnic, subcultural, and other traditions, there exists a need to build a foundation for conforming behavior. Unfortunately, as virtually every parent knows and experts tell us, children are not born with nor do they independently acquire the capacity to distinguish right from wrong or to conform their behavior to normative expectations. Rather, young children present a "blank slate," the contours of which must be filled in with appropriate messages and controls. If these messages and inner controls are missing, defective, or incomplete, children are placed at risk in conforming their behavior not only to the wishes of their parents but to the larger society as well.

Parents are initially responsible for the physiological and psychological nurturing of their children. According to many child psychologists, the earlier years are the most formative and set the stage for future lessons derived from peers, schools, churches, communities, and the like. Ideally, parents set the "limits" of acceptable behavior through training, teaching, and being positive role models. Other social institutions then carry on the work of preparing children for their future place in society and instilling in them a sense of moral worth. Problems may occur when parental skills are lacking or social institutions are ineffective in performing their roles.

Under such circumstances young people may not possess the necessary skills to channel their behavior into conventional pastimes and activities. It is true that most young people act out from time to time and behave in unconventional ways, as folklore surrounding the "terrible twos" and the "teenage years" so often recounts. It is also true, however, that most eventually adjust and find a place in mainstream society. Most indiscretions are relatively minor. While some young people are labeled deviant for a while, they usually mature out of it, some sooner than others. Thus, the majority pose no major threat to society and take their rightful place among the conforming.

On the other hand, there are a rather significant number of children and young adults who are not so fortunate. For these, the path to adulthood, aside from often being unpleasant, is one marked by more serious troubles, such as alcohol abuse, drugs, and gang activity, including contact with the juvenile justice system. Thus, their deviance not only transcends conventional standards of behavior but also includes crimes against society. These are the young people who are officially labeled as juvenile delinquents and for whom the juvenile justice system was created. Their acts may include crimes against both person and property— sometimes serious, other times less so.

Given the serious problem of delinquency, the question arises as to what factors are likely to push these people into juvenile crime? How can we account for these behaviors? What separates delinquent youths from those youths who engage in conforming behavior or at least whose transgressions are less severe? What is the extent of the problem, and are certain people differently affected? What, if anything, can be done to reclaim the lives of those who are at risk?

Theoretical Explanations

The question of why young people do or do not engage in delinquent behavior has plagued scientists for decades. Theoretical explanations for delinquent involvement have been derived from biological, psychological, and sociological fields of inquiry, which seek understanding in different aspects of human behavior. In the course of this chapter it would be difficult if not impossible to review all existing theory related to crime and delinquency. Therefore, this discussion is limited to a brief summary of those perspectives that seem most relevant toward understanding delinquency in modern society. Typically, these explanations tend to be sociological in nature, focusing on social processes and institutions. It should be emphasized at the outset that there is no one all-encompassing explanation for delinquent behavior. Rather, each perspective presents a piece of the puzzle that may be applicable in some situations but not in others.

In previous work I have reviewed those theories related to the structure of the family and delinquency.[1] While relying on that previous work, the attempt here is more broadly based, including consideration of the role of other institutions such as peers, schools, and communities and how these can be incorporated into existing theory. To begin the discussion it is useful to group existing theory into three broad categories: structure, process, and reaction.[2] *Structural* theories seek explanations in societal conditions (for example, poverty and unemployment) and their impact on individuals. *Process* theories focus on how individuals learn to deviate, whether through family, friends, or others. Finally, *reaction* theories tend to focus on the systems that define individuals as delinquent and the implications of those definitions. These theoretical orientations and their variations are described in Table 8.1.

Structural Approaches

The origins of a structural approach can be found in the pioneering work of Emile Durkheim. For Durkheim, structural conditions in society had implications for individual behavior.[3] Thus, as societies progressed from simpler to more complex forms of development, the informal rules and mores that guided conforming behavior were no longer effective. A state of anomie ("normlessness") ensued, which produced various individual pathologies such as crime, mental illness, suicide, and other forms of deviance. Later, Robert Merton expanded on Durkheim's notion of anomie to explain deviant behavior among the lower classes. In essence, what Merton argued is that everyone strives to achieve culturally valued success goals that are pervasive in modern capitalist society. The conformist attempts to achieve these goals through legitimate or conventional activities, which may include education, upward job mobility, and the like. The innovator, on the other hand, is blocked in an attempt to succeed through conventional means and thus is pushed into illegitimate channels to achieve success. One likely result of class position, a reflection of structural conditions, is criminal behavior.[4]

Cloward and Ohlin expanded upon Merton's structural approach to include variation in forms of subcultural adaptation. They discussed various forms of subcultural adaptation, based upon access, or lack thereof, to both legitimate and illegitimate opportunity structures. These adaptations could include retreatist behavior (involvement with illicit drugs), conflict (intra-gang and inter-gang fighting), and crimes of opportunity (various forms of property offenses).[5]

Silberman, in turn, used Merton's typology to examine the relationship between poverty and violent crime. According to Silberman, the factors that characterize lower-class life have their origin in the fact that American cultural goals (striving for success) transcend class lines, while the means for achieving them do not. Often, subcultural role models reinforce the idea that one can succeed through participation in the illegal economy. As Silberman notes:

> The fabric and texture in urban slums and ghettos provide an environment in which opportunities for criminal activity are manifold and in which the rewards for engaging in crime appear to be high—higher than the penalties for crime and higher than the rewards for avoiding it.[6]

Thus, Silberman adapts Merton's opportunity-structure theory, linking poverty and crime, to the emergence of a subculture that reinforces criminal and delinquent values.

Other variations on this theme include the work of Miller, Cohen, and Wolfgang and Ferracuti.[7] Miller argued that delinquent behavior resulted from conformity to values ("focal concerns") that were characteristic of a lower-class lifestyle. Coupled with female-based households (most frequently found in pov-

Table 8.1

Summary of Theoretical Perspectives Concerning the Etiology of Delinquency

Structural Approaches	Theoretical Types	Major Proponent	Theme	Emphasis	Policy Implications
Emphasis is upon structural conditions in society (e.g., poverty, unemployment) and their impact upon individuals	Anomie	Durkeim (1933, 1951) (translated writings)	Rapid progression of society and resulting pathology	Division of labor	Buffer individuals from rapid social change/regain consensus and community
		Merton (1938)	Imbalance between cultural goals and avenues for achieving them	Opportunity/inequality in life chances	Increase legitimate opportunities or lower expectations
	Subcultural	Cloward & Ohlin (1960)	Variations in cultural adaptations/gang formation	Reference groups	Provide opportunities and intervention with gang-affiliated youth
		Silberman (1978)	Importance of subcultural role models	Impact of poverty on delinquency	Economic restructuring
		Miller (1958)	Conformity to lower-class values leads to delinquency	Lower-class value structure/female-based households	Impact on value system
		Cohen (1955)	Reaction formation	Middle-class value system in schools leads to gang formation	Emphasis on improving school systems in dealing with lower-class youth
		Wolfgang & Ferracuti (1967)	Subculture of violence	Violence as an expression of lower-class value system and way of life	Impact on lower-class value system (e.g., mentoring/role model programs)

Table 8.1 *continued*

Process Approaches	Theoretical Types	Major Proponent	Theme	Emphasis	Policy Implications
Emphasis on learning both positive and negative behaviors	Social control	Hirschi (1969)	Proper socialization leads to positive bonds to society and conventional activity	Nature of bonds to society (attachment, commitment, involvement, and belief)	Enhance factors that emphasize positive bonds (e.g., families, peers, teachers, etc.)
	Social learning theory	Akers (1985) Bandura (1973) Conger (1976)	Process by which individuals learn conventional or unconventional values	Training, teaching, modeling	Provide favorable definitions and stimuli (e.g., positive role models)
	Biogenic theory	Eysenck (1977)	Various biological factors that impede positive reinforcement	Individual differences (biological) in social learning	Provide social stimulus to overcome biological dysfunction/correct biological deficiencies when possible
Reaction Approaches	**Theoretical Types**	**Major Proponent**	**Theme**	**Emphasis**	**Policy Implications**
Emphasis on system definitions and implications for individuals	Conflict	Turk (1969) Greenberg (1981) Chambliss & Seidman (1971)	Conflict and change	Differential interests and imbalance of power	Restructure structural conditions (e.g., economic differentials)
	Labeling	Gove (1980) Lemert (1951) Becker (1963) Schur (1971) Kitsuse (1962)	Focus on deviance; defining process	Who gets labeled as deviant and consequences of such labels	Reduce negative labeling; examine and restructure systems that generate negative labeling
	Radical Theory	Quinney (1970) Lynch & Groves (1986)	Power imbalance/ differentials in society	Exploitation and inquality in production and administration of law	Macro restructuring of society to emphasize social justice

Source: Adapted from Brown, S.E.; Esbensen, F.; and Geis, G. *Criminology Explaining Crime and Its Context.* Cincinnati, OH: Anderson, 1991.

erty environments), conformity to this value system increased the chances of becoming enmeshed in the justice system. Similarly, Wolfgang and Ferracuti argue that within lower-class enclaves there exists a "subculture of violence" that fosters violent responses, thus increasing the probability of arrest and imprisonment. Finally, Cohen postulated that lower-class youth often have difficulty adapting to a school system that typically espouses middle-class values. In order to obtain self-esteem, these youths engage in what Cohen terms "reaction formation," thus inverting the middle-class value system. In doing so, they tend to engage in nonconforming gang behavior.

The essence of a structural approach is that deleterious conditions in society affect individuals and lead to various forms of cultural adaptations. All of these perspectives are similar in attempting to explain crime and delinquency among the lower classes; they focus on the question of why individuals engage in nonconforming behavior. However, they are deficient in their inability to explain why, given similar circumstances, some individuals engage in law-violating behavior, while others do not—the vast majority of the urban poor are law abiding. Nor do they explain the manner in which nonconforming value systems are transmitted.

Process Approaches

Control theories begin to specify the manner in which values develop and are transmitted. Central to control theory is the process of socialization. Children do not learn by instinct but rather must be socialized into acceptable patterns of behavior. Control theory thus differs from most other perspectives in its starting premise. Rather than asking why young people commit delinquent acts, control theorists ask, "Why don't we all do it?" In other words, what bonds people to society and induces conforming behavior?

Hirschi formulated the basic tenets of control theory from a sociological perspective and tested it on a sample of high school populations. He identified four components that bond individuals to society, thus enhancing conforming behavior: (1) attachment, or the degree to which people are sensitive to the wishes and values of others; (2) commitment, or the degree to which they invest time and effort in conventional activity; (3) involvement, or the degree to which they are engrossed or immersed in conventional values and activities; and (4) belief, or the degree to which they accept the moral validity of conventional rules.

Using a self-report survey, Hirschi found that attachment to parents, school, and conventional friends were important inhibitors of delinquent activity. Youths who were sensitive to the wishes and values of their parents were less likely to be delinquent regardless of class position. Similarly, academic ability, good school performance, and sensitivity to the opinions of one's teachers were strong predictors of lawful behavior, as well as close personal associations with conventional friends.[8] Thus, control theory stresses the importance of parents, peers, and school.[9]

Similarly, social learning theory has traditionally emphasized the importance of social relationships, especially the family, in the process of socialization.[10] For example, whereas control theory focuses on the bond of the child to his or her parents, social learning theory focuses on the process whereby children learn the "rules of the game." A primary place where this learning takes place is within the context of family life. If the messages given by parents and others are positive and if the child receives them, then the child is more apt to develop in socially approved directions. Recent theories regarding family systems emphasize that children also acquire much of their social learning from schools, neighborhoods, day care programs, mass media, and the like.[11]

There is also a biogenic component to social learning theory that attempts to explain why some children are less adept than others at receiving conventional messages.[12] Thus, biological explanations may shed additional light on the perennial question of why two youths with similar backgrounds and characteristics go separate ways—one becomes the thief, and the other, the banker. One such biogenic approach is that of Eysenck, who argues that delinquents and young adult criminals are extroverts and stimulus seekers. Extroverts condition more poorly than introverts in that they need stronger reinforcement to receive and learn messages. According to Eysenck, the basis for extroversion can be found in a biologically induced precondition; thus he seeks to explain individual differences in the process of social learning.[13] Others emphasize various constitutional factors that may affect a child's temperament at birth, with some children being especially active and difficult to control from early infancy.[14] Under such conditions, interactions of parents and others with such children shape their behavioral tendencies.

Reaction Approaches

Reaction theories tend to focus on the nature of decision making within various systems such as mental health, juvenile justice, and criminal justice. Attention is centered on how decisions are made and who is at risk in coming into these social-control systems.[15] For example, various conflict theorists argue that in American society there is a marked division in treatment between the "haves" and "have-nots."[16] According to this line of reasoning, laws are often enacted to protect the interests of those in power and thus differentially impact those who are not. As a result, those who most often come in contact with the criminal and juvenile justice systems are the poor, disposed, and underprivileged.[17] Thus, the machinery of justice grinds for the powerless, whose offenses tend to be street crimes. On the other hand, the justice system tends to ignore or treat less severely crime in the suites—those committed by the more powerful segments of society.

Many conflict theorists would argue that because of the nature of law and differential enforcement policies, minorities are more at risk of exposure to and being processed through the adult and juvenile justice systems.[18] For example, it is frequently argued that minority youth (who possess fewer resources) are funneled into the juvenile system, while white youth (who possess more resources) are often funneled out of the system—the typical middle-class delinquents. Similar arguments are advanced by proponents of radical and labeling perspectives.[19] Many labeling theorists argue that official decisions are often based on the ascribed characteristics of youth, such as race, class, and gender.[20] Thus, decision making is a function not only of what one has done but also of who one is.[21] More radical arguments maintain that the adult and juvenile justice systems are not only class biased but racist as well. Thus, various levels of decision making are discriminatory in nature, accounting for the large proportion of minority youth and young adults housed in secure facilities.[22]

These theoretical orientations are exemplary of structural, process, and reaction approaches and are not meant to be exhaustive. Nonetheless, they do provide some direction and insight for filling in the blank slate noted earlier. Many of the works cited offer explanations for attitudes that may precede criminal behavior—why, for example, some youths gravitate to kinship with a few members of a gang, often at the expense of so many other members of the larger community.

The next step is to apply these three theoretical perspectives to current social conditions and examine the link to delinquency. Before doing so, however, it may prove profitable to examine some trends with regard to delinquent activity. These data point out two facts: that youthful crime is serious business, and that there is a differential impact with regard to minority youth, in that they are more likely to come into contact with the system and receive the most severe dispositions.

Trends in Juvenile Crime and Processing

When one looks at general crime patterns, it is evident that youthful involvement in criminal activity is a serious matter. For example, data derived from the Uniform Crime Reports indicate that youths under eighteen years of age accounted for 18.1 percent of those arrested for index offenses in 1988 (homicide and non-negligent manslaughter, forcible rape, robbery, aggravated assault, burglary, larceny-theft, motor vehicle theft, and arson). For violent index offenses, youths under eighteen accounted for 8.9 percent of all arrests, compared to 20.9 percent of all arrests for property offenses.

With regard to representation by race, whites comprised 71.8 percent, blacks 25.9 percent, American Indian/Alaskan native 0.9 percent, and Asian/Pacific Islander 1.4 percent of all arrests in 1988 for those under eighteen years of age.[23] For the same year, black youths accounted for approximately 30 percent of all index arrests for those under eighteen. More specifically, black youths comprised half of all arrests for forcible rape (50 percent) and over half of all arrests for robbery (64.9 percent) and murder and non-negligent manslaughter (57.1 percent). It is noteworthy that while black youths accounted for 25.9 percent of all arrests in 1988 for those under eighteen, black adults accounted for 30.3 percent of all arrests for those eighteen and over—an approximate 4 percentage point difference. Within their respective age categories, black youths accounted for a higher percentage of arrests compared to black adults for the crimes of forcible rape and robbery.[24] These figures are even more startling when it is recalled that overall blacks constitute approximately 12 percent of the United States resident population.

Case Processing

A recent report from the National Center for Juvenile Justice documents the large number of juveniles being processed through the nation's juvenile court systems. Based on data from courts with jurisdiction over 62 percent of the youth population, this report reveals a delinquency case rate of 45.3 cases per 1,000 juveniles at risk. Twenty-one percent of all youths receiving dispositions in 1988 were held in a detention facility. This represents a 4 percent increase from 1987. Moreover, 17 percent of white youths charged with a delinquency offense were detained in 1988 compared to 28 percent for black youth. Much of this difference can be attributed to drug-law violations, for which minority youth are at greater risk. As noted by Snyder et al.:

> Between 1987 and 1988, the number of white youth processed for a drug law violation increased by 1 percent, while the number of nonwhite youth processed for a drug law violation increased by 42 percent.[25]

In 1988, of those charged with a drug-law violation, 51 percent of the non-white youth were detained, compared to 21 percent of the white youth. Overall, in 1988 the nonwhite delinquency case rate was 73.7 per 1,000 youths at risk, compared to 38.4 for white youth, or nearly double. Similar discrepancies existed with regard to the number of petitions filed. Nonwhite youths were substantially more likely to have their cases petitioned (57 percent) than were white youths (44 percent).[26] To petition in juvenile court is similar to indictment in criminal (adult) court.

With regard to confinement in juvenile facilities, black youths constituted approximately 34 percent of those confined, Hispanics 12 percent, and white youths 52 percent for the year 1987.[27] Rates of confinement per 100,000 were highest for black youth, followed by Hispanic and white youth respectively. Major differences were also noted in the place of confinement. Fifty-four percent of all black and Hispanic youths were housed in public facilities, while 63 percent of all white youths were housed in private facilities. From 1975 to 1987 the confinement rate in both public and private facilities increased by 46 percent. Between 1985 and 1987 the number of black and Hispanic juveniles housed in public facilities increased by 15 and 20 percent, respectively, while the number of white juveniles declined slightly.[28]

These data emphasize the serious problem of youthful crime in general and more specifically the over-representation of minority offenders, especially black youth, in both arrests and secure facilities. Given these data and projected shifts in the age structure of the U.S. population, it is unlikely that these trends will change dramatically in the near future. If anything, one would expect the number of minority youth, especially black, held in secure facilities to increase as we move toward the twenty-first century.[29] As noted above, available data clearly show a trend in which black youth are increasingly more likely to be housed in public secure facilities while white youth are placed in more treatment-oriented private facilities.[30] Further, while the live birth rate for the white population has been declining over time, this is clearly not the case for minority populations, especially blacks.[31] Thus, in the decades to come there will be a larger pool of minority youth. As discussed below, there is evidence to suggest that minority youth are more at risk in coming into contact with the juvenile justice system in the first place and that processing decisions differentially impact minority youth in that they are more likely to receive the most severe outcomes.[32]

Implications for Delinquency

Structural theories focus on conditions in society that may have implications for criminal and delinquent behavior. Factors such as unemployment, underemployment, poverty, and the like have at one time or another been linked to increasing or decreasing rates of crime and delinquency. While overall economic fluctuations are endemic to any society, there have been some major shifts over the last few decades within the United States. Perhaps two of the most important have been the erosion of higher paying blue-collar jobs in the industrial cities coupled with the emergence of less well paying service work.[33] This has had a great impact in major metropolitan areas, with better paying jobs and services following the population shift to the suburbs. Regional variations are also noted with the relocation of industry and business from northern cities to the "sunbelt" states. In essence what is occurring is a transition from a post-industrial society to one marked by high technology on one end and the provision of services on the other. Unemployment rates are high, and higher still if "discouraged" workers are included in the counts. As Durkheim noted over a century ago, major rapid changes in economic conditions (for example, the division of labor) can have pathological results, with increasing rates of deviance.[34]

Some of the consequences of these changes include the large and increasing number of homeless in America, a reduction in home ownership, an increase in the number of young adults moving back in with their parents for economic survival, and the large number of people employed at barely subsistence-level wages. Further, there is evidence that the implications of these economic changes are not spread evenly across society. A number of scholars have noted that certain segments of the population are more at risk than others. Those residing in the "ghetto underclass" (sometimes referred to as the "urban poor") have been hit harder by these economic downturns.[35] What began to occur in the 1960s is the creation of a permanently entrenched minority underclass composed mainly of blacks. The changing nature of the economy (for example, the decline in industrial and manufacturing jobs and the erosion of many entry-level positions) has created a separate class of citizens who have little chance of competing in a largely advanced technological society.[36] In comparing Chicago's low poverty and inner-city areas Wacquant and Wilson note that joblessness and economic exclusion have triggered a process that they term "hyperghettoization."[37] Under this process the stabilizing forces of the inner city have deteriorated and, as they note:

> Social ills that have long been associated with segregated poverty—violent crime, drugs, housing deterioration, family disruption, commercial blight, and educational failure—have reached qualitatively different proportions and have become articulated into a new configuration that endows each with a more deadly impact than before.[38]

While such conditions affect all members of the underclass, they are more pronounced and have more serious implications for black adolescents.[39]

Often unable to subsist within the legal economy, many take refuge in the illegal subeconomy—engaging in prostitution, gambling, drugs, and the like—and often express frustration in acts of expressive and instrumental violence, as witnessed in the recent resurgence of youth gang activity.[40] As a result, members of the underclass comprise the bulk of juvenile and adult institutionalized populations.

In a recent article pertaining to issues of the underclass, William Julius Wilson attempts to integrate social structural and cultural arguments. He argues that cultural adaptations of the underclass are rooted not only in larger structural and economic conditions but also in variations across neighborhoods in which they reside. Structural conditions and cultural expression are intimately linked to one another.[41] According to Wilson:

> Poor individuals with similar education and occupational skills confront different risks of persistent poverty depending on the neighborhoods they reside in, as embodied in the formal and informal networks to which they have access, their prospects of marriage or remarriage to a stably employed mate, and the families or households to which they belong.[42]

Neighborhoods vary in the degree to which families are stable, school systems educate, churches instill moral worth and youth are integrated into the community. Recent work by Lemann, for example, illustrates the importance of family structure. In an examination of Chicago's black underclass, often characterized by high illegitimate-birth rates, the single most important factor associated with those who were able to escape the ghetto was having been raised in a two-parent household that stressed values conducive to hard work and success.[43]

Contrary to popular conceptions, however, in many cases families can be hazardous to one's health. For example, an early study of homicide by Wolfgang indicated that 65 percent of all homicides involved individuals in close contact (for example, friends, lovers, etc.) while over one-quarter involved family members and occurred in the home.[44] More recent research continues to support this initial finding. Available data reveal a large amount of family violence (including spouse and child abuse) reported annually,[45] with perhaps even more that is unreported. Further, there is evidence to suggest that child abuse within the home is related to later incidents of aggression, delinquency, crime, and mental health problems.[46] Although violence generally (and family abuse specifically) crosses all class lines, official statistics indicate that it tends to be more concentrated in lower-class enclaves, especially in inner-city areas. As noted earlier, structural problems of inner-city areas (extreme poverty, deficient educational opportunities, underemployment, and the like) can have a major impact on family life, resulting in a higher incidence of single-parent households, drug and alcohol abuse, unwed mothers, and other dysfunctional conditions. Many theoretical orientations (for example, control and social learning theories) stress the importance of family nurturing. Without such nurturing, many young people will not develop moral paths to guide their behavior. Hence, their choices become constrained and they are more at risk of becoming enmeshed in the juvenile justice system.

The problem becomes exacerbated when other social institutions fail to function as well. In many major metropolitan areas, school systems serve as warehouses for troublesome youth. Rather than educating and preparing students for their future roles as citizens, parents, and labor force participants, they instead serve as institutions of containment (see chapter 11). In most cities good school systems have developed in the suburbs to serve the children of the affluent. As communities have deteriorated, so has any sense of belonging. Informal systems of control that influenced and monitored youthful behavior in the past are no longer effective. Many youths, as well as adults, have become estranged in their own communities. Anderson's recent ethnographic study of poor urban communities illustrates the point. Older generation blacks (the "old heads") have become less effective as role models and guides for the younger generation of black males. The streets and the peer group have replaced them as tutors. Thus, the gangs and other problem youth have become the focal point of youthful attention, increasing the chances of delinquent behavior.[47]

Reaction theories also play a role in the web of delinquency by focusing on the role of minority status and decision making. The problem of minority over-representation within the juvenile justice system and in secure facilities has drawn increased attention at both the state and the federal levels. Attention to this problem is not unwarranted. Pope and Feyerherm recently reviewed over three decades of research examining the issue of minorities in the juvenile justice system. The majority of the literature revealed either direct or indirect race effects operating within the system, effects that worked to the disadvantage of minority youth. Approximately two-thirds of the literature reviewed found disproportionate treatment of minorities even after relevant variables were statistically controlled. These disproportionate results were not limited to any one decision point, but were manifested across various stages of juvenile processing (e.g. intake, detention, adjudication, disposition).[48]

Recent research reports from three states (Georgia, Missouri, and Florida) focusing on the juvenile justice system and minority youth reinforce the findings noted above. Each of the reports suggests that at various stages of juvenile processing nonwhites (specifically black youth) receive more severe outcomes than do whites.[49] As Bishop and Frazier note for Florida:

> Non-white youths processed for delinquency offenses in 1987 received more severe (i.e. more formal and/or more restrictive) dispositions than their white counterparts at several stages of juvenile processing. Specifically, we found that when juvenile offenders were alike in terms of age, gender, seriousness of the offense which prompted the current referral, and seriousness of their prior records, the probability of receiving the harshest disposition available at each of several processing stages was higher for non-white than for white youth.[50]

Each of the studies also supports Feld's finding in Minnesota of "justice by geography."[51] In many states there are two separate systems of juvenile justice in operation—a more legalistic court in the urban areas and one geared toward a more traditional pre-Gault model (marked by informality and lack of due process) in the rural areas, each of which provides differential treatment, for which black youth are more at risk. Indirect race effects were also noted with regard to family situation. Youths coming from intact homes in which families were willing or able to provide support generally received less severe dispositions and were more likely to be placed in treatment options. Under these circumstances, black youth were found to be more at risk than white youth.[52]

Implications for the Future

The above discussion emphasizes the importance of structural/economic factors, cultural adaptations within communities, and the very operation of the juvenile justice system in the perpetuation of delinquency, especially among minority youth. Lack of meaningful participation in the labor market directly affects the choices that families have with regard to their future. In essence, it relegates them to a life within the so-called ghetto underclass, characterized by poverty, hopelessness, and despair. It also has implications with regard to social processes and community institutions, which may vary by neighborhood. Thus families may become dysfunctional while schools deteriorate, gangs become prevalent, and community residents become estranged from one another. Processing more minority youth into the juvenile justice system and reserving the most severe outcome for them serves to perpetuate the cycle of the underclass.

Given this, the critical issue to be considered is what can be done to arrest this cycle and reclaim the lives of youth. The policy implications derived from the discussion of theory, and outlined in Table 8.1, provide some direction. From a structural perspective, efforts would focus upon providing opportunities to succeed, such as meaningful employment; improving school systems; developing positive value systems and self-esteem; and the like. Process theory would lead to an enhancement of those factors that provide positive bonds to conventional society, as well as reinforcing conforming values through training, teaching, and modeling acceptable behavior. Reaction theories such as conflict perspectives would lead to policies that reduce economic differences, while labeling approaches would focus on decision making within the juvenile justice system (or how delinquents are created). Each provides alternatives to the cycle of delinquency and gives direction to the implementation of policy and programs.

With regard to the juvenile justice system, efforts should be made to ensure fairness and equity with regard to the processing of juvenile offenders. Decisions within local systems should be based on case characteristics (e.g., nature of the current offense, prior commitments, and so forth) and not tied, either directly or indirectly, to the personal attributes of offenders, such as race, gender, and social class. In a recent report, Pope and Feyerherm made a number of recommendations in order to accomplish this goal. The first set of recommendations focused on strategies to assess whether there is a problem with regard to racial disproportionality and the exact nature of the problem if it does exist. For example, they recommended the development of a systematic monitoring procedure to determine the percent of minority and majority youth being processed through each stage of the juvenile justice system at regular intervals. The next step would include a critical examination of those stages with the widest gaps between minority and majority youth. Such an examination would include a detailed evaluation of the criteria used in reaching decisions in order to determine the role that minority status plays alone or in conjunction with other factors. Finally, a research program to test for race effects would be introduced.[53]

If race is found to be a factor in any jurisdiction's juvenile justice system, steps should be implemented to eliminate the effect. For example, consideration should be given toward staff training in order to develop sensitivity to race-related issues within the juvenile justice system. Cultural sensitivity training should be made a priority, and efforts should be made to increase the representation of minority staff. Workshops should be implemented to discuss and evaluate decision making, especially as it pertains to minority youth. Jurisdictions should carefully evaluate the criteria used in reaching decisions at any given stage in juvenile processing. Finally, consideration should be given to the development of guidelines to aid decision makers in reaching outcome decisions. The development of a guideline-based approach to decision making should be geared toward keeping youth from further penetration into the system.[54]

Efforts should also be made to reduce the number of youths coming into the juvenile justice system. Those who are dangerous and incorrigible must, of course, be incapacitated, but too many do not fall into this category. Reducing the number of entrants to the juvenile justice system could include increasing the availability and quality of diversion programs aimed at keeping youth out of the system and providing alternatives to secure confinement. Community-based alternatives should be made available to all youth. Such alternatives could include recreational programming, mentoring, academic assistance, and the like. Local community prevention programs should be enhanced, especially those that strengthen the role of the family.

Combined, structure and process theories point to the importance of family, community, and economic enhancement. Policy prescriptions in these areas have been proposed by Currie and Curtis among others.[55] Curtis argues that, in order to reduce the incidence of violent crime, family systems need to be strengthened and empowered. As an example, he cites the House of Umoja in West Philadelphia and El Centro in Puerto Rico, both of which provide support programs for troubled youth. As he notes:

> Both create self-respect in youth, provide family-like support alternatives when there are broken families, motivate the young men to take action for the benefit of themselves and the community, and channel their energy from illegal to legal market activity.[56]

With regard to the community aspects that foster delinquency, efforts should be made to empower youth and develop within them a sense of moral worth. Various community-type programs can be effective in this regard by providing opportunities and support for youth who are prone to serious delinquent activity. Such programs can be effective in reaching individual youth and should be encouraged. However, it would be naive to expect that massive changes will result from these community efforts. As Lovell and Pope note in their discussion of recreational programming for gang-affiliated youth:

> While such comprehensive efforts are important in impacting the gang cycle, these alone will not resolve our national dilemma. These are one way, the best way perhaps, to make a difference in the lives of many. Nonetheless, conditions in America are such that the gates to undesirable consequences are wide

open. Nothing short of changes in national priorities to address inner city conditions, unemployment, and the effects of social and political tension will suffice. Moreover, little will change unless and until we end political and individual denial of the extent and nature of the conditions prevalent in our inner cities, until we come to the firm realization that too many citizens are living desperate and hopeless lives in conditions not of their choosing—especially children.[57]

Perhaps the single most important issue in dealing with the nature and scope of delinquency revolves around economic well-being. Until sound efforts are made to revitalize the United States' economy and create meaningful work for all citizens, all other efforts are likely to be piecemeal at best. While reforming the juvenile justice system is the "right thing to do," it will probably not have a major impact on the problem of delinquency. Similarly, revitalization of families, neighborhoods, and communities is a worthy goal, but without economic infusion of some sort it is not likely to bring about massive change. Rampant poverty, unemployment, and underemployment are central issues that must be given national, state, and local attention—public and private. Walker, for example, states that the plight of the underclass has been exacerbated by the steady disappearance of manufacturing and entry-level positions.[58] Both Currie and Wilson, noting the importance of economic solutions, have offered specific agendas to address these problems.[59]

Failure to give such agendas serious attention could well result in large increases in the proportion of America's urban poor living in destitute conditions. If a large segment of people are made to survive under conditions so vastly different from those encountered by the mainstream of U.S. citizens, it would not be unreasonable to expect still greater differences in behavior and outcomes. Structural and economic realities of the urban ghettos are major driving forces for entry into both the adult and juvenile justice systems. Initiatives must address not only problems in the case processing of juvenile offenders and programming aimed at individual youths, their families, and their communities, but also preexisting structural and economic conditions. Only by such a broad-front attack can we have any chance of reducing crime among our youth and the disproportionate representation of minorities within the juvenile justice system.

Notes

1. Carl E. Pope, "The Family, Delinquency and Crime."

2. Stephen E. Brown, Finn-Aage Esbensen, and Gilbert Geis, *Criminology: Explaining Crime and Its Context.*

3. Emile Durkheim, *The Division of Labor* and *Suicide.*

4. Robert K. Merton, "Social Structure and Anomie."

5. Richard A. Cloward and Lloyd E. Ohlin, *Delinquency and Opportunity.*

6. Charles E. Silberman, *Criminal Violence, Criminal Justice*, p. 121.

7. Walter B. Miller, "Lower-Class Culture As a Generating Milieu of Gang Delinquency"; Albert K. Cohen, *Delinquent Boys*; Marvin E. Wolfgang and Franco Ferracuti, *The Subculture of Violence.*

8. Travis Hirschi, *Causes of Delinquency.*

9. Pope, "Family, Delinquency and Crime."

10. Ronald L. Akers, *Deviant Behavior: A Social Learning Approach*; Rand Conger, "Social Control and Social Learning Models of Delinquency: A Synthesis"; Albert Bandura, *Aggression: A Social Learning Analysis.*

11. Pope, "Family, Delinquency and Crime."

12. Clarence R. Jeffery, *Biology and Crime*; S.A. Shah and L.H. Roth, "Biological and Psychological Factors in Criminality."

13. Hans J. Eysenck, *Crime and Personality.*

14. James Q. Wilson and Richard J. Herrnstein, *Crime and Human Nature.*

15. William J. Chambliss and Robert B. Seidman, *Law, Order and Power*; Michael J. Lynch and Walter B. Groves, *A Primer in Radical Criminology*; T. Sellin, *Culture, Conflict and Crime.*

16. Austin Turk, *Criminality and the Legal Order.*

17. David F. Greenberg, *Crime and Capitalism.*

18. Brown, Esbensen, and Geis, *Criminology.*

19. George B. Vold and Thomas S. Bernard, *Theoretical Criminology.*

20. Walter R. Gove, *The Labeling of Deviance*; John I. Kitsuse, "Societal Reaction to Deviant Behavior: Problem of Theory and Method"; Edwin M. Lemert, *Social Pathology*; Edwin M. Schur, *Labeling Deviant Behavior*; H.S. Becker, *Outsiders: Studies in the Sociology of Deviance.*

21. Richard Quinney, *The Social Reality of Crime.*

22. Lynch and Groves, *Primer.*

23. Kathleen Maguire and Timothy Flanagan, *Sourcebook of Criminal Justice Statistics, 1990*, p. 431.

24. Ibid.

25. Howard Snyder et al., *Juvenile Court Statistics 1988*, pp. 5, 8.

26. Ibid., p. 9.

27. Terrence Thornberry et al., *Children in Custody 1987*, p. 6.

28. Ibid., pp. 8, 12.

29. Carl E. Pope, "Juvenile Justice in the Next Millennium."

30. Snyder et al., *Juvenile Court Statistics.*

31. Charles Britt, "The Nature of Crime in the Year 2010"; Pope, "Juvenile Justice."

32. Carl Pope, "Blacks and Juvenile Crime: A Review."

33. William Wilson, *The Truly Disadvantaged: The Inner City, the Underclass and Public Policy.*

34. Durkheim, *Division of Labor* and *Suicide.*

35. Margaret C. Simms and Samuel L. Myers, *The Economics of Race and Crime.*

36. Carl E. Pope and William Feyerherm, *Minorities and the Juvenile Justice System.*

37. L. Wacquant and William Wilson, "The Cost of Racial and Class Exclusion in the Inner City."

38. Ibid., p. 15.

39. Darnell Hawkins and Nolan Jones, "Black Adolescents and the Criminal Justice System."

40. John Hagedorn, *People and Folks: Gangs, Crime and the Underclass in a Rustbelt City.*

41. William Wilson, "Studying Inner-City Social Dislocations."

42. Ibid., p. 10.

43. Nicholas Lemann, "The Origins of the Underclass" and *The Promised Land: The Great Black Migration and How It Changed America.*
44. Marvin E. Wolfgang, *Patterns in Criminal Homicide.*
45. P.A. Klaus and M.R. Rand, *Family Violence.*
46. Michael T. Zingraff and M.J. Belson, "Child Abuse and Violent Crime."
47. Elijah Anderson, *Streetwise: Race, Class and Change in an Urban Community.*
48. Carl Pope and William Feyerherm, "Minority Status and Juvenile Justice Processing."
49. Donna Bishop and Charles Frazier, *A Study of Race and Juvenile Processing in Florida*; Kimberly Kempf, Scott Decker, and Robert Bing, *An Analysis of Apparent Disparities in the Handling of Black Youth Within Missouri's Juvenile Justice System*; L. Lockhart et al., *Georgia's Juvenile Justice System: A Retrospective Investigation of Racial Disparity.*
50. Bishop and Frazier, *A Study.*
51. Barry C. Feld, "Justice by Geography: Urban, Suburban, and Rural Variations in Juvenile Administration."
52. Kempf, Decker, and Bing, *An Analysis.*
53. Pope and Feyerherm, "Minority Status."
54. Ibid.
55. Elliot Currie, "Crimes of Violence and Public Policy: Changing Directions" and "Confronting Crime: Looking Toward the Twenty-First Century"; Lynn A. Curtis, "Neighborhood, Family and Employment: Toward a New Public Policy Against Violence."
56. Curtis, "Neighborhood, Family and Employment."
57. R. Lovell and C.E. Pope, "Recreational Interventions."
58. Samuel Walker, *Sense and Nonsense About Crime.*
59. Currie, "Confronting Crime"; Wilson, *The Truly Disadvantaged.*

References

Akers, Ronald L. *Deviant Behavior: A Social Learning Approach.* Belmont, Calif.: Wadsworth, 1985.
Anderson, Elijah. *Streetwise: Race, Class and Change in an Urban Community.* Chicago: University of Chicago Press, 1990.
Bandura, Albert. *Aggression: A Social Learning Analysis.* Englewood Cliffs, N.J.: Prentice-Hall, 1973.
Becker, H.S. *Outsiders: Studies in the Sociology of Deviance.* New York: Free Press, 1963.
Bishop, Donna, and Frazier, Charles. *A Study of Race and Juvenile Processing in Florida*, report submitted to the Florida Supreme Court Racial and Ethnic Bias Study Commission, 1990.
Britt, Charles. "The Nature of Crime in the Year 2010." In J. Klofas and S. Stojkovic, eds., *Crime and Justice in the Year 2010*, Pacific Grove, Calif.: Brooks/Cole, 1993.
Brown, Stephen E.; Esbensen, Finn-Aage; and Geis, Gilbert. *Criminology: Explaining Crime and Its Context.* Cincinnati, Ohio: Anderson, 1991.
Chambliss, William J., and Seidman, Robert B. *Law, Order and Power.* Reading, Mass.: Addison-Wesley, 1971.
Cloward, Richard A., and Ohlin, Lloyd E. *Delinquency and Opportunity.* New York: Free Press, 1960.
Cohen, Albert K. *Delinquent Boys.* New York: Free Press, 1955.
Conger, Rand. "Social Control and Social Learning Models of Delinquency: A Synthesis." *Criminology* 14 (1976): 17–40.
Currie, Elliot. "Confronting Crime: Looking Toward the Twenty-First Century." *Justice Quarterly* 6 (1989): 5–25.

————. "Crimes of Violence and Public Policy: Changing Directions." In L.A. Curtis, ed., *American Violence and Public Policy*. New Haven: Yale University Press, 1985.

Curtis, Lynn A. "Neighborhood, Family and Employment: Toward a New Public Policy Against Violence." In Curtis, ed., *American Violence and Public Policy*. New Haven: Yale University Press, 1985.

Durkheim, Emile. *The Division of Labor* (1893), tr. George Simpson. New York: Free Press, 1933.

————. *Suicide* (1897). Tr. George Simpson. New York: Free Press, 1951.

Eysenick, Hans J. *Crime and Personality*. London: Routledge and Kegan Paul, 1977.

Feld, Barry C. "Justice by Geography: Urban, Suburban, and Rural Variations in Juvenile Administration." *The Journal of Criminal Law and Criminology* 82, no. 1 (1991): 156–210.

Feyerherm, William; Pope, Carl; and Mann, Coramae. *Technical Assistance to Address Minority Overrepresentation*, grant proposal submitted to and funded by the Office of Juvenile Justice and Delinquency Prevention, Washington, D.C., 1991.

Gove, Walter R. *The Labeling of Deviance*. Beverly Hills: Sage Publications, 1980.

Greenberg, David F. *Crime and Capitalism*. Palo Alto, Calif.: Mayfield, 1981.

Hagedorn, John. *People and Folks: Gangs, Crime and the Underclass in a Rustbelt City*, Chicago: Lakeview Press, 1988.

Hawkins, Darnell, and Jones, Nolan. "Black Adolescents and the Criminal Justice System." In R. Jones, ed., *Black Adolescents*. pp. 403–25. Berkeley, Calif.: Cobb and Henry, 1989.

Hirschi, Travis. *Causes of Delinquency*. Berkeley: University of California Press, 1969.

Jeffery, Clarence R. *Biology and Crime*. Beverly Hills: Sage Publications, 1979.

Kempf, Kimberly; Decker, Scott; and Bing, Robert. *An Analysis of Apparent Disparities in the Handling of Black Youth Within Missouri's Juvenile Justice System*. St. Louis, Mo.: Department of Administration of Justice, University of Missouri, 1990.

Kitsuse, John I. "Societal Reaction to Deviant Behavior: Problem of Theory and Method." *Social Problems* 9 (1962): 247–56.

Klaus, P.A., and Rand, M.R. *Family Violence*, Bureau of Justice Statistics Special Report. Washington, D.C.: U.S. Government Printing Office, 1984.

Lemann, Nicholas. "The Origins of the Underclass." *Atlantic Monthly* (June–July 1986): pp. 31–55; 54–68.

————. *The Promised Land: The Great Black Migration and How It Changed America*. New York: Alfred A. Knopf, 1991.

Lemert, Edwin M. *Social Pathology*. New York: McGraw-Hill, 1951.

Lockhart, Lettie; Kurtz, P. David; Stutphen, Richard; and Gauger, Kenneth. *Georgia's Juvenile Justice System: A Retrospective Investigation of Racial Disparity*, research report to the Georgia Juvenile Justice Coordinating Council, Part I of The Racial Disparity Investigation. Athens, Ga.: School of Social Work, University of Georgia, 1990.

Lovell, R., and Pope, C.E. "Recreational Interventions." In A.P. Goldstein and C.R. Huff, eds., *The Gang Intervention Handbook*, pp. 319–32. Champaign, Ill.: Research Press, 268, 1993.

Lynch, Michael J., and Groves, Walter B. *A Primer in Radical Criminology*. Albany, N.Y.: Harrow and Heston, 1986.

Maguire, Kathleen, and Flanagan, Timothy. *Sourcebook of Criminal Justice Statistics, 1990*. Washington, D.C.: U.S. Government Printing Office, 1991.

Merton, Robert K. "Social Structure and Anomie." *American Sociological Review* 3 (1938): 672–82.

Miller, Walter B. "Lower-Class Culture As a Generating Milieu of Gang Delinquency." *Journal of Social Issues* 14, no. 3 (1958): 5–19.

Pope, Carl. "Blacks and Juvenile Crime: A Review." In D. Georges-Abeyie, ed., *The Criminal Justice System and Blacks*, pp. 75–94. New York: Clark Boardman, 1984.

――. "The Family, Delinquency, and Crime." In E.W. Nunnally, C.S. Chilman, and F.M. Cox, eds., *Mental Illness, Delinquency and Crime*. Beverly Hills: Sage Publications, 1988.

――. "Juvenile Justice in the Next Millennium." In J. Klofas and S. Stojkovic, eds., *Crime and Justice in the Year 2010*, pp. 1–16. Pacific Grove, Calif.: Brooks/Cole, 1993.

Pope, Carl, and Feyerherm, William. "Minority Status and Juvenile Justice Processing." *Criminal Justice Abstracts* 22, no. 3 (1990): 327–36 (Part I), 527–542 (Part II).

Pope, Carl E., and Feyerherm, William. *Minorities and the Juvenile Justice System*, final report, Office of Juvenile Justice and Delinquency Prevention, U.S. Department of Justice, Washington, D.C., 1991.

Quinney, Richard. *The Social Reality of Crime*. Boston: Little, Brown, 1970.

Schur, Edwin M. *Labeling Deviant Behavior*. New York: Harper and Row, 1971.

Sellin, T. *Culture, Conflict and Crime*. New York: Social Science Research Council, 1938.

Shah, S.A., and Roth, L.H. "Biological and Psychological Factors in Criminality." In D. Glaser, ed., *Handbook of Criminology*, pp. 101–73. Chicago: Rand McNally, 1974.

Silberman, Charles E. *Criminal Violence, Criminal Justice*. New York: Vintage Books, 1978.

Simms, Margaret C., and Myers, Samuel L. *The Economics of Race and Crime*. New Brunswick, N.J.: Transaction Books, 1988.

Snyder, Howard; Finnegan, Terrence; Nimick, Ellen; Sickmund, Melissa; Sullivan, Dennis; and Tierney, J. *Juvenile Court Statistics 1988*. Pittsburgh: National Center for Juvenile Justice, 1990.

Thornberry, Terrence; Tolnay, S.; Flanagan, Timothy; and Glynn, P. *Children in Custody 1987*. Washington, D.C.: Office of Juvenile Justice and Delinquency Prevention, 1991.

Turk, Austin. *Criminality and the Legal Order*. Chicago: Rand McNally, 1969.

Vold, George B., and Bernard, Thomas S. *Theoretical Criminology*. New York: Oxford University Press, 1986.

Wacquant, L., and Wilson, William. "The Cost of Racial and Class Exclusion in the Inner City." *The Annals* 501 (1989): 8–25.

Walker, Samuel. *Sense and Nonsense About Crime*. Pacific Grove, Calif.: Brooks/Cole, 1989.

Wilson, James Q., and Herrnstein, Richard J. *Crime and Human Nature*. New York: Simon and Schuster, 1985.

Wilson, William. "Studying Inner-City Social Dislocations." *American Sociological Review* 56, no. 1 (1991): 1–14.

――. *The Truly Disadvantaged: The Inner City, the Underclass and Public Policy*. Chicago: University of Chicago Press, 1987.

Wolfgang, Marvin E. *Patterns in Criminal Homicide*. New York: John Wiley, 1958.

Wolfgang, Marvin E., and Ferracuti, Franco. *The Subculture of Violence*. London: Social Science Paperbacks, 1967.

Zingraff, Michael T., and Belson, M.J. "Child Abuse and Violent Crime." In K.C. Hass and C.P. Alpert, eds., *The Dilemmas of Punishment*. Prospect Heights, Ill.: Waveland, 1986.

9

BONNIE FISHER

Community Responses to Crime and Fear of Crime

Since the mid-1970s, a wide range of community responses to prevent crime and reduce fear of crime have appeared in growing numbers throughout the United States, Europe, Australia, and Asia.[1] Despite their variety, community responses to crime and fear all ultimately depend on the participation of the public, the police, or both.[2] This chapter examines the motivations of the public and the police in these community responses to crime by reviewing the literature.

To understand the public–police nexus, the respective motivations for the participation of the public and the police in responses to crime within the rational model of behavior and socioeconomics theory of behavior are examined, along with different community responses to crime: crime stoppers, citizen patrols, neighborhood-block watch, and police-community involvement programs.

Motivations for Participation in Responses to Crime and Fear of Crime

The dominant neoclassical rational choice theory of behavior assumes that individuals are motivated by a quest for the maximization of their self-interested goals. Motivations for behavior beyond self-interest, such as moral or social responsibility, or altruism, are "considered exceptional, and self-interested behavior is usually thought to be the rule."[3] Consequently, motivations for behavior are based on egoistical interests that maximize one's own greatest good.[4] As Anthony Downs wrote, "every individual, though rational, is also selfish. . . . Thus, whenever we speak of rational behavior, we always mean rational behav-

Thanks to Amitai Etzioni, Brian Forst, Jane J. Mansbridge, and Nicolas Williams for their helpful comments, and to Wesley G. Skogan for initially getting me involved in writing this chapter.

ior directed towards selfish ends."[5] Proponents of rational choice theory do not limit its application to purely economic situations; rather they make strong claims about its broad application and explanatory approach.[6] Claims are made that rational choice theory "is applicable to all human behavior," including responses to crime and fear.[7]

A growing body of theoretical and empirical work has focused on the explanatory limits of the rational theory of behavior, however, and has demonstrated the importance of motivations beyond self-interest.[8] Despite the dominance of the rational theory of behavior because of its ability to explain much with little, Elster argued that "we cannot conclude . . . in general . . . on any given occasion, that selfishness is the more widespread motivation. Sometimes the world is messy, and the most parsimonious explanation is wrong."[9] He further observed that "what seems clear is that self-interest cannot be the whole story."[10]

One recent theory, the socioeconomic theory of behavior, argues that the neoclassical theory of behavior is lacking because its focus does not take into account factors other than self-interest as motivations for behavior.[11] According to Etzioni, the socioeconomics perspective assumes that individuals are simultaneously under the influence of two sets of factors: their own self-interest and their moral duty.[12] These two factors are important to motivating behavior, because as Mansbridge wrote, "When [people] define their own interests, and when they act to pursue those interests, they often give great weight both to their moral principles and to the interests of others."[13] Therefore, the socioeconomic theory of behavior argues that motivation for behavior is based not only on self-interest but also on some moral commitment or social responsibility.[14]

Motivation for behavior, as Kuttner puts it, is influenced not only by self-interested impulses but also by ethical considerations of what is good or necessary for the collectivity. Such behavior benefits the community as well as the individual.[15] As Etzioni wrote, "The need for commitment to serve shared needs and the involvement in the community that attends to these needs" is important to the development of a responsive community, along with individual freedom and rights.[16]

Self-interest and community interest are not mutually exclusive; they complement each other and are interrelated. Self-interest affects moral duty to the community, and in turn moral duty affects self-interest.[17] Self-interest and community interest are complements; hence the I&WE paradigm that Etzioni and others espouse.[18]

The discussion that follows examines motivations to participate in responses to crime and fear by the public and the police within the socioeconomics perspective. For members of the public, motivations for self-interest and community-interest responses are examined, as well as the effects of such responses on the individual and on the community. Police responses are examined in light of various policing styles that emphasize different incentives for participation.

Individual-Focused, Private-Minded Responses

Research has shown that a large proportion of individuals adopt protective behaviors that reduce the risk of victimization by avoiding threatening situations
(risk avoidance) and by making victimization more difficult or by minimizing
the loss when victimization occurs (risk management). Risk-avoidance behaviors
include staying home at night and avoiding certain parts of a city or a neighborhood. Risk-management behaviors include carrying a weapon such as a knife or
gun, carrying little or no money when out, and equipping oneself with defense
skills. Many people also adopt household "target-hardening" measures, such as
installing strong locks on doors and windows, or a security system, engraving
property with an identity number, and locking doors and windows when away.
Such measures are used to eliminate the possibility of physical intrusion or make
it more difficult, or to reduce the amount of loss that occurs when a victimization
is not prevented.

Each of these three responses, risk avoidance, risk management, and target-
hardening measures, represents self-protective behaviors intended to reduce the
individual's fear of crime or the probability of crime; they are not necessarily
intended to provide collective safety.[19] Protecting one's self-interest appears to
be a strong incentive for responding to crime and fear of crime. Research has
shown that more people participate in individually focused, "private-minded"
responses to crime than in collective, "public-minded" responses to crime, such
as block- or neighborhood-watch schemes.[20] Research has consistently found
that over 80 percent of individuals have adopted some form of private crime
prevention measures, whereas less than 10 percent participate in public-minded
programs.[21] The private security industry has grown substantially over the last
decade; private protection expenditures now exceed public.[22]

Research has indicated that private-minded responses are effective in reducing the probability of individual victimization,[23] and that people who engage in
high levels of risk-avoidance activity, especially women and the elderly, are less
likely to be victimized than people who report fewer such behaviors.[24] There is
also some evidence to suggest that people who engage in household protection
measures are less likely to be property crime victims than those who do not take
such measures.[25] Bennett and Wright's work suggests that offenders look for
household crime prevention measures when choosing a burglary target,[26] and
Reppetto has empirically supported the notion that target-hardening devices
serve as a strong deterrent to residential burglary.[27] For example, Bennett and
Wright found that the presence or absence of alarms was a prime consideration in
the choice of targets. Findings suggest that the impact on fear of crime is positive
as well. People who engage in target-hardening responses generally report lower
fear of crime, higher feelings of safety, and increased perceptions of security.[28]

Private-minded responses to crime pose a complex irony for community
safety. On the one hand, although this relationship has not been fully developed

in the literature,[29] individuals who protect themselves and their property by adopting private-minded responses may produce a collective benefit.[30] The community may be safer because a majority of the residents are staying off the streets at night or because a majority of households have better locks on windows and doors or burglary alarm systems, thereby discouraging offenders from attempting crime in the vicinity.[31]

On the other hand, some scholars have argued that an excess of private-minded responses to crime and fear may produce negative effects for the individual and for the community. Rosenbaum has argued that "avoiding risk by restricting one's behavior often is viewed as a major loss of freedom and opportunity for a better life; . . . individual protection may be increased, but often the price is heavy in terms of personal freedom and/or long-term collective safety."[32] Bottoms has further warned that "if individualism really is unstoppable, the end result, or nightmare, could ultimately be a society with massive security hardware protecting individual homes, streets, shops, while all adult citizens would carry personal alarms, and perhaps, guns, for individual protection while moving from place to place."[33]

Research is needed to determine if private-minded responses necessarily lead to the negative effects suggested by Rosenbaum and Bottoms. This type of analysis is complicated by the direction of causality (does fear cause one to adopt private-minded responses or vice versa) and whether the relationship is circular. Most researchers believe that fear is the driving force behind adopting private-minded responses rather than the reverse, although there is some evidence that suggests that investment in private-minded strategies may increase people's fear of crime, so the relationship may be recursive.[34]

So, although the community may actually be safer, the perception of safety may decrease, because people see other people carrying weapons or homes that appear to be little fortresses and become fearful.[35] Private-minded responses may cause people to be more fearful of crime and more distrustful of their neighbors because of the omnipresence of private protection. These findings concerning private-minded responses to crime imply a "radical individualism" that may also lead to negative effects on the community.[36] A report of a government agency in the Netherlands summed up this effect by stating that "society has become more individualistic; . . . in some cases this individualism leads to a tendency to satisfy personal need at the expense of others or of the community."[37] In this circumstance, self-interest may undermine collective safety and can lead to the weakening and eventual destruction of the community.[38]

This line of thinking can be found in the "broken windows" hypothesis, which suggests that as communities fall into a cycle of decline and informal social control weakens, broken windows, graffiti, and other physical and social disorders signal that no one cares, and further decline follows, thus beginning a downward spiral. Individuals no longer care about the safety or welfare of their community; rather, their own protection and survival guide their actions.[39] This self-interest may undermine the mobilization capacity of people in the community to address its problems in any collective fashion because they are focusing only on their own safety and not the safety of the community. Further adding to the self-interest character of the community, people may become so fearful that they physically withdraw from the community into their little fortresses.[40]

Such communities are viewed as consisting of residents whose self-interest is manifested through such self-maximizing protective devices as better locks on doors and windows and burglar alarms for individual housing units, rather than collective responses to crime that may strengthen commitment to the community. In his summary of the findings in the crime prevention literature, Rosenbaum noted that "when a large number of residents withdraw from the streets, this reaction may undermine the community's ability to exercise informal social control, and surveillance over public behavior, thus lowering the constraints against deviant and criminal behavior."[41] Such reactions can have devastating effects on the community. As Skogan noted, "At the extreme end of the cycle, [communities] are no longer recognizable as neighborhoods but take on an entirely different social function."[42]

Collective, Public-Minded Responses

The socioeconomic view of responses to crime assumes that individuals can act not only out of self-interest but also out of a moral or social responsibility for a safer community.[43] Besides adopting private-minded responses to crime and fear, people can also be motivated to participate in public-minded, collective responses to crime and fear (activities carried out by groups) that benefit both the individual and the community.

Research suggests that the relationship between crime and fear of crime and participation in collective crime prevention responses has some contradictions. As previously noted, some scholars view crime and fear as divisive forces that destroy the capacity of the community to take collective action. They have argued that people prefer private-minded responses over collective solutions to crime problems and fear,[44] and that they tend to be drawn into the protective environment of their homes, which undermines the capacity of the community to organize against common goals.[45]

Other scholars argue that crime and fear of crime unite the community in common purpose. Durkheim wrote, "Crime brings together upright consciences and concentrates them."[46] Erickson, in interpreting Durkheim's thesis, wrote, "When these people come together to express their outrage over the offense and to bear witness against the offender, they develop a tighter bond of solidarity than existed earlier. The excitement generated by the crime, in other words, quickens the tempo of interaction in the group."[47] Consistent with the Durkheimian view that communities faced with crime and fear can respond with collective actions, most community responses to crime and fear assume that individuals will participate in such collectives because many of them view participation as appropriate behavior or want to participate out of general concern for the community.[48] Implicit in the Durkheimian view is the assumption that individuals choose to participate not only because their values have been affronted but also out of a moral obligation to the safety of the community.[49]

The community crime prevention movement in the 1970s had its roots not only in Durkheim's thinking but also in what has been called the "community hypothesis."[50] This thesis suggests that residents of a community can be mobilized by community organizations to participate in collective crime prevention programs and that the resulting social solidarity and cohesiveness will result in reduced levels of crime and fear.[51] The hypothesis has the underlying assumption that when the opportunity to participate in collective actions exists, individuals will look beyond their self-interest in protecting themselves and their dwelling units because of some moral commitment to the safety of the community.[52] Marx commented that such collective actions rested upon an honored American tradition of self-help in which neighbors voluntarily come together to help solve problems. Such thinking has had a strong influence on the development of strategies to organize the community in response to crime and fear.[53]

There are many types of collective responses to crime and many ways of conceptualizing collective responses to crime.[54] Two distinct broad approaches that seek to strengthen informal social controls in the neighborhood have been identified in the literature: the opportunity-reduction approach and the social-problems approach. Collective strategies that developed from the opportunity-reduction approach often involve surveillance, crime reporting, and activities designed to deter or control crime in a specific area. They aim to encourage a wide range of proactive self-interest behaviors in the hopes of developing interaction and social responsibility among the residents and thereby creating a safer neighborhood for all. Neighborhood or block watches often serve as vehicles for encouraging a range of opportunity-reduction behaviors.[55] The social-problems approach typically involves the community and public service workers working together to address the "root causes" of crime, such as unemployment, lack of educational skills, cultural misunderstanding, lack of positive role models for youths, and youths on the streets getting into trouble.[56] Rather than viewing the community as a collection of attitudes and behaviors, the social-problems approach sees the community as an interlocked set of long-standing institutions actively involved in addressing the underlying causes of crime and fear and aiming to improve the quality of life by discouraging a predisposition for crime.[57] Various components of community policing, such as police and residents working together on delinquency problems or job training, are examples of the social-problems approach to crime and fear.

Past studies provide a useful portrait of patterns of participation in collective responses to crime and fear by individuals. A consistent finding is that higher rates of participation are reported in middle- and upper-income communities than in low-income communities.[58] People who have an economic investment in the community, such as owning a home, are more likely to participate in collective responses in order to protect their investment.[59] In addition, families with children and those who plan to stay in their neighborhood are more likely to report involvement in collective crime prevention responses.[60] Concern for personal well-being and the safety of property also has been shown to motivate participation in collective responses. In a study of two London neighborhoods, Bennett (1989) found that participants were more worried about being victims of burglary and robbery and were more likely to feel unsafe than nonparticipants. He also found that fear of crime was a significant predictor of participation, but it is unclear if high fear levels preceded participation or resulted from participation.[61]

Research has also shown that individuals are motivated to participate because they feel a responsibility to make their community a better place to live. "Civicmindedness" has been found to be a strong predictor of participation in collective efforts.[62] Those who have a social commitment to the community also have been found to be more likely to participate in collective responses; Bennett measured social commitment as perceived friendships in the neighborhood, as people helping each other, and as people involved with each other in home protection.[63]

Behavior that reflects social responsibility also appears to be associated with participation in collective responses to crime and fear. The most consistent finding is that those who participate in collective responses to crime and fear are more likely than those who do not participate to already be involved in the improvement of their community. Those who participate typically are involved with community organizations that are addressing a variety of neighborhood problems by promoting community improvement. These individuals tend to be "joiners," who have higher feelings of responsibility toward the community than nonparticipants.[64]

Although little multivariate analysis has been done to test whether self-interest or moral responsibility is a stronger predictor of participation, research employing a pretest-posttest design has shown that individuals who participate in collective responses felt an increased sense of community, had stronger perceptions of informal social control and stronger feelings of crime prevention efficacy, and experienced lower fear of crime than those who did not.[65]

In their study of collective crime prevention programs in fifteen neighborhoods in Chicago, Rosenbaum, Lewis, and Grant report findings contrary to the community hypothesis.[66] For example, in communities where collective crime prevention programs were implemented, respondents reported being more fearful of personal and property crimes and felt less efficacious than in communities where no programs were implemented. They report that some communities that implemented collective programs experienced either no change or an increase in their crime levels when compared to communities that did not. Others, such as Bennett, report that communities that implemented collective crime prevention programs experienced no changes in fear of personal crime and no increase in crime when compared to those communities that did not.[67]

Police Responses

Although police officers take a public service vow as part of their job require-ment, they can be motivated to participate in certain community responses to crime and fear and not to participate in others, depending on the reward structure imposed by their supervisors. Police officers can satisfy their sworn duty to provide a safe community and enhance their perceived efficacy in the eyes of most residents, as well as earning rewards such as increased pay, job perks, promotions, special assignments, and recognition.[68] In general, police officers' motivation to participate in a community response to crime and fear is influenced by outcome measures of their job performance.[69]

Performance measures for officers have changed over time, largely depending on how police commissioners and supervisors view the role and functions of the police department. Officers tend to take a narrow self-interest view of their crime-control role when performance measures are based primarily on crime statistics. When performance measures include understanding the underlying problems that can cause crime and developing a working relationship with resi-dents, community organizations, and institutions, officers tend to take a broad view of their crime-control role and to include the interests and needs of the community. At least three different police orientations have been developed to incorporate these different views of crime control: incident-oriented policing, problem-oriented policing, and community-oriented policing.[70]

Incident-Oriented Policing

Incident-oriented policing has been and continues to be the dominant strategy used by police departments to motivate officers to enforce the law. With its emphasis on crime control and criminal apprehension, incident-oriented policing relies heavily on performance measures that reflect the tabulation of crime statis-tics. The Uniform Crime Reports has become the primary standard by which police departments measure their effectiveness. Effectiveness is measured by how well they are able to control crime rates.

A variety of measures are commonly used to measure the performance of patrol officers and provide a basis for promotions within the department. The number of arrests made, the number of reports written, the number of tickets issued, and the number of crimes solved are typically used to measure officers' crime-control performance. Response time to a call for service and the number of times a patrol car passes a given point on a city street are generally viewed by public officials and the public as other measures of the effectiveness of officers. An officer who performs his or her duties well is typically rewarded by a promo-tion in the ranks of the military-like hierarchy.[71]

Incident-oriented policing attempts to control crime directly through preventive patrols and rapid response time to calls for service.[72] The primary role of the officer is passive: drive around in high-powered patrol cars and cruise neighborhoods to deter potential offenders and reassure citizens that the police are doing their jobs. Officers are removed from the public—they are there to serve and protect, not to interact. They are professionals who know better than anyone else what must be done to protect the community and enforce the law.[73]

Should a call come over the radio, the officer puts on the flashing lights and sirens and races to the scene as fast as possible so as not to lose time in pursuing the offender or gathering information and witnesses. In this respect, incident-oriented policing is very much reactionary. As Kelling summarized, "Generally, the business of police for the past thirty years has been responding to calls for service."[74] An officer's job has been to get to the scene quickly and collect relevant information that can help the detectives solve the crime. Goldstein describes an officer's typical response: "Go to a call, pacify things, and leave to get ready for another call."[75]

Overall, incident-oriented policing rewards the officer for a narrow definition of his or her role: law enforcement. The "good collar" is what the officer strives for and is ultimately rewarded for in an incident-oriented department. Incident-oriented policing tends to take a narrow view of the community, as well; community interests are defined by the number of incidents per capita and the crime rate. Officers are not necessarily rewarded for looking beyond the numbers.

Problem-Oriented Policing and Community-Oriented Policing

Over the last twenty years, significant changes have occurred within and outside police departments, transforming the interests and the motivations of officers to participate in community responses to crime. Due in part to increasing crime rates and increasing levels of fear of crime in the early 1970s, there was a growing realization by academics, politicians, and citizens that the police were limited in responding to crime and fear. With a push from several national law enforcement commissions, some police departments began to move from relying on incident-oriented policing and began to give the public a role in crime prevention. Police departments sponsored workshops in which police officers educated the public about target-hardening responses to crime and encouraged the public to mark their property, and promoted collective responses to crime and fear that stressed the public as the "eyes and ears" of the police. Citizen crime-watch groups were set up to call the police to report suspicious activity.

However, these efforts were limited. Though they hoped to use the public to help reduce crime, it was evident that the police intended to maintain their monopoly on both expertise and operational capability.[76] The public was given a limited role in helping the police, but the reward system for the patrol officer was still related to incident-oriented measures.

In the late 1970s and early 1980s, what Kelling calls "a quiet revolution" began to reshape policing.[77] In part due to 1970s research about how preventive patrols, rapid responses to calls for service, and investigative work were ineffective tactics to controlling and solving crimes, police departments began to look beyond incident-oriented policing and experiment with innovative responses to crime that took a broad view of law enforcement and crime control. Moore, Trojanowicz, and Kelling noted that police departments began to look "behind offenses to the precipitating causes of crimes, building closer relations with the community" and sought "to enhance the self-defense capacities of the communities themselves."[78]

These philosophical changes did not mean that the police abandoned their crime-control or protection responsibilities; rather, the changes expanded the crime-control and protection focus of the police.[79] Looking beyond the tabulation of crime statistics to the causes of crime and fear and to the concerns of the residents of the community, the police began to take a much wider view of their crime-control role. Along with changes in the crime-control role came changes in performance measures. Two related types of community policing developed as a result: problem-oriented policing and community-oriented policing.

Problem-oriented policing was developed to improve upon incident-oriented policing by adding proactiveness and thoughtfulness to the role of the officer. In problem-oriented policing, officers do not naturally assume that crimes are committed by predatory offenders whom they need to either deter or catch in the act.[80] Rather, officers are taught to assume that crimes could be caused by particular problems in the community such as frustrating relationships, like a noisy neighbor, an abusing spouse, or delinquent children, and they are taught to be more aware of such underlying problems, especially at the individual and household levels. Officers are encouraged to identify, analyze, and respond to the underlying circumstances that create criminal incidents, fear of crime, social and physical disorders, and neighborhood decay.[81] Problem-oriented policing thus rejects the fragmented approach in which police deal with each incident as an isolated event with neither history nor future.[82] It depends upon the initiative and skill of officers in defining problems and proposing solutions to the community. It also places special demands on police recruitment and training.

Although arrest and conviction are still used as measures of police effectiveness under problem-oriented policing, the possible causes of crime and fear and methods for controlling them are substantially widened.[83] Police officers are encouraged to use a range of responses to crime far beyond patrol, investigation, and arrests. They are taught to use negotiating and conflict-resolving skills to address disputes before they become crimes.

Community-oriented policing also expands the role and autonomy of the individual officer. In community policing, institutions such as families, schools, neighborhood associations, and business groups are viewed as key partners to the police in the creation of safe, secure communities.[84] There is a strong emphasis on the police recognizing that they work ultimately for the community. One of the goals is to develop a working relationship with the community by being responsive to community concerns. Officers are encouraged to work closely with community groups and institutions to create a close relationship between police and citizens.

Community-oriented police officers are assigned, ideally, so that they can get to know the workings of the community and the citizens' concerns. Citizens are encouraged to bring problems directly to beat officers. The emphasis is on police officers interacting with citizens to determine the type of community-level problems they are confronting and to devise solutions to those problems. Skolnick and Bayley stress that community-oriented policing is "supposed to be congruent with community priorities and inviting of public cooperation to know about and solve most crime."[85]

In community-oriented policing, officers take a view of the community beyond incidents and beyond problem solving. They see communities as partners not only in crime control and prevention but also in the enhancement of the quality of life. Both the police and the public have the responsibility for identifying and addressing the community's problems in order to make the community safer and more livable for everyone. These problems include signs of disorder like graffiti, vandalism, gangs of rowdy teenagers, and quality-of-life issues like residents' satisfaction with the neighborhood and sense of community, as well as criminal acts.

Horne has noted that since rewards continue to be powerful motivators in these police departments, a reward system that recognizes an officer's and department's achievements in problem-solving and community policing must be created if more departments and officers are to engage in community-oriented policing rather than only incident-oriented policing.[86] Although arrests, clearances, convictions, and traffic tickets are still used to measure the overall effectiveness of the police, other means are incorporated in an evaluation.[87] Citizen satisfaction with police service, the rate of citizen complaints against the police, and quality-of-life factors such as sense of citizen efficacy against crime, trust among neighbors, fear of crime, and sense of partnership with the police are currently used to evaluate police performance in community-oriented policing.[88] Individual officers are being evaluated in terms of their commitment to and interest in the well-being of the community, not just how many tickets they write or how many arrests they make. The ability to assess and solve problems and offer effectiveness in relationships with groups working with the police are also used as performance criteria.

Criteria for a reward structure are still being developed by police experts and commissioners because many departments have not learned how to reward performance systematically. Measures are still somewhat ambiguous. Skolnick and Bayley warned "that the ambiguity of evaluating and rewarding the quality of

Table 9.1

Motivation for Police and Public Participation in Different Community Responses to Crime and Fear

		Motivation for Police Participation		
		Incident-Oriented	Problem-Oriented	Community-Oriented
Motivation for Public Participation	Self-Interest	Crime Stoppers	Educational Programs Home Visits Ride-Along Programs	
	Mixed (Individual and Community)	Neighborhood or Block Watch Public Relations Campaigns Foot Patrols		
	Community Interest	Citizen Patrols	Neighborhood Improvement Programs	Police-Community Mini-Stations

community policing performance constitutes a factor, albeit not a dispositive one, in inhibiting the development of community policing."[89]

Community Responses to Crime and Fear of Crime

The motivations for public and police participation differ from program to program and vary along many dimensions. Different responses to crime are categorized in Table 9.1 along three motivations for the public: self-interest, community interest, and mixed. Motivations of police participation are also categorized along three dimensions: incident-oriented, problem-oriented, and community-oriented. The motivational categories are not mutually exclusive; rather, they reflect what may be the predominant motivation. As can be seen, each response to crime and fear offers different motivations for public and police participation. For example, the Crime Stoppers program primarily appeals to the self-interest of the public and officers who are in a department that rewards incident-oriented policing, whereas neighborhood improvement programs, such as neighborhood cleanups, primarily appeal to individuals who are interested in making the community look more attractive and developing a positive image, and to officers who are in departments that encourage communities to address their physical problems.

Crime Stoppers

The Crime Stoppers program, in which the public is encouraged to call the local police department with any information pertaining to criminal activity, not only unites the police and the public in the fight against crime but also enlists the help of the media. Typically, a selected "crime of the week" is reenacted or described for the public during peak viewing hours on television. Members of the public are then encouraged to call Crime Stoppers if they have any information that might lead to the arrest of the person or persons involved or to solving open felony cases.[90] Calls from the public are encouraged through the assurance of anonymity and the payment of cash rewards (typically from $100 to $1,000) for any information relative to the crime and or the wanted persons that leads to an arrest or an indictment.[91]

A number of police studies have demonstrated that the traditional strategies of policing that ignore the role of the public are unsuccessful; Crime Stoppers is an attempt to increase the public's participation and responsibility in the fight against crime.[92] The Crime Stoppers program has grown rapidly since its inception in 1976 in Albuquerque, New Mexico. It now covers the United States, Canada, Great Britain, Australia, New Zealand, and Puerto Rico. Crime Stoppers has estimated that there are 700 operational programs accepting calls in the United States and boasts of new programs emerging on a continual basis.[93]

This program steadfastly maintains the police's traditional incident-oriented role in solving crimes but at the same time acknowledges that the police cannot solve the crime problem alone and need the help of the public. The reenacted crimes on the television are typically "dead-end" cases that the police have experienced serious problems in solving.

The role of the public in Crime Stoppers programs is a passive but hopefully an effective one: to supply the police with critically needed information so that they can solve crimes. The motivation for the public to supply the police with helpful clues may be mostly economic—people may participate to maximize their economic self-interest by obtaining the reward money. Calling the police with a tip may also be motivated by a moral commitment to the safety of the community or by a desire to influence events or get even with someone. Some people may provide information because it could lead to the reduction of crime and fear by getting an offender off the streets. To date, no research has been done to directly investigate the forms of motivation; this type of research may be limited by a lack of data, because people who call the police are guaranteed anonymity.

One evaluation of the effects of the reward in Crime Stoppers suggested that reward size was not a strong determinant of either informant satisfaction with the reward, perceived fairness of the reward, belief in the effectiveness of Crime Stoppers, or intention to participate in the program again.[94] Economic factors, therefore, may not be the only incentive for participation. Lurigio and Rosenbaum noted that critics fear that programs such as Crime Stoppers have the potential to undermine the social fabric of our society by encouraging distrust among neighbors and discouraging participation in civic responsibilities without monetary compensation.[95]

Many police departments participate in Crime Stoppers. Police need to solve crimes in order to justify their existence and performance to the public, so they need to show positive results. One way to view the motivation behind their endorsement of Crime Stoppers is in protecting and maintaining their crime-control and prevention roles, in other words, in maintaining incident-oriented policing.

Although Crime Stoppers has emerged as one of the most rapidly expanding and highly visible community responses to crime, only a handful of evaluations of the program exist. One evaluation of Crime Stoppers in the United States revealed impressive statistics of felony arrests, convictions, and stolen property and drugs recovered. But despite the striking statistics, the impact of Crime Stoppers on community crime and fear of crime remains unknown.[96]

Neighborhood or Block Watch

Citizen involvement in collective crime prevention has grown considerably in the last fifteen years, resulting in thousands of neighborhood- or block-watch programs throughout the United States, the United Kingdom, and Canada.[97] It is estimated that one out of every five families in the United States lives in a neighborhood with a watch-type program.[98] Neighborhood- or block-watch programs (herein referred to as "the Watch Program") have become the backbone of community crime prevention not because they are necessarily the most effective form of crime prevention but partly because of their acceptance and support by community organizations, residents, and the police.[99] The Watch Program is a generic, off-the-shelf program that is typically sponsored by the police or a community organization. It is premised on community-obligation arguments made by Durkheim and others.[100]

Although the organizational structure, sponsorship, and range of functions differ, there are three primary aspects of the standard Watch Program: increased surveillance by residents over their neighborhoods, reporting of any unusual activity as accurately as possible to the police, and increased use of target-hardening activities designed to control or deter crime in dwellings. These are usually accomplished by bringing together residents of the designated area to discuss mutual crime problems, along with crime prevention and security tips, and to develop their own solutions to these problems. This leads to increased appreciation of communal needs and results in mutual cooperation and joint action among the residents.[101]

The role of the public is typically passive: watching the neighborhood and reporting suspicious behavior, crimes in progress, and relevant crime-solving information to the police. This participation does not represent a novel way of addressing crime and fear. It is incident-oriented policing with a slight twist in which the residents protect their turf by informing the police.[102] In a national survey of 550 Watch Programs, Garofalo and McLeod found that in addition to being the "eyes and ears" of the police, a majority of the programs supplemented informal neighborhood surveillance with other activities. These included private-minded security responses such as property marking and home-security surveys, as well as public-minded responses such as meeting to plan, exchange information, and resolve physical environmental concerns (graffiti, trash collection, and street-light improvement). Their study also reported that over twice the number of individuals participated in the private-minded responses than in the public-minded responses.[103] Neighborhood Watch is unique in that the three police orientations are all stressed in this response to crime and fear, which may be why the police generally support and encourage it.

Like Crime Stoppers, Watch Programs involve an admission that the police cannot address crime by themselves and residents must accept responsibility for surveillance of the community.[104] The Watch Program relies heavily on residents looking out for each other and calling the police to report suspicious behavior; it assumes that individuals will accept responsibility for the safety of another person or another's dwelling through surveillance. It also assumes that some degree of mutual interest in the well-being of the community exists among the residents beyond individual self-interest, and that as people participate in Watch Programs, the social processes outlined in the community hypothesis will develop.

Whether people will participate in crime prevention activities depends on public knowledge of and attitudes toward crime prevention initiatives.[105] In the 1984 British Crime Survey, 63 percent of respondents overall were prepared to join a local Watch Program.[106] In Canada, close to half of the respondents to the Canadian Urban Victimization Survey knew about the Watch Program.[107] Results from the British Crime Survey show the same pattern of awareness. Despite widespread enthusiasm to join and awareness of the Watch Program, however, participation rates remain rather modest: this survey found that fewer than 1 percent of the respondents were actively involved.[108] In short, willingness to join and awareness exceed active participation by a substantial margin.[109] Attitudes appear favorable but are not generally accompanied by consistent behavior in collective actions such as the Watch Program. This is not to say that people do not participate in crime prevention, but research shows that, while people take private-minded measures to make themselves and their dwellings safe from crime, they seldom actively participate in the Watch Program.[110]

Mixed results have been reported with respect to the effectiveness of neighborhood- or block-watch responses. On the positive side, quasi-experimental evaluations revealed that individuals who participated in such programs were less fearful, perceived a more informal social control, and felt a stronger sense of community than those who did not.[111] On the negative side, quasi-experimental results at the community level suggested that such programs had either no effect or a negative effect on the community. For example, in communities where the Watch Program was implemented, fear of crime either had increased or was not affected by the program.[112] Although the individual is somewhat better off by participating in the Watch Program, the community as a whole may not be.

The results of these studies also seem to suggest that members of the public participate in the Watch Program to make their dwelling units safer, not necessarily to make the community safer for everyone. Recall that Garofalo and McLeod's study reported that over 80 percent of the individuals participated in the private-minded, crime-prevention specific responses like engraving their property with identification numbers and conducting home security, whereas less than 40 percent participated in public-minded, community-oriented responses like physical environmental concerns.

Citizen Patrols

Citizen patrols are typically made up of residents of an area who engage in systematic patrolling of their neighborhood in the hopes of either deterring crime by their presence or discovering crimes in progress and intervening at some level.[113] They increase the surveillance of the community and act as protectors of the community. Like the participants in the Watch Programs, citizen patrols act as the eyes and ears of the police; but instead of sitting at home and watching for suspicious activity, they play a more active role, walking the streets. Some patrols, like the highly publicized Guardian Angels, are taught physical defensive techniques, which they use to directly intervene in a criminal situation. Other patrols are discouraged from directly intervening in any questionable activity they find: instead, they are taught to call the police for help. Some police departments find citizen patrols can supplement incident-oriented policing, and thus they may be willing to support citizen patrols to the extent that police officers get the credit for controlling and solving crimes.

Patrols are organized for various reasons, from supplementing police activity to acting as vigilantes. Those patrols that are organized to provide supplemental assistance to police are often opposed by the police, perhaps because the police dislike sharing authority over crime prevention, as well as prestige, with the patrols.[114] Concern over vigilante-like behavior of patrols when members grew bored—police patrol work is mostly quite boring—or were recruited from youth factions in the neighborhoods is articulated in the citizen patrol literature.[115] Although Yin et al. found evidence of vigilante-like behavior by some patrols, Rosenbaum noted that generally there was little support for this concern. In particular, Pennell et al. reported results that do not support the label of vigilantism often attached to the Guardian Angels by the press and representatives of law enforcement.[116]

Although the exact number of citizen patrols is unknown,[117] there were estimated to be 800 or more patrols throughout the United States in 1977.[118] In

1989, the Guardian Angels reported forty-eight chapters in the United States and Canada.[119] In the early 1980s in Philadelphia, it was estimated that 150,000 people participated in patrols, and a similar number was estimated in New York City.[120]

Motivation for participation and the effectiveness of patrols in reducing crime and fear are unclear due to the lack of empirical research, which is due in part to the short-lived nature of most of these patrols.[121] Citizen patrols typically form out of frustration against the police for not adequately protecting the community or in the aftermath of a serious crime that shocks the community.[122] For example, Troyer documented the formation of an officially sanctioned student patrol in the aftermath of a rape incident on a college campus. The group gradually disbanded due to lack of interest after further incidents did not occur.[123] This pattern is typical of citizen patrols. Once crime has been displaced and complacency returns, the patrol disbands until a new incident occurs.

Citizen patrols may be motivated by concerned, vigilant residents who have community safety as a priority because they feel that the police can not fulfill their crime control or prevention responsibilities to the community's satisfaction. Typically, the participants in these patrols live in the community that they patrol, and they appear to be motivated by a civic-mindedness toward the safety of the whole community, because they are actively patrolling the streets of the community. They are trying to cover more of the community than merely the front of their dwelling unit or block, so there is a broader concern for safety than is typical in individual crime prevention efforts.

Although citizen patrols have been praised as partially effective in reducing street crime, there has been very little evaluation research that measures their impact.[124] Anecdotal evidence suggests that patrols may be effective both in preventing crime and in increasing residents' sense of safety at home when the patrols are visible.[125] Some have suggested that their presence may reduce fear of crime rather than serving any deterrent effects.[126]

Police–Community Involvement

Unlike the traditional incident-oriented policing or the eyes-and-ears philosophy, the basic principle of police–community involvement in crime control and prevention takes a broad view of control and prevention that includes the police and the public working together to address the underlying problems that cause crime and fear. Problem-oriented policing has been defined as a "prescribed approach to addressing neighborhood concerns through the identification and analysis of specific problems, followed by the development and implementation of specific solutions."[127] Community-oriented policing has been described as "an umbrella term for a wide variety of community-oriented police activities that share a common set of values."[128] Problem-oriented policing focuses more on individual or household specific problems, whereas community-oriented policing focuses more on community-level problems. Implicit in each is the notion of shared crime control and prevention power; both seek to improve the partnership between the police and the community. Both the public and the police, therefore, share the responsibilities for promoting a shared goal, community safety, and both are viewed as having legitimate roles in the pursuit of this goal.[129]

A variety of responses to crime and fear exist that are targeted at individuals and their specific concerns or problems. Specific educational programs that focus on problems of women and families and children are part of problem- and community-oriented policing. For example, in Houston, officers fingerprinted children as an effort to have an official record of the child should the child disappear. A school program was also developed there in conjunction with school administrators to address the truancy problem.[130] Police officers in a neighborhood may be motivated to organize seminars with groups who may be at risk of being victimized or to sponsor classes on self-defense or household protection measures for members of the community. Individuals are encouraged to take advantage of the specific services or programs offered by the police in order to reduce their likelihood of victimization, reduce their fear, and in the end benefit their general well-being and quality of life. For example, in some cities police are using negotiating and conflict-resolving skills to address disputes before they become crime problems. Officers get involved in mediating disputes between neighbors, spouses, or merchants and customers without waiting for a fight to occur.[131]

Other responses encourage developing a working partnership between the police and the residents. Unsolicited visits by the police to residents are another response that police departments have encouraged. Programs focusing on individual residents, such as the distribution of police-community newsletters and recontacting victims of crime to offer sympathy, counseling, and victim services have been used to get to know the residents on an informal basis. Members of the community are also encouraged to ride along with an officer patrolling in the neighborhood in the hopes that the public will develop a better understanding of the daily work of the officer and trust in the officer, so that information can be openly exchanged between them. Neighborhood improvement programs have been sponsored by the police and community organizations to clean up the community and parks, plant flowers, paint over graffiti, and paint colorful murals on the sides of abandoned buildings to create a positive image and help develop a sense of community among the residents.

Unlike the public's reactionary role in the Watch Program, here the public works proactively with the police in addressing neighborhood concerns through identification and analysis of specific local problems that contribute to increased crime and fear. For example, the police and the public have sponsored public relations campaigns to help establish and promote their partnership in addressing crime and fear and their underlying causes.[132] Like Crime Stoppers, the public is expected to help the police in addressing their concerns by providing crime-related information, but unlike Crime Stoppers, there is no monetary incentive built in. This type of information is needed not only to solve specific crimes but also to address the many neighborhood problems that concern the community. Public relations programs can help the police in their crime-control role, as well as their problem-solving role, by helping to create a working relationship with the public and institutions in the community like businesses and community organizations.

Community policing provides an opportunity for people to look beyond their own interests, to respond to problems of crime and fear beyond themselves and their respective dwelling units. It offers them a voice in identifying and positively addressing the problems of specific individuals and of the whole community, which may lead to a decrease in crime and fear and to a better quality of life in the community. Classical and participatory democrats have long argued that this type of involvement will aid in the development of more public-minded individuals who think beyond their own needs and impulses to the concerns and needs of the community.[133]

Two responses to crime and fear that have become popular with police departments are the foot patrol and the police–community mini-station. Police foot patrols, like citizen patrols, have the officers walking around the neighborhood instead of driving. It is hoped that by having officers walk around the community, they will increase their interactions with the residents and reduce fears by deterring crime. It is hoped that residents will talk with officers about community problems, as well as offer inside information, so that the police can both control and prevent crime with their help. As Trojanowicz observed, "Because foot-patrol officers make face-to-face contact with the public, they are able to act as community organizers, dispute mediators, service brokers, and links between the community and local social service agencies."[134]

Supporters of foot patrols hope that such community-minded responses will help to get people involved in improving their community.[135] Such action is a two-way street: residents must be willing to get involved, and officers must be willing, too. In a study of foot patrol in Flint, Michigan, Trojanowicz found that "foot patrol officers showed a willingness and desire to conduct special classes for residents and, in general, saw communication and community involvement as very important."[136]

Police–community mini-stations have also been used by police as a means of getting the community involved in crime control and prevention. These stations are typically storefront offices open to all residents. Assigned officers are there to offer a variety of services to the residents, including providing information on crime prevention. Supporters of mini-stations hope that the public will support the stations as a forum for police and residents to meet and work together on addressing community issues.[137]

Although much media attention has been given to police departments and communities that have adopted community policing, the overall effectiveness of this type of response to crime is unknown due to the lack of rigorous evaluations. It remains uncertain whether police foot patrols, for example, can reduce crime,[138] but there is evidence suggesting that in areas where foot patrols are present residents feel safer and crime is perceived to be less of a problem.[139] Also, residents appear not to stress private-minded crime prevention efforts in the presence of area foot patrols.[140] Foot patrol officers are responsible for the creation of neighborhood-watch programs and goodwill toward the police.[141] There is evidence suggesting that in areas where foot patrol is implemented, individuals were satisfied with the patrol and felt that the quality of police service had improved. However, some analyses of official crime records and victimization surveys at the beat level show no change in crime for areas where there are foot patrols, whereas other analyses suggest that crime rates decreased over the life of foot patrol in areas that implemented it.[142]

Responses aimed solely at individual or household problems appear to produce mixed results. For responses focusing on individual residents, such as police–community newsletters and contacting victims of crime, Rosenbaum reported that no effects were found.[143] In a recent study in England, areas where the police contacted residents directly to gather information on problems concerning crime or quality-of-life issues, residents showed an increased sense of community, control over crime, and police satisfaction but no reduction in fear of crime.[144] Interaction between police and residents on an informal basis in which officers stop and actively meet with residents has resulted in lower levels of fear and perceptions of crime among residents.[145] The reason for these mixed findings may be due to the lack of rigorous evaluations of these responses. Overall, it appears that different forms of community policing have different levels of effectiveness.

Conclusions

Participation in responses to crime and fear by the public and the police is viewed as a key to the successful reduction of crime and fear in communities.[146] In practice, this translates into a wide range of responses including the ones highlighted in this chapter and others.[147] Despite the different types of responses and their growing numbers, unanswered questions remain with respect to participation: What is reasonable to expect from the public in terms of responding to crime and fear? What is reasonable to expect from the police?

Research documents the adoption of private-minded responses by a majority of individuals and the resultant growth of private-security businesses. The overwhelming expectation appears to be the protection of one's self, family, and property. But is this response enough to reduce crime and fear of crime in communities? Some researchers have suggested that it is not, and have pointed to the negative consequences for individuals and society when self-interested responses dominate. Others have suggested that such responses lead to a reduction in the probability of being victimized and may lead to a safer community. There appears to be little consensus as to the individual-level and community-level effects of individuals adopting only private-minded responses. This does not mean that such responses do not work and should be abandoned. What is still needed are improved evaluations of the impact of private-minded responses on individuals and communities.

Given the overwhelming adoption of private-minded responses by people, can we expect them to be motivated to participate in public-minded, collective responses?

Rosenbaum has suggested that we may have come to expect too much from these collective responses with respect to participation.[148] He may be right. Many public-minded responses have not been designed to incorporate both self and community interests as motivations of behavior. By appealing to both types of interests, perhaps a more responsive community can be developed over time. We cannot assume that individuals will participate in collective responses because they feel a responsibility toward the community, especially given the high percentage of individuals who participate in private-minded responses and the low percentage that participate in collective responses. Perhaps what is needed is to educate residents as to their responsibility both to themselves and to their communities.

In support of this line of thinking, Etzioni wrote, "Socio-economics suggests that whenever the goal of a policy is to change behavior . . . both normative and economic factors should be considered as policy levers."[149] The time may have come to rethink the incentives for participation in these responses, and to start designing and implementing responses that have a creative synthesis and balance of self-interest and community-interest incentives: educating individuals as to their responsibility to themselves, their property, and their neighborhood and instructing them that collective responses to crime and fear can satisfy their self and community interests.

What can we expect from the police? In reviewing the literature, it appears that some police departments have made and others are making progress toward community-oriented policing. One thing that we can expect is that police departments will not abandon incident-oriented policing, nor do we necessarily want them to abandon it. Crime control and criminal apprehension will continue to be their raison d'être.[150] Hopefully, what we can come to expect is visible, accessible police officers who actively communicate with the public to address each other's needs and concerns, as well as to educate the public as to their role in crime prevention.

Last, participation in responses to crime and fear should not be carried out only by individuals *or* by police officers. Neither the public nor the police can control and prevent crime on their own. Police officers and members of the public need to cooperate and work together to address crime and fear. Bottoms has taken this a step further and has suggested "inter-agency cooperation" to develop and implement responses to crime and fear in neighborhoods. Community organizations and government agencies, including the local police, work with the public to address the underlying problems that lead to crime and fear. According to Bottoms, inter-agency cooperation is such a new theme that, as yet, it has been little researched. His point is that maybe we should think more about how to pool the efforts of different government agencies, community organizations, the police, and the public to work creatively together on crime prevention responses in communities.[151]

In sum, there needs to be more research to understand what motivates individuals to participate in responses to crime and fear. Given that neither the police nor the public can prevent crime and reduce fear alone, research should begin to concentrate on the joint incentives for participation. By better understanding the motives for participation by individuals and by police officers, hopefully we can design and implement successful responses to crime and fear. Research should not stop at understanding motivation for participation but should go further and attempt to understand maintaining participation in responses to crime and fear, and individual- and community-level effects of such participation. Only by better understanding different aspects of responses to crime and fear from motivations to effects can more effective responses be developed.

Notes

1. Dennis Rosenbaum, "Community Crime Prevention: A Review and Synthesis of the Literature"; Jerome Skolnick and David Bayley, "Theme and Variation in Community Policing"; Christopher Nuthall, "Crime Prevention in Canada"; Patricia Brantingham and Paul Brantingham, "Situational Crime Prevention in Practice"; Anthony Bottoms, "Crime Prevention Facing the 1990s."

2. Susan Bennett, Bonnie Fisher, and Paul Lavrakas, "Awareness and Participation in the Eisenhower Neighborhood Program"; Bonnie Fisher, "Participatory Democracy and Participation at the Local Level: A Look at Community Crime Prevention Strategies"; Wesley G. Skogan, "Communities, Crime, and Neighborhood Organization"; Aaron Podolefsky, "Rejecting Crime Prevention Programs: The Dynamics of Program Implementation in High Need Communities." This is not to say that other actors in the criminal justice system, such as prosecutors, judges, and probation officers, are not involved in community responses to crime. For an international overview of how other criminal justice actors are responding to crime and fear, see Skolnick and Bayley, "Theme and Variation in Community Policing," and Bottoms, "Crime Prevention Facing the 1990s." There are also groups outside the criminal justice system who address specific issues with respect to crime and fear, such as those concerned with child and spouse abuse and gun control. Only the police are examined in this essay, because they are the ones who typically work directly with the residents of the community in different responses to crime and fear.

3. Mancur Olson, *The Logic of Collective Action: Public Goods and the Theory of Groups*, p. 1.

4. Mark Petracca, "The Rational Choice Approach to Politics: A Challenge to Democratic Theory"; Jane Mansbridge, *Beyond Self-Interest*; Michael Slote, *Beyond Optimizing: A Study of Rational Choice*.

5. Anthony Downs, *Economic Theory of Democracy*, p. 27.

6. Petracca, "The Rational Choice Approach."

7. Gary Becker, *The Economic Approach to Human Behavior*.

8. See Mansbridge, *Beyond Self-Interest*.

9. Jon Elster, "Selfishness and Altruism," p. 45.

10. Ibid., p. 51.

11. Amitai Etzioni, *The Moral Dimension: Toward a New Economics*.

12. Ibid., p. 63.

13. Mansbridge, *Beyond Self-Interest*, p. ix.

14. Etzioni, *The Moral Dimension*; Howard Margolis, *Selfishness, Altruism, and Rationality*.

15. Robert Kuttner, "Economists Really Should Get Out More Often."

16. Etzioni, *The Moral Dimension*, p. 8.

17. Ibid., p. 64.

18. Letter from Brian Forst to author, March 22, 1992.

19. See Rosenbaum, "Community Crime Prevention."

20. Anne Schneider, "Neighborhood-Based Antiburglary Strategies: An Analysis of Public and Private Benefits from the Portland Program."

21. Schneider, "Neighborhood-Based Antiburglary Strategies"; James Garofalo and Maureen McLeod, "Improving the Use and Effectiveness of Neighborhood Watch Programs"; Gary Marx, "Commentary: Some Trends and Issues in Citizen Involvement in Law Enforcement Process."

22. Lloyd Klein, Joan Luxenburg, and Marianna King, "Perceived Neighborhood Crime and the Impact of Private Security."

23. Steven Lab, *Crime Prevention: Approaches, Practices and Evaluations*; Rosenbaum, "Community Crime Prevention."

24. Wesley G. Skogan and Michael Maxfield, *Coping with Crime: Individual and Neighborhood Reactions*.

25. See Rosenbaum, "Community Crime Prevention."

26. Trevor Bennett and Ronald Wright, *Burglars on Burglary*.

27. Thomas Reppetto, *Residential Crime*.

28. Lab, *Crime Prevention*.

29. Ibid.

30. Rosenbaum, "Community Crime Prevention."

31. This argument is not fully developed and needs to be further examined and tested because displacement of crime from one community to another has been observed by criminologists for years. When target-hardening measures merely displace crime to more vulnerable, less "hardened" targets, one has to question whether society has gained from this type of response. For a good discussion of crime displacement, see Lab, *Crime Prevention*.

32. Rosenbaum, "Community Crime Prevention."

33. Bottoms, "Crime Prevention," p. 20.

34. Rosenbaum, "Community Crime Prevention"; Lab, *Crime Prevention*.

35. Bennett and Wright, *Burglars on Burglary*; Reppetto, *Residential Crime*.

36. Etzioni, *The Moral Dimension*, p. 181.

37. Netherlands Ministry of Justice, "Society and Crime: A Policy Plan for the Netherlands," p. 10.

38. Mansbridge, *Beyond Self-Interest*; Wesley G. Skogan, "Fear of Crime and Neighborhood Change."

39. James Q. Wilson and George Kelling, "Police and Neighborhood Safety: Broken Windows."

40. Skogan, "Communities."

41. Rosenbaum, "Community Crime Prevention."

42. Skogan, "Fear of Crime."

43. Etzioni, *The Moral Dimension*; Margolis, *Selfishness*.

44. Fred DuBow and Aaron Podolefsky, "Citizen Participation in Community Crime Prevention"; Dennis Rosenbaum, Dan Lewis, and Jane Grant, "Neighborhood-Based Crime Prevention: Assessing the Efficacy of Community Organizing in Chicago"; Trevor Bennett, "Factors Related to Participation in Neighborhood Watch Schemes."

45. Wilson and Kelling, "Police and Neighborhood Safety."

46. Emile Durkheim, *The Division of Labor in Society*, p. 102.

47. Kai Erickson, *Wayward Puritans*, p. 4.

48. Trevor Bennett, "The Effectiveness of a Police-Initiated Fear-Reducing Strategy."

49. Etzioni, *The Moral Dimension*.

50. Dennis Rosenbaum, *Community Crime Prevention: Does It Work?*

51. Fred DuBow and David Emmons, "The Community Hypothesis."

52. Ibid.; Fisher, "Participatory Democracy"; Wesley G. Skogan, "Communities, Crime, and Neighborhood Organization."

53. Marx, "Commentary"; and see Rosenbaum, "Community Crime Prevention."

54. Aaron Podolefsky and Fred DuBow, *Strategies for Community Crime Prevention, Collective Responses to Crime in Urban America*; Skogan, "Fear of Crime"; Fisher "Participatory Democracy."

55. Dennis Rosenbaum, "The Theory and Research Behind Neighborhood Watch: Is It a Sound Fear and Crime Reduction Strategy?"

56. Rosenbaum, "Community Crime Prevention."

57. Elliot Currie, "Two Visions of Community Crime Prevention"; Paul Lavrakas and Susan Bennett, "Thinking about the Implementation of Citizen and Community Anti-Crime Measures." Lavrakas and Bennett note that there has been much debate regarding the complex forces that contribute to criminality. Many agree that macrolevel forces such as population demographics, the economy, educational opportunities, and the culture's religious and moral climate play important roles in putting limits on the amount of criminality that might be expected in a society.

58. Skogan and Maxfield, *Coping with Crime*; Rosenbaum, *Community Crime Prevention*.

59. Bennett, "Factors Related to Participation"; Lab, *Crime Prevention*; Skogan and Maxfield, *Coping with Crime*.

60. Podolefsky and DuBow, *Strategies*; Rosenbaum, "Community Crime Prevention"; Lab, *Crime Prevention*.

61. Bennett, "Factors Related to Participation," pp. 215–16.

62. Paul Lavrakas et al., *Factors Related to Citizen Involvement in Personal, Household, and Neighborhood Anti-Crime Measures*.

63. Bennett, "Factors Related to Participation," pp. 213–17.

64. Bennett, "Factors Related to Participation"; Rosenbaum, "Community Crime Prevention"; Skogan, "Fear of Crime"; Lab, *Crime Prevention*.

65. Bonnie Fisher, "Block Watch or Seminars: What Works in Community Crime Prevention?"

66. Rosenbaum, Lewis, and Grant, "Neighborhood-Based Crime Prevention." Rosenbaum, Lewis, and Grant employed a pretest-posttest design with a nonequivalent comparison group. Each of their five neighborhoods that implemented collective crime prevention responses had three comparison neighborhoods where responses were not implemented.

67. Trevor Bennett, "An Evaluation of Two Neighborhood Watch Schemes in London."

68. George Kelling, Robert Wasserman, and Hubert Williams, *Police Accountability and Community Policing.*

69. Skolnick and Bayley, "Theme and Variation."

70. For an excellent overview of the police history, see George Kelling and Mark Moore, *The Evolving Strategy of Policing.*

71. Christopher Walker and Sandra-Gail Walker, "The Citizen and the Police: A Partnership in Crime Prevention"; Nuthall, "Crime Prevention in Canada"; Kelling and Moore, *Evolving Strategy*; George Kelling, *Police and Communities: The Quiet Revolution.*

72. Kelling and Moore, *Evolving Strategy.*

73. Skolnick and Bayley, "Theme and Variation."

74. Kelling, *Police and Communities*, p. 4.

75. As cited in Kelling, *Police and Communities*, p. 4.

76. Mark Moore, Robert Trojanowicz, and George Kelling, *Crime and Policing.*

77. Kelling, *Police and Communities.*

78. Moore, Trojanowicz, and Kelling, *Crime and Policing*, p. 8.

79. Skolnick and Bayley, "Theme and Variation."

80. Herman Goldstein, "Improving Policing: A Problem-Oriented Approach" and *Problem-Oriented Policing.*

81. Podolefsky and DuBow, *Strategies*; Lab, *Crime Prevention*; Rosenbaum, "Community Crime Prevention."

82. Kelling and Moore, *Evolving Strategy.*

83. Mark Moore and Robert Trojanowicz, *Corporate Strategies for Policing.*

84. Ibid.

85. Skolnick and Bayley, "Theme and Variation," p. 12.

86. Peter Horne, "Not Just Old Wine in New Bottles: The Inextricable Relationship Between Crime Prevention and Community Policing."

87. Skolnick and Bayley, "Theme and Variation," p. 25.

88. Kelling and Moore, *Evolving Strategy*; Camille Barnett and Robert Bowers, "Community Policing: The New Model for the Way the Police Do Their Jobs."

89. Skolnick and Bayley, "Theme and Variation," p. 26.

90. Klein, Luxenburg, and King, "Perceived Neighborhood Crime."

91. Dennis Rosenbaum, Arthur Lurigio, and Paul Lavrakas, "Enhancing Citizen Participation and Solving Serious Crime: A National Evaluation of Crime Stoppers Programs."

92. Rosenbaum, *Community Crime Prevention.*

93. Crime Stoppers International, *The Caller.*

94. Rosenbaum, Lurigio, and Lavrakas, "Enhancing Citizen Participation."

95. Dennis Rosenbaum and Arthur Lurigio, working paper.

96. Rosenbaum, Lurigio, and Lavrakas, "Enhancing Citizen Participation."

97. Brantingham and Brantingham, "Situational Crime Prevention"; James Garofalo and Maureen McLeod, "The Structure and Operations of Neighborhood Watch Programs in the United States."

98. U.S. Department of Justice, "Report to the Nation on Crime and Justice: The Data."

99. Rosenbaum, *Community Crime Prevention* and "Community Crime Prevention."

100. DuBow and Emmons, "The Community Hypothesis."

101. Lab, *Crime Prevention*; Skogan, "Communities"; Brantingham and Brantingham, "Situational Crime Prevention."

102. Marx, "Commentary."

103. Garofalo and McLeod, "Improving the Use and Effectiveness."

104. Garofalo and McLeod, "The Structure and Operations."

105. Julian Roberts and Michelle Grossman, "Crime Prevention and Public Opinion."

106. Michael Hough and Pat Mayhew, "Taking Accounts of Crime: Findings from the 1984 British Crime Victim Survey."

107. Solicitor General of Canada, *Crime Prevention: Awareness and Practice.*

108. Hough and Mayhew, "Taking Accounts of Crime."

109. Roberts and Grossman, "Crime Prevention."

110. Rosenbaum, "Community Crime Prevention."

111. Fisher, "Block Watch or Seminars."

112. Bennett, "An Evaluation"; Rosenbaum, Lewis, and Grant, "Neighborhood-Based Crime Prevention."

113. Lab, *Crime Prevention.*

114. Gary Marx and Dane Archer, "The Urban Vigilante."

115. Marx, "Commentary"; Susan Pennell et al., "Guardian Angels: A Unique Approach to Crime Prevention."

116. Robert Yin et al., *Citizen Patrol Projects*; Rosenbaum, "Community Crime Prevention"; Pennell et al., "Guardian Angels."

117. Lab, *Crime Prevention.*

118. Yin et al., *Citizen Patrol Projects.*

119. Pennell et al., "Guardian Angels."

120. Susan Pennell, Christine Curtis, and Joel Henderson, *Guardian Angels: An Assessment of Citizen Responses to Crime.*

121. Rosenbaum, "Community Crime Prevention."

122. Klein, Luxenburg, and King, "Perceived Neighborhood Crime."

123. Ron Troyer, "The Urban Anticrime Patrol Phenomenon: A Case Study of a Student Effort."

124. See Pennell et al., "Guardian Angels."

125. Rosenbaum, "Community Crime Prevention"; Ron Troyer and Ronald Wright, "Community Responses to Crime: Two Middle-Class Anti-Crime Patrols"; Edward Latessa and Harry E. Allen, "Using Citizens to Prevent Crime: An Example of Deterrence and Community Involvement."

126. Rosenbaum, "Community Crime Prevention"; Lab, *Crime Prevention.*

127. Rosenbaum, "Community Crime Prevention," p. 372.

128. Ibid.

129. Lab, *Crime Prevention.*

130. Wesley G. Skogan and Mary Ann Wycoff, "Storefront Police Offices: The Houston Field Test."

131. Mark Moore and Robert Trojanowicz, *Corporate Strategies for Policing.*

132. Skolnick and Bayley, "Theme and Variation."

133. Carole Pateman, *Participation and Democratic Theory.*

134. Robert Trojanowicz, "Evaluating a Neighborhood Foot Patrol Program: The Flint, Michigan, Project," p. 177.

135. Moore and Trojanowicz, *Corporate Strategies for Policing.*

136. Trojanowicz, "Evaluating a Foot Patrol Program," p. 171.

137. Skogan and Wycoff, "Storefront Police Offices."

138. Rosenbaum, "Community Crime Prevention."

139. Rosenbaum, "Community Crime Prevention"; Antony Pate, "Experimenting with Foot Patrol: The Newark Experience"; Trojanowicz, "Evaluating a Foot Patrol Program."

140. Lab, *Crime Prevention.*

141. Robert Trojanowicz and Bonnie Bucqueroux, *Community Policing: A Contemporary Perspective.*

142. Pate, "Experimenting with Foot Patrol"; Trojanowicz, "Evaluating a Foot Patrol Program."

143. Rosenbaum, "Community Crime Prevention."

144. Bennett, "The Effectiveness of a Police-Initiated Fear-Reducing Strategy."

145. Lee Brown and Mary Ann Wycoff, "Policing Houston: Reducing Fear and Improving Service."

146. Rosenbaum, "Community Crime Prevention"; Lab, *Crime Prevention.*

147. See Arthur Lurigio and Dennis Rosenbaum, "Evaluation Research in Community Crime Prevention: A Critical Look at the Field."

148. Rosenbaum, "Community Crime Prevention."

149. Etzioni, *The Moral Dimension*, p. 238.

150. Skolnick and Bayley, "Theme and Variation."

151. Bottoms, "Crime Prevention."

References

Barnett, Camille, and Bowers, Robert. "Community Policing: The New Model for the Way the Police Do Their Jobs." *Public Management* 72, no. 6 (1990): 2–6.

Becker, Gary. *The Economic Approach to Human Behavior.* Chicago: University of Chicago Press, 1976.

Bennett, Susan; Fisher, Bonnie; and Lavrakas, Paul. "Awareness and Participation in the Eisenhower Neighborhood Program." Paper presented at the American Society of Criminology, Atlanta, Georgia, October 1986.

Bennett, Trevor. "The Effectiveness of a Police-Initiated Fear-Reducing Strategy." *British Journal of Criminology* 31, no. 1 (1991): 1–13.

———. "An Evaluation of Two Neighborhood Watch Schemes in London." Executive summary of final report to the Home Office Research and Planning Unit. Cambridge, England: Cambridge University, Institute of Criminology, 1987.

———. "Factors Related to Participation in Neighborhood Watch Schemes." *British Journal of Criminology* 29, no. 3 (1989): 207–17.

Bennett, Trevor, and Wright, Ronald. *Burglars on Burglary.* Aldershot, England: Gower, 1984.

Bottoms, Anthony. "Crime Prevention Facing the 1990s." *Policing and Society* 1, no. 1 (1990): 3–22.

Brantingham, Patricia, and Brantingham, Paul. "Situational Crime Prevention in Practice." *Canadian Journal of Criminology* 32, no. 1 (1990): 17–40.

Brown, Lee, and Wycoff, Mary Ann. "Policing Houston: Reducing Fear and Improving Service." *Crime and Delinquency* 33, no. 1 (1987): 71–89.

Clark, Peter, and Wilson, James Q. "Incentive Systems: A Theory of Organizations." *Administrative Science Quarterly* 6 (1961): 129–66.

Clarke, Ronald. "Situational Crime Prevention: Theory and Practice." *British Journal of Criminology* 20, no. 2 (1980): 136–47.

Crime Stoppers International. *The Caller*, no. 53 (April 1988).

Currie, Elliot. "Two Visions of Community Crime Prevention." Paper delivered at the Home Office Conference on Communities and Crime Reduction, Cambridge, England, July 16–18, 1986.

Downs, Anthony. *Economic Theory of Democracy.* New York: Harper and Row, 1957.

DuBow, Fred, and Emmons, David. "The Community Hypothesis." In Dan A. Lewis, ed., *Reactions to Crime*, pp. 167–81. Beverly Hills: Sage Publications, 1981.

DuBow, Fred and Podolefsky, Aaron. "Citizen Participation in Community Crime Prevention." *Human Organization* 41, no. 4 (1982): 307–14.

Durkheim, Emile. *The Division of Labor in Society* (1893), tr. George Simpson. New York: Free Press, 1933.

Elster, Jon. "Selfishness and Altruism." In Jane J. Mansbridge, ed., *Beyond Self-Interest.* Chicago: University of Chicago Press, 1990.

Erickson, Kai. *Wayward Puritans.* New York: John Wiley, 1966.

Etzioni, Amitai. *The Moral Dimension: Toward a New Economics.* New York: Free Press, 1988.

Fisher, Bonnie. "Block Watch or Seminars: What Works in Community Crime Prevention?" *Journal of Crime and Justice* 16, no. 1 (1993): 1–20.

———. "Participatory Democracy and Participation at the Local Level: A Look at Community Crime Prevention Strategies." Unpublished dissertation. Northwestern University, Evanston, Illinois, 1988.

Garofalo, James, and McLeod, Maureen. "Improving the Use and Effectiveness of Neighborhood Watch Programs." National Institute of Justice, Research in Action. Washington, D.C.: Government Printing Office, 1988.

———. "The Structure and Operations of Neighborhood Watch Programs in the United States." *Crime and Delinquency* 35, no. 3 (1989): 326–44.

Goldstein, Herman. "Improving Policing: A Problem-Oriented Approach." *Crime and Delinquency* 25, no. 2 (1979): 236–58.

———. *Problem-Oriented Policing.* New York: McGraw-Hill, 1990.

Hale, Donna, and Leonik, Robert. "Planning Community-Initiated Crime Prevention." *Journal of Police Science and Administration* 10, no. 1 (1982): 76–82.

Horne, Peter. "Not Just Old Wine in New Bottles: The Inextricable Relationship Between Crime Prevention and Community Policing." *The Police Chief* (May 1991): 24–27.

Hough, Michael, and Mayhew, Pat. "Taking Accounts of Crime: Findings from the 1984 British Crime Victim Survey." London: Her Majesty's Stationery Office, 1985.

Hourihan, Kevin. "Local Community Involvement and Participation in Neighbourhood Watch: A Case-Study in Cork, Ireland." *Urban Studies* 24, no. 2 (1987): 129–36.

Kelling, George. *Police and Communities: The Quiet Revolution.* Washington, D.C.: U.S. Department of Justice; Cambridge, Mass.: John F. Kennedy School of Government, Harvard University, 1988.

Kelling, George, and Moore, Mark. *The Evolving Strategy of Policing.* Washington, D.C.: U.S. Department of Justice; Cambridge, Mass.: John F. Kennedy School of Government, Harvard University, 1988.

Kelling, George; Wasserman, Robert; and Williams, Hubert. *Police Accountability and Community Policing.* Washington, D.C.: U.S. Department of Justice; Cambridge, Mass.: John F. Kennedy School of Government, Harvard University, 1988.

Klein, Lloyd; Luxenburg, Joan; and King, Marianna. "Perceived Neighborhood Crime and the Impact of Private Security." *Crime and Delinquency* 35, no. 3 (1989): 365–77.

Kuttner, Robert. "Economists Really Should Get Out More Often." *Business Week*, April 24, 1989, p. 16.

Lab, Steven. *Crime Prevention: Approaches, Practices and Evaluations.* Cincinnati, Ohio: Anderson, 1988.

Latessa, Edward, and Allen, Harry E. "Using Citizens to Prevent Crime: An Example of Deterrence and Community Involvement." *Journal of Police Science and Administration* 8, no. 1 (1980): 69–74.

Lavrakas, Paul, and Bennett, Susan. "Thinking about the Implementation of Citizen and Community Anti-Crime Measures." Paper delivered at the Home Office Conference on Communities and Crime Reduction, Cambridge, England, July 16–18, 1986.

Lavrakas, Paul; Normoyle, Janice; Skogan, Wesley; Hertz, Elica; Salem, Gerta; and Lewis, Dan. *Factors Related to Citizen Involvement in Personal, Household, and*

Neighborhood Anti-Crime Measures. Final report to the National Institute of Justice. Evanston, Ill.: Northwestern University, Center for Urban Affairs and Policy Research, 1980.

Lavrakas, Paul, and Herz, Elica. "Citizen Participation in Neighborhood Crime Prevention." *Criminology* 20, no. 3 (1982): 479–98.

Lurigio, Arthur, and Rosenbaum, Dennis. "The Effects of Mass Media on Crime Prevention Awareness Attitudes and Behavior: The Case of Crime Stoppers." *American Journal of Community Psychology* (1990).

———. "Evaluation Research in Community Crime Prevention: A Critical Look at the Field." In Dennis P. Rosenbaum, ed., *Community Crime Prevention: Does It Work?* Beverly Hills: Sage Publications, 1986.

Mansbridge, Jane. *Beyond Self-Interest.* Chicago: University of Chicago Press, 1990.

Margolis, Howard. *Selfishness, Altruism, and Rationality.* Cambridge: University of Cambridge, 1982.

Marx, Gary. "Commentary: Some Trends and Issues in Citizen Involvement in Law Enforcement Process." *Crime and Delinquency* 35, no. 3 (1989): 500–519.

Marx, Gary, and Archer, Dane. "The Urban Vigilante." *Psychology Today* 6, no. 1 (January–February 1973): 45–50.

McPherson, Marlys, and Silloway, Glenn. "Planning to Prevent Crime." In Dan A. Lewis, ed., *Reactions to Crime,* pp. 149–65. Beverly Hills: Sage Publications, 1981.

Moore, Mark, and Trojanowicz, Robert. *Corporate Strategies for Policing.* Washington, D.C.: U.S. Department of Justice; Cambridge, Mass.: John F. Kennedy School of Government, Harvard University, 1988.

———. *Policing and Fear of Crime.* Washington, D.C.: U.S. Department of Justice; Cambridge, Mass.: John F. Kennedy School of Government, Harvard University, 1988.

Moore, Mark; Trojanowicz, Robert; and Kelling, George. *Crime and Policing.* Washington, D.C.: U.S. Department of Justice; Cambridge, Mass.: John F. Kennedy School of Government, Harvard University, 1988.

Netherlands Ministry of Justice. "Society and Crime: A Policy Plan for the Netherlands." The Hague: Ministerie van Justitie, 1985.

Nuthall, Christopher. "Crime Prevention in Canada." *Canadian Journal of Criminology* 32, no. 3 (1989): 477–85.

Olson, Mancur. *The Logic of Collective Action: Public Goods and the Theory of Groups.* Cambridge, Mass.: Harvard University Press, 1971.

Pate, Antony. "Experimenting with Foot Patrol: The Newark Experience." In Dennis P. Rosenbaum, ed., *Community Crime Prevention: Does It Work?* Beverly Hills: Sage Publications, 1986.

Pateman, Carole. *Participation and Democratic Theory.* London: Cambridge University Press, 1970.

Pennell, Susan; Curtis, Christine; and Henderson, Joel. *Guardian Angels: An Assessment of Citizen Responses to Crime,* vol. 2. Technical report. San Diego: San Diego Association of Governments, 1985.

Pennell, Susan; Curtis, Christine; Henderson, Joel; and Tayman, Jeff. "Guardian Angels: A Unique Approach to Crime Prevention." *Crime and Delinquency* 35, no. 3 (1989): 378–400.

Petracca, Mark. "The Rational Choice Approach to Politics: A Challenge to Democratic Theory." *The Review of Politics* 53, no. 2 (1991): 289–319.

Podolefsky, Aaron. "Rejecting Crime Prevention Programs: The Dynamics of Program Implementation in High Need Communities." *Human Organization* 44, no. 1 (1985): 33–40.

Podolefsky, Aaron, and DuBow, Fred. *Strategies for Community Crime Prevention, Collective Responses to Crime in Urban America*. Springfield, Ill.: Charles C. Thomas, 1982.

Reppetto, Thomas. *Residential Crime*. Cambridge, Mass.: Ballinger, 1974.

Roberts, Julian, and Grossman, Michelle. "Crime Prevention and Public Opinion." *Canadian Journal of Criminology* (January 1990): 75–89.

Roehl, Janice, and Cook, Royer. *Evaluation of the Urban Crime Prevention Program*. Washington, D.C.: Department of Justice, National Institute of Justice, 1984.

Rosenbaum, Dennis. *Community Crime Prevention: Does It Work?* Beverly Hills: Sage Publications, 1986.

———. "Community Crime Prevention: A Review and Synthesis of the Literature." *Justice Quarterly* 5, no. 3 (1988): 323–94.

———. "The Theory and Research Behind Neighborhood Watch: Is It a Sound Fear and Crime Reduction Strategy?" *Crime and Delinquency* 33, no. 1 (1987): 103–34.

Rosenbaum, Dennis; Lewis, Dan; and Grant, Jane. "Neighborhood-Based Crime Prevention: Assessing the Efficacy of Community Organizing in Chicago." In Dennis P. Rosenbaum, ed., *Community Crime Prevention: Does It Work?* Beverly Hills: Sage Publications, 1986.

Rosenbaum, Dennis, and Lurigio, Arthur. Working paper, University of Chicago, 1990.

Rosenbaum, Dennis; Lurigio, Arthur; and Lavrakas, Paul. "Enhancing Citizen Participation and Solving Serious Crime: A National Evaluation of Crime Stoppers Programs." *Crime and Delinquency* 35, no. 3 (1989): 401–20.

Schneider, Anne. "Neighborhood-Based Antiburglary Strategies: An Analysis of Public and Private Benefits from the Portland Program." In Dennis P. Rosenbaum, ed., *Community Crime Prevention: Does It Work?* Beverly Hills: Sage Publications, 1986.

Skogan, Wesley G. "Communities, Crime, and Neighborhood Organization." *Crime and Delinquency* 35, no. 3 (1988): 437–57.

———. "Fear of Crime and Neighborhood Change." In Albert J. Reiss and Michael Tonry eds., *Crime and Justice: A Review of Research*. Chicago: University of Chicago Press, 1986.

Skogan, Wesley G., and Maxfield, Michael. *Coping with Crime: Individual and Neighborhood Reactions*. Beverly Hills: Sage Publications, 1981.

Skogan, Wesley G,. and Wycoff, Mary Ann. "Storefront Police Offices: The Houston Field Test." In Dennis P. Rosenbaum, ed., *Community Crime Prevention: Does It Work?* Beverly Hills: Sage Publications, 1986.

Skolnick, Jerome, and Bayley, David. "Theme and Variation in Community Policing." In Michael Tonry and Norval Morris, eds., *Crime and Justice: A Review of Research*. Chicago: University of Chicago Press, 1988.

Slote, Michael. *Beyond Optimizing: A Study of Rational Choice*. Cambridge, Mass.: Harvard University Press. 1989.

Solicitor General of Canada. 1984. *Crime Prevention: Awareness and Practice*. Canadian Urban Victimization Survey Bulletin 3. Ottawa: Research and Statistics Group, Programs Branch, 1984.

Trojanowicz, Robert. "Evaluating a Neighborhood Foot Patrol Program: The Flint, Michigan, Project." In Dennis P. Rosenbaum, ed., *Community Crime Prevention: Does It Work?* Beverly Hills: Sage Publications, 1986.

Trojanowicz, Robert, and Bucqueroux, Bonnie. *Community Policing: A Contemporary Perspective*. Cincinnati, Ohio: Anderson, 1990.

Troyer, Ron. "The Urban Anticrime Patrol Phenomenon: A Case Study of a Student Effort." *Justice Quarterly* 5 (1988): 397–419.

Troyer, Ron, and Wright, Ronald. "Community Responses to Crime: Two Middle-Class Anti-Crime Patrols." *Journal of Crime and Justice* 10, no. 3 (1985): 199–210.

U.S. Department of Justice, Bureau of Justice Statistics. "Report to the Nation on Crime and Justice: The Data." Washington, D.C.: U.S. Department of Justice, 1986.

Walker, Christopher, and Walker, Sandra-Gail. "The Citizen and the Police: A Partnership in Crime Prevention." *Canadian Journal of Criminology* 32, no. 1 (1990): 125–35.

Wilson, James Q. and Kelling, George. "Police and Neighborhood Safety: Broken Windows." *Atlantic Monthly* 249, no. 3 (1982): 29–38.

Yin, Robert; Vogel, M.; Chaiken, Jan; and Both, D. *Citizen Patrol Projects*. Washington, D.C.: Government Printing Office, 1977.

10

JEFFREY FAGAN

Social Structure and Spouse Assault

Introduction

Social scientists are fond of saying that family violence is a "classless" problem. This conventional wisdom states that the abuse of women and children occurs in all social classes, across occupational types, in all racial and ethnic groups, in all types of neighborhoods, in cities and rural areas, and among the young and the old.[1] Gelles and Cornell rank the popular belief that family violence is confined to the lower classes as the *second* most pervasive myth about family violence.[2]

Acceptance of a socially unbounded distribution of family violence is no small matter for theory and research. Social class and associated social factors such as poverty and social disorganization having presumably been eliminated as causes of family violence; explanations of family violence have focused on cultural factors and individual or family pathologies.[3]

But the claim that family violence is independent of social structural influences runs counter to empirical evidence about the social epidemiology of violence between spouses and other intimates. Violence toward spouses is more common among lower-income groups[4] and non-whites,[5] and is concentrated spatially in central cities where there are greater concentrations of poor people.[6] These trends suggest that indeed there are social structural influences on the distribution of spouse assault.

Yet the "classless" interpretation of spouse assault may also be valid: spouse assault is not limited to the lower socioeconomic groups. Although general population studies show that spouse assault victimization rates may be higher for women with lower socioeconomic status (SES), effect sizes rarely are reported and SES measures vary considerably across studies. For example, a 1979 replica-

This research was supported in part by a grant from the Harry Frank Guggenheim Foundation. Thanks to Joel Garner for his comments on earlier versions of this manuscript and to Christopher Maxwell for invaluable assistance in data analysis.

tion in Kentucky of the Straus, Gelles, and Steinmetz. National Family Violence Survey found only a 3 percent difference between spouse assault rates for low-income women (11 percent) and women whose family incomes exceeded $25,000 (8 percent).[7] A secondary analysis of the Straus, Gelles, and Steinmetz data found no differences among low and high SES women in their reports of the prevalence of verbal assault and minor violence directed at them,[8] but significant differences in the likelihood of severe assault.[9] And after controlling for race, income, and education, the effects of male unemployment on rates of spouse assault are negligible.[10] It seems that evidence of social structural influences on spouse assault may reflect definition, measurement, and analysis decisions more so than substantive differences.[11]

In this chapter, we examine the social structure of spouse assault. The debate over whether spouse assault is a societal problem or one predominantly affecting only poor or minority people is a highly charged and contextualized debate, encompassing nothing short of the state of minority (primarily African-American) families, the origins of interpersonal violence, and the design of social interventions to control violent behavior. The conflicting assertions and evidence on the social, demographic, and economic correlates of spouse assault suggest that we reconsider its social epidemiology and the distribution of injuries and deaths caused by family members. We also consider here the mediating effects of social structure and social area on the effectiveness of legal interventions for spouse assault, processes that bear on the theory and practice of deterrence.

The assumption that spouse assault is classless has important implications for theory and policy. First, if spouse assault does not share the social structural correlates of stranger violence, then there is reason to believe that some of the origins and explanations of interpersonal violence may be distinct from stranger assault. Interpersonal violence involving strangers is mediated by social structural factors that are influential at both the individual and community levels.[12] If spouse assault is unrelated to these factors, we might reasonably assume that it is influenced by etiological processes separate from those involved in stranger assaults, as well as involving different individuals. This assumption in turn suggests that the unique context of families itself is an etiological factor in spouse assault and diminishes the importance of ecological factors or social position in explaining this form of interpersonal violence.

Although family violence may be evident in all social *classes*, some forms of it may be concentrated in specific social *areas*. Victimization of women by intimates (spouses, boyfriends, or nonmarital cohabitants) is more likely in central cities.[13] Central cities tend to have greater concentrations of poor people and minorities as well as higher rates of interpersonal violence overall.[14] Social controls generally are weaker in cities and especially in their poorer areas, contributing to higher rates of interpersonal violence.[15] Thus, the question of whether social structural variables influence spouse assault also raises the question of the extent to which stranger and spouse assault are related or distinct phenomena.

Second, the social structure of spouse assault has implications for the effectiveness of interventions and social controls for violent partners. If the causes of spouse assault are unrelated to social class (that is, if spouse assault is "classless"), then social controls are likely to be equally effective regardless of the assailant's social position or social area. This would reflect the dominant influence of the unique context of the family in the genesis and control of spouse assault and its independence from the informal and formal restraints on violence in neighborhood and workplace milieus.

Social controls on stranger violence do reflect the social structure of individuals, if not the neighborhoods they live in. Access to services for victims vary by social area as well as the social position of victims. Certainly, economic circumstances can influence a victim's decision to leave an abusive partner[16] and the decision to make use of public services such as shelters or private remedies.[17] The salience of informal social controls within neighborhoods also may reflect the social capital within the neighborhood[18] and the willingness of its residents to invoke social sanctions or opprobria for violence toward spouses. The efficacy of legal sanctions for spouse assault may reflect the reciprocity between (formal) sanctions imposed by legal institutions and informal social sanctions in regulating family behaviors.[19] Social controls also may reflect assailants' perceptions of the social and economic benefits of stopping their violence, benefits that derive from the social structure of the neighborhood and surrounding community. Accordingly, the social structure of neighborhoods and families may be important influences on whether laws and norms regarding family violence are respected.

I begin the chapter by reviewing empirical research on the social correlates of spouse assault. Analyses of recent national survey data will show the social and economic correlates of spouse assault in a general population study of American couples. I briefly review data from the National Crime Survey to show another view of the social structure of spouse assault. Also reviewed are injuries and fatalities, extremes of spouse assault that are undersampled in the general population studies. I then analyze the growing literature on the influence of social structure and social area on the effectiveness of legal interventions for spouse assault. The chapter concludes with an analysis of theoretical perspectives that integrate social structural perspectives with contemporary theories on the occurrence and control of spouse assault.

The Social Epidemiology of Spouse Assault

Empirical reports of violence between adults in families first appeared in the social science literature in the 1960s.[20] Early studies relied on small samples of battered women, men, or couples involved in the criminal justice system, or violent couples who defined themselves as experiencing family violence before being included in the research.[21] In 1977, the first epidemiological estimates of family violence were published, based on data from the National Family Violence Survey (NFVS)[22] and the National Crime Survey (NCS).[23] The NFVS was repeated a decade later,[24] while the NCS is a continuing survey whose results are reported annually.[25]

Estimates of the prevalence and social correlates of spouse assault are quite sensitive to sampling, analysis, and measurement decisions.[26] Official records and reports from service agencies have obvious sampling biases resulting from selection processes by police and individuals seeking help. In self-report studies, segments of the population at risk for intimate or spouse assault are often excluded: for example, those who do not speak English fluently,[27] the very poor who lack telephones, the homeless, homosexual couples, college students, couples in short-term relationships of less than one year, and persons hospitalized, institutionalized, or incarcerated. Many of these groups are spatially concentrated in cities and are from low socioeconomic groups. Their exclusion obviously bears heavily on the assessment of the social structure of spouse assault.

Ethnicity and race often are confounded, particularly in the case of Hispanic couples.[28] Gross categorizations of diverse Spanish-speaking cultures as "Hispanics" mask differences in normative family processes among separate ethnic groups. Selection biases also limit empirical knowledge among Hispanic families. Many are recent immigrants to the United States who may not participate in self-report studies due to language skills, lack of familiarity with social surveys, and (for illegal immigrants) fears of detection and deportation.[29] The confounding of race, class, education, and urbanism also limits conclusions about social class and spouse assault among African-Americans.[30]

The 1985 NFVS provides a unique opportunity to disentangle the effects of urbanism, race, and social class on spouse assault. The probability sample (N = 6,002 households) includes two oversamples (508 African-American and 516 Hispanic households) that were added to assure sufficient representation across income and education groups, and especially in urban areas. The sample was then weighted to adjust for the oversamples, providing a representative sample of the U.S. population.[31] It also includes households with both intact couples and recently divorced or separated adults. These data are used to estimate the effects of social structure on spouse assault by either partner in the home in the past year.

In addition to estimating rates by ethnicity, education, and income, the estimates control for the macrosocial influences of urbanism. There is consistent evidence that interpersonal violence rates are higher in cities,[32] and that urbanism has both direct and indirect influences on interpersonal assault.[33] Urban areas have higher concentrations of poor and minority people and greater residential mobility.[34] Although urbanism includes dimensions of density and heterogeneity, it is size of place that most often is emphasized in research on urbanism.[35] Size of place implies density, since size is usually determined by political boundaries. And with density comes greater anonymity and weaker social controls, social processes that are associated with higher rates of interpersonal violence.[36] However, the effects of place on spouse assault have yet to be tested.

Estimates of prevalence and offending rates of spouse assault were computed based on reports of spouse assault by *any* adult respondent within the home, either as victim or as assailant.[37] The use of a frequency measure recognizes the distinction between prevalence and incidence measures of spouse assault and their conceptual importance for assessing risks.[38] The use of both male and female reports avoids the limitations of relying solely on either male or female reports. For example, previous analyses of these data showed that males and females report similar prevalence rates of victimization, but males report lower rates of serious assaults against their partners.[39]

Table 10.1 shows the overall spouse assault rates for couples in central cities, suburbs, or rural areas by the couple's income, age, marital status, ethnicity,[40] the highest education of either partner, and whether anyone in the home is employed. Overall, rates are highest in central cities, with 20.3 per 100 couples reporting spouse assault by one or both partners in the past year. This rate was higher than the rates for couples in suburbs (15.3 per 100 couples) and in rural areas (13.7 per 100 couples). These trends persist after controlling for family income, marital status, ethnicity, education, and employment.

Within central cities, participation rates are significantly higher for African-American and Hispanic couples than for white couples and other ethnic groups. Yet there were no significant differences among ethnic groups outside central cities. These trends may reflect disparities in income, housing, and employment faced by African-American and Hispanic families in inner cities, as well as differences in social processes in neighborhoods with concentrations of poor, nonwhite households. Such disparities have long been associated with both individual and aggregate rates of interpersonal violence and homicide.[41]

Spouse assault rates were highest in central cities for low-income groups, low-education couples, and couples with no household members working; rates declined with urbanism for all these groups. But the effects of low education and income were not evident outside central cities. Outside central cities, high income and education were protective factors for spouse assault, but the effects of poverty were not evident beyond central cities. Only the effects of unemployment were evident in suburbs and rural areas. Accordingly, the effects of low socioeconomic status are reflected in spouse-assault rates primarily under conditions of urbanism. It seems that the effects of social structural factors on spouse assault at the individual level may be mediated by the ecological context where couples reside.

In more detailed race-income analyses (not shown), spouse assault rates were consistently over 30 percent for African-American families earning less than $10,000 annually, whether in cities, suburbs, or rural areas. These rates were nearly three times the general population rate reported by Straus and Gelles.[42] Although spouse-assault rates for African-American families decline with in-

Table 10.1

Participation of Any Adult Household Members in Spouse Assault by Social and Demographic Characteristics, Controlling for Area Size

	Area Size		
	Central City	Suburban	Rural
N	1,362	2,634	1,365
N with One or More Incidents	276	404	187
Percent with One or More Incidents	20.3	15.3	13.7
Social and Demographic Characteristics			
Age			
≤ 21	39.4	23.4	43.1
22 – 26	37.8	32.5	26.8
27 – 35	25.0	22.6	20.3
36 – 50	17.0	12.9	9.9
≥ 51	8.9	5.5	6.3
p (Chi-square)	.000	.000	.000
Marital Status			
Nonmarried Cohabitants	42.0	32.4	24.6
Married	17.7	14.3	13.4
Separated/Divorced	50.4	27.3	14.6
p (Chi-square)	.000	.000	.193
Ethnicity			
White	18.7	15.2	13.2
African-American	27.4	20.0	24.9
Hispanic	25.9	18.2	19.4
Other	16.0	15.8	16.1
p (Chi-square)	.017	.592	.109
Household Income			
≤ $10,000	29.3	18.8	12.9
$10,001–20,000	23.8	16.0	14.4
$20,001–30,000	22.4	19.4	14.7
≥ $30,000	17.8	13.3	13.7
p (Chi-square)	.017	.004	.950
Educational Attainment			
High School Graduate or Less	23.2	14.9	15.1
Some College or More	18.5	15.6	11.0
p (Chi-square)	.035	.619	.090
Household Member Working			
Working	15.7	9.7	10.4
Not Working	21.3	16.3	14.5
p (Chi-square)	.053	.0001	.078

creasing income in suburban and rural areas, their rates remain high (nearly 30 percent) in central cities independent of income.[43] There is no consistent pattern for Hispanic couples. For white couples, spouse-assault rates are inversely associated with income in central cities but not elsewhere. Yet their rates remain lower than the rates for nonwhites at all income levels.

These trends suggest that poverty for African-American families is a stronger risk factor for spouse assault than among white or Hispanic families. But there also are stresses on African-American families within central cities that occur independently of income or educational status and are not present in suburbs. There seem to be mediating processes in the social and ecological contexts of neighborhoods where African-American families live that may contribute to spouse assault, independent of social structural variables or other factors. Neighborhood effects will be discussed further later in this chapter.

Unlike income or other structural factors, age and marital status differences persist even after controlling for "place." Prevalence rates were highest among couples in which respondents were twenty-six years of age or less, regardless of whether they resided in cities, suburbs, or rural areas. The highest prevalence rates were reported by respondents eighteen to twenty-one years of age in cities and rural areas, and respondents twenty-two to twenty-six years of age in the suburbs. Rates also were highest for nonmarried couples, with over 40 percent of the cohabiting couples reporting one or more types of spouse assault. The differences persisted across areas but declined with decreasing area size. In all three types of areas, marriage was a protective factor, relative to any other marital status, from spouse assault.

The prevalence rates for younger respondents in the NFVS are consistent with the rates obtained in the National Youth Survey, a longitudinal study with a nationwide probability sample of 1,725 young adults ages eighteen to twenty-four. Elliott, Huizinga, and Morse reported rates for the 1983 wave that were more than three times higher than the rates obtained by Straus and colleagues in either the 1975 or 1985 NFVS iterations. The trends in the NYS and NFVS mirror the high participation rates for stranger violence among general populations in this age range,[44] and suggest similar age structures for marital and stranger violence.

Table 10.2 shows spouse-assault offending rates for the past year for any adult member of a household by the same social structural variables. Here, I compare the frequency of spouse assault by any member of the household, only for those households reporting at least one incident in the past year. Separate analyses were completed for respondents within central cities, suburbs, and rural areas. Based on the findings in Table 10.1 regarding age, age was included as a covariate in analyses of incidence rates by income, marital status, ethnicity, education, and employment.

Table 10.2 shows that, after controlling for age, spouse-assault offending rates overall are higher for people living in central cities and decline with area size.

Table 10.2

Spouse-Assault Offending Rates for Adult Household Members by Social and Demographic Characteristics

	Area Size		
	Central City	Suburban	Rural
N	1,362	2,634	1,365
N with One or More Incidents	276	404	187
Percent with One or More Incidents	20.3	15.3	13.7
Social and Demographic Characteristics			
Age			
≤ 21	14.3	11.4	14.2
22 – 26	8.4	10.6	7.9
27 – 35	10.0	8.8	6.8
36 – 50	5.9	7.8	14.4
≥ 51	6.2	10.4	4.8
p (F):	.164	.857	.167
Marital Status[a]			
Nonmarried Cohabitants	5.4	5.4	2.1
Married	1.3	1.2	1.2
Separated/Divorced	7.1	1.7	.9
p (F):	.000	.000	.960
Ethnicity			
White	7.2	9.6	7.8
African-American	10.0	6.8	21.7
Hispanic	13.5	6.7	4.7
Other	8.2	5.8	11.5
p (F):	.175	.733	.129
Household Income			
≤ $10,000	18.0	15.7	14.6
$10,001–20,000	7.2	11.5	10.8
$20,001–30,000	7.7	7.3	6.8
≥ $30,000	6.6	6.9	7.6
p (F):	.002	.034	.470
Educational Attainment			
High School Graduate or less	10.2	10.8	10.7
Some College or more	7.2	7.9	5.7
p (F):	.106	.143	.093
Household Member Working			
Not Working	14.0	11.5	9.9
Working	7.7	8.8	8.6
p (F):	.005	.413	.346

[a]For all three areas, p(F) = .000 for age as a covariate. Age was not a significant covariate for income, education, ethnicity, or employment.

This relationship is consistent for marital status, income, and employment but not for educational attainment. Although Table 10.1 shows that age is significantly associated with *participation* in spouse assault, the results in Table 10.2 show that age is not a significant covariate in the frequency of spouse assault other than with marital status.

Incidence rates are highest for nonmarried cohabitants in cities and suburbs and for divorced/separated women in cities. Incidence rates are lowest among married couples, again suggesting the protective function of marriage as a risk factor for frequent assault. Assuming that there are few differences in the types of people who choose to live together in cities versus other areas, the importance of area size is apparent in the decline in incidence rates with declining urbanism.

Among ethnic groups, spouse assault occurs most often among nonwhite couples in central cities and rural areas, but rates are highest in the suburbs among white couples. Rates are highest among the populations with the lowest incomes regardless of social area. Although rates decline with area size among the very poorest populations, the rates are consistent across area size for people with annual household incomes above $10,000. Rates are higher in couples in which no one is working, and this effect is most pronounced in central cities.

The effects of poverty on spouse assault seem strongest in urban areas: the highest rates were observed for the poorest households in central cities. As with participation rates in Table 10.1, these trends again suggest that the social context of urban areas heightens the risks for spouse assault from low socioeconomic status. There appear to be processes within urban settings that increase the already sizable risks for spouse assault posed by low income and unemployment.

To sort out the relative influences of these social structural factors on individual rates by area size, Table 10.3 shows the results of logistic regressions[45] that estimate the likelihood of spouse assault within the past year for each of the three areas and again for the total sample. In the latter model, dummy variables were included for suburbs and rural areas. Dummy variables for specific ethnic groups were included. Age was controlled in this analysis since it is a strong correlate of stranger violence[46] and also is a proxy for the length of the relationship.[47] Interaction terms for race, income, and age by each of the other predictors were included; results are reported only for those interaction terms that entered any of the models.

In the full model (all areas), the significant negative coefficient for suburbs and rural areas illustrates the unique risks associated with urbanism. The likelihood of spouse assault increases significantly in central cities among younger couples, African-Americans, nonmarried couples, and low-income couples. The interaction terms suggest that unemployed African-American couples are more likely to experience spouse assault. These factors describe a cluster of structural variables that are associated with urbanism—concentrations of younger, poorer, nonmarried and minority couples—and also with the features of "persistent poverty" that are present in urban areas nationwide.[48]

Table 10.3

Logistic Regression on Participation of any Adult Household Member in Spouse Assault, Controlling for Area Size (Logit Coefficient, Standard Error, Significance of T)[a]

| | Area Size | | | |
	Central City	Suburban	Rural	All Areas
Constant	3.14 (1.58)*	−1.53 (1.89)	−4.68 (2.36)*	.54 (1.17)
Area[b]				
Suburb				−.21 (.10)*
Rural				−.33 (.11)**
Age	−.04 (.007)***	−.06 (.006)***	−.06 (.008)***	−.05 (.004)***
Ethnicity				
African-American	.54 (.20)**	3.45 (1.52)*	5.27 (1.95)**	2.13 (.82)**
Hispanic	.15 (.25)	−.04 (.32)	.18 (.54)	.11 (.18)
Other	−3.41 (1.32)**	−.31 (.25)	−.04 (.32)	−1.18 (.46)**
Marital Status				
Single (Cohabitating)	.69 (.23)**	.43 (.22)*	.40 (.47)	.50 (.15)***
Separated/Divorced	1.56 (.57)**	.88 (.50)	−.38 (.80)	.82 (.33)*
Household Income	−.42 (.16)**	−.22 (.08)**	.30 (.10)**	−.17 (.07)*
Household Education	−.26 (.16)	−.65 (.31)*	.68 (.42)	−.16 (.09)
Household Member Working	.14 (.28)	1.81 (.92)*	1.60 (1.13)	.78 (.50)

Table 10.3 continued

	Area Size			
	Central City	Suburban	Rural	All Areas
African-American x Work	.39 (.15) **	-1.71 (.81) *	-2.32 (1.04)*	-.86 (.43) *
Other x Income		.11 (.05) *		.14 (.06) *
Education x Income			-.18 (.06) **	
Model Statistics				
Model Chi-square	8.4 **	9.9 **	11.7 **	9.5 ***
Log-likelihood	-600.9	-975.5	-471.8	-2116
Classification (percentage)				
No Assault	98.3	99.7	100	99.8
Assault	9.3	1.3	0	1.1

[a] Significance of T: * p .05; ** p .01; *** p .001
[b] Variables entered only for model for all areas.

The specific models for each area reflect different concentrations of risk factors. As in the full model, the likelihood of spouse assault in central cities is predicted by variables that describe populations characterized by "persistent poverty." The absence of interaction terms suggests that their effects are not conditioned by one another, but rather are independent predictors of spouse assault. In suburbs, the significant interaction term indicates that unemployment among African-Americans is a specific risk factor. But labor force participation (work) was *positively* associated with spouse assault in the suburbs, suggesting that there are multiple risk factors and groups experiencing spouse assault. In rural areas, a smaller group of predictors was significant, but again the special circumstances facing unemployed African-Americans is evident in the interaction term. Unlike the other areas, marital status in rural areas was unrelated to spouse assault. And in sharp contrast to cities and suburbs, income was *positively* associated with spouse assault.

The higher rates for spouse assault in central cities suggest that distinct social processes within urban neighborhoods intensify the risks of spouse assault that already are stimulated by poverty, low investment in marriage, minority ethnic status, weak educational attainment, and other deficits in human capital within couples. Since residential segregation and poverty in central cities primarily affect African-Americans,[49] the results in Table 10.3 reflect the specific contexts in cities where African-Americans are concentrated.[50] These results once again suggest that the effects of social structural factors are conditioned by area size and the unique social processes within urban neighborhoods.

This intersection of structure and social context suggests that there are independent and important contributions to spouse assault from the social processes of communities. This does not imply that culture explains the distinct patterns within ethnic groups. If cultural influences exist, they are bound up with the structural circumstances and features within which ethnic and racial groups live within social areas. How else can we explain variation within race, such as the lower rates of spouse assault among all ethnic groups for higher-income groups? In fact, cultural explanations are conscientiously avoided in this chapter, as are explanations tied to racial differences. Rather, it is the social structural correlates of communities—including racial concentration but dominated by material concerns tied to jobs and education—that seem to explain the variations in spouse-assault rates by community rather than the aggregate characteristics of the individuals who live in them.

Assuming that the causes of spouse assault are not unique for any racial or ethnic group, these trends suggest that we turn instead to the specific social organization and dynamics of different ecological contexts—communities—to understand variation in rates of spouse assault within different structural contexts. But we must also bear in mind the effects of social structure on the dynamics of communities. I return to these constructs at the conclusion of the chapter.

Spouse Homicide

Homicides in the United States are committed disproportionately by family members, often in marital relationships, and women disproportionately are the victims and perpetrators of spouse homicides.[51] Browne and Williams (1989) show that although the homicide (commission) rate in 1975–84 for female spouses was 56 percent of the rate of male spouses, female involvement in homicide disproportionately involved spouse homicides. Outside the family, women committed only 14 percent of all murders, compared to 38 percent within the home. Women also disproportionately are victims of spousal homicides: twice as many wives are killed by husbands than husbands killed by wives.[52] Comparing homicides between cohabitants and spouses, Mercy and Saltzman reported that women were 1.3 times more likely to be killed than were men.[53]

Spouse-homicide rates vary by ethnicity, and gender-ethnicity interactions are evident. Only Jurik and Winn found that race was not a significant predictor of gender differences in spouse homicides.[54] Mercy and Saltzman found that African-Americans account for 45.4 percent of all spouse-homicide victims, and their rate is 8.4 times higher than the white rate. But white wives had twice the risk of spousal homicide, while African-American women had lower spouse-homicide victimization rates than African-American males.[55] Block's analysis of 1965–81 domestic homicides in Chicago found substantially fewer marital homicides among Latinos than among African-Americans and whites. Although the percentage of marital homicides committed by males varied by ethnicity (from 33.6 percent for African-Americans to 53.2 percent for whites), marital homicides as a percentage of domestic homicides were relatively constant across racial groups.[56] From police incident reports, Saltzman et al. found that the risk of fatal assaults in Atlanta was three times greater for nonwhites than whites.[57]

Gender-ethnicity interactions in spouse homicides may also vary by residential area.[58] For example, Kuhl found gender–region–race interactions in analysis of spousal homicides in California from 1974 to 1986. Latino women more often were victims of spousal homicide than other race or ethnic groups outside Los Angeles County, but African-American males were victims most often within that county.[59]

If whites and nonwhites live in unique and disparate social contexts within cities and suburbs, reinforced by patterns of residential segregation,[60] differences in rates of spouse homicide may reflect the social structural factors and neighborhood processes that distinguish ethnic neighborhoods. Unfortunately, there has been little research on spouse homicide that has considered the risks associated with gender, ethnicity, and other social structural factors, and the variation in these risks by area size.

Area Studies in Spouse Homicide

The importance of social structure also is evident in macrosocial research on spouse homicide that compares rates across areas. Homicide research has long emphasized the importance of social areas[61] and factors associated with urbanism,[62] as well as the conceptual importance of victim–offender interactions.[63] Research on variations in homicide rates by social areas illustrates three themes: economic deprivation,[64] subcultures of violence,[65] and routine activities.[66] If social structure influences spouse assault, we would expect to see similar themes emerging when comparing spouse-homicide rates across jurisdictions.

Research on the social structural correlates of spouse homicides is more recent, taking advantage of the creation of data sets such as the Supplemental Homicide Reports (SHRs), part of the Uniform Crime Reports, that disaggregate homicide rates by victim-offender relationship and geographic area. Browne and Williams found that urbanism and the male homicide rate predicted the female homicide rate, suggesting an urban concentration to female-perpetrated partner homicides.[67] Williams and Flewelling showed that homicides resulting from family conflict were highly correlated with two indicators of poverty: percentage African-American and percentage of the population below the poverty level.[68] These studies suggest that resource deprivation and social disorganization (measured by the divorce rate) have a pervasive impact on city-to-city variations in all forms of homicide, including both family and nonfamily fatalities.

Parker and Toth tested the interaction of subculture, economic-deprivation, and routine-activities influences on spouse-homicide rates from 1973 to 1975 in 299 U.S. cities. Although family intimate homicides (involving spouses) were associated with social disorganization (infant mortality rates, percent African-American population), factors associated with urbanism (total population and population density, unemployment rates) and inequality (income disparities, percent below poverty) were not significant predictors. But when the definition of "spouse assault" is broadened to include unmarried intimates (cohabitants with a sexually intimate relationship), several social structural factors emerged as predictors: percentage poor, percentage young, percentage African-American population, and the unemployment rate. Parker and Toth conclude that the social structural context of cities influences homicides between "intimates," regardless of their marital status.[69]

Results from these two traditions of homicide research—microlevel studies within cities or areas and macrolevel studies across cities—suggest that spouse (or intimate) homicide is an urban phenomenon that occurs more often in social areas that typify the problems of urban areas: poverty, residential mobility, weak family structures, and concentrations of minority populations. Although spouse abuse appears to be ecologically concentrated, more specific studies are needed that tie homicides to specific locales, measure their social area characteristics, and disaggregate homicides by race, social status, and abuse histories of the participants.

The Spatial Distribution of Marital Violence

Research on the social locations of domestic violence also suggests that there may be spatial or ecological concentrations. Research in Kansas City showed that 5.2 percent of police calls for disturbances were dispatched to addresses with five to eight calls in the same year.[70] Sherman, Gartin, and Buerger analyzed data on locations of repeat calls for service for "domestic disturbances," a broad category that includes loud stereos, family fights, neighbor disputes, and family violence. Nearly 25,000 domestic disturbances in Minneapolis in 1986 (from December 1985 to December 1986) were recorded in 8.6 percent of all locations; 9.1 percent of the addresses with at least one domestic disturbance call accounted for 35.9 percent of all domestic calls.[71] Sherman, Gartin, and Buerger reported results of a 1988 Boston study by Pierce, Spaar, and Briggs in which 9 percent of apartments reporting any calls for "family trouble" over a five-year period accounted for about 28 percent of all such calls.[72]

Yet the criminogenic influence of place on domestic disturbances remains ambiguous. Many of the areas where calls were concentrated involved high-rise buildings with multiple addresses. In these settings, close proximity between neighbors may result in greater reporting of disturbances. Sherman, Gartin, and Buerger also posit that these areas or buildings may be receptors for the types of people most likely to experience, or call police about, domestic problems. Without knowing either specific addresses or the nature of the calls, the correlation of domestic disturbance with place remains only speculative.

Weisburd, Sherman, and Maher argued that situation-specific models of crime commission would naturally lead to identification of "hot spots" of specific crime types, such as violent offenses. Instead, they found strong correlations between domestic disturbances and other crime types reported within residences, such as residential burglaries and robberies of persons. In general, although these were areas that manifested incivilities that suggest growing social disorganization, Weisburd, Sherman, and Maher found no evidence of crime-specific patterns regarding violence within or outside the home.[73]

There appear to be only weak correlations between specific locations or microareas and reports to the police of violent crimes among nonstrangers or in domestic situations. Rather than signifying causal relationships, the concentration of spouse assault among low SES groups suggests evidence that ecological factors may facilitate or support marital violence. These relationships also may reflect reciprocal causal processes; for example, men who are assaultive and threatening with their families may also exhibit problematic behaviors at work and experience job or income loss, problems that further aggravate the social context of spouse assault.

Overall, evidence of the direct effects of place (social location) on spouse assault are equivocal. Although places themselves may be criminogenic, it is unclear whether places directly contribute to marital violence, simply host individuals who are more likely to engage in it (that is, concentration effects), or indirectly facilitate crime through weak social controls. The unique context of the home itself seems to contribute to the disproportionate occurrence of victimization of spouses or partners. Yet families and couples are socially embedded in communities and subject to the forces that influence social controls and in turn shape behavioral norms. Whether indirectly through social structural risk factors or indirectly through sociocultural processes within neighborhoods, ecological factors in socially disorganized areas place certain couples at greater risk for spouse assault than they might be in other social areas.

The evidence on ecological clustering of spouse homicides also shows a modest association. Research on domestic homicides in Kansas City in the 1970s showed that police had responded to at least five prior calls for service in about 50 percent of the addresses where domestic homicides occurred in the two years preceding the homicide.[74]

But Sherman, Gartin, and Buerger contend that residential mobility among both domestic and stranger homicide victims and perpetrators mitigates any linkage between addresses and individuals. They found weak predictions of domestic homicides from recurring prior calls for service linked to individuals among domestic homicides in Milwaukee. They also contend that the addresses considered in the Kansas City study primarily were apartment buildings with multiple residences; the calls for service may have aggregated the calls of the individual apartment dwellers.[75] Homicide victims evidently reside in the types of buildings that have high prevalence and frequency of police calls for recurring domestic disturbances. These studies suggest that a safer conclusion would attribute residential patterns and ecological processes to types of places rather than individuals in establishing social locations of domestic homicides.

Social Structure and the Social Control of Spouse Assault

The emergence of family violence as a social problem in the 1960s opened family social interactions to formal social control and legal sanctions. This trend took place within a larger context of expansion of governmental regulation of the traditionally private realm of family life.[76] In turn, social and legal institutions were mobilized to increase their involvement in marital relations and develop new mechanisms of social control of families.

The social and legal controls that emerged varied according to the explanations and causal theories of spouse assault.[77] Social control through law most often occurred through criminal justice interventions that made salient the risks and costs of spouse assault. Legal controls focused on the victim and the assailant in the context of law violation with associated punishment costs. They were rooted in assumptions of both specific[78] and general deterrence[79]

If legal control is a last resort option after other social controls have failed,[80] the mobilization of legal institutions to regulate spouse assault hinted at the perceived limitations or ineffectiveness of nonlegal social controls.[81] Despite the broader interpretation of spouse assault that informed other approaches to social control of family violence, legal control replaced other formal and informal social controls as the *first* resort for regulation of family relationships.[82]

However, research on the effectiveness of law as social control for spouse assault has provided contradictory results: Experiments under a range of sampling conditions have yielded no consistent support for specific deterrent effects of arrest.[83] There is only weak evidence of *general* deterrent effects of arrest.[84] Instead, there is consistent evidence that spousal violence is well controlled by informal (nonlegal) social controls,[85] while the social costs associated with arrest (job loss, stigma, relationship loss) are more salient in the *perceived* deterrent effects of arrest than are the expected costs of punishment.[86]

These forms of social control converge with the informal and formal social controls that influence violent crime more generally and reflect the social structure, social organization, and social capital of neighborhoods and communities.[87] In turn, the salience of both legal and informal social controls for spouse assault will undoubtedly reflect the social structure of the neighborhood contexts of spouse assault. These developments provide opportunities for further development of the theoretical basis for the social control of spouse assault and an examination of the ways in which social structure influences the effectiveness of formal and informal social controls.

The Influence of Social Structure on Social Control

Social control of spouse assault through legal sanctions has been examined as a process of legal mobilization and implementation of the law[88] and as the internalization of the perceived costs of law violation.[89] However, if the "quantity of law" or governmental social control invoked is inversely related to nonlegal (informal) social control,[90] the salience of legal controls of spouse assault can be understood only as it is influenced by other types of informal social controls that surround intimate relationships.

Arrest of spouse assailants may result in deterrence processes that operate through both formal social controls (legal sanctions)[91] and informal social controls (loss of self-esteem, disrupted social ties, job loss, and shame).[92] These effects were observed in paradigms using both hypothetical scenarios and actual arrests.[93] Offenders who desist from further violence following arrest may be responding not only to the potential legal costs but also to the implications of arrest for relationships with peers, employers, spouses, and neighbors.[94] Thus, the deterrent effects of legal sanctions for spouse assault depend on raising both social costs and punishment costs. Raising social costs in turn requires that there are meaningful threats from possible job loss, social stigmatization, and relationship loss associated with spouse assault.

These perspectives suggest that the salience of social costs depends on whether an assailant has anything to lose—that there is a job with economic and social value to lose, that relationships are stable and have value, and that the assailant is socially embedded in a neighborhood or work context that accords status. Toby referred to an individual's "stake in conformity" to predict the effects of legal sanctions on criminality. To the extent that social costs concurrently reflect an individual's stake in conformity or social bonds within a neighborhood and long-term labor market prospects available within the city or region, the deterrent effects of social controls are likely to reflect both the individual's social class and the neighborhood's opportunity structure.[95]

In fact, the salience of legal and social controls seems to be influenced by social structural characteristics: gender and race,[96] age,[97] occupational status,[98] and labor force participation.[99] Evidence from quasi-experimental studies on arrest[100] and experimental studies in three cities[101] show that the deterrent effects of arrest are greater for individuals with higher "stakes in conformity."

Not only does unemployment compromise the deterrent effect of arrest, but violence appears to escalate for arrested persons with weak labor market and marital attachments. For example, arrests with short custody terms had a criminogenic effect on unemployed persons in Milwaukee, a "rustbelt" city with declining labor market participation for African-Americans.[102] Similar long-term criminogenic effects of arrest were reported in Charlotte, North Carolina,[103] Miami,[104] and Omaha.[105] In Colorado Springs, a city with an expanding labor market, the deterrent effects of arrest for employed persons suggest that "stakes" may enhance the salience of legal sanctions.[106] In each of these studies, respondents were disproportionately poor and nonwhite, and the majority of arrests were concentrated in areas with high concentrations of similarly situated people.[107]

Other studies also have suggested that social and legal sanctions interact to deter spouse assault. Fagan et al. found that legal interventions had the strongest deterrent effects for better-educated and employed assailants with no prior record. They also tended to have less serious or even no prior records.[108] Bowker's interviews with women whose spouses had stopped their assaults also suggested that legal interventions were less effective than social sanctions (especially relationship loss) for males with blue-collar jobs, but legal interventions were more effective in promoting desistance among men with white-collar jobs.[109]

While these studies point to an interaction between social position and social control of spouse assault, the evidence is hardly conclusive. In the arrest experiments, the samples disproportionately come from poor areas or poor backgrounds, with too few cases from other areas to address possible interactions between characteristics of areas and individuals. Other studies, using quasi-experimental designs or lacking control groups, also offer limited evidence. The results thus far seem to be limited to arrestees living in areas of concentrated poverty or reports from self-selected victim samples. Obviously, further experiments with more heterogeneous samples are needed to assess the interaction among social area, social class, and the effects on social and legal controls for spouse assault.

Reciprocity between Social Control and Social Structure

Research on both general and specific deterrence of spouse assault points toward a reciprocal relationship between social and legal sanctions in the social control of spouse assault. Deterrence theorists have long acknowledged a conditional relationship between formal and informal sanctions where formal legal sanctions may initiate societal reactions that complement the legal costs of punishment.[110] Others suggest that formal sanctions cannot be effective in the absence of informal social sanctions.[111] Both the direct costs to the offender of legal sanctions (the intrinsic punitive consequences of arrest) and the social costs of legal sanctions are salient as controls, although the effects of legal sanctions seem to be indirect and work through their facilitation of social controls.[112]

Research on deterrence of spouse assault suggests that although a violent act may not produce such informal controls, they may be set in motion or facilitated by formal sanctions.[113] Results of experiments on arrest and prosecution suggest how these processes may be set in motion, and how such informal social controls are invoked by victims once empowered through an alliance with legal institutions.[114] Controls that are facilitated by legal sanctions create a coercive context in which social costs are made more salient and the victim's security is enhanced.

But social controls for spouse assault, particularly informal controls that rely on contextualized social processes, involve more than the interactions between victims and assailants and the interventions of legal institutions. Social control involves the normative processes and ethics of social interaction that regulate everyday social life,[115] as well as the mobilization of community that occurs in response to problem behaviors. Thus, informal social controls are effective in several ways: inhibition of problem behaviors, facilitation of conformity, and restraint of social deviance once it appears.

Informal social controls are facilitated and perhaps made more salient by the reciprocity between legal and social controls. Williams and Hawkins suggest that community knowledge of an individual's probable involvement in a violent act is necessary for the activation of informal social controls. Such knowledge may accrue either from a formal intervention (arrest) or from information networks independent of the formal sanctioning agents. These informal, often interpersonal, social controls often involve explicit or remedial actions to raise the social costs of spouse assault. Williams and Hawkins identify three types of informal controls and social costs that may interact with formal (legal) sanctions: social disclosure (commitment costs), relationship costs (attachment costs), and shame (stigma costs).[116] In other words, the effectiveness of these controls requires that an assailant perceive that his social ties and accomplishments will be jeopardized by his actions. These costs in turn arise from the person's "stakes in conformity."[117]

Each of these social costs reflects the social structure of the neighborhood context in which offenders live or work. Commitment costs include the possible loss of employment chances, educational opportunities, and integration in other social contexts such as church or peer group.[118] Attachment costs include the loss of valued friendships as well as marriage prospects or cohabitational partners. Stigma is associated with social opprobria and damage to reputation from social disclosure of the offender's violence.

These informal controls are likely to be effective under fairly specific social conditions. The perceived (social) costs of violence depend on the salience of these costs to the individual.[119] If the costs are minimal, the effects of informal controls or formal sanctions will be weak.[120] Thus, the material costs of sanctions and the social censure attached to them will directly influence the effectiveness of social controls.[121] These material factors and the social networks in which spouses are embedded will reflect the social structure and social cohesion of their immediate social contexts.

Accordingly, whether social control is effective for spouse assault will depend quite directly on the socioeconomic factors that set the various costs attached to informal controls. Employment rates and the social organization of work will determine whether the possibility of lost employment and education opportunities are salient commitment costs. Where labor force participation and wages are low, especially among younger nonwhite males, whose spouse-assault rates are highest, commitment costs are likely to be relatively low. Marriage and divorce rates, as well as norms of parenting, will influence the definitions and expectations of intimate relationships and in turn set the attachment costs.

Attachment costs will be low in neighborhood contexts where family life is seen as temporary or impermanent, where attachments of male parents to children are weak, and where social networks disproportionately involve poor people and are weakened by residential mobility. Social cohesion among neighbors, social capital that regulates behavioral norms across generations, residential mobility, and general crime and violence rates in neighborhoods will influence the stigma attached to disclosure of spouse assault. Indeed, families and couples themselves are embedded in the social networks of communities.[122]

The discount in these social costs of spouse assault reflects the dimensions of urban areas where spouse-assault rates also are highest. These trends suggest that not only is spouse assault mediated by the social structural characteristics of urban areas, but so too is the salience of social controls that may affect it. In the following section, we turn to the social processes that convey the effects of these structural characteristics on participation in and control of spouse assault.

The Mediating Effects of Social Structure on Spouse Assault

Like other forms of interpersonal violence, spouse assault seems to be concentrated among poor and low-socioeconomic-status people. But there is no reason to believe that the sources of spouse assault are different for upper- and lower-income people or for whites and nonwhites. Even within income or race groups, rates were higher in central cities than elsewhere. Given these within-group similarities across ecological contexts, we must ask instead whether people in each context are differentially exposed to criminogenic structural conditions, especially those factors that lead to spouse assault. We also must begin to wrestle with the possibility of intrinsic social processes within the contexts of central cities that may be criminogenic with respect to interpersonal violence generally and specifically to spouse assault.

Although processes intrinsic to urban contexts have been shown to influence delinquency rates, rates of adult violence, and family interactions,[123] their effects on spouse assault seem to point to ecological effects independent of other etiological factors. Research on child maltreatment, for example, suggests that there are ecological concentrations of child abuse that reflect social structure.[124] Variations in child-abuse rates have been traced to variations in community structure including poverty, residential mobility, and single-parent households.[125] These patterns of social disorganization often are concentrated in urban areas and also are associated with high rates of stranger violence.

Yet structure alone is insufficient to explain variations in spouse-assault rates. Within-race, within-income, and within-city variations in family violence suggest that the effects of structural and ecological factors on child abuse and other forms of intrafamily violence are conditioned by neighborhood processes. Garbarino and Sherman compared two neighborhoods matched on socioeconomic and demographic characteristics but that varied dramatically on the rates of child maltreatment. Through interviews with families and neighborhood informants, they identified neighborhood risk factors for child abuse that reflected the urban social context of these neighborhoods rather than their socioeconomic status. These risk factors included what they termed "social impoverishment," a milieu characterized by family social isolation, insubstantial social networks, and weak social supports among family caretakers.[126]

The implications of these risk factors for child abuse suggest that neighborhood processes also will influence spouse-assault rates for individuals in socially impoverished neighborhoods. First, childhood exposure to family violence, whether as victim of child abuse or witness to parental violence, is a strong risk factor for long-term patterns of interpersonal violence generally and for assaults against spouses.[127] Assailants' childhood violence exposure was the strongest predictor of the frequency and severity of spouse assault (as well as the severity of injuries), based on reports from women in shelters and other intervention programs.[128] If childhood violence experiences are more common among families in socially disorganized (urban) neighborhoods, then we may expect this risk factor for spouse assault to be ecologically concentrated in similarly structured areas.[129]

Second, the co-morbidity of stranger and spouse assault seems to be highest in central cities.[130] The prevalence of domestic assault is highest among unmarried couples, especially those recently separated or divorced, and also among nonmarried cohabitants (compared to married couples). Self-reports by males of their violence toward *strangers* are highest for nonmarried cohabitants, while *spouse*-assault rates are highest for divorced or separated males. The latter group also reported the highest rates of general violence toward *both* spouses and strangers, and these rates were highest for males living in central cities.

Female reports showed that divorce or separation posed an extraordinary risk for victimization of women by a former spouse or partner: over one in four (28.4 percent) divorced/separated males assaulted their spouses in the past year.[131] These rates are even higher for women living in central cities. Marriage seems to be a protective factor for all forms of interpersonal violence, but especially spouse assault and especially in the context of urban life. Yet marriage rates are lowest in central cities and family supports are weakest, indicating a concentration of these risk factors in urban areas.

Accordingly, many of the risk factors for spouse assault seem to converge in central cities with many of the risk factors for other forms of interpersonal violence: high rates of child maltreatment, social disorganization (high rates of residential mobility, poverty, divorce or family disruption, and female-headed families with children), and weak social networks leading to social isolation. To the extent that these processes describe what Kasarda and Janowitz call a "systemic" model of social disorganization,[132] they are symptomatic of what more recently has been termed "structural" forms of social disorganization—focusing less on the spatial or even geographic dimensions of community than on the structure of social networks within them.[133]

It is at this level of explanation that we propose social processes that explain the concentration of spouse assault within central cities and among the poorest communities of those areas. Our goal here is to describe processes that explain the *concentration* of spouse assault in central cities and among low SES groups, recognizing that spouse assault also is prevalent elsewhere and throughout social strata.

The Social Organization of Spouse Assault

The differences between central cities and other areas in spouse-assault rates, and the different reactivity of income or ethnic groups to these conditions, suggest that we look more closely at the unique social processes that are brought forth by the structural conditions of communities within such areas. These processes, and the interaction of community and structure, represent what Anderson calls the interconnected realities born of the difficult social conditions in poor communities.[134] The relevant dimensions of community—the interaction of structure and social process—for understanding spouse assault include the level of social control within the community, the social networks within which people and couples are embedded, and the social capital within the community.

Social Controls

The concentration of social structural deficits in urban areas weakens both informal and formal social controls for spouse assault. If social costs are tied to the
threat of relationship loss, then these costs are discounted in neighborhoods with
high rates of family disruption and dissolution or with low marriage rates. Marriage itself becomes a less desirable option for both men and women in an
economic context in which young men are systematically excluded from stable
employment and consigned to persistent poverty.[135] The decline in family-
sustaining jobs denies many young men in urban areas, especially areas where
labor force participation has declined, the opportunity to pursue an economically
self-sufficient family.[136]

For young males, the declining interest in marriage as a long-term goal skews
male-female relationships and the meaning of manhood. In this political economic context, sexual prowess is one of the few opportunities left to gain and
display personal power and accomplishment.[137] Their exploitation of women,
coupled with their weak economic futures, makes these young men less desirable
marriage partners for women,[138] leading to more transient sexual relationships
and an increasing prevalence of female-headed families with children.[139]
Hannerz noted that in considering marriage, "there is an awareness among ghetto
dwellers that they may be literally 'taking a chance on love.' "[140] If marriage is a
protective factor for spouse assault, then the risks of spouse assault grow with the
decline in marriage tied to the declining economic fortunes of young men.

In addition to the social costs of spouse assault, social controls reflect the
structure of social interactions within a community. In particular, the stigma
costs of spouse assault may be discounted in low SES neighborhoods by factors
associated with urbanism: residential mobility, anonymity, and heterogeneity.[141]
Residential mobility is greater in neighborhoods with lower socioeconomic status. Rapid population change undercuts the capacity of a community to exercise
informal social controls by increasing the anonymity among neighbors and decreasing their involvement with one another in informal relationships as well as
their participation in formal institutions (churches, school groups, economic interactions).[142]

When neighbors know little of each other or feel little responsibility for what
happens in areas surrounding their home, an assaultive spouse may be uncon-
cerned about perceptions formed when violence in the home becomes apparent.
That is, stigma costs are low when there is little cohesion among neighbors. With
little stake in the neighborhood, witnesses to spouse assault have little inclination
to either directly cast their sanction on the offender or report the behavior to the
police. They also have less motivation to intercede personally to offer help to
victims or to develop and express social norms against that behavior. These
processes are especially important for establishing community intolerance for
spouse assault and aiding its victims.[143]

To the extent that these processes are shaped by the social and economic context in which neighborhoods are embedded, the salience of informal social controls on spouse assault will directly reflect the social structure of the community. Larger economic forces such as segregation, migration, and economic transformation will influence the patterns and rates of social interaction that may inhibit spouse assault.

Social Networks and Social Isolation

The importance of social networks in spouse assault is illustrated both from our understanding of its risk factors and the ability of victims to invoke informal social controls. Social isolation is a risk factor both for spouse assault[144] and child abuse.[145] Families that are cut off physically (no telephones, closed blinds, no transportation) and socially (weak friendship ties, few contacts with neighbors, limited participation in social organizations) are more often involved in both forms of family violence. Cazenave and Straus, using the 1985 NFVS data, found that network embeddedness is associated with low spouse-assault and parent–child violence regardless of income and occupational status. They also found that while spouse-assault rates were higher for African-American families, these differences disappeared after controlling for network embeddedness.[146]

Bowker suggested that assaultive spouses were socially embedded in male-dominated networks that fostered attitudes supportive of spouse abuse. He suggested that the more time assaultive males spent in male-only settings, the more serious, frequent, and intractable was their violence. Bowker also showed the importance of social networks for women seeking to escape these relationships. Their networks not only invoked informal social sanctions for assailants, they provided material resources and options that enabled women to escape abusive relationships.[147]

Social networks, especially those involving families, are protective factors against spouse assault. Kinship networks generally are more prevalent among lower social-class families as well as nonwhite families; higher SES families tend to rely on occupational networks rather than kin-based networks.[148] Among low-income African-American families, these networks depend on regular interactions among network members, close living arrangements, and shared resources such as child supervision, food, and shelter.[149]

Similarly, the intricate relationships among natural extended families or ritual kin relations (compadres) are a sociocultural process central to socialization in Puerto Rican neighborhoods.[150] In these networks, the family serves as the cornerstone of the culture, defining and determining individual and social behaviors. Relatives by blood and ceremonial ties, as well as friends of the family, are linked in an intricate network of reciprocal obligations that promote collective sharing of both misfortunes and good times.[151] Among adolescents from families with low income, absent fathers, or troubled family relationships, the value of familism may be invoked by parents or other family members to restrain their involvement in antisocial behavior.[152]

As with other social processes, social isolation affects microsocial (individual) interactions and communities. Residential mobility has far-reaching consequences for disruption of social networks. To the extent that networks are composed of family relationships, the decline in two-parent families in poorer neighborhoods signals a narrowing of the kinship networks that form around marriage and children. Other social networks have become increasingly composed of people with low incomes or low occupational status in central cities as middle-income nonwhites and whites have moved away from traditional neighborhoods.[153]

For those left behind, especially nonwhites, access to family-sustaining work becomes more difficult, and the networks increasingly reflect the behaviors and norms of those marginalized within closed neighborhoods. The risks for spouse assault increase as the protective networks of kinship change or weaken within central cities. Intimate relationships suffer from the weakening of social networks, the frustration of material deprivations, and behavioral influences from other jobless families in the neighborhood.[154]

The effects of social isolation also increase the risks of spouse assault at the community level. Increasing residential segregation[155] and isolation of residents from the social and economic institutions that represent mainstream society weaken the influence of the larger society on interpersonal behaviors. The absence of more conventional patterns of husband–wife interactions, patterns otherwise facilitated by working families embedded in stable kinship or friendship networks, facilitates the transmission and reification of more violent norms.[156] The rare and skewed contacts of neighborhood residents with people in other social contexts (such as work or commercial transactions) allow norms and attitudes supportive of violence in intimate relationships to prevail over nonviolent norms. In turn, young people considering coupling or marriage are more likely to be exposed to violent interactions between adult intimates. Eventually, these norms are internalized as their transmission becomes more efficient.

These themes are evident throughout the ethnographic literature on inner-city life going back to the 1930s,[157] consistently noting the routine incidence of spouse assaults within segregated, socially isolated, and disorganized communities.[158] Liebow, for example, describes violent transactions between men and women that often followed struggles over (scarce) money. He concluded that:

> the widespread violence between streetcorner husbands and their wives seems to be more a product of persons engaged in an always failing enterprise than merely the "style" or "characteristic feature" of streetcorner husband–wife relationships.[159]

Liebow goes on to describe male violence toward spouses that is contextualized in their frustration over failing to meet a wife's legitimate expectations for herself and her children, and a context for "angry aggression" among household members.[160] Marriage becomes an occasion for failure, and the inability to support a family results in loss of self-esteem and social status among neighbors and transfers marital power to the woman.[161] The tension between maintaining the public image of "breadwinner" and a dominant role in the home on the one hand and the economic and social problems in achieving that role on the other creates strains within marriages that often lead to violent conflicts and breakup.[162] It also creates a cautiousness in coupling and marriage that fosters a high rate of divorce or dissolution.

Within socially isolated neighborhoods where structural conditions foster marital relations that are transient and frequently conflicted, spouse assault (like other forms of violence) may become routinized and normative. Married couples with higher incomes, having protective factors against spouse assault, have increasingly left central cities.[163]

Young people forming definitions of marriage or male-female relations are more likely to see violence as a way of family life when their social learning experiences are unduly influenced by the weakened families that remain. Adolescents and young adults may be more likely to witness violence between spouses, be taught these norms in their own families or among immediate neighbors, and be exposed to adult role models who have engaged in these behaviors. To the extent that these processes are shaped by the social structural factors—especially segregation, residential mobility, and concentrated poverty—a system of values may emerge regarding expectations of conduct. These may become what Liebow calls "shadow cultures" that influence socialization and social development.[164]

Social Capital

The third intervening process between social structure and spouse assault is *social capital*. Coleman defines social capital as the structure of relations among people, particularly relations that lead to social action "making possible the achievements of certain ends."[165] It fosters the processes by which behavioral norms are set and regulated, and by which they are transmitted from one generation to the next and across social networks. Coleman sees deficits in social capital as symptomatic of communities with limited social networks and weak cohesion among their residents. To the extent that networks are attenuated, they may become ineffective at controlling behaviors and sustaining norms that oppose violence within marriage.[166]

Social capital is intrinsic to forming and maintaining social networks in a community. The structure of relations among families and between generations in a community is a particularly important dimension of social capital. Social capital requires that these relationships transcend families and encompass the broader sets of relations between families and across generations, as well as between families and institutional networks: parent–teacher relationships, religious affiliations, economic relationships that cross generations, and legal institutions.[167] Accordingly, the influences of social capital are greater than any that could occur within a single family or kinship network. And the relationships within a single network or family alone cannot produce social capital.[168]

Social capital accrues when individual behaviors occur in multiple contexts and are subject to multiple reactions. The young person experiencing marital conflict may encounter reactions from family members, work-related acquaintances, or neighbors. If these relationships exist within fairly dense networks of acquaintances, obligations, and expectations, the reactions (or sanctions) of people within these networks to those experiencing problems will be more consistent and have greater salience.

The extent to which social capital is depleted under conditions of social disorganization and structural deficits should be fairly obvious.[169] Not only are kinship and economic networks subject to breakup under structural conditions of unemployment, poverty, and residential mobility, but so too do demographics work against the formation of social capital. The concentration of female-headed families with children compromises the effectiveness of cross-family intergenerational relationships.[170]

To some degree, these relationships depend on modeled behaviors based on exposure of young people to adults. The depletion of the "marriage pool" of adult males certainly threatens social capital.[171] The limited contacts between males of younger and older generations in these contexts not only truncate the learning and mentoring relationships that develop but also weaken the informal social controls that regulate the behaviors of young males and females. These relationships teach and reinforce lessons about intimate relationships and tolerance (or rejection) of violence within them. They also provide important gateways for connections to the wider society through jobs, social ties, and friendship networks. Accordingly, the depletion of social capital helps sustain social isolation.

To the extent that social capital is present, norms opposing spouse assault can develop and be transmitted across generations. Victims can better invoke the negative sanctions of the community and make more salient the threat of social disclosure (and stigma costs) when there is contact in networks beyond immediate family members. The process of instilling norms opposing spouse assault is made more efficient when connections exist across generations and between networks. And the ability of young males and females to achieve their expectations for intimate relationships and for their individual lives is enhanced through involvement in interlocking networks of commitments and obligations that offer support for child care, job prospects, and rewarding social interactions.

Conclusions

Explanations for the concentration of spouse assault in urban areas and among lower socioeconomic groups require an understanding of the ways that social structure fosters social processes that either impede or facilitate violence between intimates. This of course does not deny the occurrence of spouse assault among all social strata and in all spatial areas. Yet the concentration of spouse assault among the poor and minority populations in central cities, similar to other forms of interpersonal violence, indicates that there are factors tied to social structure and social area that contribute to higher participation and offending rates.

Although race and poverty are confounded in the United States, variations in within-race rates of interpersonal violence suggest that neighborhood social processes are more likely to reflect their social structure than the aggregate characteristics of individuals within them.[172] For example, neighborhoods with high residential mobility or weak economic activity may attenuate social networks, regardless of the race and income distribution of the community.[173] Nevertheless, the association among place, race, and poverty leads to a greater concentration of these effects in African-American and Latino communities.[174] These intersections also suggest that many of the contextual processes intrinsic to interpersonal violence more generally will be relevant to spouse assault, and that the social contexts of spouse assault and stranger violence may share common processes. Moreover, the factors within communities that are criminogenic with respect to interpersonal violence are also contributors to spouse assault.

Within the poorer communities of urban areas, rates of interpersonal violence vary inversely with the strengths of social networks and other informal social controls.[175] These processes also address the special circumstances of violence between intimates. If we view interpersonal violence along a continuum of intimacy of its victims, we may begin to see how the broader ecological processes of communities may influence violence at the most "intimate" end of the continuum. These processes may determine where on that continuum victimization will occur: in communities with stronger informal controls, interpersonal violence may be confined to the home with its more intimate victims and greater privacy. In socially disorganized areas, victimization may be more likely to occur at both ends of the continuum of intimacy.

Implicit in these processes that convey the effects of structural conditions is the role of political economy of place in generating the structural contexts. If both marriage and violence patterns reflect the integration of communities with the larger society, neighborhood isolation in inner cities may launch social processes that skew behaviors and weaken the ability of communities to regulate them. For spouse assault particularly, these processes reflect the skewed notions of manhood that derive from waning alternative roles as wage earners or family heads. The deficits in power and control that accrue to men in these conditions, and the devaluation of life that occurs in impoverished communities, are strong risk factors for spouse assault.[176]

While these concepts help explain the occurrence of spouse assault within areas, further conceptual development is needed to explain events and individual differences within communities. The day-to-day interactions within socially impoverished communities create an unending supply of the triggers, motivations, and arousal to escalate routine conflicts into "angry aggression."[177] The specific motivations may range from the accumulated anger of a "devalued life"[178] to the routinized violence among victims and offenders[179] to the emotional arousal of powerlessness,[180] and the deindividuation of violence.[181] Together with skewed norms regarding emotional intimacy and male-female relations and weak controls against violence generally, community also shapes the immediate contexts in which spouse assault is likely to occur and influences the arousal and triggers that precede violent events.

To further specify this framework, research is needed that compares within-race spouse-assault rates in communities that vary by social structural dimensions. This involves community studies that examine not only patterns of victimization but also specific events and patterns of violence within couples over time. The importance of social structure for spouse assault is evident in the neighborhood processes that shape behaviors as well as in the specific interactions leading to violence between intimates. Experiments on sanctions for spouse assault will provide empirical assessments of the reactivity of individuals across communities that vary not only social structural characteristics but also on the mediating processes that support or inhibit interpersonal violence. Finally, research across neighborhoods will reveal the social processes and informal controls that interact with social structural factors to restrain or intensify rates of spouse assault.

Notes

1. Murray A. Straus, Richard J. Gelles, and Suzanne Steinmetz, *Behind Closed Doors: Violence in the American Family*; D.A. Gaguin, "Spouse Abuse: Data from the National Crime Survey"; J. Garbarino, "The Incidence and Prevalence of Child Maltreatment"; A.J. Sedlak, "Prevention of Wife Abuse."

2. Richard J. Gelles and Claire P. Cornell, *Intimate Violence in Families*. The most pervasive myth is that family violence is confined to mentally ill or sick people (Gelles and Cornell, *Intimate Violence*). Until the 1980s, popular media and the arts portrayed spouse assault as primarily a working-class phenomenon and deeply entangled in alcohol abuse. Note the images in Tennessee Williams's *A Streetcar Named Desire*, when a drunken Stanley Kowalski strikes his pregnant wife, Stella, and later on rapes and beats his sister-in-law, Blanche DuBois (herself a former alcoholic) on the night that Stella delivers their first baby. In *The Brothers Karamazov*, Dostoevski hints that alcohol may have led Dmitri to kill his father. Similar episodes occurred in Edward Albee's *Who's Afraid of Virginia Woolf*, when George and Martha drink through the night and become increasingly abusive to each other, though only verbally.

3. Jeffrey A. Fagan and Angela Browne, "Violence between Spouses and Intimates: Physical Aggression between Women and Men in Relationships."

4. Patricia A. Klaus and M.R. Rand, *Family Violence*; Straus, Gelles, and Steinmetz, *Behind Closed Doors*; Carolyn W. Harlow, "Female Victims of Violent Crime."

5. Gelles and Straus, *Intimate Violence*; H.R. Lentzner and M.M. DeBerry, *Intimate Victims: A Study of Violence among Friends and Relatives*; M.A. Straus and C. Smith, "Violence in Hispanic Families in the United States: Incidence Rates and Structural Interpretations."

6. See Robert Nash Parker and A.M. Toth, "Family, Intimacy and Homicide: A Macrosocial Approach," regarding family homicide; Harlow, "Female Victims," regarding spouse assault; and Susan J. Zuravin, "The Ecology of Child Abuse and Neglect: Review of the Literature and Presentation of Data," and Robert J. Sampson, "Family Management and Child Development: Insights from Social Disorganization Theory," regarding child abuse. Similarly, stranger violence is stratified by race and class, and also is concentrated in urban areas marked by persistent poverty and weak social controls (Albert J. Reiss, Jr., and Jeffrey A. Roth, *Understanding and Controlling Violence*; R.J. Sampson and J. Lauritsen, "Individual and Community Factors in Violent Offending and Victimization"). The convergence of correlates for family and stranger violence suggests that the unique context of the family may not be etiologically relevant to spouse assault but may provide a situational context that facilitates its occurrence.

7. Evan Stark and Anne Flitcraft, "Violence among Intimates: An Epidemiological Review."

8. Gerald T. Hotaling and D.B. Sugarman, "A Risk Marker Analysis of Assaulted Wives."

9. Socioeconomic status in this study was determined from a factor analysis of the 1980 National Family Violence Survey data (Straus, Gelles, and Steinmetz, *Behind Closed Doors*). The SES factor included high factor coefficients for "Husband's occupational prestige" and "Family income." The explained variance and eigenvalue for the factor were not reported.

10. Stark and Flitcraft, "Violence among Intimates."

11. Weis, "Family Violence Research Methodology and Design"; Fagan and Browne, "Violence between Spouses and Intimates." For example, National Crime Survey data from 1979–87 show that white women were more likely to be assaulted by spouses than other types of partners, but African-American women were more likely to be assaulted by boyfriends than spouses or ex-spouses (Harlow, "Female Victims").

12. Sampson and Lauritsen, "Individual and Community Factors."

13. Harlow, "Female Victims."

14. Judith Blau and Peter M. Blau, "The Cost of Inequality: Metropolitan Structure and Violent Crime"; John A. Laub, "Urbanism, Race and Crime"; William C. Bailey, "Poverty, Inequality, and City Homicide Rates: Some Not So Unexpected Results"; Robert J. Sampson, "Urban Black Violence: The Effect of Male Joblessness and Family Disruption."

15. Delbert S. Elliott and David Huizinga, "The Mediating Effects of the Social Structure in High Risk Neighborhoods"; Sampson and Lauritsen, "Individual and Community Factors."

16. Lenore E. Walker, *The Battered Women*; A. Browne, *When Battered Women Kill*.

17. Jeffrey Fagan et al., *The National Family Violence Evaluation: Final Report, Volume I—Analytic Findings*.

18. James S. Coleman, in "Social Capital in the Creation of Human Capital" and *Foundations of Social Theory*, defines *social capital* as the resources for supervision and control that result from networks of interlocking relationships among families, neighbors, coworkers, and people within institutions such as schools.

19. Jeffrey Fagan, "The Social Control of Spouse Assault."

20. For example, Raymond Parnas, "Police Responses to Domestic Violence"; David J. Pitman and William Handy, "Patterns in Criminal Aggravated Assault."

21. See, for example, M. Elbow, "Theoretical Considerations of Violent Marriages."

22. Murray A. Straus, "Wife Beating: How Common and Why?"

23. Gaguin, "Spouse Abuse."

24. Murray A. Straus and Richard J. Gelles, "Societal Change in Family Violence from 1975 to 1985 As Revealed by Two National Surveys"; Richard J. Gelles and Murray A. Straus, *Intimate Violence.*

25. To measure spouse assault, the NFVS used the *Conflict Tactics Scales* (CTS) (Murray A. Straus, "Measuring Family Conflict and Violence: The Conflict Tactics Scale"). The CTS contains eight items ranging in severity from throwing objects to using a gun or knife. Threats of violence were considered nonviolent acts (Murray A. Straus and Richard J. Gelles, *Physical Violence in American Families: Risk Factors and Adaptations to Violence in 8,145 Families*). An additional item on "choking" was included in the 1985 survey. Also, questions on marital rape (forced sexual relations) were excluded from the 1975 study but were added to the 1985 survey separately from the CTS items. Interviews with a probability sample of 2,143 intact couples yielded estimates that 16 percent of all marital couples experienced physical aggression during the year before the survey; 28 percent had experienced physical aggression at some point in their relationship (Straus, "Wife Beating"). Among those reporting at least one act of violence in the past year, over one in three involved acts of severe violence: punching, kicking, biting, hitting with the fist, hitting or trying to hit with an object, beating up, threatening with a gun or knife, using a gun or knife. Straus and his colleagues found that 3.8 percent of female respondents and 4.6 percent of the males reported being victims of at least one of these acts of "severe violence." The 1985 survey included a larger sample (N = 6,002) with divorced/separated respondents in addition to intact couples. The interviews were conducted by telephone. The prevalence estimates for spouse assault from the 1985 survey were consistent with the 1975 effort (M.A. Straus and R.J. Gelles, "Societal Change").

NCS estimates of spouse assault were based on items asking whether the respondent had been physically assaulted in the past six months and whether the assailant was a spouse or ex-spouse, another "intimate," or a stranger.

26. Annual prevalence estimates of spouse-assault victimization based on the CTS range from 110 to 470 per 1,000 population (Fagan and Browne, "Violence between Spouses and Intimates"), depending on the sample and method. For example, telephone interviews may produce lower rates of spouse assault compared to face-to-face interviews (Diane E. H. Russell, *Rape in Marriage*; Irene H. Frieze and Angela Browne, "Violence in Marriage"; Straus and Gelles, *Physical Violence in American Families*). Whether the respondent is male or female also influences prevalence estimates: although males and females agree on the prevalence of marital violence, males tend to "minimize" their own spouse assault: they report lower rates of their own severe violence compared to female reports of male severe violence (Fagan and Browne, "Violence between Spouses and Intimates").

27. Ko-lin Chin, "Out-of-Town Brides: International Marriage and Wife Abuse among Chinese Immigrants."

28. See Murray A. Straus and C. Smith, "Violence in Hispanic Families"; S.B. Sorenson and C.A. Telles, "Self-Reports of Spouse Violence in a Mexican-American and Non-Hispanic White Population."

29. Sorenson and Telles, "Self-Reports."

30. Robert L. Hampton, R.J. Gelles, and J.W. Harrop, "Is Violence in the Black Family Increasing? A Comparison of 1975 and 1985 National Survey Rates."

31. Straus and Gelles, *Physical Violence in American Families*, p. 530.

32. Robert J. Sampson, "Crime in Cities: The Effects of Formal and Informal Social Control"; Laub, "Urbanism, Race and Crime."

33. Charles R. Tittle, "Influences on Urbanism: A Test of Predictions from Three Perspectives"; Colin Loftin and Ellen MacKenzie, "The Incidence and Prevalence of Violent Victimization."

34. P.J. Brantingham and Paul L. Brantingham, "Notes on the Geography of Crime."

35. Louis Wirth, *Culture of Cities*; Tittle, "Influences on Urbanism."

36. Albert J. Reiss, Jr., "Why Are Communities Important in Understanding Crime?"

37. *Offending rates* are the annual frequency of assaults for those reporting at least one assault in the past year.

38. See Carol Petrie and Joel Garner, "Is Violence Preventable?" for a review.

39. Fagan and Browne, "Violence between Spouses and Intimates."

40. *Age* was the respondent's age. For *ethnicity*, the partners' ethnicity was the same in nearly all cases. The few cases with mixed ethnicity were excluded from the tables. However, separate analyses showed that the prevalence of spouse assault did not differ for mixed-ethnicity couples from the rates for the total sample.

41. Sampson and Lauritsen, "Individual and Community Factors"; Steven F. Messner, "Poverty, Inequality and the Urban Homicide Rate" and "Regional Differences in the Economic Correlates of the Urban Homicide Rate: Some Evidence on the Importance of Context."

42. Straus and Gelles, "Societal Change in Family Violence."

43. Over one in three African-American couples reported at least one incident of spouse assault in the past year, compared to one in four white couples.

44. Delbert S. Elliott, David Huizinga, and Barbara Morse, *The Dynamics of Delinquent Behavior: A National Survey Progress Report*; Michael Gottfredson and Travis Hirschi, *A General Theory of Crime*; Greenberg, "Age, Crime and Explanation."

45. G. Maddala, Limited Dependent and Qualitative Variables in Econometric Research.

46. Greenberg, "Age, Crime and Explanation"; Sampson and Lauritsen, "Individual and Community Factors."

47. Spouse assault is more likely to occur in shorter relationships, in part because of the over-representation of younger partners in newer relationships and the longer tenure of nonviolent relationships (Hotaling and Sugarman, "A Risk Marker Analysis").

48. Paul Jargowsky and Mary J. Bane, "Ghetto Poverty in the United States, 1970-80"; William J. Wilson, "Studying Inner-City Social Dislocations: The Challenge of Public Agenda Research"; Loic Wacquant, "The Specificity of Ghetto Poverty: A Comparative Analysis of Race, Class, and Urban Exclusion in Chicago's Black Belt and the Parisian Red Belt."

49. Douglas S. Massey and Mitchell L. Eggers, "The Ecology of Inequality: Minorities and the Concentration of Poverty 1970–80"; Reynolds Farley, "Residential Segregation of Social and Economic Groups among Blacks, 1970–80."

50. These trends also may reflect selection processes leading to the concentration in cities of poorer within-ethnic groups. The migration of middle-income African-Americans to suburbs beginning in the 1970s left behind in central cities the poorest among African-Americans, setting off neighborhood processes that weakened social controls and compromised social networks (William J. Wilson, *The Truly Disadvantaged: The Inner City, the Underclass, and Urban Policy* and "Studying Inner-City Social Dislocations). However, within-race variation in crime rates in urban areas suggests that there are neighborhood processes that are either protective or facilitative of violence generally (Robert J. Sampson and William J. Wilson, "Race, Crime and Urban Inequality") and argue against selection processes as an exclusive explanation of violence rates within areas.

51. See Fagan and Browne, "Violence between Spouses and Intimates," for a review. For example, Mark Reidel, Margaret A. Zahn, and Lois Mock (*The Nature and Patterns*

of American Homicides), using UCR Supplemental Homicide Reports (SHRs) from eight cities, showed that 18.7 percent of all homicides from 1978 occurred within families. Straus, "Wife-Beating" calculated that nearly half of intrafamily homicides (48 percent) were spouse murders. Using SHRs, James A. Mercy and Linda E. Saltzman ("Fatal Violence among Spouses in the United States, 1976–85") identified 16,595 homicides among legal or common-law spouses between 1976 and 1985, or 8.8 percent of all homicides nationally over the ten-year period. And using pre-sentence investigations for 158 homicide defendants, Nancy Jurik and Russell Winn ("Gender and Homicide: A Comparison of Men and Women Who Kill") found that 52 percent of female perpetrators killed partners or ex-partners, compared to 10 percent of males.

52. Murray A. Straus, "Domestic Violence and Homicide Antecedents"; Angela Browne and Kirk R. Williams, "Exploring the Effects of Resource Availability and the Likelihood of Female-Perpetrated Homicides."

53. Mercy and Saltzman, "Fatal Violence."

54. Jurik and Winn, "Gender and Homicide."

55. Mercy and Saltzman, "Fatal Violence."

56. Carolyn Rebecca Block, "Lethal Violence at Home: Racial/Ethnic Differences in Domestic Homicide in Chicago, 1965 to 1981."

57. Linda E. Saltzman et al., "Magnitude and Patterns of Family and Intimate Assaults in Atlanta, Georgia, 1984."

58. Block, "Lethal Violence"; Franklin E. Zimring, S.K. Mukherjee, and B.J. Van Winkle, "Intimate Violence: A Study of Intersexual Homicide in Chicago."

59. Anna Kuhl, "Patterns of Victimization in Spousal Homicide in California, 1974–1986."

60. Massey and Eggers, "Ecology of Inequality."

61. Messner, "Poverty, Inequality and the Urban Homicide Rate."

62. Colin Loftin and Robert Nash Parker, "An Errors-Invariable Model of the Effect of Poverty on Urban Homicide Rates"; Kirk R. Williams and Robert L. Flewelling, "The Social Production of Criminal Homicide: A Comparative Study of Disaggregated Rates in American Cities."

63. Marvin E. Wolfgang, *Patterns in Criminal Homicide*; Paul J. Goldstein et al., "Crack and Homicide in New York City, 1988: A Conceptually-Based Event Analysis."

64. Blau and Blau, "The Cost of Inequality"; Kirk R. Williams, "Economic Sources of Homicide: Reestimating the Effects of Poverty and Inequality"; Douglas A. Smith and Robert Nash Parker, "Type of Homicide and Variation in Regional Rates."

65. Messner, "Poverty, Inequality and the Urban Homicide Rate."

66. Lawrence E. Cohen and Marcus Felson, "Social Change and Crime Rate Trends: A Routine Activities Approach."

67. Browne and Williams, "Exploring the Effects."

68. Williams and Flewelling, "Social Production."

69. Parker and Toth, "Family, Intimacy and Homicide."

70. J.K. Meyer and T.D. Lorimor, "Police Intervention Data and Domestic Violence: Exploratory Development and Validation of Prediction Models."

71. Lawrence W. Sherman, Patrick R. Gartin, and Michael E. Buerger, "Hot Spots of Predatory Crime: Routine Activities and the Criminology of Place."

72. Ibid.

73. David L. Weisburd, Lawrence W. Sherman, and Lisa Maher, "Contrasting Crime-Specific and Crime-General Theories: The Case of Hot Spots of Crime"; Wesley Skogan, *Disorder and Decline.*

74. R.K. Breedlove et al., "Domestic Violence and the Police: Kansas City." Domestic homicides include both spouses and other related adults or family members. However, most of these involved homicides among adults and also in primary (sexually intimate) relationships including spouses and cohabitants (boyfriends/girlfriends).

75. Sherman, Gartin, and Buerger, "Hot Spots."

76. N. Gilbert, *Capitalism and the Welfare State: Dilemmas of Social Benevolence.*

77. Fagan and Browne, "Violence between Spouses and Intimates"; Jeffrey Fagan and Sandra Wexler, "Crime in the Home and Crime in the Streets: The Relation between Family Violence and Stranger Crime." Fagan and Browne distinguish between feminist, social service, and social control paradigms. These three approaches were not exclusive. Feminist approaches converged with the expansion of legal controls through the proliferation of victim-witness programs, creating favorable conditions for shifting the focus of social control to the legal system. Victim-witness programs proliferated in the 1970s and were magnets within the criminal justice system for female victims of *both* family and stranger violence. Victimization as a social movement reflected concerns of several constituencies with divergent interests. Groups opposed to what they perceived as lenient sentencing of offenders saw the victims "movement" as a force to balance the rights of the accused with the rights of the victims. Citing tort theory, they viewed crime as a failure of the state to fulfill its part of the social contract, in turn creating an obligation to compensate. The needs of women and children for protection both from offenders and from shabby treatment from criminal justice agencies were seen by victims rights advocates as staking legitimate claims to their share of the "finite rights" in criminal law. Of course, these approaches were disproportionately invoked for victims and families whose backgrounds reflected clients in the criminal justice system.

78. Lawrence W. Sherman and Richard A. Berk, "The Specific Deterrent Effects of Arrest for Domestic Assault"; Richard A. Berk and Phyllis J. Newton, "Does Arrest Really Deter Wife Battery? An Effort to Replicate the Findings of the Minneapolis Spouse Abuse Experiment"; G.A. Goolkasian, "Confronting Domestic Violence: The Role of Criminal Court Judges."

79. Kirk R. Williams and Richard Hawkins, "Controlling Male Aggression in Intimate Relationships." Deterrence theory informed the development of criminal justice responses to marital violence. This approach emphasized the application of legal sanctions through arrest and prosecution of assailants, or invoking the threat of legal sanction through civil remedies that carried criminal penalties if violated. Legal action was designed to exact a cost, and to the extent that further violence was not evident, its suppression was attributed to the intrinsic consequences of legal sanctions (D. Dutton et al., "Arrest and the Reduction of Repeat Wife Assault"). Mandatory arrest policies for incidents in which there is probable cause of wife assault reflect this approach to social control of marital violence (Lawrence W. Sherman and Ellen G. Cohn, "The Impact of Research on Legal Policy: The Minneapolis Violence Experiment"; Fagan and Browne, "Violence between Spouses and Intimates").

80. Donald Black, *The Behavior of the Law*; R. Emerson, "On Last Resorts"; Susan Miller and Sally Simpson, "Courtship Violence and Social Control: Does Gender Matter?"

81. Williams and Hawkins, "Controlling Male Aggression."

82. J.A. Fagan, "Contributions of Family Violence Research to Criminal Justice Policy on Wife Assault: Paradigms of Science and Social Control"; K.R. Williams and R. Hawkins, "The Meaning of Arrest for Wife Assault."

83. Fagan and Browne, "Violence between Spouses and Intimates." The evidence from experiments will be reviewed later in this chapter. Also, Williams and Hawkins ("The Social Costs of Wife Assault") suggest that the general deterrent effects of these policies have been overlooked in research that examines only the specific deterrent ef-

fects. They argue that social costs are risked by both arrest and the violent acts that may outweigh other costs associated with legal actions (that is, punishment).

84. Diane C. Carmody and Kirk R. Williams, "Wife Assault and Perceptions of Sanctions"; Williams and Hawkins, "Controlling Male Aggression"; Fagan, "The Social Control of Spouse Assault."

85. Lee Bowker, *Beating Wife-Beating* and "Coping with Wife Abuse: Personal and Social Networks"; Berk and Newton, "Does Arrest Really Deter?"; Jeffrey Fagan, "Cessation of Family Violence: Deterrence and Dissuasion"; Williams and Hawkins, "The Social Costs."

86. Williams and Hawkins, "The Meaning of Arrest."

87. Sampson and Wilson, "Race, Crime and Urban Inequality"; Elliott and Huizinga, "The Mediating Effects of the Social Structure in High Risk Neighborhoods."

88. Black, *The Manners and Customs of the Police*; Sherman and Berk, "The Specific Deterrent Effects of Arrest for Domestic Assault"; Franklin E. Zimring, "Toward a Jurisprudence of Family Violence"; Franklin W. Dunford, David Huizinga, and Delbert S. Elliott, "The Role of Arrest in Domestic Assault: The Omaha Police Experiment"; J. David Hirschel, Ira W. Hutchison, III, and Charles Dean, "The Failure of Arrest to Deter Spouse Abuse"; D.A. Ford, "Prosecution As a Victim Power Resource: A Note on Empowering Women in Violent Conjugal Relationships."

89. Carmody and Williams, "Wife Assault"; Williams and Hawkins, "The Meaning of Arrest"; Miller and Simpson, "Courtship Violence"; Dutton et al., "Arrest and Reduction."

90. Black, *Behavior of the Law.*

91. Sherman and Berk, "Specific Deterrent Effects"; Dutton et al., "Arrest and Reduction."

92. Berk and Newton, "Does Arrest Really Deter?"; Franklin W. Dunford, David Huizinga, and Delbert S. Elliott, *The Omaha Domestic Violence Police Experiment.* Bowker (*Beating Wife-Beating*) included loss of spouse and/or children as an explicit cost of legal intervention.

93. Williams and Hawkins, "The Meaning of Arrest" and "Controlling Male Aggression"; Dutton et al., "Arrest and Reduction."

94. Dutton et al. ("Arrest and Reduction") report that the weight accorded to the threat of jail time is greater for research on arrestees than was observed in the studies using "hypothetical" arrests.

95. Jackson Toby, "Social Disorganization and Stake in Conformity: Complementary Factors in the Predatory Behavior of Hoodlums"; R.J. Sampson and W.B. Groves, "Community Structure and Crime: Testing Social Disorganization Theory."

96. Miller and Simpson, "Courtship Violence."

97. Fagan, "Cessation of Family Violence."

98. Bowker, *Beating Wife-Beating* and "Coping with Wife Abuse."

99. Lawrence W. Sherman et al., "From Initial Deterrence to Longterm Escalation: Short Custody Arrest for Poverty Ghetto Domestic Violence."

100. Berk and Newton, "Does Arrest Really Deter?"

101. Sherman et al., "From Initial Deterrence to Longterm Escalation"; Lawrence W. Sherman and Douglas A. Smith, "Crime, Punishment and Stake in Conformity: Legal and Extralegal Control of Domestic Violence"; Anthony Pate, Edwin Hamilton, and Sampson Annan "Formal and Informal Deterrents: Dade County Experiment"; Richard A. Berk et al., "The Deterrent Effects of Arrest: A Bayesian Analysis of Four Field Experiments."

102. Sherman et al., "From Initial Deterrence to Longterm Escalation"; Hagedorn with Macon, *People and Folks: Gangs, Crime and the Underclass in a Rustbelt City.*

103. Hirschel, Hutchison, and Dean, "The Failure of Arrest."

104. Pate, Hamilton, and Annan, "Formal and Informal Deterrents."

105. Dunford, Huizinga, and Elliott, *Omaha.*

106. Berk et al., "The Deterrent Effects of Arrest."

107. In the Omaha experiment, 43 percent of the domestic-violence arrestees were African-Americans; over half were nonwhite, including Latinos and Native Americans. Arrestees in the Charlotte and Milwaukee experiments predominantly were African-American (70 percent and 71 percent of eligible cases, respectively).

108. Fagan et al., *National Family Violence Evaluation.*

109. Bowker, *Beating Wife-Beating.*

110. Franklin E. Zimring and Gordon Hawkins, *Deterrence: The Legal Threat in Crime Control.*

111. Jack Gibbs, *Social Control;* Tittle and Logan, "Sanctions and Deviance: Evidence and Remaining Questions"; Matthew Silberman, "Toward a Theory of Criminal Deterrence."

112. The relationship between formal and informal sanctions also may be seen as *additive*—where both sources of sanctions combine to deter offenders—or as *replacement*—where legal controls replace the effects of social sanctions or controls (see Harold Grasmick and Robert Bursik, Jr., "Conscience, Significant Others, and Rational Choice: Extending the Deterrence Model," for a review). These relationships have been tested primarily through survey research in general populations (with predominantly white populations) and rarely with arrestees.

113. Kirk R. Williams and Richard Hawkins, "The Meaning of Arrest."

114. Franklin W. Dunford, David Huizinga, and; Ford, "Prosecution as a Victim Power Resource." and Delbert S. Elliott, *Omaha.*

115. Daniel Doyle and David Luckenbill, "Mobilizing Law in Response to Collective Problems: A Test of Black's Theory of Law."

116. Kirk R. Williams and Richard Hawkins, "Perceptual Research on General Deterrence: A Critical Review."

117. Howard Becker, *Outsiders.*

118. Williams and Hawkins, "Perceptual Research," p. 565.

119. Toby, "Social Disorganization"; Sherman and Smith, "Crime, Punishment and Stake in Conformity."

120. Williams and Hawkins, "Perceptual Research," p. 566.

121. Daniel Nagin and Raymond Paternoster, "The Preventive Effects of the Perceived Risk of Arrest: Testing an Expanded Conception of Deterrence."

122. Coleman, "Social Capital"; Sampson, "Family Management."

123. Sampson and Groves, "Community Structure and Crime."

124. Zuravin, "The Ecology of Child Abuse and Neglect"

125. James Garbarino, "A Preliminary Study of Some Ecological Correlates of Child Abuse: The Impact of Socioeconomic Stress on Mothers"; J. Garbarino and A. Crouter, "Defining the Community Context for Parent–Child Relations: The Correlates of Child Maltreatment."

126. James Garbarino and Deborah Sherman, "High-Risk Neighborhoods and High-Risk Families: The Human Ecology of Child Maltreatment" ("social impoverishment" on p. 196). They also noted that "high-risk families may drift toward high-risk neighborhoods" (p. 196), creating a compositional or aggregation effect.

127. Cathy Spatz Widom, "The Cycle of Violence"; Hotaling and Sugarman, "A Risk Marker Analysis"; P.L. Caesar, "Exposure to Violence in Families of Origin among Wife Abusers and Maritally Nonviolent Men"; Fagan and Browne, "Violence between Spouses and Intimates."

128. Jeffrey Fagan, Douglas Stewart, and Karen V. Hansen, "Violent Men or Violent Husbands? Background Factors and Situational Correlates of Domestic and Extra-Domestic Violence."

129. However, such intergenerational transmission of violence itself is mediated by social structural factors (Cathy Spatz Widom, "Child Abuse, Neglect and Violent Criminal Behavior"): childhood violence victimization was a stronger risk factor for white and nonpoor families than among poor families or families located in poor neighborhoods.

130. See Fagan and Browne, "Violence between Spouses and Intimates," for analyses of the 1985 NFVS data.

131. Fagan and Browne, "Violence between Spouses and Intimates."

132. John Kasarda and Morris Janowitz, "Community Attachment in Mass Society."

133. Sampson and Wilson, "Race, Crime and Urban Inequality."

134. Elijah Anderson, *Streetwise: Race, Class, and Change in an Urban Community*, p. 112.

135. See Wilson, *The Truly Disadvantaged*, regarding the pool of marriageable young men.

136. Anderson, *Streetwise*.

137. Ibid.

138. Wilson, *The Truly Disadvantaged*.

139. In this context, young men may be seen as burdens or risks rather than assets in achieving the passage of setting up her own household (Anderson, *Streetwise*, p. 128).

140. Ulf Hannerz, *Soulside: Inquiries into Ghetto Culture and Community*, p. 71.

141. Sampson and Wilson, "Race, Crime and Urban Inequality."

142. Ralph Taylor and Jeanette Covington, "Neighborhood Changes in Ecology and Violence."

143. Bowker, *Beating Wife-Beating* and "Coping with Wife Abuse."

144. Hotaling and Sugarman, "A Risk Marker Analysis."

145. Garbarino, "Incidence and Prevalence."

146. Neal A. Cazenave and Murray A. Straus, "Race, Class, Network Embeddedness, and Family Violence: A Search for Potent Support Systems."

147. Bowker, *Beating Wife-Beating*.

148. Claude S. Fischer et al., *Networks and Places: Social Relations in the Urban Setting*.

149. Carol Stack, *All Our Kin: Strategies for Survival in a Black Community*.

150. J.P. Fitzpatrick, "Drugs and Puerto Ricans in New York City."

151. Felix Padilla, *The Gang As an American Enterprise. Familism* has been defined as a value system in support of the family that emphasizes the bonds and obligations among relatives and the duty to help and express concern for them (Lloyd Rogler and Rosemary S. Cooney, *Puerto Rican Families in New York City: Intergenerational Processes*). Ties between families are cemented by the establishment of *compadrazco* (god-parent–godchild) relationships. The godparents at baptism or sponsors at confirmation are the *padrinos* of the child and become co-parents with the natural parents. Witnesses at a wedding become *compadres* of the married couple (Fitzpatrick, "Drugs and Puerto Ricans"). These serious relationships involve reciprocal obligations that often are as demanding as natural family relations. Within this milieu, the well-being of the individual is subordinated to the welfare of the family or kinship network.

152. N. Busch-Rossnagel and L. Zayas, "Hispanic Adolescents."

153. Wilson, *The Truly Disadvantaged* and "Studying Inner-City Social Dislocations."

154. Sampson and Wilson, "Race, Crime and Urban Inequality."

155. Douglas S. Massey, "American Apartheid: Segregation and the Making of the Underclass."

156. See Anderson, *Streetwise*, and Hannerz, *Soulside*, for example.

157. William F. Whyte, *Street Corner Society*.

158. See Oscar Lewis, *La Vida: A Puerto Rican Family in the Culture of Poverty, San Juan and New York*; Stack, *All Our Kin*; Lee Rainwater, *Behind Ghetto Walls: Black*

Families in a Federal Slum; G.D. Suttles, *The Social Order of the Slum: Ethnicity and Territory in the Inner City*; Elijah Anderson, *A Place on the Corner* and *Streetwise*; Hannerz, *Soulside*; Chin, "Out-of-Town Brides"; Elliot Liebow, *Tally's Corner*.

159. Liebow, *Tally's Corner*, p. 127.

160. Thomas J. Bernard, "Angry Aggression among the 'Truly Disadvantaged.'"

161. Liebow, *Tally's Corner*, p. 130.

162. Hannerz, *Soulside*; Anderson, *Streetwise*; Elliot Liebow, *Tally's Corner*.

163. Wilson, *The Truly Disadvantaged*.

164. Liebow, *Tally's Corner*.

165. Coleman, *Foundations*, p. 98. This is distinguished from human capital that is tangible: skills, resources, and knowledge.

166. Coleman, "Social Capital" and *Foundations*.

167. Coleman, *Foundations*, p. 318.

168. Sampson, "Family Management."

169. But social capital also may fail to accrue even under more benign structural conditions, particularly in neighborhoods marked by infrequent contacts between families or limited cross-generational and cross-family integration within the contexts of schools or other institutions.

170. See Robert J. Sampson, "Urban Black Violence: The Effect of Male Joblessness and Family Disruption."

171. Wilson, *The Truly Disadvantaged*.

172. The intervening neighborhood processes specifically avoid the problem of "individualistic fallacy," in which individual-level correlations are spuriously related to community-level processes or the selection effects that result in persons of low socioeconomic status being surrounded by persons of similar status.

173. See Sampson and Wilson, "Race, Crime and Urban Inequality."

174. The higher rates of spouse assault for African-Americans regardless of social area suggest that they are subject to stresses that extend beyond the context of community. For example, encounters with workplace job discrimination are commonplace in the lives of African-American males (Neckerman and Kirschenman, "Hiring Strategies, Racial Bias, and Inner-City Workers"), as is disparity within legal institutions (Mark Maurer, *Young Black Men and the Criminal Justice System: A Growing National Problem*). To the extent that these interactions create a perceptual framework or landscape of societal discrimination, the processes of socially isolated urban areas may be carried over to African-American families living outside the central city. Wacquant ("The Specificity of Ghetto Poverty"), for example, observes that racial domination in American society extends well beyond the physical ghetto, despite the concentration of race, place, and poverty.

175. Taylor and Covington, "Neighborhood Changes"; Sampson, "Urban Black Violence"; Sampson and Lauritsen, "Individual and Community Factors."

176. Darnell F. Hawkins, "Devalued Lives and Racial Stereotypes: Ideological Barriers to the Prevention of Family Violence among Blacks"; Fagan and Browne, "Violence between Spouses and Intimates"; Donald Dutton, "Profiling of Wife Assaulters: Preliminary Evidence for a Trimodal Analysis."

177. Bernard, "Angry Aggression."

178. Hawkins, "Devalued Lives."

179. Jeffrey Fagan, Elizabeth S. Piper, and Yu-teh Cheng, "Contributions of Victimization to Delinquency."

180. Angela Browne and Donald G. Dutton, "Risks and Alternatives for Abused Women: What Do We Currently Know?"

181. Donald Dutton, "Severe Wife Battering As Deindividuated Violence."

References

Anderson, Elijah. *A Place on the Corner*. Chicago: University of Chicago Press, 1978.
————. *Streetwise: Race, Class, and Change in an Urban Community*. Chicago: University of Chicago Press, 1990.
Bailey, William C. "Poverty, Inequality, and City Homicide Rates: Some Not So Unexpected Results." *Criminology* 22 (1984): 531–50.
Becker, Howard. *Outsiders*. New York: Free Press, 1960.
Berk, Richard A.; Campbell, Alec; Klap, Ruth, and Western, Bruce. "The Deterrent Effects of Arrest: A Bayesian Analysis of Four Field Experiments." *American Sociological Review* 57 (1992): 698–708.
Berk, Richard A., and Newton, Phyllis J. "Does Arrest Really Deter Wife Battery? An Effort to Replicate the Findings of the Minneapolis Spouse Abuse Experiment." *American Sociological Review* 50 (1985): 253–62.
Bernard, Thomas J. "Angry Aggression among the 'Truly Disadvantaged.'" *Criminology* 28 (1990): 73–96.
Black, Donald. *The Behavior of the Law*. New York: Academic Press, 1976.
————. *The Manners and Customs of the Police*. New York: Academic Press, 1980.
Blau, Judith, and Blau, Peter M. "The Cost of Inequality: Metropolitan Structure and Violent Crime." *American Sociological Review* 47 (1982): 114–29.
Block, Carolyn Rebecca. "Lethal Violence at Home: Racial/Ethnic Differences in Domestic Homicide in Chicago, 1965 to 1981." Paper presented at the Annual Meeting of the American Society of Criminology, Chicago, November 1987.
Bowker, Lee N. 1983. *Beating Wife-Beating*. Lexington, Mass.: D.C. Heath, 1983.
————. "Coping with Wife Abuse: Personal and Social Networks". In A.R. Roberts, ed., *Battered Women and Their Families*. New York: Springer, 1984.
Brantingham, Paul J., and Brantingham, Patricia L., "Notes on the Geography of Crime." In Brantingham and Brantingham, eds., *Environmental Criminology*, 2d ed., Prospect Heights, Ill.: Waveland Press, 1991.
Breedlove, R.K.; Kennish, J.W.; Sanker, D.M.; and Sawtell, R.K. "Domestic Violence and the Police: Kansas City." In *Domestic Violence and the Police: Studies in Detroit and Kansas City*, pp. 22–33. Washington, D.C.: Police Foundation, 1977.
Browne, Angela. *When Battered Women Kill*. New York: Free Press, 1987.
Browne, Angela, and Dutton, Donald G. "Risks and Alternatives for Abused Women: What Do We Currently Know?" In R. Roesch, D.G. Dutton, and V.F. Sacco, eds., *Family Violence: Perspectives in Research and Practice*. Vancouver, B.C.: Simon Fraser University, 1990.
Browne, Angela, and Williams, Kirk R. "Exploring the Effects of Resource Availability and the Likelihood of Female-Perpetrated Homicides." *Law and Society Review*, 23 (1989): 75–94.
Busch-Rossnagel, N., and Zayas, L. "Hispanic Adolescents." In R. Lerner, A. Peterson, and J. Brooks-Gunn, eds., *Encyclopedia of Adolescence*. New York: Garland, 1992.
Caesar, P. Lynn. "Exposure to Violence in Families of Origin among Wife Abusers and Maritally Nonviolent Men." *Violence and Victims* 3, no. 1 (1988): 49–64.
Carmody, Diane C., and Williams, Kirk R. "Wife Assault and Perceptions of Sanctions." *Violence and Victims* 2 (1987): 25–38.
Cazenave, Neal A., and Straus, Murray A. "Race, Class, Network Embeddedness, and Family Violence: A Search for Potent Support Systems." In M.A. Straus and R.J. Gelles, eds., *Physical Violence in American Families: Risk Factors and Adaptations to Violence in 8,145 Families*, pp. 321–40. New Brunswick, N.J.: Transaction Press, 1990.

Chin, Ko-lin. "Out-of-Town Brides: International Marriage and Wife Abuse among Chinese Immigrants." *Journal of Comparative Family Studies* (1993).

Cohen, Lawrence E., and Felson, Marcus. "Social Change and Crime Rate Trends: A Routine Activities Approach." *American Sociological Review* 44 (1979): 588–607.

Coleman, James. *Foundations of Social Theory.* Cambridge, Mass.: Harvard University Press, 1990.

———. "Social Capital in the Creation of Human Capital." *American Journal of Sociology* 94 (1988): S95–S120.

Dibble, Ursula, and Straus, Murray A. "Some Social Structure Determinants of Inconsistency between Attitudes and Behavior: The Case of Family Violence." In M.A. Straus and R.J. Gelles, eds., *Physical Violence in American Families: Risk Factors and Adaptations to Violence in 8,145 Families,* pp. 167–80. New Brunswick, N.J.: Transaction Press, 1990.

Doyle, Daniel, and Luckenbill, David. "Mobilizing Law in Response to Collective Problems: A Test of Black's Theory of Law." *Law and Society Review* 25 (1991): 103–16.

Dunford, Franklin W.; Huizinga, David; and Elliott, Delbert S. *The Omaha Domestic Violence Police Experiment.* Final Report, Grant 85-IJ-CX-K435, National Institute of Justice. Washington, D.C.: U.S. Department of Justice, 1989.

———. "The Role of Arrest in Domestic Assault: The Omaha Police Experiment." *Criminology* 28, no. 2 (1990): 183–206.

Dutton, Donald. "Profiling of Wife Assaulters: Preliminary Evidence for a Trimodal Analysis." *Violence and Victims* 3 (1988): 5–30.

———. "Severe Wife Battering as Deindividuated Violence." *Victimology: An International Journal* 7 (1982): 13–23.

Dutton, D.; Hart, S.G.; Kennedy, L.W.; and Williams, K.R. "Arrest and the Reduction of Repeat Wife Assault." In E. Buzawa and C. Buzawa, eds., *Domestic Violence: The Changing Criminal Justice Response.* Westport, Conn.: Greenwood, 1991.

Elbow, M. "Theoretical Considerations of Violent Marriages. *Social Casework* 58 (1977): 515–26.

Elliott, Delbert S., and Huizinga, David. "The Mediating Effects of the Social Structure in High Risk Neighborhoods." Paper presented at the Annual Meeting of the American Sociological Association, Washington D.C., August 1990.

Elliott, Delbert S., Huizinga, David, and Morse, Barbara. *The Dynamics of Delinquent Behavior: A National Survey Progress Report.* Boulder, Colo.: Institute of Behavioral Sciences, University of Colorado, 1985.

Emerson, R. "On Last Resorts." *American Journal of Sociology* 87 (1981): 1–22.

Fagan, Jeffrey. "The Social Control of Spouse Assault." In F. Adler and W. Laufer, eds., *Advances in Criminological Theory, Volume IV.* New Brunswick, N.J.: Transaction Press, 1992.

———. "Contributions of Family Violence Research to Criminal Justice Policy on Wife Assault: Paradigms of Science and Social Control." *Violence and Victims* 3 (1988): 159–86.

———. "Cessation of Family Violence: Deterrence and Dissuasion." In L. Ohlin and M. Tonry, eds. *Family Violence.* Chicago: University of Chicago Press, 1989.

Fagan, Jeffrey, and Browne, Angela. "Violence between Spouses and Intimates: Physical Aggression between Women and Men in Relationships." In A.J. Reiss, Jr., and J.A. Roth, eds., *Understanding and Controlling Violence.* Washington, D.C.: National Academy Press, forthcoming.

Fagan, Jeffrey; Friedman, E.; Wexler, S.; and Lewis, V. *The National Family Violence Evaluation: Final Report, Volume I—Analytic Findings.* Washington, D.C.: Office of Juvenile Justice and Delinquency Prevention, 1984.

Fagan, Jeffrey; Piper, Elizabeth S.; and Cheng, Yu-teh. "Contributions of Victimization to Delinquency." *Journal of Criminal Law and Criminology* 78 (1987): 586–613.

Fagan, Jeffrey; Stewart, Douglas; and Hansen, Karen V. "Violent Men or Violent Husbands? Background Factors and Situational Correlates of Domestic and Extra-Domestic Violence." In D. Finkelhor, R. Gelles, G. Hotaling, and M.A. Straus, eds., *The Dark Side of Families*. Beverly Hills: Sage Publications, 1983.

Fagan, Jeffrey, and Wexler, Sandra R. "Crime in the Home and Crime in the Streets: The Relation between Family Violence and Stranger Crime." *Violence and Victims* 2 (1987): 5–21.

Farley, Reynolds. "Residential Segregation of Social and Economic Groups among Blacks, 1970–80." In C. Jencks and P.E. Peterson, eds., *The Urban Underclass*. Washington, D.C.: Brookings Press, 1991.

Fischer, Claude S.; Jackson, R.M.; Stueve, C.A.; Gerson, K.; Jones, L.M.; and Boldassare, M. *Networks and Places: Social Relations in the Urban Setting*. New York: Free Press, 1977.

Fitzpatrick, J.P. "Drugs and Puerto Ricans in New York City." In R. Glick and J. Moore, eds., *Drugs in Hispanic Communities*, pp. 77–102. New Brunswick, N.J.: Rutgers University Press, 1990.

Ford, David A. "Prosecution As a Victim Power Resource: A Note on Empowering Women in Violent Conjugal Relationships." *Law and Society Review* 25 (1991): 313–34.

Frieze, Irene H., and Browne, Angela. "Violence in Marriage." In L. Ohlin and M. Tonry, eds., *Family Violence*. Chicago: University of Chicago Press, 1989.

Gaguin, D.A. "Spouse Abuse: Data from the National Crime Survey. *Victimology: An International Journal* 2, nos. 3, 4 (1977): 632–42.

Garbarino, James. "The Incidence and Prevalence of Child Maltreatment." In L. Ohlin and M. Tonry, eds., *Family Violence*, pp. 219–62. Chicago: University of Chicago Press, 1989.

———. "A Preliminary Study of Some Ecological Correlates of Child Abuse: The Impact of Socioeconomic Stress on Mothers." *Child Development* 47 (1976): 178–85.

Garbarino, James, and Crouter, A. "Defining the Community Context for Parent–Child Relations: The Correlates of Child Maltreatment." *Child Development* 49 (1978): 604–16.

Garbarino, James, and Sherman, Deborah. "High-Risk Neighborhoods and High-Risk Families: The Human Ecology of Child Maltreatment." *Child Development* 51 (1980): 188–98.

Gelles, Richard J., and Cornell, Claire P. *Intimate Violence in Families*. Beverly Hills: Sage Publications, 1985.

Gelles, Richard J., and Straus, Murray A. *Intimate Violence*. New York: Simon and Schuster, 1988.

Gibbs, Jack. *Social Control*. Beverly Hills: Sage Publications, 1975.

Gilbert, N. *Capitalism and the Welfare State: Dilemmas of Social Benevolence*. New Haven: Yale University Press, 1983.

Goldstein, Paul J.; Brownstein, Henry H.; Ryan, Patrick; and Belluci, Patricia A. "Crack and Homicide in New York City, 1988: A Conceptually-Based Event Analysis." *Contemporary Drug Problems* 16 (1989): 651–87.

Goolkasian, Gail A. "Confronting Domestic Violence: The Role of Criminal Court Judges." *Research in Brief.* Washington, D.C.: National Institute of Justice, 1986.

Gottfredson, Michael, and Hirschi, Travis. *A General Theory of Crime*. Palo Alto, Calif.: Stanford University Press, 1990.

Grasmick, Harold, and Bursik, Robert, Jr. "Conscience, Significant Others, and Rational

Choice: Extending the Deterrence Model." *Law and Society Review* 24 (1990): 837–61.

Greenberg, D. "Age, Crime and Explanation." American Journal of Sociology, vol. 91, pp. 1–21.

Hagedorn, John, with Perry Macon. *People and Folks: Gangs, Crime and the Underclass in a Rustbelt City.* Boulder, Colo.: Westview Press, 1988.

Hampton, Robert L.; Gelles, Richard J.; and Harrop, J.W. "Is Violence in the Black Family Increasing? A Comparison of 1975 and 1985 National Survey Rates." *Journal of Marriage and the Family* 51 (1989): 969–80.

Hannerz, Ulf. *Soulside: Inquiries into Ghetto Culture and Community.* New York: Columbia University Press, 1969.

Harlow, Caroline W. "Female Victims of Violent Crime." Report NCJ-126826, Bureau of Justice Statistics, Office of Justice Programs, U.S. Department of Justice. Washington, D.C.: Government Printing Office, 1991.

Hawkins, Darnell F. "Devalued Lives and Racial Stereotypes: Ideological Barriers to the Prevention of Family Violence among Blacks." In R.L. Hampton, ed., *Violence in the Black Family.* Lexington, Mass.: D.C. Heath, Lexington Books, 1987.

Hirschel, J. David; Hutchison, Ira W.; and Dean, C. "The Failure of Arrest to Deter Spouse Abuse." *Journal of Research in Crime and Delinquency* 29 (1992).

Hirschel, J. David; Hutchison, Ira W., III; Dean, Charles W.; Kelley, J.J.; and Pesackis, C. "Charlotte Spouse Assault Replication Project: Final Report." Grant 87-IJ-CX-K004, National Institute of Justice. Washington, D.C.: U.S. Department of Justice, 1991.

Hotaling, Gerald T., and Sugarman, D.B. "A Risk Marker Analysis of Assaulted Wives." *Journal of Family Violence* 5 (1990): 1–13.

Jargowsky, Paul, and Bane, Mary J. "Ghetto Poverty in the United States, 1970-80." In C. Jencks and P.E. Peterson, eds., *The Urban Underclass.* Washington, D.C.: Brookings Press, 1991.

Jurik, Nancy, and Winn, Russell. "Gender and Homicide: A Comparison of Men and Women Who Kill." *Violence and Victims* 5 (1990): 227–42.

Kasarda, John, and Janowitz, Morris. "Community Attachment in Mass Society." *American Sociological Review* 39 (1974): 328–39.

Kennedy, Leslie W., and Dutton, Donald G. "The Incidence of Wife Assault in Alberta." *Canadian Journal of Behavioural Science* 21 (1989): 40–54.

Klaus, Patricia A., and Rand, M.R. *Family Violence.* Special Report, Bureau of Justice Statistics, Office of Justice Programs, U.S. Department of Justice. Washington, D.C.: U.S. Government Printing Office, 1984.

Kuhl, Anna. "Patterns of Victimization in Spousal Homicide in California, 1974–1986." Unpublished. Sacramento, Calif.: Office of the Attorney General, 1989.

Laub, John A. "Urbanism, Race and Crime." *Journal of Research in Crime and Delinquency* 20 (1983): 183–98.

Lentzner, H.R., and DeBerry, M.M. *Intimate Victims: A Study of Violence among Friends and Relatives.* Washington, D.C.: U.S. Department of Justice, Bureau of Justice Statistics, 1980.

Lewis, Oscar. *La Vida: A Puerto Rican Family in the Culture of Poverty, San Juan and New York.* New York: Random House, 1965.

Liebow, Elliot. *Tally's Corner.* Boston: Little, Brown, 1967.

Loftin, Colin, and MacKenzie, Ellen. "The Incidence and Prevalence of Violent Victimization." In A.J. Reiss, Jr., D.P. Farrington, and J.A. Roth, eds., *Understanding and Controlling Violent Behavior.* Washington, D.C.: National Academy Press, 1993.

Loftin, Colin, and Parker, Robert Nash. "An Errors-Invariable Model of the Effect of Poverty on Urban Homicide Rates." *Criminology* 23 (1985): 289–312.

Maddala, G. 1983. *Limited Dependent and Qualitative Variables in Econometric Research.* Cambridge: Cambridge University Press, 1983.

Massey, Douglas S. "American Apartheid: Segregation and the Making of the Underclass." *American Journal of Sociology* 96 (1990): 329–57.

Massey, Douglas S., and Eggers, Mitchell L. "The Ecology of Inequality: Minorities and the Concentration of Poverty, 1970–80." *American Journal of Sociology* 95 (1990): 1153–88.

Maurer, Mark. *Young Black Men and the Criminal Justice System: A Growing National Problem.* Washington, D.C.: Sentencing Project, 1990.

Mercy, James A., and Saltzman, Linda E. "Fatal Violence among Spouses in the United States, 1976–85." *American Journal of Public Health* 79 (1989): 595–99.

Messner, Steven F. "Poverty, Inequality and the Urban Homicide Rate." *Criminology* 20 (1982): 103–14.

———. "Regional Differences in the Economic Correlates of the Urban Homicide Rate: Some evidence on the Importance of Context." *Criminology* 21 (1983): 477–88.

Meyer, J.K., and Lorimor, T.D. "Police Intervention Data and Domestic Violence: Exploratory Development and Validation of Prediction Models." Paper prepared under Grant R 01 MH27918, National Institute of Mental Health. Kansas City, Mo.: Kansas City Police Department, 1977.

Miller, Susan, and Simpson, Sally. "Courtship Violence and Social Control: Does Gender Matter?" *Law and Society Review* 25 (1991): 335–67.

Nagin, Daniel and Paternoster, Raymond. The Preventive Effect of the Perceived Risk of Arrest: Testing an Expanded Conception of Deterrence." *Criminology* 29 (1991): 561–89.

Neckerman, Katherine M., and Kirschenman, Joleen. "Hiring Strategies, Racial Bias, and Inner-City Workers." *Social Problem* 38 (1991): 433–77.

Padilla, Felix. *The Gang As an American Enterprise.* New Brunswick, N.J.: Rutgers University Press, 1992.

Pagelow, Mildred. *Family Violence.* New York: Praeger, 1984.

Parker, Robert Nash, and Toth, A.M. "Family, Intimacy and Homicide: A Macrosocial Approach." *Violence and Victims* 5 (1990): 195–211.

Parnas, Raymond. "Police Responses to Domestic Violence." *Wisconsin Law Review* 31 (1967): 914–60.

Pate, Anthony; Hamilton, Edwin; and Annan, Sampson. "Formal and Informal Deterrents: Dade County Experiment." *American Sociological Review* 57 (1992): 691–98.

Petrie, Carol, and Garner, Joel. "Is Violence Preventable?" In D.J. Besharov, ed., *Family Violence: Research and Public Policy Issues.* Washington, D.C.: AEI Press, 1990.

Pitman, David J., and Handy, William. "Patterns in Criminal Aggravated Assault." *Journal of Criminal Law and Criminology* 55 (1964): 462–67.

Rainwater, Lee. *Behind Ghetto Walls: Black Families in a Federal Slum.* Chicago: Aldine-deGruyter, 1970.

Reidel, Mark; Zahn, Margaret A.; and Mock, Lois. *The Nature and Patterns of American Homicides.* Washington, D.C.: U.S. Government Printing Office, 1985.

Reiss, Albert J., Jr. "Why Are Communities Important in Understanding Crime?" In A.J. Reiss, Jr., and M. Tonry, eds., *Communities and Crime,* pp. 1–33. Chicago: University of Chicago Press, 1986.

Reiss, Albert J., Jr., and Roth, Jeffrey A. *Understanding and Controlling Violence.* Washington, D.C.: National Academy Press, 1992.

Rogler, Lloyd, and Cooney, Rosemary S. *Puerto Rican Families in New York City: Intergenerational Processes.* Maplewood, N.J.: Waterfront Press, 1984.

Russell, Diana E.H. *Rape in Marriage.* New York: Macmillan, 1982.

Saltzman, Linda E.; Mercy, James A.; Rosenberg, Mark L.; Elsea, W.R.; Napper, George;

Sikes, R.K.; Waxweiler, Richard; and the Collaborative Working Group for the Study of Family and Intimate Assaults in Atlanta. "Magnitude and Patterns of Family and Intimate Assaults in Atlanta, Georgia, 1984." *Violence and Victims* 5 (1990): 3–18.

Sampson, Robert J. "Crime in Cities: The Effects of Formal and Informal Social Control". In A.J. Reiss, Jr. and M. Tonry, eds., *Communities and Crime*, pp. 29–69. Chicago: University of Chicago Press, 1986.

————. "Family Management and Child Development: Insights from Social Disorganization Theory." In Joan McCord, ed., *Facts, Forecasts, and Frameworks*, pp. 63–92. New Brunswick, N.J.: Transaction Press, 1992.

————. "Urban Black Violence: The Effect of Male Joblessness and Family Disruption." *American Journal of Sociology* 93 (1987): 348–82.

Sampson, Robert J., and Groves, W. Byron. "Community Structure and Crime: Testing Social Disorganization Theory." *American Journal of Sociology* 94 (1989): 774–802.

Sampson, Robert J., and Lauritsen, Janet. "Individual and Community Factors in Violent Offending and Victimization." In A.J. Reiss, Jr., D.P. Farrington, and J.A. Roth, eds., *Understanding and Controlling Violent Behavior*. Washington, D.C.: National Academy Press, forthcoming.

Sampson, Robert J., and Wilson, William J. "Race, Crime and Urban Inequality." In J. Hagan, ed., *Crime and Inequality*. Chicago: University of Chicago Press, forthcoming.

Sedlak, Andrea J. "Prevention of Wife Abuse." In V.B. Van Hasselt, R.L. Morrison, A.S. Bellack, and M. Hersen, eds., *Handbook of Family Violence*, pp. 319–58. New York: Plenum Press, 1988.

Sherman, Lawrence W., and Berk, Richard A. "The Specific Deterrent Effects of Arrest for Domestic Assault." *American Sociological Review* 49 (1984): 261–72.

Sherman, Lawrence W., and Cohn, Ellen G. "The Impact of Research on Legal Policy: The Minneapolis Violence Experiment." *Law and Society Review* 23 (1989): 117–44.

Sherman, Lawrence W.; Gartin, Patrick R.; and Buerger, Michael E. "Hot Spots of Predatory Crime: Routine Activities and the Criminology of Place." *Criminology* 27 (1989): 27–55.

Sherman, Lawrence W.; Schmidt, Janelle D.; Rogan, Dennis P.; Gartin, Patrick R.; Cohn, Ellen G.; Collins, D.J.; and Bacich, A.R. "From Initial Deterrence to Longterm Escalation: Short Custody Arrest for Poverty Ghetto Domestic Violence." *Criminology* 29 (1991): 821–50.

Sherman, Lawrence W., and Smith, Douglas A. "Crime, Punishment and Stake in Conformity: Legal and Extralegal Control of Domestic Violence." *American Sociological Review* (1992).

Silberman, Matthew. "Toward a Theory of Criminal Deterrence." *American Sociological Review* 41 (1976): 442–61.

Skogan, Wesley. *Disorder and Decline*. New York: Free Press, 1990.

Smith, Douglas A., and Parker, Robert Nash. "Type of Homicide and Variation in Regional Rates." *Social Forces* 59 (1980): 136–47.

Sorenson, Susan B., and Telles, Cynthia A. "Self-Reports of Spouse Violence in a Mexican-American and Non-Hispanic White Population." *Violence and Victims* 6 (1991): 3–16.

Stack, Carol. *All Our Kin: Strategies for Survival in a Black Community*. New York: Harper and Row, 1974.

Stark, Evan, and Flitcraft, Anne. "Violence among Intimates: An Epidemiological Review." In V.B. Van Hasselt, R.L. Morrison, A.S. Bellack, and M. Hersen, eds., *Handbook of Family Violence*, pp. 293–317. New York: Plenum Press, 1988.

Straus, Murray A. "Domestic Violence and Homicide Antecedents." *Bulletin of the New York Academy of Medicine* 62 (1986): 446–65.

————. "Measuring Family Conflict and Violence: The Conflict Tactics Scale." *Journal of Marriage and the Family* 41 (1979): 75–88.

————. "Wife Beating: How Common and Why?" *Victimology* 2 (1978): 576–84.

Straus, Murray A., and Gelles, Richard J., eds., *Physical Violence in American Families: Risk Factors and Adaptations to Violence in 8,145 Families.* New Brunswick, N.J.: Transaction Press, 1990.

————. "Societal Change in Family Violence from 1975 to 1985 As Revealed by Two National Surveys." *Journal of Marriage and the Family* 48 (1986): 465–79.

Straus, Murray A.; Gelles, Richard J.; and Steinmetz, Suzanne. *Behind Closed Doors: Violence in the American Family.* New York: Anchor Press, 1980.

Straus, Murray A., and Smith, C. "Violence in Hispanic Families in the United States: Incidence Rates and Structural Interpretations." In M.A. Straus and R.J. Gelles, eds., *Physical Violence in American Families: Risk Factors and Adaptations to Violence in 8,145 Families*, pp. 341–68. New Brunswick, N.J.: Transaction Press, 1990.

Suttles, G.D. *The Social Order of the Slum: Ethnicity and Territory in the Inner City.* Chicago: University of Chicago Press, 1968.

Taylor, Ralph, and Covington, Jeanette. "Neighborhood Changes in Ecology and Violence." *Criminology* 26 (1988): 553–90.

Tittle, Charles R. "Influences on Urbanism: A Test of Predictions from Three Perspectives." *Social Problems* 36 (1989): 270–88.

Tittle, Charles R., and Logan, Charles H. "Sanctions and Deviance: Evidence and Remaining Questions." *Law and Society Review* 7 (1973): 371–92.

Toby, Jackson. "Social Disorganization and Stake in Conformity: Complementary Factors in the Predatory Behavior of Hoodlums." *Journal of Criminal Law, Criminology, and Police Science* 48 (1957): 12–17.

Wacquant, Loic. "The Specificity of Ghetto Poverty: A Comparative Analysis of Race, Class, and Urban Exclusion in Chicago's Black Belt and the Parisian Red Belt." Presented at the Chicago Urban Poverty and Family Life Conference, University of Chicago, October 1991.

Walker, Lenore E. *The Battered Women.* New York: Harper and Row, 1979.

————. "The Battered Woman Syndrome Study." In G. Hotaling, D. Finkelhor, J.T. Kirkpatrick, and M.A. Straus, eds., *Family Abuse and Its Consequences: New Directions for Research*, pp. 139–48. Newbury Park, Calif.: Sage Publications, 1983.

Weis, Joseph G. "Family Violence Research Methodology and Design." In L. Ohlin and M. Tonry, eds., *Family Violence.* Chicago: University of Chicago Press, 1989.

Weisburd, David L.; Sherman, Lawrence W.; and Maher, Lisa. "Contrasting Crime-Specific and Crime-General Theories: The Case of Hot Spots of Crime." Presented at the Annual Meeting of the American Sociological Association, San Francisco, August 1989.

Whyte, William F. *Street Corner Society.* Chicago: University of Chicago Press, 1943.

Widom, Cathy Spatz. "Child Abuse, Neglect and Violent Criminal Behavior." *Criminology* 27 (1989): 251–71.

————. "The Cycle of Violence." *Science* 244 (1989): 160–66.

Williams, Kirk R. "Economic Sources of Homicide: Reestimating the Effects of Poverty and Inequality." *American Sociological Review* 49 (1984): 283–89.

Williams, Kirk R., and Flewelling, Robert L. "The Social Production of Criminal Homicide: A Comparative Study of Disaggregated Rates in American Cities." *American Sociological Review* 53 (1988): 421–31.

Williams, Kirk R., and Hawkins, Richard. "Controlling Male Aggression in Intimate Relationships." *Law and Society Review* 23 (1989): 591–612.

Williams, Kirk R., and Hawkins, Richard. "The Meaning of Arrest for Wife Assault." *Criminology* 27 (1989): 163–81.

Williams, Kirk R., and Hawkins, Richard. "Perceptual Research on General Deterrence: A Critical Review." *Law and Society Review* 20 (1986): 545–72.

Williams, Kirk R., and Hawkins, Richard. "The Social Costs of Wife Assault." *Journal of Research in Crime and Delinquency* 29, no. 3 (1992): 292–310.

Wilson, William J. "Studying Inner-City Social Dislocations: The Challenge of Public Agenda Research." *American Sociological Review* 56 (1991): 1–14.

————. *The Truly Disadvantaged: The Inner City, the Underclass, and Urban Policy.* Chicago: University of Chicago Press, 1987.

Wirth, Louis. *Culture of Cities.* New York: Appleton Century and Crofts, 1969.

Wolfgang, Marvin E. *Patterns in Criminal Homicide.* New York: John Wiley, 1958.

Zimring, Franklin E. "Toward a Jurisprudence of Family Violence." In L. Ohlin and M. Tonry, eds., *Family Violence, Volume 11 of Crime and Justice: An Annual Review of Research.* Chicago: University of Chicago Press, 1989.

Zimring, Franklin E., and Hawkins, Gordon. *Deterrence: The Legal Threat in Crime Control.* Chicago: University of Chicago Press, 1973.

Zimring, Franklin E.; Mukherjee, S.K.; and Van Winkle, B.J. "Intimate Violence: A Study of Intersexual Homicide in Chicago." *University of Chicago Law Review* 50 (1983): 910–30.

Zuravin, Susan J. "The Ecology of Child Abuse and Neglect: Review of the Literature and Presentation of Data." *Violence and Victims* 4 (1989): 101–20.

11

JACKSON TOBY

School Violence and the Breakdown of Community Homogeneity

Newspaper editors used to tell cub reporters that they should crunch a lot of detail into the first sentence or two of a story. What happened? Where? To whom? When? In reviewing newspaper accounts of many stories of school violence in a number of countries, I find that, by and large, the stories fulfill these criteria. They are true in detail. But they are often not illuminating to readers who want to understand what was going on.

The distinction made by the psychologist Max Wertheimer a half century ago among Tt, Ft, Tf, and Ff is apropos.[1] Tt accounts, which are correct as generalizations and correct in detail, are what journalists and social scientists alike hope to achieve. Unfortunately, real-world accounts often depart from this standard. Tf accounts are correct in the large but wrong in detail. The worst departure from the ideal is Ff, false not only in overall impression but in detail. But almost as bad—and less likely to be identified as misleading—are Ft accounts, which are correct in detail but misleading in the large. They employ true stories to convey a false impression.

Les Misérables, the famous novel of crime and punishment, first published in 1862, illustrates the point. Victor Hugo had read in a provincial newspaper the true story of Pierre Maurin, sentenced in 1801 to five years in the galleys for breaking into a bakery, assaulting the baker, and stealing a loaf of bread.[2] After release in 1806, Maurin was befriended by a kindly bishop, became a courageous soldier, and perished in the battle of Waterloo. Hugo could not get the case out of his mind. Years later, when he began writing his novel, he changed the thief's name to Jean Valjean; he made Jean an orphan living with his widowed sister and her seven fatherless children; he made the theft of the loaf of bread a nonviolent offense. Finally, and most important, he explained Jean's motivation by having him lose his job as an agricultural laborer and describing him as unable to look on while his sister and his sister's children starved before his eyes.

Whether the account of Jean Valjean's offense described the real-life case accurately or not, *Les Misérables* could at best be considered an Ft account, not a Tt account. Hugo convinced readers by means of a brilliant case study that thieves typically steal because they are driven by hunger and the desire to feed their families. Hugo probably believed this, but it was an inaccurate portrayal of the motivation of most theft, not only in Hugo's time but today as well.

Newspaper Accounts of School Violence

Like fiction, journalistic accounts suggest typicality. Readers of accounts of school violence in newspapers and magazines cannot be blamed for generalizing. In reading newspaper reports of school violence, not only in American newspapers but in newspapers from Great Britain, France, and other countries, I have been asking myself why these accounts are not meaningful to their readers.

They are, in detail, less untrue than the story of Jean Valjean. But they fail to provide the context necessary for understanding the underlying reality. Let me, by way of illustration, recount some stories about school violence in British and French newspapers. What did the sociologically naive British or French reader make of them?

> A schoolgirl of 13 was recovering yesterday after being savagely attacked by six older girls.
>
> Francesca Shone was punched and kicked and left unconscious in a gutter during a blizzard. It was some time before she was found and taken to hospital with head and internal injuries.
>
> Yesterday police were interviewing other girls from her school, the Alderman Callo comprehensive in Coventry, and tracing witnesses. . . .
>
> Today, school governors will hold an inquiry into Friday's incident, which began with a row during a physical education class when a trampoline was dropped on Francesca's foot.
>
> Some hours later as she was on her way home . . . she was surrounded by six girls aged about 15 and kicked senseless. The attackers ran away and Francesca was eventually found by a district nurse.
>
> Francesca's mother, Mrs. Eileen Shone, said at her home in Newcombe Road, Earlsdon, Coventry: "She was unconscious for nearly three hours. . . . She was punched as well as kicked, but the girls really got at her with their feet when she was on the ground. In these days you can half expect that with boys, but she was so upset when she told me this had been done by other girls in her school."[3]

> A 14-year-old boy stabbed his teacher 22 times in the abdomen after failing to rape her in an empty classroom, a Manchester teachers' leader alleged yesterday.
>
> Mr. Joe Lowerey was speaking outside the National Association of Schoolmaster/Union of Women Teachers conference in Blackpool, where he had earlier told delegates that he had a file a foot thick as a result of a survey of violent assaults on teachers in the city over the past six months.

The stabbing happened last month at the end of the school day when the boy had stayed behind after a music lesson, ostensibly to help the teacher to clear up.

After the attack, he escaped, locking the door behind him, and it was more than an hour before the woman's cries for help in the empty school were heard by the caretaker.[4]

Not only are the *children* in the schools disorderly and violent on occasion, but their relatives come into the schools and add to the disorder. For instance, thirteen-year-old Sammy Xuereb called his teacher, Ashiq Hussain, a "Paki bastard." Mr. Hussain, who had taught in England for seventeen years since leaving Pakistan, reprimanded the boy. Sammy, his fourteen-year-old brother, Charlie, also a student at the South East London Boys School, and his six-foot seventeen-year-old brother, Terry, a nonstudent, later entered Mr. Hussain's classroom. Terry punched the fifty-year-old five-foot six-inch teacher "with a ringed fist, causing injuries that required five stitches." Mr. Hussain's clothes were so blood-stained that they had to be thrown away, and he stayed out of school for three weeks to convalesce. Mr. Hussain was popular among the 700 students at the school, many of whom were from West Indian, Turkish, Cypriot, and other minority backgrounds. Some students offered to "do over" the Maltese boys who had beaten him up.[5]

In a different case, the West Indian mother of seven-year-old Brenda Alcendor eventually received a suspended sentence of three months in jail for bursting into her daughter's class and shoving the teacher, Suzanne Puttock, to the floor, causing her to be badly bruised. Mrs. Alcendor, angry at the teacher because Brenda had been suspended for disrupting lessons, had previous convictions for violent behavior, including seven for assaults upon police. In the initial stages of the case, a magistrate had rebuked the teacher for bringing the case to court at all; the newspapers reported him as saying that bringing such a charge was a waste of public funds. He explained that violence is an occupational hazard for teachers and that Ms. Puttock should expect to be assaulted six or seven times in the course of a teaching career. Questioned about the case on the floor of the House of Commons, the prime minister at the time, Margaret Thatcher, expressed shock and disbelief at the magistrate's comment and launched an investigation. Another magistrate imposed the sentence.[6]

Similar cases of school violence have appeared in the French press. Charles Cabin, principal of a school near Paris with 1,150 pupils, was attacked in his office by the older brother of one of them, angry because his brother had been accused of stealing and selling a bicycle.[7] A teacher in a school in Toulon was hospitalized because his jaw was injured by the father of a student.[8]

In a Strasbourg school, twelve-year-old Jean was kept after school for five minutes by his teacher, Francis Gillman, because he did not complete some schoolwork. His older brother had been waiting for Jean with a friend. When Jean did not appear, the elder brother and his companion burst into the classroom; one of them stabbed the teacher in the arm twice before fleeing. Mr. Gillman and a colleague who tried unsuccessfully to help him ward off the attack went to the police to press charges, but they also applied for a transfer to a safer school because they were afraid of reprisals from the friends or families of the two boys.[9]

French newspaper accounts say that older adolescents extort money and valuables from younger ones by threats of violence. Newspapers write about "the law of the jungle in high school" and "racketeers in short pants." Apparently, threats are usually enough, but weapons are used when necessary. For example, Thierry Heimo, a seventeen-year-old student at a technical high school in Grenoble, was stabbed several times with a scissors for encouraging a fifteen-year-old to resist demands for money.[10] Teachers are also victims of extortion, although more rarely. A teacher in a Paris high school had to walk home in his stockinged feet because he was given the alternatives of being beaten up or surrendering his shoes.[11]

The newspapers report that serious injuries are mainly the result of fights or assaults rather than of robberies, and the two main victimization surveys generally confirm this.[12] In the course of a quarrel in a Paris school, Sinislac Dinic, the twelve-year-old only son of a widowed Yugoslavian charwoman, was stabbed fatally in the stomach by a smaller West Indian classmate.[13]

Crucial pieces of cultural context are missing from these stories. Without that context the stories are interesting, shocking, maybe even entertaining, but they cannot truly convey to the reader—in the sense referred to as Tt—the reason school violence is a problem in some public secondary schools in the urban centers of affluent industrial countries. E.D. Hirsch, Jr., in his book, *Cultural Literacy*, has argued that readers cannot grasp what they are reading if they simply know what the words mean. They must also share knowledge about cultural contexts, or they will miss key points.[14] Thus, "school" is not merely a building containing desks, textbooks, teachers, and computers. For those immersed in the mainstream of American culture—or in compatible ethnic subcultures like the Japanese, "school" means an opportunity to acquire the knowledge and the skills that will make a well-remunerated and interesting career possible. For those living in third world enclaves within Western societies, school means something quite different.

Two trends that gained momentum after the end of World War II have transformed unselective schools of developed societies from the orderly places they once were to places where order is more precarious. This is the essential context for understanding contemporary school violence. One trend is the rising level of compulsory school attendance; the second trend is the increasingly diverse school clientele, especially in urban areas.

Compulsory School Attendance

In Great Britain and France, as in most of the states of the United States, the law requires youngsters to attend school until the age of sixteen. Such laws are justified as providing universally the education children need to function in a modern economy. Recall how this came about: In the nineteenth century, governments opened public schools for youngsters whose parents wished to take advantage of state-sponsored secular education for their children. Later, school attendance became compulsory in the early grades, partly to prevent children from working in factories and mines at an early age, partly out of a widespread conviction that formal education was needed for adequate adult functioning, and partly because industrial societies were rich enough to afford the cost. Gradually, the age for voluntary school leaving was raised. If some education is good, more education is better.

One unintended consequence of rising levels of compulsory education has been to trap unwilling students in school. Why should they be unwilling to take advantage of a free opportunity? In some cases, they cannot take advantage of public schooling because of emotional, physical, or intellectual problems that a mass educational system cannot cope with. In other cases, particular teachers have not done a good job, and children lose their way. In still other cases, personal or family problems may have interposed situational obstacles to learning. Whatever the explanation, however, the fact is that some children grow alienated at school. They leave school in third world countries, even countries where education is nominally compulsory, because public education is expensive, and overcrowded schools have all the *willing* students they can handle.

But industrialized countries refuse to take no for an answer. Truant officers round up youngsters enrolled but not attending school. In some cities with high truancy rates, they are literally plucked off the streets and bused back to school. Juvenile courts hold hearings in which judges threaten youngsters and their parents.[15] Dropout-prevention programs mobilize both carrots and sticks in an effort to get every child to graduate from high school. Some school districts pay potential dropouts to attend school; some states revoke the driver's licenses of students who drop out.[16]

A consequence of all this effort is that some schools—mainly in urban areas—accumulate high concentrations of unwilling students with little or no stake in conformity. There are two unfortunate consequences of this: First, the educational process suffers; it is difficult for teachers to teach effectively and for students to learn what they are supposed to be learning in a tense custodial atmosphere in which the main priority necessarily is managing students who pay little attention when they go to classes, don't do homework, and undermine teacher authority by defiant behavior. Second, teachers and students become targets of assaults, not only from students who regard themselves as prisoners rather than learners but also from intruders from the community where the school is located. Often these intruders are former students or friends or enemies of currently enrolled students.[17]

A Tale of Two Big-City High Schools: One Violent, One Safe

In February 1992, two students at Thomas Jefferson High School in Brooklyn, New York, were fatally shot by an angry classmate; at that same school a student was killed in November 1991 in a fusillade of shots that also critically wounded a teacher. Clearly Thomas Jefferson is one of the most violent high schools of New York City, but even at Jefferson most of the violence is assault or predatory shakedowns of lunch money or gold chains, not murder. The lethal violence probably would not have occurred without the guns and knives that students brought into the school despite security officers who screen for weapons with magnetometers.

Why the weapons? Students blame the violent neighborhood in which the school is located; they say that they are afraid for their own safety without a weapon for self-protection.[18] Indeed, fifty Jefferson students have died in the neighborhood over the past five years, most of them in street violence. In an effort to increase safety at Thomas Jefferson, New York City plans to have more security guards and more metal detectors to search for weapons. Such measures, though marginally useful, do not address the issue of why some students are violence prone. Of course, it takes an aggressive personality to set out to shoot one's schoolmates, but the more basic factor is a cultural climate in which education takes second place to other values. On any given day one-fourth of enrolled students at Thomas Jefferson are absent. Included in this statistic are chronic truants, who may be roaming the streets on more than half of school days. Chronic truants come to school when it is raining or cold, when they want to see a girlfriend, to attack an enemy, to buy or sell drugs, or to play basketball in the gym. They cut most of their classes and wander the halls in pursuit of entertainment like throwing firecrackers or rotten fruit at passing teachers. This behavior intimidates teachers and makes them afraid to attempt to control students more amenable to school discipline.

In short, the indirect cause of student violence at inner-city schools like Thomas Jefferson High School is that a significant minority of enrolled students look and smell like students but are not students at all. They are transplanted street thugs. The cultural climate in Thomas Jefferson makes it more likely for some students to treat the building as a shooting gallery than a temple of learning.

In the aftermath of the recent murders at Jefferson, reporters visited other schools of New York City, trying to find out why, in contrast to Jefferson, most New York high schools are reasonably safe and some are academically superb. A sixteen-year-old student at Forest Hills High School explained why her school is safe: "It's not because of the security guards. It's not because of the neighborhood. It's because of the kids. I think the kids are proud of this school, and they like learning here."

Some of the safe New York City high schools with academically motivated students are selective. Students apply in far greater numbers than can be admitted to such schools as the Bronx High School of Science and Stuyvesant High School. Consequently, applicants from all over New York City take competitive examinations for scarce places at such schools and are jubilant if they are admitted. But other safe high schools are neighborhood schools that will enroll any junior high school graduate in its catchment area.

Seward Park High School, located on the drug-infested Lower East Side of Manhattan, is a neighborhood school, yet it is not dangerous.[19] Why, despite the violence in the surrounding streets, is Seward Park High School an oasis of safety? A former New York Times reporter, Samuel G. Freedman, spent a year observing the school and wrote a best-selling book, Small Victories, showing how a dedicated teacher, Jessica Siegel, gave twelfth-grade journalism students a superb education. Like Thomas Jefferson, Seward Park has a high dropout rate. More than 40 percent of entering freshmen drop out before graduating. As Freedman wrote: "What diminishes violence in Seward Park is . . . an urban version of natural selection in which the most dangerous teenagers on the Lower East Side do not bother going to high school."[20]

Certainly the high dropout rate helps to make Seward Park High School safe, but it cannot be the whole explanation.[21] The dropout rate is higher at Thomas Jefferson. The more important factor is that the students who remain to graduate from Seward Park share high educational aspirations similar to those of the children of Jewish immigrants who attended Seward Park a half century ago. Seward Park is lucky to be located within walking distance of Chinatown, and its Chinese students are usually very diligent. They may not be the most academically able children in the area—those tend to prefer selective schools like Stuyvesant or Brooklyn Tech—and their English may be poor, but their attitude toward education makes them a pleasure to teach. That is part of the reason why the turnover rate for teachers at Seward Park is so low and why 90 percent of Seward Park graduates go on to colleges and universities.

Increasingly Diverse School Clienteles

Exacerbating the school violence problem is the increasing heterogeneity of all modern societies, as migration, legal and illegal, undermines the cultural homogeneity that once provided social glue. In many of the large cities of Great Britain, France, Germany, and Spain, foreign-born workers and their children live in subcultural enclaves. With parents from Pakistan, Turkey, Greece, Yugoslavia, Cyprus, Morocco, Algeria, Tunisia, and the West Indies, children may not hear fluent English, French, German, or Spanish in their homes. But the reasons they do not do well in school go deeper than unfamiliarity with the language of the country: their family and peer cultures do not necessarily place a high value on education and on the teachers who transmit it. Many of their foreign-born parents are not immigrants; they are sojourners attracted by employment opportunities, who intend to return to their country of origin.

The United States also faces the difficulty of absorbing large numbers of people from diverse cultures. More than half a million legal immigrants come to the United States each year, as well as several hundred thousand illegal immigrants.[22] This is a smaller proportion of the American population than was absorbed between 1890 and 1914, but the new immigrants are harder to acculturate. Recent immigrants come from Latin America, Asia, and Africa as well as from Europe. In contrast, the migration from 1890 to 1914 was predominantly European. For these older cohorts of immigrants, it was easier to find compatriots who had migrated earlier and who were already attached to American institutions.

Equally important, the migrants of a century ago *had* to adjust to American society. Since welfare services were rudimentary—often private voluntary organizations rather than government bureaucracies—survival depended on adults and sometimes children finding work. Frank Lloyd Wright described his philosophy of teaching his children to swim; he threw them off the dock into a lake. American society of a century ago had a similar approach to absorbing immigrants: cruel to those who had difficulty making it on their own but apparently fairly effective in terms of outcomes.[23] In the contemporary United States, multicultural curricula, bilingual education, and generous welfare programs cushion the adjustment, but an unintended consequence of these cushions is that immigrants and their children are not under relentless pressure to learn English and to get a job quickly.

Much has been written about the excellence of Japanese secondary education. What is not always mentioned is that Japan is remarkably homogeneous culturally, a unique situation for a developed society. This cultural homogeneity means that Japanese schoolchildren face consistent expectations for high levels of effort at school, not only from teachers but from parents and peers as well.[24] By contrast, the United States is a cultural mosaic. Children hear the cultural message that education is important, but they receive other cultural messages as well, including the desirability of having lots of fun.

In the short run, study is not fun. It is tempting to cut class and go out with one's friends rather than face the drudgery of studying boring schoolbooks. Students will be more likely to choose present drudgery over present fun, however, if, like Japanese students, they share a value of the importance of performing well in school.[25] What parents seek intuitively when they look for a good school for their children is a school good in the sense that its microculture encourages sustained effort.

Policy Implications

When journalists write about school violence, even intelligent and well-informed journalists rarely say anything about compulsory education laws. And when mention is made of the ethnic group from which the perpetrator comes, it is treated as almost irrelevant. Yet, if I am correct in my interpretation of school violence in contemporary societies, most of it arises because we compel all children—for their own good—to get exposed to as much formal education as possible; yet such a universal rule does not receive equally enthusiastic support from all of the subgroups of ethnically heterogeneous societies (e.g., North African Arab immigrants in Paris and other French cities and Turks in German cities). And ethnic heterogeneity seems to be increasing in the modern world in response to economic and social forces that drive large numbers of people across national boundaries. School violence is the predictable result of creating in public schools a group of students with little stake in self-control.

While the high level of school violence in some urban schools can be understood partly in terms of family disorganization and individual pathology, violence is also a result of diverse ethnic communities that do not share common values about schools, studying, teachers, lifestyles, and occupational objectives.[26] As Nathan Glazer put it, contrasting the success of New York City schools two generations ago with the violence and academic failure of many contemporary urban schools, "Mothers were for the most part at home to prepare lunch, fathers were present and worked or sought work, families were for the most part intact, education for the most part was seen as the way to improvement, teachers and principals were respected."[27]

All schools—including inner-city schools like Thomas Jefferson—can be safe. To accomplish this requires not more security guards or more metal detectors but studious students. It requires setting high educational goals for enrolled students. They must do homework every day, attend regularly, restrain horseplay so that they and their classmates can concentrate on the lesson. Those youngsters who, for whatever reason, cannot or will not subordinate the impulses of the moment to the long-term goal of academic achievement should withdraw until they are ready to be studious. Once enrolled youngsters share the academic values of their teachers, teachers become empowered. When students care about the outcome of the educational process, they necessarily are sensitive to the positive and negative reactions of their teachers. In addition, the authority of teachers can be buttressed by administrative policies, such as giving more weight to teacher input in disciplinary procedures as opposed to vesting discipline entirely in specialized roles such as assistant principals and guidance counselors.

This strategy for reducing school violence assumes that the obligation of society is to guarantee educational opportunity by protecting the integrity of the educational process in all public schools. And what are the implications of this policy for those youngsters now interfering with the education of their classmates and making some schools dangerous? Some will shape up academically rather than allow themselves to be excluded from the social center of adolescent lives, the school. Most of their parents will push for this choice rather than the choice of drifting onto the streets and toward a bleak adult future. But some youngsters—how many we do not know—are not self-disciplined enough to become real students. They will continue to threaten the safety of the school, no longer as students but as intruders. The main function of security guards will be to keep them out.

Society does not want to deny them educational opportunities; and the door should be open for their return—as soon as they are ready to take education seriously. But public schools cannot put the welfare of phantom students ahead of the welfare of real students. Schools are not recreation centers or rehabilitation centers for delinquents. Truth requires that someone deliver this message if American educational policy is to be realistic and effective. If the calling of sociology is the enlightenment of opinion, as Edward Shils has assured us,[28] a sociologist may have to assume this burden.

Notes

1. Max Wertheimer, "On Truth."
2. Victor Hugo, *Les Misérables*, pp. 10–11.
3. *Guardian*, January 11, 1982.
4. *Guardian*, April 16, 1982.
5. *Guardian*, June 25, 1982.
6. *Guardian*, January 21, March 17, April 2, 1982.
7. *Le Figaro*, June 2, 1978.
8. *Le Figaro*, June 15, 1979.
9. *Le Figaro*, October 9, 1979.
10. *Le Figaro*, March 10, 1980.
11. *Le Figaro*, December 3, 1980.
12. U.S. Department of Health, Education, and Welfare, *Violent Schools—Safe Schools: The Safe Schools Report to the Congress.* Lisa Bastian and Bruce M. Taylor, *School Crime: A National Crime Victimization Survey Report.*
13. *Le Figaro*, October 21, 1979.
14. E.D. Hirsch, Jr., *Cultural Literacy: What Every American Needs to Know.*
15. Gilbert Geis and Arnold Binder, "Sins of Their Children: Parental Responsibility for Juvenile Delinquency."
16. Jackson Toby and David Armor, "Carrots or Sticks for High School Dropouts?"
17. Jackson Toby, "Violence in School" and "Crime in the Schools."
18. Jackson Toby, "To Get Rid of Guns in Schools, Get Rid of Some Students."
19. Jackson Toby, review of *Small Victories.*
20. Samuel G. Freedman, *Small Victories: The Real World of a Teacher, Her Students, and Their High School*, p. 339.
21. Jackson Toby, "Of Dropouts and Stayins: The Gershwin Approach" and "Coercion or Choice."
22. U.S. Bureau of the Census, *Statistical Abstract of the United States: 1991*, p. 9.
23. U.S. Congress, Senate Committee on Immigration, *Abstract of Reports of the Immigration Commission.*
24. U.S. Department of Education, *Japanese Education Today*; Thomas P. Rohlen, *Japan's High Schools.*
25. Rohlen, *Japan's High Schools.*
26. Leonard Covello, *The Social Background of the Italo-American School Child.*
27. Nathan Glazer, "The Real World of Urban Education," pp. 74–75.

28. Edward Shils, *The Calling of Sociology and Other Essays on the Pursuit of Learning*, pp. 3–92.

References

Bastian, Lisa, and Taylor, Bruce M. *School Crime: A National Crime Victimization Survey Report*. Washington, D.C.: Bureau of Justice Statistics, 1991.

Covello, Leonard. *The Social Background of the Italo-American School Child*. Leiden, The Netherlands: E.J. Brill, 1967.

Le Figaro. June 2, 15, 1978; March 10, October 9, 21, 1979; December 3, 1980.

Freedman, Samuel G. *Small Victories: The Real World of a Teacher, Her Students, and Their High School*. New York: Harper & Row, 1990.

Geis, Gilbert, and Binder, Arnold. "Sins of Their Children: Parental Responsibility for Juvenile Delinquency." *Notre Dame Journal of Law, Ethics, and Public Policy* 5, no. 2 (1991): 303–22.

Glazer, Nathan. "The Real World of Urban Education." *The Public Interest* (Winter 1992): 57–75.

The Guardian. January 11, 21, March 17, April 2, 16, June 25, 1982.

Hirsch, E.D., Jr. *Cultural Literacy: What Every American Needs to Know*. Boston: Houghton-Mifflin, 1987.

Hugo, Victor. *Les Misérables* (1862), ed. Maurice Allem. Paris: Librairie Gallimard, 1951.

Rohlen, Thomas P. *Japan's High Schools*. Berkeley: University of California Press, 1983.

Shils, Edward. *The Calling of Sociology and Other Essays on the Pursuit of Learning*. Chicago: University of Chicago Press, 1980.

Toby, Jackson. "Coercion or Choice?" *The Public Interest*, no. 96 (Summer 1989): 134–36.

———. "Crime in the Schools." In James Q. Wilson, ed., *Crime and Public Policy*, pp. 69–88. San Francisco: Institute for Contemporary Studies, 1983.

———. "Of Dropouts and Stayins: The Gershwin Approach." *The Public Interest*, no. 95 (Spring 1989): 3–13.

———. Review of *Small Victories*. *Commentary* 90 (August 1990): 61–62.

———. "To Get Rid of Guns in Schools, Get Rid of Some Students." *The Wall Street Journal*, March 3, 1992.

———. "Violence in School." In Michael Tonry and Norval Morris, eds., *Crime and Justice: An Annual Review of Research, Vol. IV*, pp. 1–47. Chicago: University of Chicago Press, 1983.

Toby, Jackson, and Armor, David. "Carrots or Sticks for High School Dropouts?" *The Public Interest* (Winter 1992): 76–90.

U.S. Bureau of the Census. *Statistical Abstract of the United States: 1991*. Washington, D.C.: Government Printing Office, 1991.

U.S. Department of Education. *Japanese Education Today*. Washington, D.C.: Government Printing Office, 1987.

U.S. Department of Health, Education, and Welfare. *Violent Schools—Safe Schools: The Safe Schools Report to the Congress*. Washington, D.C.: U.S. Government Printing Office, 1978.

U.S. Congress. Senate Committee on Immigration. *Abstract of Reports of the Immigration Commission*, vol. 1. Washington, D.C.: U.S. Government Printing Office, 1911.

Wertheimer, Max. "On Truth." *Social Research* 1 (May 1934): 135–46.

Part IV
The Criminal Justice System

12

JAMES J. FYFE

"Good" Policing

According to Peter K. Manning, the social mandate of the American police is a hodgepodge of conflicting duties and responsibilities that has developed with little input from the police themselves.[1] He is correct. Firefighting, the uniformed public service frequently compared to policing, has a clear mandate that firefighters have helped to fashion: the fire service exists to prevent fires and to extinguish as quickly and as safely as possible all those it did not prevent. It is virtually impossible to derive a similarly succinct and comprehensive statement of the police role. Instead, it is safe to say only that police perform a variety of services that must be available seven days a week, twenty-four hours a day, that may require the use or threat of force, and that are not readily available from any other public agency or private institution.[2]

Doing What Nobody Else Does

Police responsibility for these tasks not handled by others has meant that the police sometimes are called upon to do the impossible or to attempt to provide services they have not been adequately prepared to perform. The historic reluctance of police to intervene in domestic disputes,[3] for example, probably has more to do with the difficulty of straightening out other people's arguments in the middle of the night than with the purported danger to police of such assignments. A line of research has recently demonstrated that *domestics* are not nearly the police job hazard they were assumed to be.[4] The difficulty of resolving such arguments while they are at flashpoint, however, has long been clear and is a task that might better be handled by social workers provided with protective police escorts. Social workers understandably have not volunteered to play such a role. Consequently, the police have been stuck with it on grounds that they are available and that their duties include order maintenance.

In the past, the ready, round-the-clock availability of the police has caused them to be assigned to many duties that fit under this *order maintenance* rubric only by the most liberal definition. In the late nineteenth century, Philadelphia police provided lodging for more than 100,000 people every year. Early in the twentieth century, New York police stations were the distribution points for food and coal doled out to the poor under "home relief" programs.[5]

In addition, the close ties of the police to the powerful have, in many places, made police departments a major vehicle of job patronage. A major factor in historic analyses of policing is the great extent to which attainment of formally stated police goals has continually been affected by use of police departments as a means of politically dispensed upward mobility for newly arrived ethnic groups and recently empowered racial minorities.[6]

The closeness of the police to communities and to politicians has also led to corruption, especially in inner cities, where police have been charged with enforcing laws that had been enacted by conservative rural-dominated legislatures, but that found little support in the hurly-burly of urban life. In such places, it became the job of locally controlled police to protect illegal businesses—most notably, gambling and prostitution—from disruptions caused by other law enforcement agencies and unruly clients who might scare off paying customers.[7]

This trend reached a peak during Prohibition, when official corruption became the standard operating procedure of many American police departments.[8] By the time Prohibition ended, however, the United States was deep in the Great Depression, and a constricted job market made policing an attractive career option to well-educated people who in better times would have gone into more traditional white-collar and professional work. In many cases, this new breed was repulsed by old-school corruption and sought to turn policing into a respectable undertaking.

Police As Crime Fighters

Two icons of these new professionals were J. Edgar Hoover, whose FBI waged a bloody and successful war against the gangsters of the early 1930s, and August Vollmer, who had earlier made the Berkeley Police Department an exemplar of efficiency and technological excellence.[9] These two role models led many local police to attempt to do away with the ambiguity of their mandate by redefining themselves first and foremost as professional crime fighters. These new professionals among police believed that, like FBI agents, local police would win their war by adopting the selective personnel standards and high technology employed with such apparent success by both Hoover and Vollmer. Unfortunately, the police were to find over the long run that the experiences of Hoover and Vollmer were not readily generalizable to other times and places.

J. Edgar Hoover

Hoover's depression-era successes came not in a broad-fronted war but in a series of skirmishes against a small number of spectacular outlaws. When local police attempted to apply this same model of the resolute and professional lawman on the track of bad guys, however, they eventually became stymied. Police used this strategy over three decades and took great credit for the comparative domestic tranquility that then prevailed. Then, in the 1960s, American crime exploded. Since that watershed decade, the police have learned that the techniques that had been so useful to the FBI in its war against a few colorful characters meant little when a huge baby-boomer generation entered its crimeprone adolescent years, or in inner-city crime factories that systematically turn out criminals in overwhelming numbers. Hoover could declare victory when his agents had rounded up or killed the likes of John Dillinger, "Pretty Boy" Floyd, "Babyface" Nelson, and other legendary bandits of the era. But no such easy victory is possible over the rampant and ubiquitous street crime that has consumed many inner cities.

August Vollmer

In the same way that police were misled by Hoover's victories, their attempts to emulate Vollmer's example generally have been based on an inexact analogy. Without question, Vollmer turned the Berkeley Police Department into the early twentieth-century American ideal. The Berkeley department was extremely selective, allowing only the very best young men to wear its uniforms. Under Vollmer, the department's apparent success in stifling crime, combined with its great responsiveness to the needs of the *good people* of the community, won it universal admiration at home.[10] But history suggests that, like the "service"-style police departments studied by James Q. Wilson during the 1960s[11]—the Nassau County (New York) Police Department, for example—the Berkeley Police Department enjoyed such apparent success and exalted status largely because it was serving an ideal community that didn't need much from it.

When Vollmer was the police chief of Berkeley, the city was a fast-growing, prosperous, homogeneous, and well-educated home to wealthy families who had been scared out of San Francisco by the crime, disorder, bawdiness, earthquake, and fire for which that bigger city on the bay was best known at the time. Berkeley also was home to the first campus of the University of California, an industry of the type that did not draw employees or clients likely to cause the police much trouble. Indeed, if early twentieth-century Berkeley undergraduates sought to raise hell, it was easy enough for them to ferry across the bay to the more exciting Sodom of San Francisco or to simply walk across the city line to the Gomorrah of Jack London's Oakland waterfront.

Wilson studied Nassau County, the Long Island suburb adjacent to New York City, when policing there was the same sort of cakewalk that Vollmer's staff had enjoyed a half century earlier in Berkeley. Until World War II, Nassau County consisted largely of farms, a few small towns, and estates like those occupied by Fitzgerald's Jay Gatsby and friends. During the War, Long Island's expansion began with the growth of its defense industries and aircraft manufacturers. In the years immediately after the war, Nassau County became a booming suburb that, except for its larger population, was much like those that sprouted around Los Angeles at the same time. Generous GI financing, a new highway system, and quick construction methods combined with the desire for the good life—a patch of green away from mean city streets—overnight turned potato fields into tract housing. By the time Wilson observed its police department, the population of Nassau County had nearly doubled during the 1950s—to 1.3 million by 1960— and the county boasted a tax base larger than all but a small handful of U.S. cities. The nonwhite population in areas served by the county police (as opposed to the generally more exclusive towns policed by a few small independent departments) was 2.5 percent, and was located largely in a few small and long-established enclaves that had started as the homes for domestic help to the wealthy.[12] The county's homicide rate was less than one-sixth the national average, and, despite the fact that its ratio of cars to population was far higher than the national norm, Nassau's vehicle theft rate was only one-third the national average.[13]

Like Vollmer's Berkeley Police Department, Nassau selected its officers carefully, paid and equipped them well, and asked them to give friendly service to a homogeneous populace who sought to share peace, quiet, and stability with their neighbors. Wilson's Nassau differed from Vollmer's Berkeley chiefly in size and by virtue of the high percentage of its population that wore blue collars at work. Both places enjoyed freedom from poverty, inequity, class and ethnic conflict, and social discord of any other type. Both had ideal police departments because both were populated by people of means who had chosen to move there from elsewhere in order to be part of an idyllic community.

In the years since Vollmer's tenure and Wilson's studies, both Berkeley and Nassau have changed. Neither has remained homogeneous, uniformly prosperous, or untroubled by decay, conflict, social discord, homelessness, unemployment. Regardless of the quality and competence of its chief executives or what they may have accomplished since Vollmer's halcyon days, nobody in policing regards the Berkeley Police Department as *the* local American law enforcement agency that stands in a class by itself, *the* role model for professional policing. Nobody studies policing in Berkeley,[14] and nobody in policing knows much about what may be going on there. Nor has any scholar recently studied police in Nassau County. There, while the number of residents has declined slightly over the last three decades, the population has grown much more heterogeneous. The percentage of nonwhite residents has increased fivefold to 13.3 percent, and Hispanics—virtually unknown in the county at the time of Wilson's work—comprise another 3.3 percent.[15] In addition, crime rates have increased, and closings of defense and aircraft manufacturers have severely hurt the economy; even the most casual observer would not expect a replication of Wilson's work to come up with the same rosy picture he found a quarter century ago.[16]

Lessons Learned?

The two lessons of these experiences have not been easily digested by either the police or the public. The first of these lessons is that *neither the low crime rates during the golden years of J. Edgar Hoover and August Vollmer nor the great increases since then have had much to do with the police or law enforcement.* Despite Vollmer's good efforts, Berkeley boasted low crime rates during his years because it was a fast-growing, prosperous, homogeneous, and highly educated town in which the major employer was the state's flagship university. Around the country during the depression years of Hoover's climb to fame, most people were concerned with putting bread on the table and were too beaten down to be aggressive. Thus, minor property crime was common, but—except for a rash of well-publicized kidnappings and one-man crime waves of the type he vigorously stifled—violent crime generally was not much of a concern.

With the exception of a few defense-industry boomtowns, the home front remained quiet during World War II, because most young men of crime-prone age were either in the military or busy working overtime to supply or fill in for the boys overseas. Crime remained low throughout the 1950s, probably because the generation then at peak crime age (roughly sixteen to twenty-four) was small in number: it had been born in the depression, when birth rates had dropped.

The 1960s changed all that. Urban crime rates soared virtually everywhere regardless of whether police conformed to the ideal of professional-warrior-against-crime. The increase in crime was attributable to several converging forces, but two probably are most important. The huge baby-boom generation entered adolescence, so that an unusually large percentage of the population was in its most crime-prone years. In addition, cities changed. For years, blacks and Hispanics had steadily been replacing white city dwellers who had fled to suburbs like Nassau County, taking businesses, jobs, and the cohesiveness of their former neighborhoods with them. This pattern came to a head in the 1960s: old communities broke up to be replaced by impersonal and densely populated projects. Racial, cultural, and class conflicts arose. Urban tax bases eroded, municipal services declined, and all the ills of the inner city flourished as they had not since the great waves of European immigration a half century earlier. Since the 1960s, the death of Jim Crow, the increased mobility of the black middle class, and cutbacks in social programs have aggravated these conditions. With few strong community institutions or positive role models for young people, inner cities have grown even more desolate and hopeless.

Thus, it is unrealistic to model the police on Hoover's FBI or even to think of the police as our first line of defense against crime. In large measure, the presence or absence of crime has nothing to do with the police. Indeed, even though many people continue to think of *police* and *law enforcement* almost interchangeably, the boom in scholarly studies of policing that began in the 1960s has shown with some consistency that only a small proportion of street police officers' time—in the neighborhood of a quarter—involves law enforcement or investigation of crime. Eric Scott, for example, studied more than 26,000 calls for police service in three urban areas; 2 percent of these involved reports of violent crime, 17 percent involved reports of nonviolent crime, and 5 percent concerned people or circumstances that had aroused citizens' suspicions. The remaining 76 percent concerned interpersonal conflict (7 percent), requests for medical assistance (3 percent), traffic problems (9 percent), dependent persons in need of police care (3 percent), noise and other public nuisances (11 percent), calls for miscellaneous assistance (12 percent), requests for information (21 percent), provision of noncrime-related information (8 percent), and various police internal matters (2 percent).[17] In short, although the clientele of the FBI consists almost exclusively of criminal suspects and victims and witnesses to crime, most of the people with whom the police interact need help with problems not related to crime.

The second lesson is that *policing can probably be regarded as ideal only in places that are themselves idyllic and untroubled.* This is a message with important implications for police reformers, many of whom currently urge adoption of new *community-oriented* and *community-based* policing models. According to Trojanowicz and Bucqueroux:

> Community Policing is a new philosophy of policing, based on the concept that police officers and private citizens working together in creative ways can help solve contemporary problems related to crime, fear of crime, social and physical disorder, and neighborhood decay. The philosophy is predicated in the belief that achieving these goals requires that police departments develop a new relationship with the law-abiding people in the community, allowing them a greater voice in setting local police priorities and involving them in efforts to improve the overall quality of life in their neighborhoods. It shifts the focus of police work from handling random calls to solving community problems.[18]

Trojanowicz and Bucqueroux go on to say that this new model requires the designation of some patrol officers as "Community Policing Officers." Each of these CPOs should be assigned on a continuing basis to the same small geographic area. There, from their patrol cars and with substantially less responsibility for responding to radio calls, CPOs can develop collaborative relationships with community members. These relationships, in turn, will allow "people direct input in setting day-to-day, local police priorities, in exchange for their cooperation and participation in efforts to police themselves."[19]

While there certainly is room for greater and more imaginative police interaction with the communities they serve, it often is difficult to distinguish these new community-oriented models from Wilson's *service* style of policing and from such police arrangements as the democratic team-policing alternative of John E. Angell and neighborhood team policing.[20] Indeed, I can find virtually nothing in descriptions of recent community policing models that differs from my own experience in two New York City police precincts that included Neighborhood Police Teams more than two decades ago.

But these prior attempts to rearrange police departments and their relationships with communities have either been discarded or, as in the case of Wilson's service style, apparently have been feasible only so long as there exists a monolithic community to which the police can become oriented.[21] Unfortunately, in the areas most in need of high quality police services—however such quality is defined—the *community* and its needs are neither readily identifiable nor monolithic.[22] Instead, as Wilson suggested, such neighborhoods are marked by great social, racial, and political cleavages and by divergent views about law enforcement and order-maintenance policies and practices.[23] As long as this is so, virtually every police policy or action will offend some interests in the community, and near unanimous approval of the police, as in Vollmer's Berkeley or 1960s Nassau County, will remain unattainable. Further, as long as communities define the police role in the expectation that police will merely respond unquestioningly to their wishes, the police mandate will continue to be amorphous and unclear.

Consequences of Unclear Direction

Priority Setting

The consequences of vague definition of the police role and minimal police participation in specifying it are widespread. Police have not been given much direction for setting priorities among the melange of duties and responsibilities they have been assigned. The police are expected both to maintain order and to enforce the law, but in important instances these two obligations may conflict. Uniformed officers assigned in response to citizens' complaints that specific streets have become open-air drug markets, for example, usually are instructed by their superiors to enforce the law aggressively. But officers who follow such instructions by arresting the first minor offender they see may find themselves off the street and caught up in the booking and court processes for hours. While these officers are gone, their beats remain open territory, dealers do uninterrupted land-office business, and law-abiding citizens wonder what happened to the cops they had asked for. The final frustration in such cases usually comes when arrestees are slapped on the wrist by the courts, treated like public nuisances rather than the purveyors of poison that officers and residents see.

A better alternative might be to direct officers to avoid making arrests except in major cases and, instead, attempt to drive dealers off the street by maintaining as high a degree of presence as possible. If this were done, police officers might rid their beats of drug trafficking and restore order to lawless streets, just as they routinely have done in neighborhoods marred by street prostitution and other annoying public order offenses. Importantly, however, such a strategy would generate little of the enforcement "activity" so often used to justify police budget requests.[24]

Trying to Quantify Quality

Quantitative measures of police activity—numbers of tickets, arrests, calls for service, minutes and seconds required to respond to calls—often mislead. They say nothing about the vigor or quality of police service or, as in this street drug-dealing example, about whether the numbers presented have had any substantial effect on the problem the police were marshaled to address.[25] But, regardless of their limited usefulness as a measure of police effectiveness—or their questionable accuracy—numbers are part and parcel of American policing. From the annual figures of the FBI's Uniform Crime Reports through the flashy charts and bar graphs that characterize police departmental annual reports to the monthly activity reports of patrol officers and traffic cops, policing revolves around numbers.

Herman Goldstein called this tendency to measure police performance in quantitative terms a "means-ends syndrome." It exists, he suggests, because of the ease of toting up the frequency and rapidity with which police use the tools available to them—arrests, tickets, response time—and the difficulty of sitting down and resolving Manning's dilemma by clearly defining police goals, measures of the extent to which they have been achieved, and some notion of whether the police actions involved in achieving them may have created or aggravated other problems.[26] From a desk in police headquarters, it is very easy and often very convincing to report to a concerned city councilperson that the police response to complaints about drug dealing on 25th Street has resulted in *n* arrests. It is not so easy to go out and measure the level of apparent drug activity on 25th Street, or to determine whether police presence has displaced it to 24th Street. Even when such measures are attempted, the absence of impressive arrest numbers often makes them less than convincing.

Prevention and Apprehension

This situation is a conundrum and a contradiction of the principles enunciated by Sir Robert Peel when he established the first modern urban police in Dublin and in London in 1829.[27] Before Peel's "Bobbies," police forces existed in continental Europe, but these generally focused their activities on political criminals and on after-the-fact investigations of crime; the notoriously persistent Javert of Hugo's *Les Misérables* is a case in point. But Peel, inspired by the Enlightenment view of man as a rational and ultimately redeemable creature, designed the London Metropolitan Police to be *preventive* rather than punitive. The widespread presence on the streets of police in distinctive but purposely nonmilitary uniforms, Peel reasoned, would convince potential criminals that successful crime was impossible. Accordingly, Peel also reasoned, the best measure of police success in crime-fighting would be the *absence* of crime, disorder, and related police business, rather than the measures of law enforcement activity currently in vogue in the United States.

Certainly, police today also are expected to prevent crime. A considerable amount of research, however, suggests that their ability to do so, especially in sprawling, multicultural American cities, is more limited than Peel, Hoover, or Vollmer believed.[28] Further, the incentive to develop more sophisticated prevention strategies is diminished by news and entertainment media that grant police their greatest glory for arresting those whom they have failed to deter in the first place. Cops 'n' robbers make for spectacular headlines and sensational docudrama, but the work of police crime-prevention officers has never been the focus of any movie or TV series. This emphasis and glorification of apprehension over prevention spills down to the lowest level of policing, where the greenest beat cops learn early in their careers that "important arrests" are enthusiastically counted and rewarded, while nobody knows—or seems to care—how many crimes did not occur because of officers' vigilance.

On occasion, the consequences of this apprehension-oriented incentive system are bizarre and certainly not what Peel intended. In some departments, instead of cruising by bars at closing time to make sure that drunks do not attempt to drive home, officers hide in darkened cars a block or two away to catch them after they have gotten into their cars and driven off. In using this technique to gain credit for arrests, officers allow drunks to commit the very same life-endangering acts one might expect the police to prevent. In Los Angeles, an elite squad has for years refrained from intervening while, as its officers anticipated, armed burglars and robbers have victimized unsuspecting citizens. Instead of preventing these victimizations, officers have stood by and watched in order to confront their quarry—often with bloody results—after all doubt about their intentions has been removed. "Public safety is certainly a concern," the unit's commander told the Los Angeles *Times*, "but we have to look beyond that, because if we arrest someone for attempt, the likelihood of a conviction is not as great."[29]

Accusations of Discrimination

At the same time that police are charged to enforce the law firmly and fairly, they also are expected to be judicious and selective in their enforcement efforts. Unfortunately, the police have received little guidance in establishment of criteria to distinguish between unfair discrimination and discretion that serves some legitimate social end. Consequently, "selective enforcement" often is little more than individual officers' ad hoc decisions about which driver should receive a ticket and which should not; which loud-mouthed kid should be arrested, which taken home to his parents.

Regardless of how judicious a police department may be, the absence of meaningful decision-making standards dictates that any agency that polices a pluralistic constituency will be the subject of regular criticism and dissatisfaction on the part of one or more subpopulations. Further, the absence of such standards means that the best-intended police officers in a department will be left confused and vulnerable to accusations of arbitrariness. Motorists know that cops do not issue tickets for all the traffic violations they witness. Consequently, every experienced cop has heard bitter motorists allege that the tickets they have just been handed were motivated by questions of race or class rather than by the need to enforce laws against traffic violations that so many others commit without punishment.[30]

Further, in a society in which race and class are as closely related as ours, it often is hard to draw a line between discretion and discrimination. The fundamental precept of the juvenile justice system—to *help and reform*, rather than to *punish*—generally dictates that police interventions into kids' minor delinquencies should be no more intrusive and formal than whatever may be necessary to accomplish two goals. First, the action selected—ranging anywhere from warning through arrest and booking—should give officers some sense that the youngsters involved have learned the errors of their ways. Second, officers should be assured that, after they leave the scene, responsible parties will carefully supervise the miscreants and keep them on the straight and narrow. But when cops act on these precepts, their dispositions of juveniles who have been involved in minor delinquencies result in numbers heavily skewed by class and, therefore, by race. Middle-class kids are skilled at ingratiating themselves to people who can affect their futures. When the police bring such kids home or to police stations after they have done wrong, the police meet concerned, stable families from nice neighborhoods. Most important, the police get convincing assurances from moms and dads that it will be a long time before Junior—who is by now teary-eyed and apologetic—has another opportunity to misbehave. Consequently, the police typically take no formal action, but leave such kids to the care of their parents.

Street kids learn early to challenge authority. In the ghetto, where life often includes no thoughts of the future beyond tomorrow, the middle-class skill of ingratiating oneself with people who can affect one's future is meaningless and denigrated. Often, ghetto kids come from home environments in which no meaningful control is exercised over their conduct. In such circumstances, cops are likely to conclude that helping kids to find the straight and narrow can be accomplished only by invoking the formal juvenile justice system. This, of course, has two effects. First, it punishes these youngsters by attaching formal delinquent labels to them. Second, it generates statistics that can be used to put police on the defensive by those who claim that cops' decisions routinely are racist. In fact, the statistics may hide well-intended decisions to arrest or release juveniles that, like police and judicial decisions related to adults' bail and pre-trial release, appropriately are driven by variables independent of the instant offense. Judges' bail decisions and police releases on adult suspects' own recognizance are based on assessments of the probability that defendants will be back in court on schedule. Cops' decisions about what to do with young violators often are based on officers' assessments of the probability that police will have no further contact with the youngsters involved. Thus, the goals of these decisions—to achieve the hope of seeing subjects again in the first case; to achieve the hope of never seeing them again in the second—are different, but the criteria used in making the decisions should be similar. Unlike police and court discretion related to adult criminal defendants,[31] however, police decisions concerning juvenile offenders generally are unbounded by rules or guidelines and, therefore, remain subject to criticism.

Defining Good Policing

The discussion to this point suggests the overarching dilemma caused by the absence of a clear police mandate: beyond some prescriptions for specific field situations in which closure is rapid and clearly identifiable, we have yet to derive a widely accepted definition of police effectiveness. Within policing, the absence of such a definition reverberates at every level.

The requirements for entry into an occupation, for example, should be those that best predict satisfactory job performance. But the absence of clearly articulated standards for assessing police effectiveness means that police entry requirements can be no more than guesses about which candidates are likely to be abusive, to beget scandals, or, through physical disability or acts that create legal liability, to impose great financial losses on those to whom they have applied for employment. Some police candidates are screened out on the basis of bizarre personal histories or criminal records. Others, however, survive this screening and demonstrate their lack of suitability for policing only after they have been locked into it by civil service tenure. Equally important, the imprecision inherent in searches to fill jobs that are not clearly defined undoubtedly results in the loss of fine candidates whose membership in policing would increase its representativeness of the population.

The Absence of the Satisfaction of a Job Well Done

Those who make it through the screening find that police work carries many rewards. Although no honest police officer ever becomes rich from policing, policing in most parts of the United States pays a decent wage, which, despite the last couple of decades' police layoffs in financially strapped cities, also is very dependable. In the busiest jurisdictions, the police workday goes very quickly and, in the words of a recruiting poster in use when I began my police career, often includes "a view of life your deskbound friends will never see."

Certainly, this view is not always pleasant or fulfilling: the things police see cause some to become chronically distrustful and hardened, ultimately leading to problems in their private lives. Other officers, however, draw from their work a greater appreciation of their own comparative good fortune. However trying, regular exposure to violence, exploitation, greed, madness, cruelty, poverty, hopelessness, addiction, and the rest of humankind's most serious ills puts into perspective and makes less insurmountable the annoyances of middle-class life.

Specific police actions—cracking a big case, pulling a driver from a burning car, talking an emotionally disturbed person out of a suicide attempt—also provide a great deal of satisfaction and official praise for police officers. But, absent the opportunity to engage in such heroics, cops may try their hardest without ever knowing whether they are doing well or whether their work has made a difference, and without ever receiving formal acknowledgment of their efforts.

This issue involves much more than the salving of cops' tender egos. A quarter century ago, Arthur Neiderhoffer reported that New York City police patrol officers, the street cops who performed the most familiar but most ill-defined and least prestigious work in their department, had higher levels of cynicism than any other officers he studied. Over time, Neiderhoffer suggested, the intractability of patrol officers' work and their inability to get out of it and into more glamorous assignments may lead to a sense of frustration and victimization.[32] These, in turn, may alienate officers—and, indeed, whole police departments—from the community, causing the dysfunctional *us and them* relationship between police and citizens found in many jurisdictions and manifested by incidents like the 1991 beating of Rodney King. It was no accident that the King incident involved the Los Angeles Police Department, the agency that, more than any other big-city U.S. police department, had come to define itself as a beleaguered thin blue line that protects ungrateful and undeserving citizens from themselves.[33]

Indeed, Carl Klockars suggests that the gap between what police are expected to achieve and what they can achieve encourages them to brutality, perjury, and fabrications of evidence against guilty people who would otherwise go free. Anxious to achieve the noble end of seeing that offenders receive deserved punishment, good cops, asserts Klockars, become frustrated by a criminal justice system that too often seems to dismiss cases for reasons that have nothing to do with whether arrestees actually committed the offenses of which they were accused.[34] Then, like Clint Eastwood's movie character, "Dirty Harry" Callahan, some of these officers render a violent brand of street justice and/or lie from the witness stand in order to assure that the guilty get what they deserve. The infamous videotape showing Los Angeles police beating Rodney King while he is on his hands and knees memorialized the first half of such an episode. Had it not been for George Holliday and his videocam, the episode's second half would have been the prosecution the police had initiated against Mr. King before they knew they had been caught on videotape. At the court proceeding, the police who arrested and beat King might well have offered perjured testimony to the effect that King was standing upright and physically attacking them when they used no more than necessary force to subdue him.

Cops' Rules

Elizabeth Reuss-Ianni has written that police estrangement may extend to conflicting "street cop" and "management cop" subcultures within police departments. Where these exist, street cops see themselves as excluded from a management system that espouses lofty ideals and employs meaningless statistics and other forms of smoke and mirrors in order to give the illusion that these ideals are being achieved. Consequently, street cops often see their leadership as an illegitimate and naive obstacle that must be surmounted if *real* police work is to be accomplished.[35]

Like the values constructed and honored by lower-class delinquent boys in response to rejection by middle-class teachers,[36] however, street cops' definitions of admirable behavior are developed without input from above and, in addition to serving as guideposts to survival in a harsh world, often are antithetical to those publicly espoused by official police spokespersons. Reuss-Ianni's astute observations of New York City police led her to formulate a list of the rules that govern street cops' interactions with each other and with their supervisors and administrators:

> Watch out for your partner first and then the rest of the guys working the tour [shift];
>
> Don't give up another cop;
>
> Show balls [physical courage];
>
> Be aggressive when you have to, but don't be too eager;
>
> Don't get involved in anything in another guy's sector [car beat];
>
> Hold up your end of the work;
>
> If you get caught off base, don't implicate anybody else;
>
> Make sure the other guys [officers, but not supervisors or administrators] know if another cop is dangerous or "crazy";
>
> Don't trust a new guy until you have checked him out;
>
> Don't tell anybody else more than they have to know; it could be bad for you, and it could be bad for them;
>
> Don't talk too much or too little;
>
> Don't leave work for the next tour;
>
> Protect your ass;
>
> Don't make waves;
>
> Don't give [supervisors] too much activity;

Keep out of the way of any boss from outside your precinct;

Don't look for favors just for yourself;

Don't take on the patrol sergeant by yourself;

Know your bosses;

Don't do the bosses' work for them [e.g., let them discover miscreant officers without assistance];

Don't trust bosses to look out for your interest.[37]

The adversarial relationship between street cops and management cops suggested by many of these rules has its roots in the pyramidal, military style of police organization that so sharply distinguishes between administrators and those on the front lines.[38] Thus, as we see over and over again in both examples of great heroism and officers' reluctance to expose the wrongdoing of colleagues,[39] street cops' primary loyalties are to each other rather than to the bureaucracies in which they work or to the taxpayers who pay their salaries. In the absence of formal recognition of what street cops justifiably regard as good work, street cops' reward systems consist primarily of their peer groups' status rankings of their members, and the highest status in this system is the recognition that one is *a cop's cop*. The irony that those who win this high accolade from their peers often are regarded with antagonism and suspicion by police administrators is evidence of the depth of the cleavage between management and street cops.

What to Do

Several scholars have suggested solutions to all or part of this dilemma of the vague police mandate. Manning argues that police should focus on enhancing their ability as crime-fighters and on delegating to other agencies as many of their traffic-control and other noncrime-related service tasks as possible.[40] However easy this proposal might appear to make police lives and evaluation of police performance, it is unrealistic. There is no evidence that any other agencies are anxious to fill the police role as round-the-clock-first-responders to the wide variety of nonenforcement tasks currently handled by police. Further, it is not easy to distinguish in advance between crime-fighting and police noncrime service tasks. Most police services are rendered in response to citizens' telephone calls for help of some kind or other. In some cases, 911 operators can determine very quickly that those who respond to assist must be authorized and equipped to use force and to enforce laws. In most cases, however, this is not possible, and officials must actually arrive at the scene to determine whether a call for service requires use of force, law enforcement, or both. Hence, it probably is wishful thinking to plan for police delegation to other authorities of such nonenforcement tasks as handling domestic calls, resolving neighbors' disputes, chasing noisy street-corner groups, dealing with emotionally disturbed street people, and responding to vehicle accidents.

Klockars sees severe punishment of officers who use dirty means to achieve noble ends as the appropriate approach to the "Dirty Harry problem." But, paradoxically, even he recognizes that this solution is unsatisfactory:

> In urging the punishment of policemen who resort to dirty means to achieve some unquestionably good and morally compelling end, we recognize that we create a Dirty Harry problem for ourselves and for those we urge to effect such punishments. It is a fitting end, one which teaches once again that the danger in Dirty Harry problems is never in their resolution, but in thinking that one has found a resolution with which one can truly live in peace.[41]

Klockars's realization that it would be difficult to live in peace with this resolution is correct but for reasons he seems not to take into account. Punishment achieved by end runs around due process is no more an "unquestionably good and morally compelling end" than is family prosperity obtained by a breadwinner's thefts from his or her employer. In both cases, the most peaceful and satisfying resolution might be achieved not by punishing the wrongdoer but by preventing the wrongdoing in the first place. This might be accomplished by demonstrating to the people on whose behalf the wrongdoing is likely to be conducted—the public in Klockars's case; the family in my analogy—that their desires are unrealistic and likely to impose other, unquestionably bad, costs.

Breadwinners usually can bring the desires of overly demanding families into line with reality by pointing out the limits of family resources and that the immorality and costs of stealing apply regardless of whether one is caught with a hand in the till. Public officials should make sure that their constituents know that the widespread desire to ignore constitutional limits so that *justice may be done* is contradictory and equally immoral and costly. Punishing wrongdoers without regard to the process that has been prescribed by 200 years of American experience weakens the entire society, perpetuates the myth that society can rely on the police as its primary defense against crime, and encourages society's policy makers to allow the continued festering of the social conditions that have turned our inner cities into crime factories. Unfortunately, in this era of concern over law and order and apparent resolve to address the crime problem by harshness alone, few public officials seem willing to bring forth this message.

Mastrofski's suggestions seem closer to the mark and are more strongly supported by the work and experiences of other scholars. He suggests that the broad and vague mandate of the police is here to stay. He indicates also that the extent to which it is accomplished is best assessed at close range, at the microlevel of the quality of police officers' daily encounters with citizens:[42]

What police officers themselves know about good policing has to do with how officers respond to the particular circumstances they are called to handle. This is the craft of policing, about which a great deal is known, yet uncodified: making good arrests, deescalating crises, investigating crimes, using coercion and language effectively, abiding by the law and protecting individual rights, developing knowledge of the community, and imparting a sense of fairness by one's actions.[43]

There is reason to believe that this is a feasible approach to the eventual derivation of a definition of *good policing*. As Bayley and Garofalo have reported, line police officers are excellent assessors of their peers' talents. These two researchers asked groups of street officers to identify the most outstanding of their number. Subsequently, Bayley and Garofalo observed both the officers identified as outstanding and their colleagues at one of their most difficult police tasks, intervention in disputes. They report finding quantifiable differences between the manners and techniques employed by the *cops' cops* and the rest, most notably that the officers who had been identified as outstanding were less judgmental and more helpful than their peers in their dealings with disputants. Thus, even though the officers Bayley and Garofalo had asked to rate their peers had not been requested to specify *why* they thought some officers better than others, it appears that these officers had observed something different about the work of cops' cops that could subsequently be documented empirically.[44]

Hans Toch and his colleagues Douglas Grant and Raymond Galvin had earlier approached much the same problem from a different angle. They identified a group of Oakland police officers who frequently were involved in on-the-job violence they seemed to provoke or manufacture. These violence-prone officers were themselves asked to analyze the problem of violence between police and citizens and to develop solutions to it. The most intriguing result of this work was the creation by these officers of an officially approved Peer Review Panel, consisting mostly of violence-prone officers.[45] This panel met regularly with officers whose apparent violent activities had been brought to light in incident reports or by supervisory referral, and was

> designed (1) to stimulate the subject to study his violence-related arrests over time and to help him tease out cues to his contributions to violent incidents and (2) to assist the subject to define and formulate alternative strategies for coping with violence-precipitating incidents.[46]

This program was, by all measures, a success. It allowed the most violent-prone street cops to diagnose their own problems, to analyze the more generic problem of police–citizen violence, and to devise solutions to it. It enhanced their analytic sophistication and helped to break down the adversarial relationship between street cops and management. Involvement in violent incidents by officers who participated in the program declined *vis-à-vis* that of other officers.[47]

Further, and just as important as substantive results, the Oakland work showed that:

> Programs that are usually resisted as arbitrary interferences with the officers' autonomy can become experiments in whose outcome the officers have a proprietary interest and a substantial stake.[48]

This early exercise in what has since come to be known as *problem-oriented policing*—identifying a problem and the most desirable outcome of attempts to resolve it, carefully analyzing the problem and devising appropriate means of resolving it[49]—was the basis for a project I subsequently directed in Dade County, Florida.[50] There, a task force consisting of Metro-Dade Police Department street officers, trainers, investigators, and field supervisors was assembled and asked to analyze a random sample of reports of police–citizen encounters that had *gone wrong*, in the sense that they had resulted in citizens' complaints against officers, use of force by officers, or injuries to officers. The analysis required task force members to identify every decision and action of the officers in each encounter; to describe its effects (in terms of increasing or decreasing whatever potential for violence may have existed); and, where appropriate, to prescribe alternative decisions or actions that may have better served to defuse potential violence. The goals of this analysis were to identify the most satisfactory resolutions of several types of frequently encountered potentially violent encounters between police and citizens[51] and to construct a detailed list of Do's and Don't's that would help officers to achieve these resolutions.

In other words, the project enlisted officers to define jobs well done in street cops' most challenging work, and to identify the steps most likely to help officers to do such jobs well. This project, conducted under rigid social science experimental conditions, eventually resulted in a five-day "violence reduction training program" that was delivered to all Dade County officers between February 1988 and February 1989. In the three years since then, Metro-Dade police records show that complaints against officers, use of force by officers, and injuries to officers all have declined between 30 and 50 percent.

All of this signals that street cops know more than anybody about what is good policing and who are the cop's cops. But, until the groundbreaking work of Toch, Grant, and Galvin, nobody had asked them. When they have been asked, street officers have responded with remarkable accuracy. In Oakland, street cops—notably, the most violent street cops—were empowered to address the problem of which they were the major part, and came up with solutions. Bayley and Garofalo asked street cops to identify the stars among themselves, and the answers appear to have been substantiated by observations of cops at work. I asked street cops, trainers, and supervisors below the policy-making level to define good policing in a variety of challenging situations. The answers resulted in a course of training that has been followed by remarkable reductions in police–citizen violence in one of the country's most volatile policing environments.[52]

The implications seem clear. As Manning has noted, the police mandate is vague, internally inconsistent, and generally uninformed by the police themselves.[53] If we are to derive a clear statement of the police mandate and how well it is accomplished, we should start by asking street cops to define good policing at the microlevel of their one-on-one interactions with citizens. Then, brick-by-brick, we will build meaningful macrolevel definitions of the police mandate, good policing, good police departments, and good cops.

Notes

1. Peter K. Manning, *Police Work: The Social Organization of Policing.*

2. This definition owes much to the work of Egon Bittner and Herman Goldstein.

3. Here I distinguish between domestic disputes and domestic *violence*. In my view, the role of the police in situations involving violence of any kind is clear-cut: to see that no violence occurs after the police have arrived on the scene and to arrest those who have engaged in criminal violence before the arrival of the police.

4. See, for example, Mona Margarita, "Killing the Police: Myths and Motives"; David Konstantin, "Homicides of American Law Enforcement Officers"; Joel Garner and E. Clemmer, *Danger to Police in Domestic Disturbances: A New Look.*

5. Erik Monkonnen, *Police in Urban America, 1860–1920*, pp. 81–106.

6. Robert M. Fogelson, *Big-City Police*; Samuel Walker, *A Critical History of Police Reform: The Emergence of Professionalism*; James Q. Wilson, "Generational and Ethnic Differences among Career Police Officers."

7. See, for example, James Q. Wilson's description of "watchman" police agencies in *Varieties of Police Behavior.*

8. Citizens' Police Committee, *Chicago Police Problems.*

9. Gene E. Carte and Elaine H. Carte, *Police Reform in the United States: The Era of August Vollmer, 1905–1932.*

10. Ibid.

11. Wilson, *Varieties of Police Behavior.*

12. Ibid., p. 224.

13. Ibid., pp. 86–93.

14. The most recent exception to my assertion apparently is a 1978 doctoral dissertation that compares dispositions of citizens' complaints in Berkeley, Contra Costa County (California), Kansas City, Oakland, and San Jose (Douglas Perez, "Police Accountability: A Question of Balance").

15. U.S. Department of Commerce, *1990 Census of Population and Housing, Summary of Population and Housing Characteristics, New York*, p. 72.

16. In addition to changes in Nassau County specifically, a more general trend to increased accountability for police actions has meant that activities regarded as acceptable at the time of Wilson's study would today be condemned as both indiscriminate and wasteful. Of Nassau County's special "burglary patrol," for example, Wilson (*Varieties of Police Behavior*, p. 204) noted:

> During 1965 this patrol, operating in high-risk areas of the county, stopped and searched over twelve thousand vehicles and questioned over fourteen thousand "suspicious persons." Eighty-six arrests resulted, but only nine were for burglary.

17. Eric J. Scott, *Calls for Service: Citizen Demand and Initial Police Response*, pp. 28–30; see also Albert J. Reiss, Jr., *The Police and the Public*; John Webster, "Police Time and Task Study"; Wilson, *Varieties of Police Behavior.*

18. Robert Trojanowicz and Bonnie Bucqueroux, *Community Policing: A Contemporary Perspective*, pp. 5–6.

19. Ibid., p. 5.

20. James R. Wilson, *Varieties of Police Behavior*; John E. Angell, "Toward an Alternative to the Classic Police Organizational Arrangements: A Democratic Model"; Lawrence W. Sherman, Catherine H. Milton, and Thomas V. Kelly, *Team Policing: Seven Case Studies.*

21. The more successful of the two Neighborhood Police Teams in precincts where I worked was in Brooklyn Heights, a highly organized brownstone neighborhood populated largely by upper-middle-class residents who were very anxious to see that their community remained fashionable and expensive. The second NPT, in the tough Hell's Kitchen area of Manhattan's West Side, engendered considerably less interest and enthusiasm among residents.

22. Monolithic community norms related to the police and their role in the community are not necessarily a good thing. In ethnically or racially changing neighborhoods, for example, the most powerful sentiment regarding the police may be a bigoted desire for their assistance in harassing the newcomers back to whence they came (Stephen D. Mastrofski, "Community Policing As Reform: A Cautionary Tale").

23. Wilson, *Varieties of Police Behavior*, pp. 288–89; see also Stephanie W. Greenberg and William M. Rohe, "Informal Social Control and Crime Prevention in Modern Urban Neighborhoods."

24. Jonathan Rubinstein, *City Police.*

25. See, for example, Rubinstein, *City Police.*

26. Herman Goldstein, "Improving Policing: A Problem Oriented Approach."

27. Stanley H. Palmer, *Police and Protest in England and Ireland 1780–1850.*

28. George L. Kelling et al., *The Kansas City Preventive Patrol Experiment: Summary Report*; Police Foundation, *The Newark Foot Patrol Experiment.*

29. David Freed, "Citizens Terrorized As Police Look On"; Jerome H. Skolnick and James J. Fyfe, *Above the Law: Police and the Excessive Use of Force.*

30. In my own sixteen years of police experience, the specific race or class of the ticketed violator did not matter as much as the perception that police treated *others* with great leniency. I have heard whites insist, "You wouldn't give me this ticket if I were black," because, for example, "You know they run this city," as often as I have heard the converse claim from black violators. Similarly, obviously well-heeled violators bemoaned their tickets with claims that police enforcement efforts would be better directed at people driving dangerous "clunkers"; people in clunkers argued that enforcement should focus more heavily on luxury-car drivers who "think they own the road" and could better afford tickets.

31. See, for example, Wayne H. Thomas, *Bail Reform in America*; Jeffrey Roth and Paul Wice, *Pretrial Release and Misconduct in the District of Columbia.*

32. Arthur Neiderhoffer, *Behind the Shield*, pp. 95–108.

33. See, for example, Daryl F. Gates, *Chief: My Life in the LAPD.*

34. Carl Klockars, "The Dirty Harry Problem."

35. Elizabeth Reuss-Ianni, *Two Cultures of Policing: Street Cops and Management Cops.* Former Los Angeles police officer Mike Rothmiller has painted a similar picture of his department, where street officers used the pejorative term "pogues" to refer to their naive, and often venal, police supervisors and administrators (Mike Rothmiller and Ivan G. Goldman, *L.A. Secret Police*).

36. Albert K. Cohen, *Delinquent Boys: The Culture of the Gang.*

37. Reuss-Ianni, *Two Cultures of Policing*, pp. 14–16.

38. I have argued elsewhere that the military organizational model is a historical accident that probably is the single most inappropriate way to structure police organizations (James J. Fyfe, "Lessons of Los Angeles"; Skolnick and Fyfe, *Above the Law*).

39. Warren Christopher et al., *Report of the Independent Commission on the Los Angeles Police Department*; Robert Daley, *Prince of the City: The True Story of a Cop Who Knew Too Much*; Peter Maas, *Serpico.*

40. Manning, *Police Work*, p. 374.

41. Klockars, "The Dirty Harry Problem," p. 47.

42. Mastrofski, "Community Policing As Reform."

43. Ibid., p. 63.

44. David H. Bayley and James Garofalo, "The Management of Violence by Police Patrol Officers."

45. Hans Toch, J. Douglas Grant, and Raymond T. Galvin, *Agents of Change: A Study in Police Reform.*

46. Hans Toch, "Mobilizing Police Expertise," p. 60.

47. Toch, Grant, and Galvin, *Agents of Change.*

48. Toch, "Mobilizing Police Expertise," p. 61.

49. See, for example, Herman Goldstein, *Problem-Oriented Policing.*

50. James J. Fyfe, *The Metro-Dade Police/Citizen Violence Reduction Project: Final Report.*

51. The research showed that the most frequent potentially violent encounters between Dade County police and citizens were routine traffic stops; responses to reports of crimes in progress or police investigations of suspicious persons; disputes; and "high-risk vehicle stops" of cars occupied by persons suspected of criminal activity (Fyfe, *Metro-Dade Project*).

52. It is more than modesty that causes me to refrain from attributing this decline in police–citizen violence and tension exclusively to the project I directed. The training was part of a wide variety of personnel, training, and administrative changes that began in the early 1980s and that have resulted in a major philosophical shift in the Metro-Dade Police Department. It is today a much more community-oriented and representative police department than it was a decade ago.

53. Manning, *Police Work.*

References

Angell, John E., "Toward an Alternative to the Classic Police Organizational Arrangements: A Democratic Model." *Criminology* 9 (1971): 185–206.

Bayley, David H., and Garofalo, James. "The Management of Violence by Police Patrol Officers." *Criminology* 27 (February 1989): 1–25.

Carte, Gene E., and Carte, Elaine H., *Police Reform in the United States: The Era of August Vollmer, 1905–1932.* Berkeley: University of California Press, 1975.

Christopher, Warren, et al. *Report of the Independent Commission on the Los Angeles Police Department.* City of Los Angeles, 1991.

Citizens' Police Committee. *Chicago Police Problems* (1931). Reprint. Montclair, N.J.: Patterson Smith, 1969.

Cohen, Albert K. *Delinquent Boys: The Culture of the Gang.* New York: Free Press, 1955.

Daley, Robert. *Prince of the City: The True Story of a Cop Who Knew Too Much.* Boston: Houghton Mifflin, 1978.

Fogelson, Robert M. *Big-City Police*. Cambridge, Mass.: Harvard University Press, 1977.

Freed, David. "Citizens Terrorized as Police Look On." *Los Angeles Times*, September 25, 1988, pp. 1, 3–5.

Fyfe, James J. "Lessons of Los Angeles." *Focus*. Joint Center for Political and Economic Studies, Washington, D.C., August 1992.

_____. *The Metro-Dade Police/Citizen Violence Reduction Project: Final Report*. Washington, D.C.: Police Foundation, 1988.

Fyfe, James J., and Flavin, Jeanne. "Differential Police Processing of Assault Complaints." Paper presented at Annual Meeting of Law and Society Association, Amsterdam, June 1991.

Garner, Joel, and Clemmer, E. *Danger to Police in Domestic Disturbances: A New Look*. Washington, D.C.: National Institute of Justice, 1986.

Gates, Daryl F. *Chief: My Life in the LAPD*. New York: Bantam Books, 1992.

Goldstein, Herman. "Improving Policing: A Problem Oriented Approach." *Crime and Delinquency* 25 (April 1979): 236–58.

_____. *Problem-Oriented Policing*. New York: McGraw- Hill, 1990.

Greenberg, Stephanie W., and Rohe, William M. "Informal Social Control and Crime Prevention in Modern Urban Neighborhoods." In R.B. Taylor, ed., *Urban Neighborhoods: Research and Policy*, pp. 79–118. New York: Praeger, 1986.

Kelling, George L.; Pate, Tony; Dieckman, Duane; and Brown, Charles E. *The Kansas City Preventive Patrol Experiment: Summary Report*. Washington, D.C.: Police Foundation, 1974.

Klockars, Carl. "The Dirty Harry Problem." *Annals of the American Academy of Political and Social Science* 452 (November 1980): 33–52.

Konstantin, David. "Homicides of American Law Enforcement Officers." *Justice Quarterly* 1 (March 1984): 29–37.

Maas, Peter. *Serpico*. New York: Viking Press, 1973.

Manning, Peter K. *Police Work: The Social Organization of Policing*. Cambridge, Mass.: MIT Press, 1977.

Margarita, Mona. "Killing the Police: Myths and Motives." *Annals of the American Academy of Political and Social Science* 452 (November 1980): 72–81.

Mastrofski, Stephen D. "Community Policing As Reform: A Cautionary Tale." In Jack R. Greene and Stephen D. Mastrofski, eds., *Community Policing: Rhetoric or Reality*, pp. 47–68. New York: Praeger, 1988.

Monkonnen, Erik. *Police in Urban America: 1860–1920*. Cambridge: Cambridge University Press, 1981.

Neiderhoffer, Arthur. *Behind the Shield*. Garden City, N.Y.: Doubleday, 1967.

Palmer, Stanley H. *Police and Protest in England and Ireland 1780–1850*. Cambridge: Cambridge University Press, 1988.

Perez, Douglas. "Police Accountability: A Question of Balance." Ph.D. dissertation, University of California, Berkeley, 1978.

Police Foundation. *The Newark Foot Patrol Experiment*. Washington, D.C.: Police Foundation, 1981.

Reiss, Albert J., Jr. *The Police and the Public*. New Haven: Yale University Press, 1971.

Reuss-Ianni, Elizabeth. *Two Cultures of Policing: Street Cops and Management Cops*. New Brunswick, N.J.: Transaction Books, 1983.

Roth, Jeffrey, and Wice, Paul. *Pretrial Release and Misconduct in the District of Columbia*. Washington, D.C.: Institute for Law and Social Research, 1980.

Rothmiller, Mike, and Goldman, Ivan G. *L.A. Secret Police*. New York: Pocket Books, 1992.

Rubinstein, Jonathan. *City Police*. New York: Farrar, Straus and Giroux, 1973.

Scott, Eric J. *Calls for Service: Citizen Demand and Initial Police Response.* Washington, D.C.: Government Printing Office, 1981.

Sherman, Lawrence W.; Milton, Catherine H.; and Kelly, Thomas V. *Team Policing: Seven Case Studies.* Washington, D.C.: Police Foundation, 1973.

Skolnick, Jerome H., and Fyfe, James J. *Above the Law: Police and the Excessive Use of Force.* New York: Free Press, 1993.

Thomas, Wayne H. *Bail Reform in America.* Berkeley: University of California Press, 1976.

Toch, Hans. "Mobilizing Police Expertise." *Annals of the American Academy of Political and Social Science* 452 (November 1980): 53–62.

Toch, Hans, and Grant, J. Douglas. *Police As Problem Solvers.* New York: Plenum Press, 1991.

Toch, Hans; Grant, J. Douglas; and Galvin, Raymond T. *Agents of Change: A Study in Police Reform.* Cambridge, Mass.: Schenkman, 1975.

Trojanowicz, Robert, and Bucqueroux, Bonnie. *Community Policing: A Contemporary Perspective.* Cincinnati: Anderson Publishing Co., 1990.

U.S. Department of Commerce. *1990 Census of Population and Housing, Summary of Population and Housing Characteristics., New York,* CPH–1–34. Washington, D.C.: Government Printing Office, 1991.

Walker, Samuel. *A Critical History of Police Reform: The Emergence of Professionalism.* Lexington, Mass.: Lexington Books, 1977.

Webster, John. "Police Time and Task Study." *Journal of Criminal Law, Criminology and Police Science* 61 (1970): 94–100.

Wilson, James Q. "Generational and Ethnic Differences among Career Police Officers." *American Journal of Sociology* 69 (March 1964): 522–28.

_____. *Varieties of Police Behavior.* Cambridge, Mass.: Harvard University Press, 1968.

13

BRIAN FORST

The Prosecutor and the Public

The power of the prosecutor in the United States has been well documented. According to former U.S. attorney general and Supreme Court justice Robert H. Jackson, "The prosecutor has more control over life, liberty, and reputation than any other person in America."[1] Yale criminologist Albert Reiss asserts that the prosecutor exercises "the greatest discretion in the formally organized criminal justice network."[2] Wall Street investment bankers indicted for securities trading violations in the 1980s will attest to the might of the U.S. attorney for the Southern District of New York.[3] Many citizens claimed that the U.S. attorney for the District of Columbia abused his discretionary authority by his "selective prosecution" of the mayor of the district in the highly publicized cocaine case of *The United States v. Marion Barry*.

Concern about the abuse of prosecutorial discretion is, clearly, not unique to a particular quarter of the political spectrum. Abusive exercise of discretion has been charged by much of the nation's African-American community on behalf of black defendants, and it has been made just as fervently by *The Wall Street Journal* and other conservative sentinels in criticizing the zeal of U.S. attorneys prosecuting affluent individuals under the amorphous Racketeer Influenced and Corrupt Organization (RICO) statute. An issue that such diverse factions can agree is critical cannot be easily dismissed. Under a Constitution that ensures equal protection for all, it is a concern that runs much deeper than the culpability of any particular offender or class of offenders.

This concern raises questions about the proper limits of the prosecutor's exercise of discretion: How can that discretion be exercised to serve the interests of the community most effectively? Does the prosecutor's discretionary authority to select certain individuals and reject others for prosecution leave too much room to act out of political motives rather than motives that are more purely legal, sensible, and community spirited? What are the prospects for structuring such exercise of discretion—both for the sake of making the rules more explicit and to reduce unwarranted disparity—without diminishing the prosecutor's ability to make effective decisions in each case and manage the caseload efficiently? What else can the prosecutor do to serve the community better?

Prosecution by the Numbers

We can begin to address these issues by considering the role of the prosecutor in processing felony cases. Viewing case management as a production process—an appropriate perspective especially in the large felony caseload settings of most urban and suburban jurisdictions—the prosecutor's initial responsibility is to screen arrests brought by the police, to determine which cases are worthy of filing with the court and which are not. Those who have studied the prosecutor's screening decisions have found that the decision is based primarily on three sets of factors: the strength of the evidence, the seriousness of the crime, and the dangerousness of the offender, as revealed by his or her criminal record.[4] Because the evidentiary standard for a guilty verdict in trial ("proof beyond a reasonable doubt") is much higher than for making an arrest ("probable cause" that the suspect committed the offense), some 40 percent of all adult felony arrests are either rejected at the initial screening stage or dropped soon afterward—typically because of problems with witnesses or with tangible evidence.[5]

Cases that survive felony screening are quite strong in most jurisdictions. About 80 percent end up as convictions, the vast majority of those guilty pleas rather than guilty verdicts after trial.[6] The other 20 percent are cases in which the judge dismisses the charges (about 10 percent), the jury acquits the defendant (about 5 percent), or the defendant fails to appear after pretrial release (about 5 percent).

Discretion and Disparity

Prosecutors do not think naturally of case processing as we have described it above, as a production process. Law school trains prosecutors-to-be in the elements of criminal law, not management. Prosecutors are sworn to bring to justice those who violate the law. Where the law is less than explicit, they are left to exercise discretion to ensure that cases are processed justly and effectively. The less explicit the law, the greater the discretion; the greater the discretion, the greater the opportunity for unevenhanded treatment of cases—for disposition in a manner driven by the individual prosecutor. Thus, the attorneys in some 8,000 state and local prosecution agencies and 94 federal offices throughout the United States weigh not only legal considerations, but practical and political ones as well in deciding the fate of many millions of persons arrested each year.[7]

The opportunities for unevenhanded action run through the entire process. Prosecutors decide which arrests and police charges to file in court and which to reject, how much attention to give each case, whether to induce and accept pleas and reduce charges, how much to reduce charges, whether to induce some defendants to plead guilty to reduced charges in return for evidence against other defendants, and what sentences to recommend to judges.

How those decisions are made depends on a variety of factors, starting with the chief prosecutor's goals. One office might show more concern than another about drug crimes, even when the two jurisdictions have comparable drug problems. Some offices emphasize crime control and set up "career criminal" units to target defendants with serious criminal records. An office with a serious street crime problem may target white-collar offenders.

Different views about how to achieve a particular goal can create further variation in practice. Three offices may all give high priority to drug offenders: the first may target users of drugs, the second low-level traffickers, and the third high-level distributors. Two offices may pursue convictions with equal zeal; the first may be much more willing to convict offenders by engaging in plea bargaining than the second.

Where evidence is available, it points fairly clearly in the direction of disparity among prosecutors. Even in neighboring federal regions with similar case mixes and with resources balanced by the Justice Department according to caseloads, prosecutors tend to engage in plea negotiations at significantly different rates. In 1984, the 6th U.S. Circuit (Kentucky, Missouri, Ohio, and Tennessee) had 5.8 pleas for each trial, while the neighboring 5th U.S. Circuit (Louisiana, Mississippi, and Texas) had 50 percent more—8.7 pleas per trial. The Southern District of West Virginia had 9.9 pleas per trial, while the neighboring Western District of Virginia had less than half that—4.2.[8]

Variations in plea bargaining practices are even more pronounced among local jurisdictions. A study sponsored by the Bureau of Justice Statistics, an arm of the U.S. Department of Justice, found that in Manhattan, for every felony arrest that went to trial in the early 1980s, twenty-four defendants pled guilty; during approximately the same period in Washington, D.C., only five pled guilty for every one that went to trial.[9] The difference is primarily a matter of policy rather than heavy caseloads in New York. In the early 1980s, District Attorney Robert Morgenthau's Manhattan office rejected only 3 percent of all felony arrests; the local crime unit in U.S. Attorney Jay Stephens's Washington, D.C., office rejected 15 percent.[10] Prosecutors generally aim to pleas, in a manner of speaking; but some, like U.S. Attorney Stephens, devote considerably more effort to trials than others.

The Prosecutor's Goals, the Community's Interests

These sharp cross-jurisdictional differences in prosecution policies may correspond to unique community needs. In light of the distance that most prosecutors keep from the public, however, and the absence of attempts to articulate *how* the differences correspond to community needs, it appears more likely that the differences correspond to the arbitrary forces that shape policy in many public bureaucracies, a process that is well insulated from community awareness. Although usually an elected public official, the prosecutor in most jurisdictions is less visible than the police or the judiciary. A member of the community is more likely to learn about a sensational police act or judge's decision on the evening news than about a prosecutor's action. Except for the rare sensational case, the prosecutor's operations are generally well hidden from public view. The policies of the office are often unknown, and unknowable, to the community that the prosecutor professes to serve.

One factor that works to keep those operations shrouded in secrecy is the adversarial nature of prosecution. The prosecutor has little to gain and much to lose by revealing pertinent aspects of case-processing policy to the other side— either to the defense in the case at hand or to potential criminals generally. Prosecutors know that many people will be inclined to violate laws that, because of policy, are not prosecuted.

Another factor is this: under the Anglo-American system of law the prosecutor is the legal advocate on behalf of the *state*, not the victim. The prosecutor is under no special obligation to take care of victims, including the provision of information about what is being done in their cases, except to the extent that doing so strengthens the case by keeping the victim involved and supportive, willing to provide useful testimony against the defendant.

The potential for such a process to alienate victims, and thus alienate the community, is considerable. One of the cliches of our contemporary system of criminal justice is that victims are victimized twice, first by the offender and then by the system. A process in which the defendant has a formal advocate but the victim does not has led many victims to feel that they are "treated more like pieces of evidence than like human beings."[11] Many prosecutors have established special programs to serve the needs of victims and witnesses beyond their roles as providers of testimonial evidence, usually with funding outside of normal operating budget channels, but there is still substantial room to improve the treatment given to victims, regardless of whether separate funding is available. Improved treatment of victims might even improve conviction rates. In any case, prosecutors who succeed in convicting offenders may still fail the community by showing institutional indifference to victims.

Controlling the Prosecutor's Exercise of Discretion

The prosecutor's operations are not kept hidden from the lay public alone. In the United States, the prosecutor is part of the executive branch of government, so the prosecutor's policies are shielded also from judicial and legislative review under the Constitutional principle of separation of powers. Prosecutors may go public with their general philosophies, but they are rarely more specific than that, so as not to tie their own hands. Different prosecutors with different goals, combined with varying approaches to achieving given goals, clearly can result in uneven application of the law.

Such disparities in prosecution violate fundamental notions of equity. The community's victims are not served when the cases they are associated with receive less prosecutorial attention than other, similar cases. The community's defendants are not served when the prosecutor selects some of their cases for greater attention than other, similar cases. The justice system itself is not served when the community comes to believe that criminal cases are handled in a capricious manner.

It is surely in order to examine how the prosecutor's contribution to these disparities, both real and perceived, can be brought under control. An extreme position is to eliminate prosecutorial discretion altogether. The German criminal justice system allows the prosecutor virtually no room to exercise discretion, especially in serious crimes.[12] The state of Alaska, concerned about the exercise of prosecutorial discretion in plea bargaining, attempted to abolish the practice in 1975. Studies of felony case processing in Alaska afterward revealed an increase in the ratio of trials to pleas,[13] but the ultimate effect of the "abolition" was inconclusive. The vast majority of convictions continued to be in the form of pleas rather than guilty verdicts, and researchers have been unable to establish with any degree of certainty the effects of the policy change on the prosecutor's screening policies, nor have they been able to rule out the possibility that some of the voluntary pleas of guilt were in fact related to a reduction in charges by the prosecutor.[14]

Judicial controls have also been invoked to limit excesses in prosecutorial discretion, but those controls have been used only in the most egregious abuses by the prosecutor. In the nineteenth-century case of *Yick Wo v. Hopkins*, the Supreme Court upheld the right of a judge to overrule the prosecutor's decision to file charges against a defendant when the decision is based on racial or religious discrimination, or when it is in retaliation to the defendant's legitimate exercise of expression.[15] In the more recent case of *Oyler v. Boles*, however, the Court explicitly restrained itself from intruding into the prosecutor's domain.[16]

Perhaps the most viable opportunity for controlling the prosecutor's exercise of discretion is with the use of guidelines. Explicit, published guidelines have been suggested before, but guidelines that have been put in place have been either inexplicit or unpublished, or both.[17]

It is quite possible that the most effective way to establish meaningful prosecutorial guidelines is with some legislative and judicial involvement. A strong precedent for such guidelines does exist: sentencing guidelines for judges. Judicial excesses in the exercise of sentencing discretion were documented statistically in a series of studies funded by the U.S. Department of Justice in the 1970s and 1980s.[18] Those disclosures led to legislation that limited judges' discretion and established sentencing guidelines, first in several states and then, with the passage of the Sentencing Reform Act of 1984, at the federal level. The guidelines have been found to work: a National Institute of Justice study of 10,000 felony sentences in North Carolina—5,000 before that state's guidelines were enacted and 5,000 after—revealed that the guidelines shortened the interquartile range (that is, the distance from the twenty-fifth to the seventy-fifth percentile) from 3 to 10 years to 2 to 6 years.[19] The judiciary has not been eager to have their exercise of discretion narrowed, but they have adapted nonetheless, and many prefer not to have to worry about how their sentences stack up against those of their brethren. The narrowing of sentencing discretion at both the federal and state levels has, in any case, resulted in no apparent loss of either deterrent effectiveness or "pure justice."

The laws that have long governed prosecution are every bit as broad in some areas as were pre-guideline sentencing statutes. RICO and drug conspiracy laws serve as two examples of statutes that give prosecutors extraordinary latitude to pick and choose certain defendants and ignore others. The loose wording of these laws cannot help but contribute to prosecutorial excesses; they deserve to be more sharply defined, as do the prosecutor's targeting policies, so that citizens can know more clearly the limits of legal behavior.

Take one prominent example: the ugly spectacle of *U.S. v. Barry*. The U.S. attorney and his team of assistants attempted to justify singling out Marion Barry from the immense crowd of prosecutable drug users by using the metaphor of Mayor Barry as turncoat general of the army in the war against drugs in the district. But they did so in the absence of explicit guidelines that supported such an argument. In finding Barry guilty of only a single misdemeanor drug possession charge, the jury in the case indicated that they did not buy the argument. Had a set of published federal prosecution guidelines existed that explicitly call for the targeting of high public officials who break laws, the appearance that the prosecution was motivated primarily by racial or political considerations might have been lessened.

Many prosecutors may regard the notion of limiting their discretion as an attempt to take the teeth out of the law, but limiting prosecutorial discretion need not strengthen the hand of the criminal. Reducing discretion would not give criminals more freedom to menace society any more than reduced sentencing disparity has necessarily resulted in either more lenient or more severe sentencing policy. (Sentences became tougher under the federal guidelines; North Carolina's and Minnesota's guidelines had the opposite effect.) The sharpening of laws that provide a playground for more politically motivated prosecutors, together with published prosecutorial guidelines, would simply mean a narrowing of discretion in areas now too broadly defined—areas in which complaints of arbitrary or "selective" prosecution have been strongest and most numerous.

Prosecutors have tenaciously protected their exercise of discretion and resisted attempts to commit their rules to widespread publication, arguing that separation of powers prohibits either the courts or legislative bodies from altering the discretionary aspects of prosecution. Abuses of their discretionary authority, however, impose costs on the community that may be too great to bear. Such abuses are bound eventually to lead to encroachments by either or both of the other two branches of government.

Prosecutors may differ on a particular goal of prosecution, or on a particular method of achieving a goal, but it is difficult to object to a more coherent and consistent basis for making case-processing decisions on behalf of the community. Prosecutors themselves can take the initiative in identifying those areas in which guidelines are most needed and putting them in place—and then sticking to them—so that their practices can be made both more explicit and more even-handed. If they do not, others are likely to do it for them.

If we are truly a "government of laws, and not of men," as John Adams wrote in 1774, we will begin to take measures to ensure that members of the community are less susceptible to arbitrary prosecution, and to ensure more generally that the prosecutor's incentives are closely aligned with the community's interests.

Getting Closer to the Community

Thus, guidelines may be a vehicle for improving ties with the community. But why should the prosecutor aim to improve such ties? There really is no reason under the law. Politically minded prosecutors should care about their ties to the community for the sake of public relations, and prosecutors will certainly care about their ties to the community to the extent that they see themselves as public servants.

Prosecutors who wish to align themselves more closely with the community's interests can do so, first, by becoming aware of the barriers that have for so long distanced the prosecutor from the community and then stripping them away. Prosecutors may have something to learn from the police, who have begun to climb down from the perch of "professionalism" that has alienated them from the community for so long. As Fisher and Fyfe suggest in chapters 9 and 12, the police can make this change in a way that strengthens law enforcement rather than compromises it.

What are the prospects for a more community-oriented system of prosecution? They may not be as bright as the prospects for policing—the primary workplace of the police *is* the community—but there are some hopeful signs of prosecutorial reform. A recent survey of prosecutors revealed that the rate at which prosecutors notify police and victims of the outcomes of their cases more than doubled from 1974 to 1990.[20] Prosecutors are not required to provide such information; they do it largely to maintain goodwill with the people who may be able to repay the favor later, and because prosecutors are becoming more sensitive to the public's right to know certain basic facts.

Tina McLanus has documented explicit community-oriented reforms in two offices: the Office of the State's Attorney for Montgomery County, Maryland, and the Office of the District Attorney for the borough of Brooklyn, New York.[21] In 1990, Andrew Sonner, state's attorney for Montgomery County, launched a Community-Oriented Prosecution system to replace the traditional practice of assigning cases based on the nature of the offense with assignment based on the location of the crime. Sonner reorganized the office into five geographically based divisions, each corresponding to one of the county's five police patrol districts. A primary purpose: to improve coordination with the police department. Poor police–prosecutor coordination has been cited as a major factor in the finding that about half of all felony arrests nationwide do not end in conviction,[22] and Montgomery County has had its share of chronic coordination problems with the Montgomery County Police Department over the years. Each assistant state attorney in Sonner's office is assigned a geographic area within the district and is expected to become familiar with the police officers assigned to that area and to become familiar with the community itself.

Robert Dean, one of Sonner's chief assistants, is responsible for Montgomery County's Wheaton Division. He likes the new arrangement: "We're known as the Wheaton Wolverines now. There's a sense of ownership—it's your area."[23] Dean and his assistants operate differently under the new system; "ride-alongs" with the police are much more common now, as are meetings with school principals and other community leaders. An assistant of Dean's recently noticed a fugitive on the street in a ride-along, and the officer arrested the offender—an extraordinary example of police–prosecutor coordination. With the 1991 appointment of a new chief committed to community policing in Montgomery County, the relations between prosecutors and the police are better than they have been for years.

After nearly two years in operation, Sonner is sold on the new system: "Community policing is too important to be left to the police alone."[24]

Brooklyn's counterpart to the Montgomery County Community-Oriented Prosecution system is the Brooklyn Community Prosecution Program. Created in September 1991, Brooklyn's reorganization resembles Montgomery County's in its partitioning of the borough into five zones based on police precinct boundaries (from four to six police precincts per zone) and community characteristics. Brooklyn's system, however, involves judges as well as prosecutors: each of the five zones is the responsibility of seven judges, with three prosecutors assigned to each judge. A major advantage of this system is that it reduces substantially the number of different judges each prosecutor must deal with, reducing scheduling conflicts and other inefficiencies. As in Montgomery County, the prosecutors in Brooklyn are expected to familiarize themselves with the police in the area and with the community.

In both Montgomery County and Brooklyn, the prosecutors are learning that each community has unique needs—based on the patterns of complaints from the residents and merchants in the area and the prevalence of certain types of crimes—and that serving those needs does not have to come at the expense of evenhanded enforcement of the laws of the state.

With the decline of community—perhaps because of it—the public has become increasingly disenchanted with public institutions. They have become more dissatisfied generally with prosecutors and judges than with police in jurisdictions throughout the country.[25] Prosecutors in Montgomery County and

Brooklyn have taken significant steps to reintroduce into large urban environments elements of familiarity between the adjudication system and the community that characterized an earlier era.

It remains to be seen how this new perspective on prosecution will work out. If it does prove successful, the long-term prospects for such fundamental reform in other offices seem more encouraging than the short-term prospects. Prosecution has traditionally not been quick to change.

There is, clearly, ample opportunity for prosecutors to move farther away from the worst of worlds: arbitrary case-processing decisions with the appearance of politics in prosecution and aloofness from the community. A few prosecutors appear already to have discovered, as have many police officials before them, that there is little tension between the two goals, that justice may be more effectively served when the conventional notion of professionalism is reconstructed so that it recognizes that the community is the patron.

Notes

1. Robert H. Jackson, "The Federal Prosecutor," p. 18.
2. Albert Reiss, "Discretionary Justice in the United States."
3. A central figure in Tom Wolfe's eerily prescient *Bonfire of the Vanities* was prosecutor Lawrence Kramer, a cartoon of the New York City prosecutor. Wolfe had Kramer muse at one point, "What are all the limestone facades of Fifth Avenue and all the marble halls and stuffed-leather libraries and all the riches of Wall Street in the face of *my* control over *your* destiny and your helplessness in the face of the Power?" (p. 591). Without attempting to speculate on the extent to which real-world prosecutors harbor such attitudes, I would say that some prosecutors appear clearly to select cases and prosecute them in a way that gives the prosecutor more political visibility. New York prosecutors have surely been known to operate sensationally and then run for public office; Thomas E. Dewey and Rudolph Giuliani are two examples. Dewey achieved national prominence as federal prosecutor by obtaining convictions against seventy-two New York City racketeers in the 1930s; he then served as district attorney for Manhattan, rose to governor, and eventually ran unsuccessfully for president of the United States. Giuliani, the federal prosecutor who presided over the wave of Wall Street prosecutions in the 1980s, ran unsuccessfully for mayor of New York in 1989.
4. These three factors, and sometimes a fourth—characteristics of the victim—have been cited in several empirical studies of prosecution. Brian Forst and Kathleen Brosi, "A Theoretical and Empirical Analysis of the Prosecutor," pp. 177–91; Richard S. Frase, "The Decision to File Federal Criminal Charges: A Quantitative Study of Prosecutorial Discretion," pp. 246–330; Joan Jacoby, *The American Prosecutor: A Search for Identity;* William McDonald, *Police–Prosecutor Relations in the United States.*
5. There is little evidence to suggest that the large case-dropout rate is due to Fourth Amendment exclusionary rule factors—such as police search-and-seizure errors or failure to warn arrestees of their right to remain silent—as many have suggested. Analyses of arrest rejections have revealed that fewer than 1 percent of all felony arrests are dropped due to such factors; for each arrest rejected due to an exclusionary rule violation, about twenty are rejected because the police failed to produce sufficient tangible or testimonial evidence. Kathleen Brosi, *A Cross-City Comparison of Felony Case Processing*; Barbara Boland and Ronald Sones, *Prosecution of Felony Arrests.*

6. The statistics reported here are from Brosi, *Cross-City Comparison*, and from Boland and Sones, *Prosecution*. For further details regarding the ratio of pleas to trials, see text accompanying note 9.

7. The number was 13.8 million in 1988. Federal Bureau of Investigation, *Uniform Crime Reports for the United States*.

8. Administrative Office of the U.S. Courts, *Annual Report*, Table D6.

9. Brian Forst and Barbara Boland, "The Prevalence of Guilty Pleas," p. 2.

10. See Boland and Sones, *Prosecution*.

11. Gilbert Geis, "Victim and Witness Assistance Programs," p. 1600. See also Frank J. Cannavale, Jr., *Witness Cooperation*; Morton Bard and Dawn Sangrey, *The Crime Victim's Book*.

12. John H. Langbein and Lloyd L. Weinreb, "Continental Criminal Procedure: 'Myth' and Reality," pp. 1549–69.

13. Michael L. Rubinstein, Stevens H. Clarke, and Teresa J. White, *Alaska Bans Plea Bargaining*.

14. Albert W. Alschuler, "Plea Bargaining and Its History," pp. 1–42, and "The Changing Plea Bargaining Debate," pp. 652–730.

15. 118 U.S. 356 (1886).

16. "The conscious exercise of some selectivity in enforcement is not in itself a federal constitutional violation." *Oyler v. Boles*, 368 U.S. 448, 456 (1962).

17. Two prominent precursors to guidelines have been published: the *Uniform Charging Standards*, developed by the California District Attorneys Association, and the *Principles of Federal Prosecution* published by the U.S. Department of Justice. The former has not been translated into guidelines by local district attorneys, and the latter is widely regarded as too vague to be useful. Norman Abrams, "Prosecutorial Charge Decision Systems," pp. 1–56.

18. John Hogarth, *Sentencing As a Human Process*; Shari S. Diamond and Hans Zeisel, "Sentencing Councils: A Study of Sentence Disparity and Its Reduction"; Brian Forst and Charles Wellford, "Punishment and Sentencing: Developing Sentencing Guidelines Empirically from Principles of Punishment"; Alfred Blumstein et al., eds., *Research on Sentencing: The Search for Reform*.

19. Stevens H. Clarke, "North Carolina's Fair Sentencing Act: What Have the Results Been?" p. 14.

20. In 1974, 44 percent of prosecutors surveyed routinely reported case outcomes to the police, and 35 percent routinely reported outcomes to the victim; in 1990, 93 percent routinely reported case outcomes to the police, and 93 percent routinely reported them to the victim. Bureau of Justice Statistics, "Prosecutors in State Courts, 1990."

21. McLanus writes about Montgomery County in "Community Criminal Justice: Decentralized and Personalized Prosecution," pp. 15–16; she writes about Brooklyn in "Community Criminal Justice: Brooklyn Establishes 'Community Courts'," pp. 15–16.

22. Brian Forst, Judith Lucianovic, and Sarah Cox, *What Happens After Arrest?* especially pp. 61–92; McDonald, *Police–Prosecutor Relations in the United States*; Brian Forst, "Prosecution and Sentencing," especially pp. 181–82.

23. McLanus, "Community Criminal Justice: Decentralized," p. 15.

24. Personal communication, April 24, 1992.

25. Jolene C. Hernon and Brian Forst, *The Criminal Justice Response to Victim Harm*, p. 46.

References

Abrams, Norman. "Prosecutorial Charge Decision Systems." *UCLA Law Review* 23 (1975): 1–56.

Administrative Office of the U.S. Courts. *Annual Report.* Washington, D.C.: U.S. Courts, 1984.

Alschuler, Albert W. "The Changing Plea Bargaining Debate." *California Law Review* 69 (1981): 652–730.

————. "Plea Bargaining and Its History." *Columbia Law Review* 79 (1979): 1–42.

Bard, Morton, and Sangrey, Dawn. *The Crime Victim's Book.* New York: Basic Books, 1979.

Blumstein, Alfred; Cohen, Jacqueline; and Nagin, Daniel, eds. *Research on Sentencing: The Search for Reform.* Washington, D.C.: National Science Foundation, 1983.

Boland, Barbara, and Sones, Ronald. *Prosecution of Felony Arrests.* Washington, D.C.: Bureau of Justice Statistics, 1981, 1986.

Brosi, Kathleen. *A Cross-City Comparison of Felony Case Processing.* Washington, D.C.: Bureau of Justice Statistics 1979.

Bureau of Justice Statistics. "Prosecutors in State Courts, 1990." *BJS Bulletin* (March 1992).

Cannavale, Frank J., Jr. *Witness Cooperation.* Lexington, Mass.: Lexington Books, 1976.

Clarke, Stevens H. "North Carolina's Fair Sentencing Act: What Have the Results Been?" *Popular Government* 49 (Fall 1983): 14.

Diamond, Shari S., and Zeisel, Hans. "Sentencing Councils: A Study of Sentence Disparity and Its Reduction." *University of Chicago Law Review* 43 (1975): 109.

Federal Bureau of Investigation. *Uniform Crime Reports for the United States.* Washington, D.C.: U.S. Department of Justice, 1989.

Forst, Brian. "Prosecution and Sentencing." In James Q. Wilson, ed., *Crime and Public Policy.* San Francisco: Institute for Contemporary Studies, 1983.

Forst, Brian, and Boland, Barbara. "The Prevalence of Guilty Pleas." *Bureau of Justice Statistics: Special Report.* Washington, D.C.: U.S. Department of Justice, 1984.

Forst, Brian, and Brosi, Kathleen. "A Theoretical and Empirical Analysis of the Prosecutor." *Journal of Legal Studies* 6 (January 1977): 177–91.

Forst, Brian, and Wellford, Charles. "Punishment and Sentencing: Developing Sentencing Guidelines Empirically from Principles of Punishment." *Rutgers Law Review* 33 (1981): 799–837.

Forst, Brian; Lucianovic, Judith; and Cox, Sarah. *What Happens After Arrest?* Washington, D.C.: Institute for Law and Social Research, 1977.

Frase, Richard S. "The Decision to File Federal Criminal Charges: A Quantitative Study of Prosecutorial Discretion." *University of Chicago Law Review* 47 (1980): 246–330.

Geis, Gilbert. "Victim and Witness Assistance Programs." *Encyclopedia of Crime and Justice.* New York: Macmillan/Free Press, 1983.

Hernon, Jolene C., and Forst, Brian. *The Criminal Justice Response to Victim Harm.* Washington, D.C.: U.S. Department of Justice, 1984.

Hogarth, John. *Sentencing As a Human Process.* Toronto: University of Toronto Press, 1971.

Jackson, Robert H. "The Federal Prosecutor." *Journal of the American Judicial Society* 24 (1940): 18.

Jacoby, Joan. *The American Prosecutor: A Search for Identity.* Lexington, Mass.: Lexington Books, 1980.

Langbein, John H., and Weinreb, Lloyd L. "Continental Criminal Procedure: 'Myth' and Reality." *Yale Law Journal* 87 (1978): 1549–69.

McDonald, William. *Police–Prosecutor Relations in the United States.* Washington, D.C.: National Institute of Justice, 1982.

McLanus, Tina. "Community Criminal Justice: Brooklyn Establishes 'Community Courts.' " *Footprints* 4 (Winter/Spring 1992): 15–16.

————. "Community Criminal Justice: Decentralized and Personalized Prosecution." *Footprints* 3 (Spring/Summer 1991): 15–16.

Oyler v. Boles, 368 U.S. 448, 456 (1962).

Reiss, Albert. "Discretionary Justice in the United States." *International Journal of Criminology and Penology* 2 (1974): 195.

Rubinstein, Michael L.; Clarke, Stevens H.; and White, Teresa J. *Alaska Bans Plea Bargaining*. Washington, D.C.: U.S. Department of Justice, 1980.

Wilson, James Q., ed. *Crime and Public Policy*. San Francisco: Institute for Contemporary Studies, 1983.

Wolfe, Tom. *Bonfire of the Vanities*. New York: Farrar, Straus, and Giroux, 1987.

Yick Wo v. Hopkins, 118 U.S. 356 (1886).

14

NORVAL MORRIS

The Honest Politician's Guide to Sentencing Reform

Dear Honest Politician:

The prisons and jails overflow, and under the ceaseless pressure of numbers, probation and parole supervision in the cities has become tokenism. Meanwhile, in most of America, crime rates continue their steady small decline of the past decade, but not in the destroyed inner cities, where the plagues of crime and delinquency grow worse.

I will not trouble you with the numbers to support those sad propositions, unless you wish me to send them to you to add verisimilitude to any public orations you are planning. The data are reliable, and they will establish a rate of incarceration, a rate of control by the criminal justice system, and rates of crime far, far higher than those of any country with which we would wish to compare ourselves. The incarceration rate for the United States is many times higher than for any European country and higher even than South Africa's rate!

Does this mean that Americans are innately more wicked, more criminous, than citizens of other countries? Surely not. And, even if they were, you could hardly make that proposition a plank in your political platform. So, if you are indeed an honest politician, you must be prepared to recognize that our astoundingly high rates of punishment, and our booming rates of violence and homicide, are not a product of anything other than generations of failure by your political predecessors, and the continuance of their deceptive populist practices by your contemporary political peers.

You quibble, sotto voce: surely it is our racial mix, you say, which is another way of saying it is those criminally inclined African-Americans. Let me take the point head on. African-American (hereinafter "black," to be in contrast to the equally misleading "white") rates of incarceration are more than seven and a half times higher than white rates of incarceration. Why is this so? The question has been exhaustively researched. The best judgment is that about one-fifth of this discrepancy is reasonably to be attributed to unjust discrimination against black criminals by the police and by prosecutors and judges (added together), and four-fifths to blacks' disproportionate involvement in those types of crime that attract jailing and imprisonment as a punishment (that is to say, not insider trading, large-scale embezzlement, and other white-collar crimes, which are almost exclusively the province of whites). If the above ratios appear to establish that it really is the criminous blacks who push up our rates of violence and incarceration, then consider this: when blacks move into the middle class, as more do each year, their crime rates and the delinquency rates of their children are indistinguishable from those of white adults and children.

The racial imbalance in crime is not genetic in origin; it is political. You didn't create this imbalance—you wouldn't bother reading this if you did—but the responsibility for changing it is primarily yours, since you took on the profession that purports to have the social welfare of our citizenry as its fundamental concern. It is therefore entirely fit and right for me to address this polemic to you.

That bastion of conservatism *The Economist*, in an excellent "Survey of America" (October 26, 1991), described as "undoubtedly America's greatest social problem, [the] inner-city slums in the old cities of the North and East, disproportionately inhabited by blacks, whose social conditions are a disgrace to a rich nation." Those slums are the fertile seedbed of crime, and of many of the other social conditions that shape one of our two nations. Inescapably, if you care for the future of this great nation, you must take on the difficult task of charting a course to reduce the impact of the scourge of crime on the fabric of this country.

If you desire to use your rage at our excessive crime rates to keep you in office, here is what you should do: Stress the need for more police, bewail the legalistic technicalities that set the guilty free, deplore the judicial tendency to impose sentimentally lenient sentences, frequently declare war on drugs or family violence or sex offenders, and promise that by larger doses of mandatory punishment you will send a powerful message to many varieties of criminals. Also, of course, in voting and in oratory, miss no occasion to favor capital punishment. You will not, as I am sure you appreciate, have any effect on crime rates, but your tenure in office will be more secure. And when you meet someone who is informed on these matters, reassure him or her that you must stay in office if you are to achieve the many good things that come from your other policies—follow, it is simple enough, the reasoning of the German judges who stayed in office to ameliorate the pains that others would inflict under their Nazi masters.

If, on the other hand, you are genuinely concerned about the suffering that crime inflicts on individual citizens and on the social fabric, you must recognize that though police, prosecutors, courts, prisons, and probation officers are essential elements of social control, their prime business is justice, and that tinkering with their processes, toward either leniency or severity, will have no measurable effect on crime rates. The problems of crime are to be sought where crime flourishes, and you know where that is. So do we all. Take any reasonably educated adult and drive him through any of our cities; he need speak to no one. Hand him a map of the city and ask him to fill in the high crime and delinquency areas: he will do it about as well as the chief of police of that city. Not surprisingly, those areas marked will be precisely the ones where disproportionately, grossly disproportionately, to be found are: excessive infant mortality, low infant birth-weights, excessive drug addiction, excessive unemployment (particularly of youths and young men), illegitimacy far in excess of nuclear families, teenage pregnancies, illiteracy, schools like prisons—all in all, what my excellent colleague William Julius Wilson has described as "the truly disadvantaged."

Perhaps, in later letters, if you find this one of interest and use, I shall set out for you in detail a variety of ways in which you can responsibly work toward reducing crime; my task in this letter is much narrower. It is to lay the foundation of a program by which you can bring principle and justice to our chaotic and criminogenic system of sentencing and punishing convicted criminals. This will not have much effect on crime rates, in either the short or the long run, but it is an essential first step before you can address the roots of crime. Regrettably, police, prosecutors, and courts cannot do much to reduce crime—though they may tell you to the contrary—but their work must be more principled than it is before you can take the other more basic steps to that end. A precondition to a serious assault on crime in this country is the creation of a just and effective system for the punishment of convicted offenders.

You would perhaps like a roadmap of the path to that end, so that you may decide whether this journey with me is worth continuing. I shall first scan the story of sentencing reforms, so-called, over the past twenty-five years. This will set the stage for a slightly more detailed statement of current problems and the path you should follow to bring justice and efficiency to the punishment of convicted criminals.

Twenty-Five Years of Sentencing Reform

I don't know which nineteenth-century Englishman said it, but it is a suitable anecdote for this topic: "Reform, Sir, reform. Don't talk to me of reform. Things are bad enough as they are!" In the same spirit, let me describe the changes in sentencing practice in the United States over the past twenty-five years, not dignifying them by the name of reform, though recognizing that most were introduced with the very best of intentions—the path to hell, I am told, but that seems an excessive sanction.

There have been radical changes in sentencing practice over this period. Nevertheless, most of the charges that were laid against American sentencing practices at the beginning of this period continue to apply with unabated force. Three lines of criticism launched the sentencing changes of the 1970s; two were offered by academics and a few judges who had studied our punishment systems, one was offered by politicians and the press.

The scholarly charges were these: first, that there was an unwarranted disparity among sentences, by which one offender would be sentenced to a much greater punishment than another who had committed an equally serious offense and had an equally bad criminal record; and second, that the prevailing indeterminate sentences, by which the judge sentenced the offender to a maximum term or to a maximum and a minimum term of imprisonment—the actual time to be served being later set by a parole board—were fundamentally unjust. This claim of injustice was based on compelling data establishing that prison behavior was no predictor of later behavior in the community, and that the hypocrisy of parole had turned prisons into schools of dramatic art by which the most hypocritical of prisoners did the least time. Sentencing to prison, argued the academics, putting these two criticisms together, must be to a fixed term (possibly modulated by a predetermined amount of "time off" for good behavior in prison) and like offenders must receive like terms.

The criticism of politicians and the press was quite different. Seeking a scapegoat for the steeply rising crime rates of the 1970s, they attacked judicial leniency, the sentimentality of judges and parole boards, and what they called "the coddling of criminals." Prison sentences must be "tough" and for a fixed term. "Bark and bite" sentencing, by which the judge barks a long sentence but the bite of the actual term served is grossly less, must stop—there must be truth in sentencing, just as in advertising. It was the "Humpty Dumpty" principle extended: if all the king's horses and all the king's men couldn't put Humpty together again; then, by Heaven, we need more horses and more men.

The academic and judicial criticisms of sentencing practice came from the political left; the popular and political criticisms from the political right and center. It was a powerful if, in the long run, unstable combination. As a result, by the late 1970s indeterminacy of punishment was on the way out in most states, and sentencing reform was on the way in.

Three broad patterns of sentencing reform emerged: voluntary sentencing guidelines developed by the judiciary; legislatively prescribed, fixed-term mandatory sentencing; and systems of presumptive sentencing guidelines. Each of these three approaches to sentencing reform has been tried in several jurisdictions and carefully evaluated. (If you would like some support for my dogmatisms, you should read the 1983 report of the National Academy of Sciences Panel on Research on Sentencing and a study by Michael Tonry in *Crime and Justice*, published in 1988.) Here are the conclusions of those evaluations, in brief form: The voluntary guidelines approach has been found ineffective in reducing sentencing disparity or significantly altering the pattern of disparate sentences that judges impose. The statutory approach increases the proportion of convicted offenders who are sent to prison and the average length of prison terms but is otherwise ineffective in reducing sentencing disparity, though this disparity is effected by the prosecutor rather than the judge. The system of presumptive sentencing guidelines set by a sentencing commission gradually seems to be winning the day, with Minnesota and Washington providing the leading exemplars and the United States Sentencing Commission the most prominent and contentious case.

The idea of a sentencing commission to establish presumptive sentencing guidelines, to monitor and provide feedback to the sentencing system, owes its origin to a proposal of Judge Marvin Frankel that was first offered in a lecture at the University of Cincinnati Law School. That proposal was elaborated in the Minnesota legislation of 1978 that led to the first working system of presumptive sentences and brought three ideas into conjunction: presumptive sentences defined by offense–offender characteristics; appellate review when the judge sentenced outside the guidelines; and a permanent commission to establish the guidelines, monitor their implementation, and modify them as experience and the growth of knowledge might dictate.

Scholarly analysis and the judgment of most Minnesota criminal justice professionals, including the judges, agree that the Minnesota guidelines system brought greater predictability and a larger justice to sentencing in that state than previously obtained. Many states and the federal system have followed in Minnesota's footsteps. Canadian and Australian commissions have urged that those countries do likewise.

Unhappily, the story of the twenty-five years of sentencing reform does not stop there. During those same decades there was another development in this country, and more extensively in western Europe, highly relevant to what you, as an honest politician, must consider if you are to bring principle to this tortured topic. Roughly three-quarters of convicted offenders under the control of the criminal justice system, now and twenty-five years ago, are not in prison; they are on probation or parole. When those responsible for sentencing reform thought about disparity in sentencing and sought to achieve a fairer system of sentencing they tended to think of only two aspects of fairness: the avoidance of unwarranted disparity between those who are sent to prison and those who are not, and the avoidance of unwarranted disparity in the duration of prison sentences imposed—fairness at the "in–out" line, and, if "in," fairness as to time in. What was neglected was extensive experimentation with punishments more severe than probation and less severe than imprisonment. It was as if the only cure for a severe head pain was either an aspirin or a lobotomy. The middle level of punishments, those involving closer control of the offender in the community, were for the most part neglected. Fairness and efficiency were being brought to the polarities of punishment; the development of a fair and efficient *comprehensive* system of punishment was neglected.

Despite this neglect of comprehensive sentencing reform, during the twenty-five years we are discussing, there was extensive experimentation in many states, indeed in all states, with a variety of community-based punishments—

community service orders, house arrest, probation hostels, residential treatment institutions for addicts and alcoholics involved in crime, and many forms of intensive probation supervision backed up by electronic and telephonic monitoring systems. Though it became clear that there were categories of offenders for whom these "intermediate punishments" constituted the most fair, efficient, and economical punishments, there was a failure to blend them into a comprehensive system of punishment; they remained promising experiments rather than institutionalized practice.

The Current Scene

I pick a date, June 30, 1991, and give you the broad figures of the clients of the criminal justice system of the United States at that date to the best of my knowledge. Some figures are lifted from publications by the Bureau of Justice Statistics, which provides the federal government's authoritative statements on these matters; some are extrapolated by my estimation from published figures for the end of the calendar year 1990.

- Over 1,100,000 adults (eighteen and above) in prison or jail in the United States.
- Over 4 1/2 million adults in the United States under some form of correctional supervision.
- One in twenty African-American males in their twenties in prison or jail.
- One in four African-American males in their twenties in prison or jail, on parole, or on probation.

George Bernard Shaw offered the proposition that "one indicator of a sensitive and perceptive person is the capacity to be moved by statistics." Do please consider what those statistics portray.

Perhaps it will help if we contrast the incarceration rates represented by the above figures with the incarceration rate in some countries with which we like to compare ourselves. The following are rates per 100,000 of population at the end of 1990:[1]

Netherlands   36
Sweden   61
United Kingdom   98 (highest in Europe)
Canada   109
South Africa   333
U.S.A.   426

[1]Data were collected from various sources by the author.

It is entirely impossible to explain the gross differences in rates of incarceration among those countries by differences in crime rates. It is true that the United States has higher rates of serious violent crime than other countries, but nothing like that much higher, and our rates of property crime are not at all far removed from those of the United Kingdom. Further, over the past decade, when our rate of incarceration increased by over 120 percent and our rate of probation by 111 percent, the broad pattern of crime revealed a steady decline. The disturbing truth is that crime rates and rates of punishment march to different drummers; clearly, they are in a remote sense connected, but they move up or down independently of one another in both time and place.

To illustrate the point, let us consider the common-sense proposition that if we increase the number of police on the street, we will reduce crime. Repeated experimentation has established, however, that unless one suffuses, swamps, an area with police, one cannot find measurable changes in crime rates. The point can be generalized. The criminal justice system—the police, the prosecutors, the courts, the jails, the prisons, and the rest of the punishment system—have a deterrent effect on the commission of crime, but, and it is a massive "but," marginal changes in any of those systems will not have a measurable effect on crime rates. There is an element of cheating in that statement in the word "measurable." It is not easy, ethically, to measure the relationships between crime and punishment—our measuring systems are gross—but such as they are, they give no comfort to one who would by varying punishment practice vary crime rates.

Cardinal Newman put this as well as I have heard it put: "As well try to steer the ship in a storm by strands of silk, as control the pride and passion of man by threat of punishment."

So, where does that leave you in your unfashionable cloak of political honesty? Fortunately, you do not have to take on the task of reducing crime by manipulating the criminal justice system. Your task is to bring fairness and efficiency to punishing convicted criminals, a much easier task than crime reduction but also no sinecure.

The Path Ahead

As you saw from my sketch of the sentencing "reforms" of the past twenty-five years, guidelines defined by a sentencing commission on powers delegated from a legislature, confining and guiding but not eliminating judicial discretion, have established themselves as the presently preferred method of bringing fairness to judicial sentencing. They are not the only possible method, but they fit the spirit of the common law by which the judge's discretion is guided by a decent respect for the opinion of others and is not left at large. These guidelines are sometimes criticized as being too complicated, too burdensome and technical, but this is a grossly misplaced criticism. No one complains of complexity in commercial adjudication or in a host of other technical aspects of the law—surely, shaping a system to achieve evenhanded justice in sentencing convicted offenders is as difficult a task as any the law faces, and technicality is not at all to be avoided if it assists to that end.

What, then, are the current defects in the emerging guidelines system, so that you can avoid them or minimize them in your political platform?

First: The coexistence of a guideline system and mandatory punishments, or mandatory minimum punishments, is a jurisprudential contradiction. If the sentencing commission is to be trusted, it must be trusted throughout. Mandatory sentences are a sin against the light; they deny the diversity of human behavior. They are political gimmicks, unworthy of any politician, but certainly of any honest politician. You must do your best to see them eliminated, even though this may cost you votes. Work behind the scenes and try to conceal your vote on this matter.

Second: Press for the sentencing commission (if your state has one; if not, you need one) to develop guidelines for the imposition of "intermediate punishments," that is, punishments other than incarceration or ordinary probation. There are many offenders who would be better and more cheaply supervised in the community than in jail or prison. Likewise, there are many offenders who need intensive supervision—by conditions of residence or of treatment rigorously enforced, sometimes buttressed by electronic and telephonic monitoring techniques. This plea for a middle level of punishment, to fill the vacuum between our overcrowded prisons and jails and our overloaded probation systems, is a plea for neither leniency nor severity; it is a plea for justice and efficiency. You should be able to make such a plea without a loss of votes from any but the most fanatical punishers in your electorate.

If you wish, I can spell out the details of this enrichment of our punishment armamentarium beyond the polarities between which it now oscillates, but that is being done by the sentencing commission in several states and even by some academic writings to which you might refer your staff as they shape the details of policy for your consideration.

Overall, the sentencing reforms I have recommended to you would provide more effective crime prevention than our present chaotic arrangements, and would speak symbolically to more than our criminal justice system. They would speak to compassion and healing in communities greatly in need of those qualities.

If your acceptance of my advice, though certainly tending toward justice in punishment, also leads to your loss of incumbency, let me add by way of parting solace that there is also a need for well-informed law teachers with political experience. You might consider the life of an academic; you would fit it with grace, and it has certain advantages, prime among which is that you are not plagued by gratuitous advice on how to behave as a politician.

Author Index

Abrams, Norman, 300*n.17*, 300
Administrative Office of the United States
  Courts, 300*n.8*, 301
Ainsworth, Mary D., 72, 79*n.49*, 86
Akers, Ronald L., 161, 173*n.10*, 174
Alexander, John K., 97, 115*nn.17,21,24*, 117
Allen, Francis A. 33*n.3*, 34
Allen, Harry E., 202*n.125*, 204
Alschuler, Albert W., 300*n.14*, 301
American Correctional Association, 142,
  153
Andenaes, Johannes, 47*n.5*, 48, 61*n.6*, 61
Anderson, Elijah, 174*n.47*, 174,
  245*nn.134,136,137,139,156*, 246*n.158*
Anderson, K. E., 68, 78*n.28*, 80
Angell, John E., 275, 287*n.20*, 288
Annan, Sampson, 243*nn.101,104*, 251
Anthony, Debra, 153*n.3*, 153
Archer, Dane, 202*n.114*, 205
Arditi, Ralph R., 153*n.5*, 153
Arkowitz, Hal S., 78*n.35*, 83
Armor, David, 264*n.16*
Arms, R. L., 77*n.12*, 82
Aronson, Elliot, 70, 78*nn.37,40*, 80, 86
Austin, J. L., 79*n.65*, 80
Ayer, A. J., 79*n.58*, 80

Bacich, A. R., 243*n.101*, 252
Bailey, William C., 238*n.14*
Bandura, Albert, 77*n.12*, 80, 161, 173*n.10*,
  174
Bane, Mary J., 240*n.48*, 250
Banfield, Edward, 112, 117
Bard, Morton, 300*n.11*, 301
Barkley, Russell, 68
Barling, Julian, 76*n.2*, 83
Barkley, Russell A., 78*n.27*, 80

Barkow, Jerome H., 43, 46, 48*nn.20,21*, 48
Barnett, Camille, 203
Baunach, Phyllis Jo, 153*n.7*, 154
Bayley, David, 187, 198*nn.1,2*,
  201*nn.69,73,79,85,87,89*, 202*n.132*,
  203*n.150*, 206, 246, 284, 285, 288*n.44*,
  288
Beccaria, Cesare, 22–23, 34
Becker, Gary, 8, 14*n.6*, 37, 38, 46, 47*n.1*,
  48*n.26*, 48, 199*n.7*, 203
Becker, Howard S., 161, 173*n.20*, 174,
  244*n.117*, 246
Bedau, Hugo Adam, 8, 19–36
Bell, Richard Q., 68, 77*n.22*, 80
Belluci, Patricia A., 241*n.63*, 249
Belson, M. J., 174*n.46*, 176
Bennett, Susan, 198*n.2*, 200*n.57*, 203, 204
Bennett, Trevor, 179, 183, 199*nn.26,35*,
  200*nn.44,48,59,61,63,64,67*, 202*n.112*,
  203*n.144*, 203
Benson-Williams, Lynn, 69, 78*n.31*, 86
Bentham, Jeremy, 8, 22, 37, 38, 48
Berk, Richard A., 242*nn.78,85*,
  243*nn.88,91,92,100,106*, 246, 252
Berkowitz, Leonard, 77*n.12*, 80
Bernard, Thomas J., 96, 115*n.16*, 116*n.44*,
  120, 173*n.19*, 176, 246*nn.160,177*, 247
Binder, Arnold, 264*n.15*
Bing, Leon, 48*n.23*, 48
Bing, Robert, 174*nn.49,52*, 175
Bishop, Donna, 169, 174*nn.49,50*, 174
Bittner, Egon, 286*n.2*
Black, Donald, 242*n.80*, 243*nn.88,90*, 247
Blau, Judith R., 117, 238*n.14*, 241*n.64*, 247
Blau, Peter M., 117, 238*n.14*, 241*n.64*, 247
Block, Carolyn Rebecca, 221, 241*nn.56,58*,
  247

Block, Jack, 72, 79n.51, 83
Block, Jeanne H., 72, 79n.51, 83
Blumenthal, Karen, 153n.7, 154
Blumstein, Alfred, 14n.5, 47n.6, 48n.22, 48, 300n.18, 301
Boggiano, Ann K., 79n.44, 80
Boland, Barbara, 299n.5, 300nn.6,9,10, 301
Boldassare, M., 245n.148, 249
Bolton, P., 77n.25, 85
Bonger, Willem A., 99–100, 116nn.34,35,36, 118
Both, D., 192, 206
Bottoms, Anthony, 180, 198, 198nn.1,2, 199n.33 203n.151, 203
Bowers, Robert, 201n.88, 203
Bowker, Lee n., 226, 242n.85, 243nn.92,98, 244n.109, 245nn.143,147, 247
Bowlby, John, 76n.4, 80
Branham, Vernon C., 116n.37
Brantingham, Patricia, 198n.1, 201nn.97,101, 203, 240n.34, 247
Brantingham, Paul, 198n.1, 201nn.97,101, 203, 240n.34, 247
Breedlove, R. K., 242n.74, 247
Britt, Charles, 173n.31, 174
Brosi, Kathleen, 299n.45, 300n.6, 301
Brown, Charles E., 287n.28, 289
Brown, Lee, 203n.145, 203
Brown, M. Craig, 107, 117n.75, 118
Brown, Stephen E., 172n.2, 173n.18, 174
Brown, Zita, 78n.37, 86
Browne, Angela, 221, 222, 237n.3, 238nn.11,16, 239n.26, 240nn.39,51, 241nn.52,67,77, 242nn.77,79,83, 244nn.127,130,131, 246nn.176,180, 247, 248, 249
Brownstein, Henry H., 241n.63, 249
Bryan, James H., 77n.12, 80
Bucqueroux, Bonnie, 202n.141, 206, 274, 287nn.18,19, 290
Buerger, Michael E., 223, 224, 241nn.71,72, 252
Bugental, Daphne B., 68–69, 78nn.29,30, 80
Bureau of Justice Statistics, 13n.1, 15, 300n.20
Burgess, Edward, 116n.64, 119
Burkhart, Kathryn, 151, 153n.6, 154
Burnett, Camille, 201n.88
Bursik, Robert, Jr., 244n.112, 249
Busch-Rossnagel, N., 245n.152, 247
Bushwall, Steven J., 76n.4, 81
Butler, Joseph, 34, 66, 76nn.6,7, 80

Caesar, P. Lynn, 244n.127, 247
Call, Justin D., 76n.2, 80
Campbell, Alec, 243n.106, 246
Canady, Herman, 118
Cannavale, Frank J., Jr., 300n.11, 301
Cantor, Nancy L., 68, 77n.18, 81
Cantor, Nathaniel, 116n.37, 118
Caporael, Linda, 68, 78n.29, 80
Card, Claudia, 33n.6, 34
Carlsmith, J. Merrill, 67, 70, 76n.4, 77n.16, 78nn.37,40, 80, 81
Carmody, Diane C., 243nn.84,89, 247
Carte, Elaine H., 286nn.9,10, 288
Carte, Gene E., 286nn.9,10, 288
Cazenave, Neal A., 232, 245n.146, 247
Chaiken, Jan, 192, 206
Chambliss, William J., 107, 114n.3, 118, 161, 173n.15, 174
Cheng, Yu-teh, 246n.179, 248
Chin, Ko-lin, 239n.27, 247
Chisholm, Roderick M., 79n.58, 81
Christopher, F. Scott, 79n.46, 81
Christopher, Warren, 288n.39, 288
Citizens' Police Committee, 286n.8, 288
Clark, Peter, 203
Clarke, Ronald, 203
Clarke, Stevens H., 300nn.13,19, 301, 302
Clemmer, E., 286n.4, 289
Cline, Victor B., 70, 78n.38, 81
Clinard, Marshall B., 104, 116n.65, 118
Cloward, Richard A., 159, 160, 172n.5, 174
Cohen, Albert K., 61n.11, 61, 159, 160, 162, 173n.7, 174, 288n.36, 288
Cohen, Bernard, 100, 116nn.39,40, 120
Cohen, Jacqueline, 14n.5, 47n.6, 48, 300n.18, 301
Cohen, Lawrence E., 241n.66, 246
Cohn, Ellen G., 242n.79, 243n.101, 252
Coleman, James S., 234, 238n.18, 244n.122, 246nn.165,166,167, 247
Collins, D. J., 243n.101, 252
Conger, Rand, 161, 173n.10, 174
Cook, Royer, 206
Cooney, Rosemary S., 245n.151, 251
Cornell, Claire P. 209, 237n.2, 249
Courrier, Stevenenneth, 70, 78n.38, 81
Couteur, A. L., 77n.25, 85
Covello, Leonard, 264n.26, 265
Covington, Jeanette, 245n.142, 246n.175, 253
Cox, Sarah, 300n.22, 301
Craig, K. D., 78n.35, 81
Crime Stoppers International, 201n.93, 203
Croft, Roger G., 70, 78n.38, 81
Crouter, A., 244n.125, 249

Cummings, E. Mark, 77*n.10*, 81
Cunningham, Charles E., 68, 78*n.27*, 81
Curry, Elliot, 33*n.14*, 34, 171, 172,
174*nn.55,59*, 174, 200*n.57*, 203
Curtis, Christine, 192,
202*nn.115,116,119,120,124*, 205
Curtis, Lynn, 104, 116*n.63*, 118, 171,
174*nn.55,56*, 174

Dafoe, Janet L., 71, 78*n.43*, 83
Darley, John M., 78*n.37*, 81
Davidson, Donald, 74, 79*nn.66,67*, 81
Davis, Michael, 33*n.19*, 34
Dayley, Robert, 288*n.39*, 288
Dean, Charles W., 243*nn.88,103*, 250
DeBerry, M. M., 238*n.5*, 250
Decker, Scott, 174*nn.49,52*, 175
Dennett, Daniel C., 74, 79*n.68*, 81
Diamond, Shari S., 300*n.18*, 301
Dibble, Ursula, 247
Dieckman, Duane, 287*n.28*, 289
Dion, Karen, 77*n.19*, 81
Dornbusch, Sanford M., 76*n.4*, 81
Downs, Anthony, 177, 198*n.5*, 203
Doyle, Daniel, 244*n.115*, 248
Drabman, Ronald S., 78*n.39*, 86
DuBois, W. E. B., 117*n.94*, 118
Dubow, Eric, 77*n.20*, 81
DuBow, Fred, 200*nn.44,51,52,54,60*,
201*nn.81,100*, 203, 206
Duff, R. A., 34*n.32*, 34, 118
Dumas, Jean E., 70, 78*n.36*, 86
Dummett, Michael, 74, 79*n.68*, 81
Dunford, Franklin W., 243*nn.88,92*,
244*nn.105,114*, 248
Durkheim, Emile, 159, 160, 166, 172*n.3*,
173*n.34*, 175, 181–82, 200*n.46*, 204
Dutton, Donald, 242*n.79*, 243*nn.89,91,93*,
246*nn.176,180,181*, 247, 248, 250

Egeland, Byron, 76*n.2*, 81
Eggers, Mitchell L., 240*n.49*, 241*n.60*, 250
Ehrenwirth, Franz, 61*n.10*, 61
Ehrlich, Isaac, 38, 47, 47*n.6*, 48*n.27*, 48
Eisenberg, Nancy, 77*n.12*, 79*n.46*, 81
Elbow, M., 239*n.21*, 248
Elliott, Delbert S., 215, 238*n.15*, 240*n.44*,
243*nn.87,88,92*, 244*nn.105,114*, 248
Elsea, W. R., 241*n.57*, 251
Elster, Jon, 178, 199*nn.9,10*, 204
Emerson, R., 248
Emery, Gena *n.*, 76*n.9*, 85
Emery, Robert E., 76*n.3*, 81
Emmons, David, 200*nn.51,52*, 201*n.100*, 203

Erickson, Kai, 181, 200*n.47*, 204
Eron, Leonard D., 76*n.2*, 77*nn.12,20*, 81, 83
Esbensen, Finn-Aage, 172*n.2*, 173*n.18*, 174
Etzioni, Amitai, *xi-xii*, 5, 14*n.8*, 15, 177, 178,
197, 199*nn.11,12,14,16,17,36*,
200*nn.43,49*, 203*n.149*, 204
Eysenck, Hans J., 77*n.11*, 85, 161, 163,
173*n.13*, 175

Fabes, Richard A., 79*n.46*, 81
Fagan, Jeffrey, 11, 209–54
Farrington, David, 40, 48*nn.9,12*, 49,
76*nn.2,3*, 77*n.12*, 78*n.42*, 81, 82
Farley, Reynolds, 240*n.49*, 248
Federal Bureau of Investigation, 300*n.7*, 301
Feinberg, Joel, 33*n.25*, 34*n.33*
Feinman, Clarice, 153*n.7*, 154
Feld, Barry C., 169, 174*n.51*, 175
Felson, Marcus, 241*n.66*, 247
Ferdinand, Theodore N., 96, 115*nn.17,20*,
116*n.54*, 118
Ferracuti, Franco, 116*n.62*, 120, 159, 160,
162, 173*n.7*, 176
Feyerherm, William, 169, 170, 173*n.36*,
174*nn.48,53,54*, 175, 176
Fingarette, Herbert, 33*n.18*, 34
Fingerhut, Lois A., 117*n.87*, 118
Finnegan, Terrence, 165, 176
Fischer, Claude S., 245*n.148*, 249
Fisher, Bonnie, 10, 177–207, 297
Fitzpatrick, J. P., 245*nn.150,151*, 249
Flanagan, Timothy, 173*nn.27,28*, 175, 176
Flavin, Jeanne, 289
Flewelling, Robert L., 222, 241*nn.62,68*, 253
Flitcraft, Anne, 238*nn.7,10*, 252
Flowers, Ronald B., 105, 117*nn.66,68*, 118
Fogelson, Robert M., 286*n.6*, 289
Follesdal, D., 74, 79*n.68*, 82
Ford, David A., 243*n.88*, 249
Forst, Brian, 3–15, 177, 199*n.18*, 291–302
Foucalt, Michel, 21–22, 26, 34
Frank, Robert H., 5–6, 14*n.10*, 15
Frankel, Marvin E., 33*n.3*, 35
Frase, Richard S., 299*n.4*, 301
Frazier, Charles, 169, 174*nn.49,50*, 174
Frazier, E. Franklin, 102, 116*nn.37,57*, 118
Freed, David, 287*n.29*, 289
Freedman, Samuel G., 261, 264*n.20*, 265
Frege, Gottlob, 74, 79*nn.60,61*, 82
Freud, Sigmund, 72
Friberg, Lars, 77*n.20*, 84
Friedman, E., 226, 238*n.17*, 243*n.108*, 248
Friedrich, Lynette Kohn, 77*n.12*, 82
Frieze, Irene H., 239*n.26*, 249

Frittner, Andreas, 61
Fulker, David W., 77*n.11*, 85
Fultz, Jim, 79, 81
Fyfe, James J., 11–12, 269–290, 297

Gaguin, D. A., 237*n.1*, 239*n.23*, 249
Gallagher, Bernard, 49
Gallimore, Ronald, 78*n.34*, 82
Galvin, Raymond, 284, 285, 288*nn.45,47*, 290
Garbarino, James, 229, 237*n.1*, 244*nn.125,126*, 245*n.145*, 249
Garland, David, 33*nn.8,10*, 35
Garmezy, Norman, 68, 77*n.23*, 85
Garner, Joel, 209, 240*n.38*, 251, 286*n.4*, 289
Garofalo, James, 191, 192, 199*n.21*, 201*nn.97,103*, 202*n.104*, 204, 284, 285, 288*n.44*, 288
Gartin, Patrick R., 223, 224, 241*nn.71,72*, 243*n.101*, 252
Gauger, Kenneth, 174*n.49*, 175
Gastil, Raymond D., 116*n.62*, 118
Gates, Daryl, 287*n.33*, 289
Geis, Gilbert, 172*n.2*, 173*n.18*, 174, 264*n.15*, 265, 300*n.11*, 301
Gelfand, Donna M., 68, 77*n.18*, 79*n.52*, 81, 82
Gelles, Richard J., 76*n.2*, 82, 209, 213, 237*nn.1,2*, 238*nn.5,9*, 239*nn.24–26,30*, 240*n.42*, 249, 252
Gerson, K., 245*n.148*, 249
Gibbs, Jack, 33*n.23*, 35, 244*n.111*, 249
Gilbert, *n.*, 241*n.76*, 249
Ginsberg, Eli, 39, 49
Glazer, Nathan, 263, 264*n.27*, 265
Glick, Ruth M., 154
Glueck, Eleanor T., 76*n.2*, 82
Glueck, Sheldon, 76*n.2*, 82
Glynn, P., 173*nn.27,28*, 176
Golab, Caroline, 107, 117*n.76*, 118
Goldberg, F., Jr., 153
Goldfarb, William, 69–70, 76*n.4*, 78*n.33*, 82
Goldman, Ivan G., 287*n.35*, 289
Goldsmith, H. H., 77*n.20*, 82
Goldstein, Herman, 185, 201*n.80*, 204, 276, 286*n.2*, 287*n.26*, 288*n.49*, 289
Goldstein, Jeffrey H., 77*n.12*, 82
Goldstein, Paul, J, 241*n.63*, 249
Goldwyn, Ruth, 76*n.2*, 84
Goodman, Robert, 68, 77*n.21*, 82
Goolkasian, Gail A., 242*n.78*, 249
Gottesman, I. I., 77*n.20*, 82
Gottfredson, Michael, 249
Gould, Stephen J., 115*n.7*, 118

Gove, Walter R., 161, 173*n.20*, 175
Grant, J. Douglas, 284, 285, 288*nn.45,47*, 290
Grant, Jane, 183, 200*nn.44,66*, 202*n.112*, 206
Grasmick, Harold, 6, 14*nn.7,11*, 15, 244*n.112*, 249
Greeley, Andrew M., 115*n.19*, 117*n.88*, 118
Green, Donald, 6, 14*nn.7,11*, 15, 79*n.45*
Greenberg, David F, 48*n.22*, 49, 161, 173*n.17*, 175, 240*n.46*
Greenberg, Stephanie W., 287*n.23*, 289
Greene, David, 71, 78*nn.43,45*, 82, 83
Griesinger, Harriet, 40, 48*n.11*, 49
Gross, Hyman, 33*n.25*, 35
Gross, Ruth T., 76*n.4*, 81
Grossman, Eugene E., 86
Grossman, Michelle, 202*nn.105,109*, 206
Groves, Walter B., 161, 173*nn.15,22–24*, 175, 243*n.95*, 244*n.123*, 252
Grunberger, Richard, 60*n.5*, 61
Grusec, Joan E., 77*n.14*, 82
Guardian, The, 264*nn.3–6*, 265

Hackney, S., 116*n.62*, 117*n.86*, 118
Hagedorn, John, 173*n.40*, 175, 249
Hale, Donna, 204
Haller, Mark H., 116*n.26*, 118
Hamilton, Edwin, 243*nn.101,104*, 251
Hampton, Robert L., 239*n.30*, 249
Handlin, Oscar, 97, 115*nn.17,22*, 118
Handy, William, 238*n.20*, 251
Hannerz, Ulf, 245*n.140*, 246*n.162*, 249
Hansen, Karen V., 244*n.128*, 248
Harding, Christopher 33*n.8*, 35
Harlow, Caroline W., 238*nn.6,11,13*, 249
Harrington, David M., 72, 79*n.51*, 83
Harrington, R., 77*n.25*, 85
Harrop, J. W., 239*n.30*, 249
Hart, H. L. A., 23, 33*nn.25,31*, 35
Hart, Henry M., Jr., 33*n.25*, 35
Hart, S. G., 242*n.79*, 243*nn.89,91,93*
Hartle, M. M., 153
Hartmann, Donald, 79*n.52*, 82
Hartup, Willard W., 77*n.25*, 82
Hastorf, Albert H., 76*n.4*, 81
Hawkins, Darnell, 9–10, 89–120, 173*n.39*, 175, 246*nn.176,178*, 250
Hawkins, Gordon, 12, 14*n.13*, 244*n.110*
Hawkins, Richard, 227, 242*nn.79,81–83,85*, 243*nn.85,86,89,93*, 244*nn.113,116,118,120*, 253
Henderson, Joel, 192, 202*nn.115,116,119,120,124*, 205
Hernon, Jolene, 300*n.25*, 301

Herrenkohl, Ellen C., 76*n.2*, 83
Herrenkohl, Roy C., 76*n.2*, 83
Herrnstein, Richard J., 115*n.7*, 120, 173*n.14*, 176
Herskovits, Melville, 102, 116*n.57*, 118
Hertz, Elica, 200*n.62*, 204, 205
Hill, Robert, 119
Hindelang, Michael J., 100, 108, 114*n.1*, 116*n.38*, 117*n.80*, 118
Hirsch, E. D., Jr., 258, 264*n.14*, 265
Hirschel, J. David, 243*nn.88,103*, 250
Hirschi, Travis, 76*nn.3,4*, 83, 161–63, 173*n.8*, 175, 249
Hirschman, Albert, 8, 37, 40, 42, 43, 45, 48*nn.14,15,19,24*, 49
Hirshleifer, Jack, 47*n.3*, 49
Hobbes, Thomas, 66, 76*n.5*, 83
Hobbs, E. A., 115*nn.17,18*, 118
Hoekema, David, 33*nn.12,25*, 35
Hoffman, Martin L., 77*n.14*, 83
Hogan, Robert, 72, 79*n.49*, 86
Hogarth, John, 300*n.18*, 301
Hollenbeck, Barbara, 76*n.10*, 81
Honderich, Ted, 33*n.12*, 35
Horne, Peter, 187, 201*n.86*, 204
Horton, Robert W., 78*n.39*, 86
Hotaling, Gerald T., 238*n.8*, 240*n.47*, 244*n.127*, 245*n.144*, 250
Hough, Michael, 202*nn.106,108*, 204
Hourihan, Kevin, 204
Hudson, Barbara, 33*n.7*, 35
Huesmann, L. Rowell, 76*n.2*, 77*nn.12,20*, 81, 83
Hughes, Graham, 8–9, 51–61
Hugo, Victor, 255, 264*n.2*, 265, 276
Huizinga, David, 215, 238*n.15*, 240*n.44*, 243*nn.87,88,92*, 244*nn.105,114*, 248
Hume, David, 66, 76*n.8*, 83
Hutchison, Ira W., 243*nn.88,103*, 250

Iannotti, Ronald, 76*n.10*, 81
Ireland, Richard 33*n.8*, 35

Jackson, R. M., 245*n.148*, 249
Jackson, Robert H., 61*n.9*, 61, 291, 299*n.1*, 301
Jacklin, Carol *n.*, *68*, 78*n.26*, 84
Jacoby, Joan, 299*n.4*, 301
Janowitz, Morris, 230, 245*n.132*, 250
Jargowsky, Paul, 240*n.48*, 250
Jeffery, Clarence R., 173*n.12*, 175
Johnson, Guy B., 103, 116*nn.37,60*, 119
Jones, L. M., 245*n.148*, 249
Jones, Nolan, 173*n.39*, 175

Jouriles, Ernest *N.*, 76*n.2*, 83
Jurik, Nancy, 221, 241*nn.51,54*, 250
Justice Statistics, Office of Justice Programs, 250

Kant, Immanuel, 72, 79*n.47*, 83
Karniol, Rachel, 79*n.45*, 85
Kasarda, John, 230, 245*n.132*, 250
Katz, Jack, 8, 37, 46, 47*n.4*, 48*n.25*, 49, 119
Kelling, George, 185–86, 199*n.39*, 200*n.45*, 201*nn.68,70–72,74–78,82,88*, 204, 205, 206, 287*n.28*, 289
Kelly, J. J., 250
Kelly, Thomas V., 287*n.20*, 290
Kemp, Bryan, 78*n.34*, 82
Kempf, Kimberly, 174*nn.49,52*, 175
Kennedy, L. W., 242*n.79*, 243*nn.89,91,93*, 248, 250
Kennish, J. W., 241*n.74*, 247
King, Marianna, 199*n.22*, 201*n.90*, 202*n.122*, 204
King, Robert A., 72, 76*n.9*, 77*n.12*, 79*n.50*
Kirschenman, Joleen, 246*n.174*, 251
Kitsuse, John I., 161, 173*n.20*, 175
Kittrie, Nicholas, 33*n.5*, 35
Klap, Ruth, 243*n.106*, 246
Klaus, P. A., 173*n.45*, 175, 238*n.4*, 250
Klein, Lloyd, 199*n.22*, 201*n.90*, 202*n.122*, 204
Kleinman, Joel C., 117*n.87*, 118
Klockars, Carl, 280, 283, 287*n.34*, 288*n.41*, 289
Konstantin, David, 286, 289
Kopel, Steven A., 78*n.35*, 83
Korner, Anneliese F., 69, 78*n.31*, 86
Kort, Fred, 43, 48*n.18*, 49
Kuhl, Anna, 221, 241*n.59*, 250
Kurtz, P. David, 174*n.49*, 175
Kutash, Samuel B., 116*n.37*
Kuttner, Robert, 178, 199*n.15*, 204

Lab, Steven, 199*nn.23,28,29,31*, 200*nn.59,60,64*, 201*nn.81,101*, 202*nn.113,117,129,140*, 203*n.146*, 204
Lacey, Nicola, 33*n.12*, 35
Lamb, Ann, 79*n.52*, 82
Landauer, T. K., 67, 77*n.16*, 81
Landis, Jean, 153*n.8*, 154
Lane, Roger, 109, 115*n.17*, 117*nn.69,83,89*, 119
Langbein, John H., 300*n.12*, 301
Lashley, R. L., 78*n.37*, 85
Latessa, Edward, 202*n.125*, 204
Lattimore, Pamela, 48*n.9*, 49

Laub, John H., 76n.4, 83, 238n.14, 239n.32, 250
Lauritsen, Janet, 238nn.6,12,15, 240nn.41,46, 246n.175, 252
Lavrakas, Paul, 198n.2, 200nn.57,62, 201nn.94,96, 203, 204, 205, 206
Le Figaro, 264nn.7–11,13, 265
Leiderman, Herbert, 76n.4, 81
Lemann, Nicholas, 168, 173n.43, 175
Lemert, Edwin M., 161, 173n.20, 175
Lentzner, H. R., 238n.5, 250
Leonik, Robert, 204
Lepper, Mark R., 67, 71, 77n.16, 78nn.41,43, 79n.45, 81, 82, 83
Levin, Harry, 78n.25, 85
Lewis, C. I., 79nn.57,58, 83
Lewis, Dan, 183, 200nn.44,62,66, 202n.112, 204, 206
Lewis, Dorothy O., 76n.2, 83
Lewis, Oscar, 103, 116n.61, 119, 245n.158, 250
Lewis, V., 226, 238n.17, 243n.108, 248
Leyens, Jacques P., 77n.12, 80
Liebow, Elliot, 233–34, 246nn.158,159,161,164, 250
Lippincott, Elaine C., 78n.39, 86
Liska, Alan E., 76n.4, 83
Locke, John, 67, 77n.15, 83
Lockhart, Lettie, 174n.49. 175
Loeber, Rolf, 76nn.3,4, 78n.25, 83, 85
Loftin, Colin, 119, 240n.33, 241n.62, 250
Logan, Charles H., 244n.111, 253
London, Perry, 77n.12, 80
Lorimor, T. D., 241n.70, 251
Lovell, R., 171, 174n.57, 175
Lovely, Richard, 76n.2, 83
Lowry, Ira S., 115n.8, 119
Lucianovic, Judith, 300n.22, 301
Luckenbill, David, 244n.115, 248
Lurigio, Arthur, 189–90, 201nn.94–96, 203n.147, 205, 206
Luxenburg, Joan, 199n.22, 201n.90, 202n.122, 204
Lynch, Michael J., 161, 173nn.15,22–24, 175
Lytton, Hugh, 68, 77n.25, 78n.28, 80, 84

Maas, Peter, 288n.39, 289
Maccoby, Eleanor E., 68, 78nn.25,26, 79n.48, 84, 85
Macdonald, H., 77n.25, 85
MacKenzie, Ellen, 240n.33, 250
Macon, Perry, 249
Maddala, G., 240n.45, 250
Maguire, Kathleen, 175

Maher, Lisa, 223, 241n.73, 253
Mahon, Mary Ann, 79n.52, 82
Main, Deborah S., 79n.44, 80
Main, Mary, 76n.2, 84
Mann, Coramae, 175
Manning, Peter K., 269, 276, 282, 286, 286n.1, 288n.40,53, 289
Mansbridge, Jane, 5, 14n.9, 15, 177, 178, 198n.4, 199nn.8,13,38, 205
Margarita, Mona, 286n.4, 289
Margolis, Howard, 205
Martinson, Robert, 32n.1, 35
Marx, Gary, 182, 199n.21, 200n.53, 201n.102, 202nn.114,115, 205
Massey, Douglas S., 240n.49, 241n.60, 245n.155, 250
Masters, Roger, 42, 48n.17, 49
Mastrofski, Stephen D., 283, 287n.22, 288nn.42,43, 289
Maurer, Mark, 246n.174, 250
Maxfield, Michael, 199n.24, 200n.59, 206
Maxwell, Christopher, 209
May-Plumlee, Tracy, 79n.46, 81
Mayhew, Pat, 202nn.106,108, 204
McClearn, G. E., 77n.20, 84
McCord, Joan, 9, 65–87
McDonald, William, 299n.4, 300n.22, 301
McGowen, Brenda, 153n.7, 154
McKay, Henry D., 116n.48, 119
McKenzie, R. D., 116n.64, 119
McLanus, Tina, 297, 300nn.21,23, 301
McLeod, Maureen, 191, 192, 199n.21, 201nn.97,103, 202n.104, 204
McPherson, Marlys, 205
Mercy, James A., 221, 241nn.51,53,55,57, 250, 251
Merton, Robert K., 116nn.41,42,46, 119, 159, 160, 172n.4, 175
Messner, Steven F., 108, 116n.62, 117n.82, 119, 240n.41, 241nn.61,65, 250
Meyer, J. K., 241n.70, 251
Miller, Walter B., 103, 104, 116n.61, 119, 159, 160, 172n.7, 175
Miller, Susan, 242n.80, 243nn.89,96, 251
Milton, Catherine H., 287n.20, 290
Mock, Lois, 240n.51, 251
Monkkonen, Eric H., 104, 115n.24, 116n.65, 119, 286n.5, 289
Morley, Lynda, 49
Moore, Kathleen Dean, 34n.35, 35
Moore, Mark, 186, 201nn.70–72,76,78,83,84,88, 202nn.131,135, 204, 205

Morris, Herbert, 33n.5, 35
Morris, Norval, 12–13, 14n.13, 15,
   303–10
Morse, Barbara, 215, 240n.44, 248
Moy, Ernest, 76n.2, 83
Moynihan, Patrick P., 116n.47, 119
Mukherjee, S. K., 241n.58
Musolino, Angela, 154
Myers, Samuel L., Jr., 42, 48n.16, 49,
   173n.35, 176

Nagin, Daniel, 14n.5, 47n.6, 48n.22, 48,
   244n.121, 251, 300n.18, 301
Napper, George, 241n.57, 251
National Commission on Law Observance
   and Enforcement, 115n.10, 119
Neale, Michael C., 77n.11, 85
Neckerman, Katherine M., 246n.174, 251
Neiderhoffer, Arthur, 280, 287n.32, 289
Nelli, Humbert S., 106, 116n.25,
   117nn.70,72, 119
Netherlands Ministry of Justice, 199n.37,
   205
Neto, Virginia, 154
Newell, H. W., 76n.4, 84
Newton, Phyllis, 242nn.78,85, 246
Nias, David K. B., 77n.11, 85
Nietzsche, Friedrich, 22, 25, 26, 35
Nimick, Ellen, 165, 176
Nisbett, Robert E., 79n.45, 83
Normoyle, Janice, 200n.62, 204
Nozick, Robert, 33nn.6,22, 35
Nutall, Christopher, 198n.1, 201n.71,
   205

Offord, David R., 76n.2, 84
Ohlin, Lloyd E., 159, 172n.5, 174
O'Leary, K. Danise, 76n.2, 83
Olson, Mancur, 198n.3, 205

Padilla, Felix, 245n.151, 251
Pagelo, Mildred, 251
Palmer, Stanley H., 287n.27, 289
Park, Robert, 116n.64, 119
Parke, Ross D., 77n.12, 80
Parker, Robert Nash, 222, 238n.6,
   241nn.62,69, 250, 251, 252
Parnas, Raymond, 238n.20, 251
Parpal, Mary, 79n.48, 84
Pate, Antony, 202n.139, 203n.142, 205,
   243nn.101,104, 251, 287n.28, 289
Pateman, Carole, 202n.133, 205
Paternoster, Raymond, 244n.121, 251
Patterson, G. R., 78n.25, 85

Paul, Steven, 79n.52, 82
Pederson, Nancy, 77n.20, 84
Pennell, Susan, 192,
   202nn.115,116,119,120,124, 205
Perez, Douglas, 286n.14, 289
Pesackis, C., 250
Peters, J. H., 153
Petracca, Mark, 198n.4, 199n.6, 205
Petrie, Carol, 240n.38, 251
Phelps, W. R., 153
Phillips, Llad, 8, 37–49
Pincoffs, Edmund, 33n.21, 35
Pincus, Jonathan, 76n.2, 83
Piper, Elizabeth S., 246n.179, 248
Pitman, David J., 238n.20, 251
Plato, 73, 76n.1, 79n.56, 84
Plomin, Robert, 77n.20, 84
Podolefsky, Aaron, 198n.2, 200nn.44,54,60,
   201n.81, 203, 205, 206
Police Foundation, 289
Pope, Carl E., 10, 116n.43, 119, 157–176
Powell, Elwin H., 109, 117n.84, 119
Price, H. H., 79n.58, 84
Primoratz, Igor, 33n.16, 35
Pulkkinen, Lea, 76n.2, 84
Pyle, Claudia, 87

Quine, Willard V. O., 74, 79nn.59,67,69,
   84
Quinney, Richard, 92, 107, 114n.3,
   115nn.11,12 117nn.71,73,74, 119, 161,
   173n.21, 176

Radke-Yarrow, Marian, 72, 76nn.9,10,
   77n.12, 79n.50, 81, 86, 87
Rainwater, Lee, 245n.158, 251
Rand, M. R., 173n.45, 175, 238n.4, 250
Rankin, Joseph H., 76n.4, 86
Rapaport, Elizabeth, 153n.2, 154
Rawls, John, 23, 33nn.25,26,28, 35
Reed, Mark D., 76n.4, 83
Reid, John B., 77n.25, 85
Reidel, Mark, 240n.51, 251
Reiss, Albert J., Jr., 238n.6, 240n.36, 251,
   287n.17, 289, 291, 299n.2, 302
Reppetto, Thomas, 179, 199n.27, 206
Reuss-Ianni, Elizabeth, 281, 287n.35,
   288n.37, 289
Rheingold, Harriet, 76n.9, 85
Richards, Daid A. J., 33n.25, 35
Riese, Marilyn L., 69, 78n.32, 85
Ritter, Philip L., 76n.4, 81
Roberts, Julian, 202nn.105,109, 206
Robins, Lea, 76n.2, 85

Roehl, Janice, 206
Rogan, Dennis P., 243*n.101*, 252
Rogler, Lloyd, 245*n.151*, 251
Rohe, William M., 287*n.23*, 289
Rohlen, Thomas P., 264*n.25*, 265
Romanoff, Richard, 77*n.20*, 81
Romney, D. M., 68, 78*n.28*, 80
Rosellini, Robert A., 78*n.37*, 85
Rosenbaum, Dennis, 180–81, 183, 190, 192, 196, 197, 198*n.1*, 199*nn.19,25,30,32,34*, 200*nn.41,44,50,53,55,56,58,60,64,66*, 201*nn.91,92,94–96,99*, 202*nn.110,112,116,121,125–28,138,139*, 203*nn.143,146–48*, 205, 206
Rosenberg, Mark L., 241*n.57*, 251
Rosenhan, D., 77*n.12*, 85
Ross, Dorothea, 77*n.12*, 80
Ross, Michael, 79*n.45*, 85
Ross, Sheila, 77*n.12*, 80
Roth, Jeffrey A., 238*n.6*, 251, 287*n.31*, 289
Roth, L. H., 173*n.12*, 176
Rothmiller, Mike, 287*n.35*, 289
Rothstein, Mitch, 79*n.45*, 85
Rubinstein, Jonathan, 287*nn.24,25*, 289, 300*n.13*, 302
Rushton, J. Philippe, 77*nn.11,12*, 85
Russell, Diana E. H., 239*n.26*, 251
Rutter, Michael, 68, 77*n.23*, 78*n.25*, 85
Ryan, Patrick, 241*n.63*, 249

Sabol, William, 42, 48*n.16*, 49
Sagotsky, Gerald, 71, 78*n.43*, 83
St. Ledger, Raymond, 49
Salem, Gerta, 200*n.62*, 204
Saltzman, Linda E., 221, 241*nn.51,53,55,57*, 250, 251
Samaha, Joel, 115*n.23*, 119
Sampson, Robert J., 76*n.4*, 83, 238*nn.6,12,14,15*, 239*n.32*, 240*nn.41,46,50*, 243*nn.87,95*, 244*nn.122,123*, 245*nn.141,143,154*, 246*nn.168,170,173,175*, 251, 252
Sanborn, Frank M., 98, 99, 116*n.30*, 119
Sangrey, Dawn, 300*n.11*, 301
Sanker, D. M., 241*n.74*, 247
Sawtell, R. K., 241*n.74*, 247
Schaefer, Richard T., 117*nn.77,88*, 119
Scharff, William H., 77*n.12*, 86
Schlottman, Robert S., 77*n.12*, 86
Schmidt, Janelle D., 243*n.101*, 252
Schmidt, Peter, 39, 47*n.8*, 49
Schneider, Anne, 199*nn.20,21*, 206

Schultz, Theodore, 39
Schur, Edwin M., 161, 173*n.20*, 176
Scott, Eric, 274, 287*n.17*, 290
Scott, Phyllis M., 77*n.13*, 86
Searle, John R., 74, 79*n.68*, 85
Sears, Robert R., 78*n.25*, 85
Sebastian, Richard J., 77*n.12*, 80
Sedlak, Andrea J., 237*n.1*, 252
Seidman, Robert B., 107, 114*n.3*, 118, 161, 173*n.15*, 174
Sellars, Wilfrid, 73, 74, 79*nn.55,63,68*, 85
Sellin, Thorsten, 99, 100, 101–03, 109, 116*nn.31–33,50–53,55,56,58,59*, 117*n.85*, 119, 173*n.15*
Shah, S. A., 173*n.12*, 176
Shaw, Clifford, 116*n.48*, 119
Shennum, William A., 68–69, 78*nn.29,30*, 80
Sherman, Deborah, 229, 244*n.126*, 249
Sherman, Lawrence W., 223, 224, 241*nn.71–73,75*, 242*nn.78,79*, 243*nn.88,91,99,101,102*, 244*n.119*, 252, 253, 287*n.20*, 290
Shils, Edward, 264, 264*n.28*, 265
Shipley, Thomas E., Jr., 78*n.37*, 85
Sickmund, Melissa, 165, 176
Sikes, R. K., 241*n.57*
Silberman, Charles E., 159, 160, 172*n.6*, 176
Silberman, Matthew, 244*n.111*, 252
Silloway, Glenn, 205
Simms, Margaret C., 173*n.35*, 176
Simon, Rita, 10, 121–54
Simonoff, E., 77*n.25*, 85
Simpson, Sally, 242*n.80*, 243*n.89*, 251
Singer, Richard, 33*n.4*, 35
Skinner, B. F. 33*n.13*, 35, 79*n.53*, 85
Skogan, Wesley G., 177, 181, 198*n.2*, 199*nn.24,38,40*, 200*nn.42,52,54,58,62,64*, 201*n.101*, 202*nn.130,137*, 204, 206, 241*n.73*, 252
Skolnick, Jerome, 187, 198*nn.1,2*, 201*nn.69,73,79,85,87,89*, 202*n.132*, 203*n.150*, 206, 269, 287*n.29*, 288*n.38*, 290
Skubiski, Sandra L., 77*n.14*, 82
Slote, Michael, 198*n.4*, 206
Smith, Adam, 46, 49
Smith, C., 238*n.5*, 239*n.28*, 253
Smith, Cathleen, 79*n.52*, 82
Smith, Douglas A., 115*n.5*, 117*n.81*, 120, 243*n.101*, 244*n.119*, 252
Snyder, Howard, 165, 173*nn.25,26,30*, 176
Socrates, 65, 73
Solicitor General of Canada, 202*n.107*, 206

Solomon, Richard L., 70, 78*n.37*, 85
Sones, Ronald, 299*n.5*, 300*nn.6,10*, 301
Sorenson, Susan B., 239*nn.28,29*, 252
Spitzer, Elinor, 76*n.2*, 83
Sroufe, Alan, 76*n.2*, 81
Stack, Carol, 244*n.149*, 245*n.158*, 252
Stark, Evan, 238*nn.7,10*, 252
Staub, Ervin, 77*n.12*, 86
Stayton, Donald J., 72, 79*n.49*, 86
Stein, Aletha Huston, 77*n.12*, 82
Steinberg, Stephen, 97, 112, 115*n.9*,
    116*nn.27,29*, 117*nn.90,91*, 120
Steinmetz, Suzanne, 237*n.1*, 238*n.9*, 252
Stevenson, Jim, 68, 77*n.21*, 82
Stewart, Douglas, 244*n.129*, 248
Stouthamer-Loeber, Magda, 76*nn.3,4*, 83
Straus, Murray A., 210, 213, 215, 232,
    237*n.1*, 238*nn.4,5,9*, 239*nn.22–26,28,31*,
    240*nn.42,51*, 241*n.52*, 245*n.146*, 247,
    249, 252, 253
Strawson, Peter F., 35
Stueve, C. A., 245*n.148*, 249
Stutphen, Richard, 174*n.49*, 175
Sugarman, D. B., 238*n.8*, 240*n.47*, 244*n.127*,
    245*n.144*, 250
Sullivan, Dennis, 165, 176
Sutherland, Edwin H., 101, 116*nn.49,51*,
    120
Suttles, G. D., 246*n.158*, 253

Tardiff, K., 119
Tarski, Alfred, 74, 79*n.62*, 86
Tauchen, Helen, 40, 48*n.11*, 49
Taylor, Ralph, 245*n.142*, 246*n.175*, 253
Tayman, Jeff, 192, 202*nn.115,116,119*, 205
Telles, Cynthia A., 239*nn.28,29*, 252
Ten, C. L., 33*n.12*, 35
Tharp, Roland G., 78*n.34*, 82
Theiss, Stephen M., 78*n.35*, 81
Thoman, Evelyn B., 69, 78*n.31*, 86
Thomas, Margaret H., 78*n.39*, 86
Thomas, Wayne H., 287*n.31*, 290
Thornberry, Terrence, 173*nn.27,28*, 176
Tierney, J., 165, 176
Tittle, Charles, 89–90, 93, 100, 104, 108,
    114*n.4*, 115*nn.5–7,15,16*, 116*n.45*,
    117*nn.67,81*, 120, 240*n.33*, 244*n.111*,
    253
Toby, Jackson, 11, 226, 243*n.95*, 244*n.119*,
    253, 255–65
Tolnay, S., 173*nn.27,28*, 176
Toch, Hans, 284, 285, 288*nn.45–48*, 290
Tonry, Michael, 306
Toth, A. M., 222, 238*n.6*, 241*n.69*, 251

Trojanowicz, Robert, 186, 195,
    201*nn.76,78,83,84*,
    202*nn.131,134–36,139,141*, 203*n.142*,
    205, 206, 274, 287*nn.18,19*, 290
Troyer, Ron, 193, 202*nn.123,125*, 206
Turk, Austin, 161, 173*n.16*, 176
Twentieth Century Fund, 33*n.4*, 35

United States Bureau of Census, 264*n.22*, 265
United States Department of Commerce,
    286*n.15*, 290
United States Department of Education,
    264*n.24*, 265
United States Department of Health,
    Education, and Welfare, 264*n.12*, 265
United States Department of Justice,
    201*n.98*, 206
United States Immigration Commission,
    115*n.10*, 116*n.28*, 120
United States Senate Committee on
    Immigration, 264*n.23*, 265
United States Sentencing Commission, 35

Van Vechten, C. C., 92, 115*n.12*, 120
Van Winkle, B. J., 241*n.58*
Villemez, Wayne J., 115*n.5*, 117*nn.67,81*,
    120
Vogel, M., 192, 206
Vold, George B., 96, 115*n.16*, 116*n.44*, 120,
    173*n.19*, 176
von Hirsch, Andrew, 33*nn.4,6*, 35
Votey, Harold L., Jr., 40, 47*nn.2,7*,
    48*nn.10,13*, 49

Wacquant, L., 167, 173*nn.37,38*, 176,
    240*n.48*, 246*n.174*, 253
Wagner, Elizabeth, 87
Wahler, Robert G., 70, 78*n.36*, 86
Walker, Christopher, 201*n.71*, 206
Walker, Lenore E., 238*n.16*, 253
Walker, Samuel, 172, 174*n.58*, 176, 286*n.6*,
    290
Walker, Sandra-Gail, 201*n.71*, 206
Walster, Elaine, 78*n.37*, 86
Warner, Barbara D., 107, 117*n.75*, 118
Wasserman, Robert, 201*n.68*, 204
Wasserstrom, Richard A., 33*n.25*, 35
Waxler, Carolyn Zahn, 77*n.13*, 86
Waxweiler, R., 241*n.57*, 251
Webster, John, 287*n.17*, 290
Weinreb, Lloyd L., 300*n.12*, 301
Weis, Joseph F., 238*n.11*, 253
Weisburd, David L., 223, 241*n.73*, 253
Wells, L. Edward, 76*n.4*, 86

Wellford, Charles, 300n.18, 301
Wertheimer, Max, 255, 264n.1, 265
West, Donald J., 49, 78n.42, 82
West, Steven, 77n.12, 80
Western, Bruce, 243n.106, 246
Wexler, S., 226, 238n.17, 243nn.77,108, 248
White, Glenn M., 77n.12, 85, 86
White, Teresa J., 300n.13, 302
Whyte, William F., 245n.157, 253
Wice, Paul, 287n.31, 289
Widom, Cathy S., 76n.2, 86, 244nn.127,129, 253
Wilbach, Harry, 120
Wilkens, Judy L., 77n.12, 86
Williams, Hubert, 201n.68, 204
Williams, Kirk R., 221, 222, 227, 241n.52, 241nn.62,67,68, 242nn.79,81–83, 243nn.85,86,89,91,93, 244nn.113,116,118,120, 247, 248, 253
Williams, Nicolas, 177
Wilson, James Q., 3, 6, 13n.2, 14nn.3,4,11, 15, 32n.2, 35, 53, 61nn.7,8, 61, 115n.7, 120, 173n.14, 176, 199n.39, 200n.45, 203, 206, 271, 274–75, 286nn.6,7,11–13,16, 287nn.17, 20,23, 290, 302
Wilson, William J., 112, 117n.93, 167, 172, 173nn.33,37,38,41,42, 176, 240nn.48,50, 243n.87, 245n.133, 245nn.135,138,141,153,154, 246nn.160,171,173, 252, 253, 305

Winn, Russell, 221, 241nn.51,54, 250
Wirth, Louis, 240n.35, 253
Wispé, Lauren, 77n.14, 86
Witte, Ann, 39, 47n.8, 48nn.9,11, 49
Witte, Kenneth L., 86
Wittgenstein, Ludwig, 79nn.58,64, 86
Wolfe, Tom, 299n.3, 302
Wolfgang, Marvin E, 100, 107, 116nn.39,62, 117n.78, 120, 159, 160, 162, 168, 173nn.7,44, 176, 241n.63, 254
Wright, Ronald, 179, 199nn.26,35, 202n.125, 203, 206
Wycoff, Mary Ann, 202nn.130,137, 203n.145, 203, 206

Yarmel, Patty, 77n.20, 81
Yarrow, Leon J., 78n.25, 86
Yarrow, Marian Radke, 77n.13, 86
Yin, Robert, 192, 206

Zahn, Margaret A., 240n.51, 251
Zahn-Waxler, Carolyn, 72, 76nn.9,10, 77n.12, 79n.50, 81, 86, 87
Zayas, L., 245n.152, 247
Zeisel, Hans, 300n.18, 301
Zimring, Frank E., 33n.7, 35, 241n.58, 243n.88, 244n.110, 254
Zingraff, Michael T., 174n.46, 176
Zuravin, Susan J., 238n.6, 244n.124, 254

Subject Index

African-Americans
 and crime, 89, 92, 96–101, 111–12,
  113–14, 164–65, 303–04
 incarceration rates, 303–04
 spouse assualt, 210, 213–22, 232,
  236, 240*nn.43,50*, 245*n.174*
 see also Crime and ethnicity
Altruism, 46, 67, 72
Anomie, 100, 159
Arrest data, 123–34
Asian-Americans
 and crime, 92, 106, 109–10
 see also Crime and ethnicity
Attica prison riot, 20

Barry, Marion, 291, 296
Berkeley (California) Police Department,
 270, 271, 275
Beyond Self-Interest (Mansbridge), 5
Biogenic theory, 161, 163
Block watch programs. *See* Neighborhood
 watch programs
Bonfire of the Vanities (Wolfe), 299*n.3*
British Crime Survey, 191
Broken windows (hypothesis), 180–81
 police response to, 187
Brooklyn (New York) Community
 Prosecution, 298–99

Canadian Urban Victimization Survey,
 191
Capital punishment, 21–22, 38
Carjacking, *xi*
Character. *See* Crime and character
Chicano-Americans and crime. *See* Hispanic-
 Americans and crime
Child abuse research findings, 229

Citizen crime-watch programs. *See*
 Neighborhood watch programs
Communication and behavior, 72–76
Communitarianism, 10
Community-oriented policing, 185–88,
 193–96, 274–75
 citizen ride-along approach, 194
 door-to-door approach, 194
 effectiveness of, 195–96
 foot patrol approach, 195–96
 future prospects of, 197
 mini-station approach, 188, 195
 newsletter approach, 194
Community responses to crime, 10, 59–60,
 181–98
 motivations for, 177–78
 see also Fear of crime, community
  responses to
Compassion, 13
Conflict Tactics Scale (CTS), 239*n.25*
Conflict theory, 161, 164
Conscience and family, 72–76
Consequentialism. *See* Punishment and
 consequentialism
Construct theory, 9, 73–75
Continuing Criminal Enterprises (CCE), 8,
 51–52
Convictions and gender, 136–42
Crime
 and character, 6–7, 13
 costs, 3
 and culture, 9, 11, 43, 89–120
 and economic inequality, 93–101, 110
 and education, 40, 168
 and ethnicity, 9–10, 89–120
 and family, 9, 47, 65–87, 168
 and gangs, 45

Crime *(continued)*
   and gender, 10, 121–54
   and poverty, 9, 159, 163, 217
   private defenses against, 179–81
   and rationality, 3–4, 9, 55–57
   responses to, 3, 10
   "root causes" of, 182
   and socioeconomic status, 90–91,
     159–62, 209–10, 213
   and unemployment, 40
   see also Delinquency; Fear of crime;
     School violence; Spouse assault
Crime Stopper programs, 10, 188–90, 191,
   194–95
Criminal justice system, 11–13, 59–60
Criminologists, 3–4, 14*n.14*
Cultural Literacy (Hirsch), 258
Cultural variance perspective, 93–95,
   101–04, 110–11
Culture. *See* Crime and culture

Death Penalty. *See* Capital punishment
Delinquency, 10, 157–76
   process theories of, 158, 161–63, 170,
     171
   reaction theories of, 158, 161, 163–64,
     169–70
   structural theories of, 158–62, 166,
     170, 171
   theoretical explanations for, 158–64
   and unemployment, 160, 166,
   see also Crime
Deontology, 24, 27–29
Deterrence, 4, 9, 20, 38–40, 52–55, 58
   and need for credible punishment, 30
Dewey, Thomas, 299*n.3*
Dillinger, John, 271
Domestic violence. *See* Spouse assault
Drug kingpins, 51
Drug law violations, 165, 275
Drug war, *xi*, 296

Economic inequality. *See* Crime and
   economic inequality
Economics and crime, 37–51
   neoclassical, *xi-xii*, 3–7, 10, 14*n.6*,
     55–57
Education. *See* Crime and education
Egoistic theory of human nature, 65–67
Equal Rights Amendment, 150
Ethnicity. *See* Crime and ethnicity
Exit, 37–38, 42–43
Exit, Voice, and Loyalty (Hirschman), 37, 49
Experiments on behavior, 67–73

Familism, 245*n.151*
Family. *See* Crime and family, Conscience
   and family
Family violence. *See* Spouse assault
Fear of crime, 180, 181, 183, 186
   community responses to, 188–96
Federal Sentencing Guidelines, 21
Flint (Michigan) foot patrol study, 195
Floyd, "Pretty Boy," 271
Frankel, Marvin, 307
Freudian theory, 72

Gangs. *See* Crime and gangs
Gender. *See* Crime and gender
Giuliani, Rudolph, 299*n.3*
Guardian Angels, 192–93

Hedonism, 66
Hispanic-Americans
   and crime, 89, 92, 102, 106, 109, 112,
     165–66
   spouse assault, 212, 213, 215, 221, 236
   see also Crime and ethnicity
Homelessness, 166
Homicide, 7, 110, 117*n.79*, 134–35, 168
   spouse, 221–22, 240*n.51*
Hoover, J. Edgar, 270–71, 273, 277
House of Umoja, 171

I&We paradigm, 5
Imprisonment and gender, 142–50
Incapacitation, 20
Incarceration rates, international
   comparisons, 303, 308
Incident-oriented policing, 184–85, 186, 188,
   189
   see also Police
Irish-Americans
   and crime, 96–97, 102, 106–07, 109,
     111
   see also Crime and ethnicity
Italian-Americans
   and crime, 97, 102, 106–07, 109, 111
   see also Crime and ethnicity

Just desserts. *See* Sentencing, just desserts in
Juvenile delinquency. *See* Delinquency
Juvenile justice, 10, 157–76
   case processing, 164–66, 169
   confinement rates, 165–66
   evidence of discrimination in system,
     169, 278–79
   fundamental precept of, 278
   improving system, 170

King, Rodney, 280–81

Labeling, 90, 161
Labor force participation rate, 121
Latino-Americans and crime. *See* Hispanic-
  Americans and crime
Legal sanctions, limits of, 8–9, 51–61
Les Misérables (Hugo), 255–56, 276
Logical positivists, 73
London Metropolitan Police Department, 276
Los Angeles Police Department, 280–81
Loyalty, 37, 42–43

Mafia, 97, 113
Metapreferences, 40–41
Metro-Dade (Florida) Police Department,
  285, 288*nn.51,52*
Montgomery County (Maryland)
  Community-Oriented Prosecution,
  297–98
Morgenthau, Robert, 293

Nassau County (New York) Police
  Department, 271–72, 275
National Academy of Sciences Panel on
  Research on Sentencing, 306
National Center for Juvenile Justice, 165
National Crime Survey (NCS), 212, 239*n.25*
National Family Violence Survey, 210,
  211–12
National Youth Survey, 215
Nationality. *See* Crime and ethnicity
Native Americans and crime, 89, 92, 106,
  109, 114, 164
  see also Crime and ethnicity
Neighborhood watch programs, 10, 182, 185,
  188, 190–92, 194
Nelson, "Babyface," 271
New York City Police Department, 275, 281,
  287*n.21*

Opponent process theory, 70

Peel, Sir Robert, 276–77
Philosophy of justice and punishment, 8,
  19–36
  "foundations" of, 19–20, 22
Plea bargaining, 292, 293
  attempt to ban in Alaska, 295
Police, 11–12, 269–290
  accusations of discrimination by,
    277–79, 287*n.30*
  brutality, 280–81
  and community, 184–88

Police *(continued)*
  compared to fire protection service,
    269
  consequences of unclear direction,
    275–79
  corruption, 270
  as crime fighters, 270–75
  defining good policing, 279–86
  "Dirty Harry" problem, 280, 283
  frustrations, 279–80
  historical role of, 270–73
  nature of calls for service, 274
  peer review, 284
  performance measures for, 184, 187,
    276–77
  preventive vs. punitive strategy,
    276–77
  priority setting, 275–76
  and public responsibility for crime, xi
  styles, 274–75
  unwritten rules of conduct, 281–82
  violence-prone awareness and
    training, 284–85
  see also Community-oriented
    policing; Incident-oriented
    policing; Problem-oriented
    policing
Poverty. *See* and Crime and poverty
Prison furlough programs, 152
Prison overpopulation, *xi*, 303, 308
Probation, 21
Problem-oriented policing, 185–88, 193–94,
  285
Process theories, 100
  of delinquency. *See* Delinquency,
    process theories of
Prosecution, 12, 58, 291–302
  aspects of discretion, 292–93
  and the community, 293–94, 297–99
  examples of excesses in use of
    discretion, 291
  goals, 293–94
  guidelines, 295–97
  hidden nature of operations, 293–94
  Supreme Court rulings on discretion,
    295
  variation in plea rates, 293
  see also Plea bargaining
Punishment
  and behavior, 69–72, 75
  and consequentialism, 23–24, 27–29
  cruel and unusual, 30
  defining, 23, 24
  and deontology, 27–29

Punishment *(continued)*
    fair, 31
    justifying, 23–31
    legitimacy of, 26, 30, 57–59
    liberal justification of, 29–31
    nonnecessity of, 25
    proportionality of, 30
    recent history of, 20–23
    severity of, 28
    specifying goals of, 26
    theory of, 23–24

Race and crime. *See* Crime and ethnicity
Racketeer Influenced and Corrupt
    Organizations (RICO), 8, 52, 291,
    296
Radical theory, 161
Rationality. *See* Crime and rationality
Reaction theories. *See* Delinquency,
    reaction theories of
Rehabilitation, 9, 20–21, 53
Retribution, 24, 27–29, 31
    See also Sentencing, just desserts in
Reward and behavior, 69–72

Sanctions
    additivity of formal and informal,
        244n.112
    legal, 51–61
    social, 6–7, 32
Schooling
    and cultural context, 258
    compulsory attendance, 258–59
School violence, 11, 255–65
    and cultural diversity, 261–62
    importance of neighborhood, 260
    newspaper accounts of, 256–58
    policy implications, 262–64
    role of weapons, 260
Self-interest, 5, 46
    and community interest, 177–78
    as justification for punishment, 30
Sentencing, 4, 12–13, 303–10
    determinate, 20–21
    fairness in, 20–21
    guidelines, 295–96, 310
    indeterminate, 20–21
    intermediate sanctions, 308
    just desserts in, 20, 53
    legislated mandatory terms, 306
    presumptive guidelines, 307
    reform, 305–08, 309–10
    voluntary guidelines, 306
Sentencing Reform Act of 1984, 21, 52

Seward Park High School (Manhattan), 261
Serious offenders, 44–45
Signs of crime. *See* Broken windows
    hypothesis
Small Victories (Freedman), 261
Social class and crime. *See* Crime and
    socioeconomic status
Social control, 5–7, 211
    theory, 161
Social disorganization factors, 230
Social learning theory, 161
Socialization process, 163
Socio-economics, *xi-xii*, 5, 177, 178, 197
Sonner, Andrew, 297–98
Spouse assault, 10, 209–54
    deterred by social capital, 234–35
    difficulty in measuring, 212
    and "hot spots" of crime, 223
    Milwaukee arrest quasi-experiment,
        226
    Milwaukee replication sites, results,
        226, 243n.107
    social structure and social control of,
        224–35
    spatial distribution of, 223–24
    stimulated by social isolation,
        233–34
    victim-witness programs, 242n.77
    see also African-Americans and
        crime, spouse assault; Homicide,
        spouse
Stephens, Jay, 293
Strain theories, 100
Stranger violence, 211
Structural theories. *See* Delinquency,
    structural theories of
Student patrols, 193
Subculture of violence, 103–04, 160

Target hardening, 179–80
Thatcher, Margaret, 257
Thomas Jefferson High School (Brooklyn),
    260-61, 263
Twins, studies of, 66–67, 69

Underclass, 167
    see also Crime and poverty; Crime and
        socioeconomic status
Unemployment. *See* Crime and
    unemployment
Uniform Crime Reports (UCR), 92, 100,
    105–06, 110, 115n.13, 142, 164, 184,
    222, 276
United States Immigration Commission, 97

United States Sentencing Commission, 21, 307
Utilitarian position, 4
    see also Punishment and consequentialism

Victim-witness programs. *See* Spouse assault, victim-witness programs
Vigilantism, 192

Voice, 37–38, 42–43
Vollmer, August, 270, 271–73, 275, 277

Watch programs. *See* Neighborhood watch programs
White collar crime, 100, 121, 127, 304
Women's prisons, 150–52
Wright, Frank Lloyd's teaching philosophy, 262

About the Contributors

Hugo Adam Bedau is Austin Fletcher Professor of Philosophy at Tufts University. He received his Ph.D. degree from Harvard University in 1961. He is author of *Justice and Equality* (1971), *The Case Against the Death Penalty* (1973), *The Courts, the Constitution, and Capital Punishment* (1977), and *Death is Different* (1987); editor of *The Death Penalty in America* (1982); and author of numerous articles on the philosophy of punishment and the death penalty.

Jeffrey Fagan is Associate Professor, School of Criminal Justice, Rutgers University. Co-author of *Drug Use and Delinquency Among Inner-City Youth* (1993) and editor of the *Journal of Research in Crime and Delinquency*, Dr. Fagan has published widely on domestic violence, drug abuse, juvenile delinquency, and inner-city crime. He received the Ph.D. degree from the State University of New York, Buffalo, in 1975.

Bonnie Fisher is Associate Professor at the University of Cincinnati's Department of Political Science. Author of *Participatory Democracy and Crime Prevention: The Effects of Participation on the Individual* (1988), she has written extensively on community crime prevention and the fear of crime. She received her Ph.D. degree from Northwestern University in 1988.

Brian Forst is Associate Professor in the Department of Justice, Law and Society, School of Public Affairs, The American University. He was Director of Research at the Institute for Law and Social Research from 1977 to 1985 and at the Police Foundation from 1985 to 1989. Author of *Power in Numbers* (1987) and *The Representation of Uncertainty in Expert Systems: An Application in Criminal Investigation* (1992) and co-author of *What Happens After Arrest?* (1977), he has written widely on prosecution and sentencing, law enforcement, the deterrent effect of the death penalty, quantitative methods, and information technology. He received his Ph.D. degree from The George Washington University in 1993.

James J. Fyfe is Professor of Criminal Justice at Temple University. A former lieutenant with the New York City Police Department, his research contributed to the Supreme Court's sharply restricting police policies involving the shooting of fleeing felons in the landmark case of *Tennessee v. Garner*. Dr. Fyfe is co-author of *Above the Law: Police and the Excessive Use of Force* (1993) and co-editor of *Contemporary Issues in Law Enforcement* (1981). He has published an array of articles on police use of deadly force, legal constraints on police search and arrest practices, and police personnel policy. He received his Ph.D. degree from the State University of New York, Albany, in 1978.

Darnell Hawkins is Professor of Sociology and Director of Undergraduate Studies, Black Studies Program, the University of Illinois, Chicago. He edited *Homicide Among Black Americans* (1986) and has published widely on crime in the African-American community, homicide, and the correctional system. He received his Ph.D. at the University of Michigan in 1976 and a Juris Doctor degree at the University of North Carolina in 1980.

Graham Hughes, Professor of Law at New York University, is an international authority on criminal law. He authored *The Conscience of the Courts: Law and Morals in American Life* (1975), co-authored *Jurisprudence* (1957), edited *Law, Reason, and Justice: Essays in Legal Philosophy* (1969), and has written numerous articles on jurisprudence, legal philosophy, and morals and the law. He received law degrees at the University of Wales (1951) and New York University (1961).

Joan McCord is Professor of Criminal Justice at Temple University. She is a fellow of the American Society of Criminology, and was president of the Society during 1988–89. Dr. McCord co-authored *Psychopathy and Delinquency* (1956) and *Origins of Crime* (1959) and has published an array of articles on psychological development and crime, the criminogenic effects of child abuse and neglect, delinquency, and alcoholism. Dr. McCord was author of the landmark Cambridge-Somerville Youth Study retrospective. She received her Ph.D. degree from Stanford University in 1968.

Norval Morris is Julius Kreeger Professor of Law and Criminology and former Dean of the University of Chicago Law School. Author of *The Future of Imprisonment* (1974), co-author of the classic, *The Honest Politician's Guide to Crime Control* (1970), and co-editor of the annual *Crime and Justice: A Review of Research*, he has written extensively about sentencing and prison reform, capital punishment, and criminal responsibility of the mentally ill. He received his LL.B. from Melbourne University in 1946 and his Ph.D. from London University in 1949.

Llad Phillips is Professor of Economics and Provost of the College of Letters and Science at the University of California, Santa Barbara. Co-editor of *Eco-*

nomic Analysis of Pressing Social Prolems (1974) and *The Economics of Crime Control* (1974), he has published widely on the economics of crime and justice, deterrence, and population demographics. He received his Ph.D. from Harvard University in 1969.

Carl E. Pope is Professor of Criminal Justice at the University of Wisconsin, Milwaukee. He received the Ph.D. degree from the State University of New York, Albany, in 1975. Author of *Sentencing of California Felony Offenders* (1975) and co-editor of *Race, Crime and Criminal Justice* (1981), Dr. Pope has published several articles on delinquency, race and crime, burglary, and criminal justice data.

Rita Simon is University Professor at The American University's Department of Justice, Law and Society and former Dean of the University's School of Justice. A fellow of the American Society of Criminology, she is also former editor of the *American Sociological Review* and *Justice Quarterly*. Author of *The Jury and the Defense of Insanity* (1967) and *Women and Crime* (1975), Dr. Simon has written widely on women and crime, transracial adoption, the jury, and immigration. She received the Ph.D. degree from the University of Chicago in 1957.

Jackson Toby is Director of the Institute for Criminological Research at Rutgers University. He studied with Talcott Parsons at Harvard University, receiving his Ph.D. degree in 1950. Co-author of *Social Problems in America* (1972) and *Delinquency* (1973) and frequent contributor to *The New York Times, The Wall Street Journal,* and *The Public Interest,* Dr. Toby has written extensively on education policy and crime in the schools.